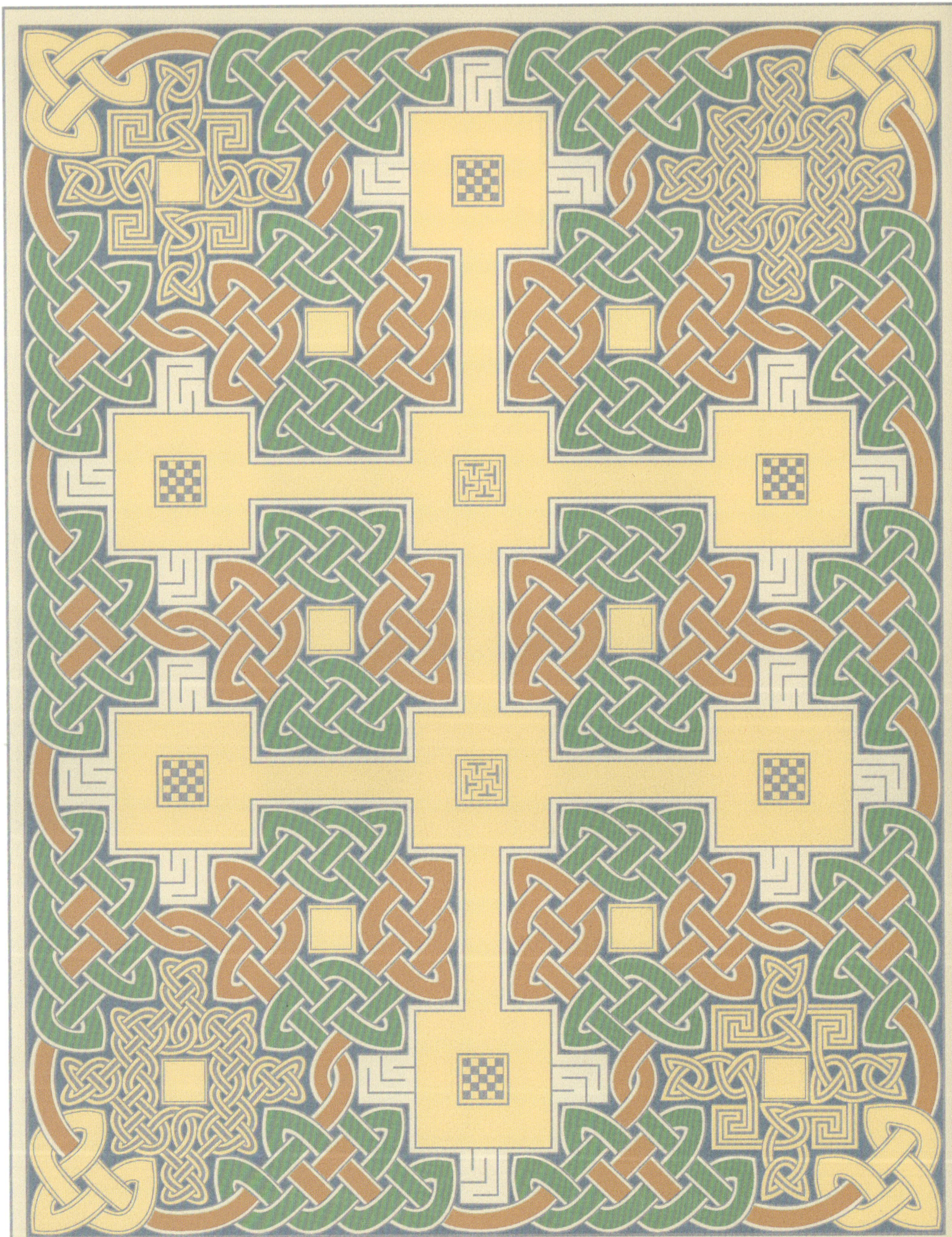

Celtic and Anglo-Saxon Art
Geometric Aspects

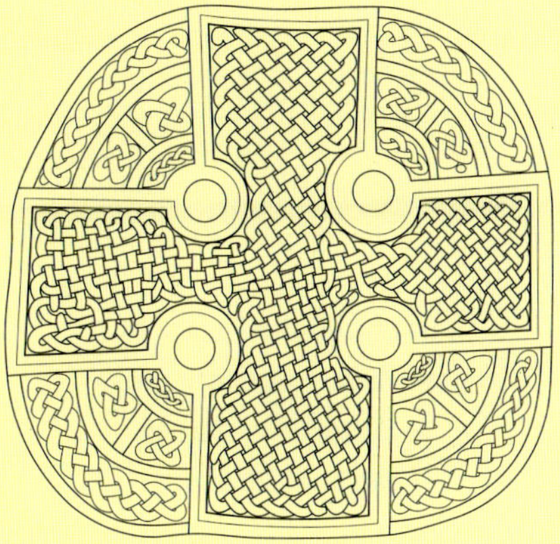

Celtic and Anglo-Saxon Art
Geometric Aspects

DEREK HULL

LIVERPOOL UNIVERSITY PRESS

First published 2003 by
Liverpool University Press
4 Cambridge Street
Liverpool L69 7ZU

British Library Cataloguing-in-Publication data
A British Library CIP record is available

ISBN 0-85323-549-X

Designed by axisgraphicdesign.co.uk
Printed and bound by
Editoriale Bortolazzi Stei, Verona

Contents

The general forms being first cared for, these should be subdivided and ornamented by general lines; the interstices may then be filled in with ornament, which may again be subdivided and enriched for closer inspection.

Proposition 7 in Owen Jones,
The Grammar of Ornament (1856)

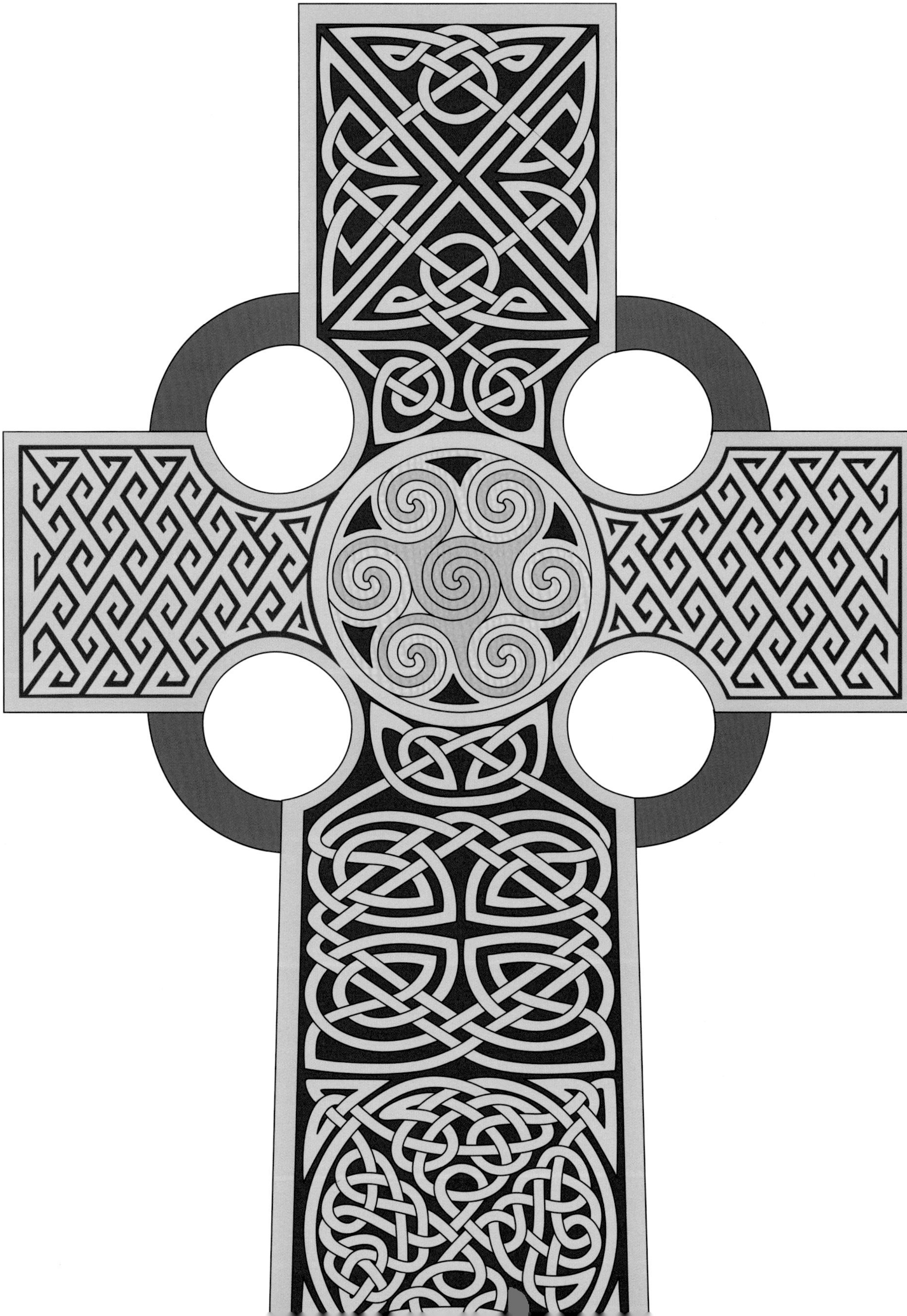

Preface

This book tells a story of exploration. It could be called a life story because I have always been fascinated by patterns – in art, in nature and, more specifically, in my own academic subject of the science of materials. A few years ago, at a time when I was completing a book about observing and interpreting the complex patterns that are formed on the surfaces of solids – rocks, glasses, metals, plastics and composite materials – when they break, I saw a simple interlacing pattern on an old stone cross in a churchyard. This was the start of a new and exciting exploration. It has taken me to remote parts of the British Isles and Ireland to see ancient sculptured stones and to a study of manuscripts, stone monuments and metal artefacts in museums and libraries. Hundreds of hours have been spent searching the world-wide web and in discussions and correspondence with scholars who have long experience in archaeology and the history of art.

Every pattern tells a story. Quite innocently, as I looked at the interlacing on the stone cross, I asked myself – how was this pattern produced? There are, of course, many other questions to be asked about the pattern and the cross. Who created the cross? When was it made? What was it meant to represent or symbolise? From where did the inspiration for the design come? Why was it used on this particular piece of stone? What skills were required to carve this intricate pattern? What does the stone tells us about the people who commissioned the work? In the story of exploration recorded in this book I have concentrated on my first question – how was this pattern produced? The other questions have to be answered by those who have skills, knowledge and experience in archaeology, history, social sciences and art. They are beyond my capacity but, like others, I can speculate.

Shortly after I first became aware of these patterns, and with a touch of serendipity, I came across George Bain's splendid book *Celtic Art* in a bookshop at Theatr Clwyd in north Wales. I quickly discovered that there was a vast treasure house of early medieval art in manuscripts, on stone monuments and on metalwork. In this art relatively simple motifs – interlacing, key, spiral, zoomorphic and foliate – are combined to create complex and exotic designs. These works of art were produced during a period once referred to as the Dark Ages, by craftspeople and artists who must have had remarkable skills in illuminating, carving and metalworking. Even with the benefits of modern technology and computer graphics it would be difficult to produce such sophisticated work today.

In studying Bain's book it became apparent that there was a strong element of geometric construction both in the layout and in the very fine artwork. Some of the detail, as for example in the Book of Kells, is on such a fine scale that a magnifying glass is required to resolve it. More remarkably, the geometric constructions must have been achieved using only a straight-edge and compasses. What an incredible story and what an incredible achievement!

It took me many months of study to appreciate and follow the detail in Bain's book. It led me to explore how early medieval artists used straight-edge and compasses in their work. They must have been familiar with the geometric skills of the Egyptians, Romans and Greeks. The principles involved are really quite simple but the way they were applied in producing masterpieces of ornamental art is one of the highlights of the history of art.

Some people find geometry, however simple, difficult to grasp. I have included geometric details to persuade those familiar with geometric methods that these methods were, indeed, used by the original artists. Fortunately there is no need to follow the detail to appreciate the underlying approach and enjoy the wonder of it all. In a similar vein, I have included references to a selection of authoritative sources. They provide an introduction to the vast amount of scholarship on early medieval art for those who wish to pursue some of the topics further.

This book answers my own question – how was the interlacing pattern produced? My approach has been to consider examples, simple and complex, from a wide range of early medieval art and attempt to discover in simple terms the stages of geometric construction that must have been used. In most cases this is far from obvious and there is the 'excitement of the chase' and the ultimate 'Eureka' experience that is arguably the greatest thrill for a scientist. There is also the sense of wonder and mystery, a gift to all people, in enjoying and celebrating the beauty and sense of creativity offered by this art.

The book has a straightforward structure. The background topics in the Introduction set the scene for Chapter 2 which describes the importance of panels and the use of primary, secondary and tertiary grids in laying out designs. This is developed further in Chapter 3 with a description of the way that panels, each filled with a single form of motif, are combined to create composite panel designs.

Chapter 4 is a comprehensive treatment of the geometric constructions used in drawing and laying out the main motifs. It includes an introductory treatment of symmetry and repetition, which are the bases of regular, ordered patterns. The constructions used in complex designs are described in Chapter 5.

Chapter 6 demonstrates how the application of basic rules and geometric principles, developed in the earlier chapters, can be applied to the reconstruction of incomplete patterns in works of art that have suffered the ravages of wear and erosion, corrosion and wanton damage. The theme of Chapter 7 is metamorphosis. Much of the early work in the sixth to ninth centuries was highly disciplined, so that the underlying rules can be established readily. In later times changes in style and the introduction of new motifs produced profound changes. Some of the rigour of geometric construction disappeared and some new approaches to design were developed.

My exploration has benefited enormously by having access to the resources of the Library and Special Collections of the Sidney Jones Library of the University of Liverpool as well as the John Moores University Library and the Central Libraries of the City of Liverpool. The Special Collections include facsimile editions of some of the great Gospel books. My thanks go to the staff of all these libraries who have courteously and patiently responded to my requests.

I have valued the help and advice of many curators, librarians and experts elsewhere. I am particularly grateful to Jamie Camplin, Niamh Deegan, Günter Hägele, Isabel Henderson, Bernard Meehan, Michael Pinder, Bob Pond, Mark Redknap, Ian Scott, Susan Seright, and Alison Sheridan. I was particularly fortunate to make contact with Dr Nancy Edwards of the University of Wales in Bangor. She responded very warmly and constructively to my enquiries and generously gave her time to reading and reviewing the whole of the text. Pauline, my wife, has, as ever, tolerated my enthusiasm and joined in many expeditions to all corners of the islands. She has also patiently read the text. I offer my sincere thanks to all who have helped in any way.

Derek Hull
May 2003

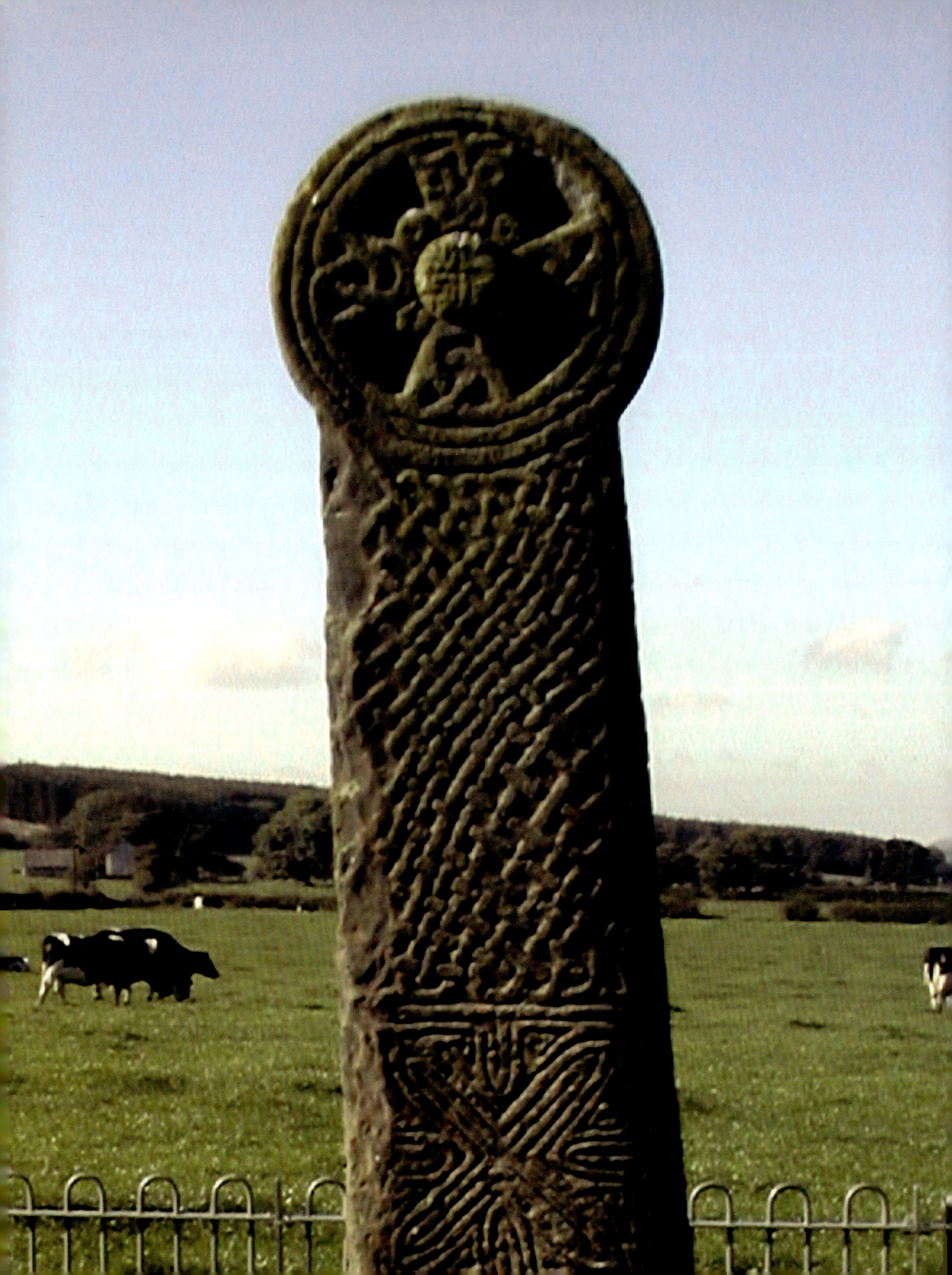

1

Introduction

FROM CALLANISH TO MAEN ACHWYFAN

The stones of Callanish in the Outer Hebrides (Fig. 1.1) reflect on the story of the people of all the islands, large and small, that lie off the north-west coast of mainland Europe. One can only speculate about the reasons for raising and aligning these slender irregular columns, some over 4.5 m high, and about the purposes for which they were used. Was it a temple of the Druids 'admirably adapted, both by its position and construction to produce the greatest possible effect on a vast concourse of people, assembled to witness their dreadful sacrifices', as suggested by Col. Sir Henry James in 1866, shortly after the site was first excavated? One can never know.

What is certain is that stone monuments of this kind played no part in the everyday life of the hunter-gatherers and farmers of the Stone and Bronze Ages. Rather, in some strange way, they seem to be a human response to a deeply felt awareness of mystery, of a sense of transcendence, of the vastness of time and space, of vulnerability and insignificance, and of a fear of the unknown, particularly of the prospect of life beyond death. They were sacred places, shrines for unknown and unknowable gods.

The stones of Callanish were hewn from local metamorphic rocks. The coarse foliated structure of the crystalline gneiss made it possible to split the rock along the layers to produce thin slabs. The surfaces of the stones reveal the structure of the layers fashioned into exotic patterns by wind, rain and frost. The patterns of nature tell their own story.

The stone sculpture known as Maen Achwyfan (Fig. 1.2) was raised and fashioned about 4000 years after the first stone circle at Callanish was

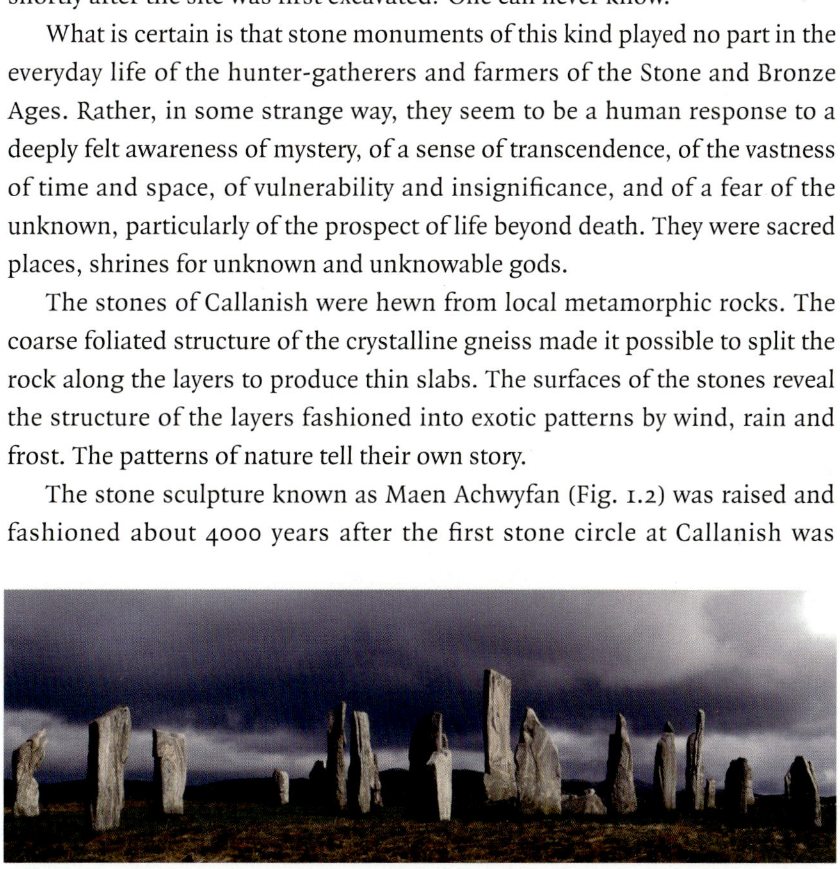

Figure 1.1
The Standing Stones of Callanish form a closed circle surrounding a chambered cairn with other stones in rows that radiate from the circle. The stones are on the spine of a shallow ridge that overlooks Loch Roag close to the Atlantic coast of the Isle of Lewis in the Outer Hebrides.

created. This elegant sandstone monolith was originally called Maen Machwyfan, meaning 'the stone of Cwyfan's field', and is now sometimes know as the 'Stone of Lamentations'. It stands in rolling countryside in the hills of north Wales close to Whitford in Flintshire. An intricate array of complex patterns has been carved on the four faces of the stone and an equal-armed cross, set inside a circle, forms a cross-head. Recent archaeological and art-historical studies by Edwards (1999) suggest, from the design of the patterns and the shape of the cross, that Maen Achwyfan was erected in the late tenth or early eleventh century by sculptors influenced by the influx of Viking people in north-east Wales. The stories told by the patterns span many centuries and speak of myths, legends, beliefs and art forms of peoples and cultures from all over the known world.

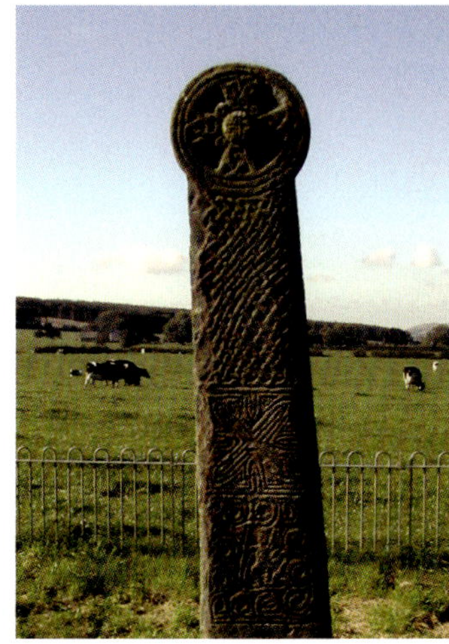

Figure 1.2
Maen Achwyfan, a sculptured stone, sometimes referred to as the 'Stone of Lamentations', standing in open countryside near Whitford in north Wales.

Although the meaning and significance of many of the motifs used to form the patterns carved on the stone are obscure, to the point of being unknown today, it is certain that they had great significance to the artists who designed the stone and the people who commissioned it. Maen Achwyfan has a rich array of symbols that reflect beliefs in Christianity, witnessed by the cross, as well as in the traditions and gods of the Vikings. In displaying these symbolic images there is a reaching out to human experiences that are beyond words – of belonging, of identity, of allegiances, of fears and hopes, of beliefs in life and life to come. The patterns are poetry in stone, the art of generations that lived 1000 years ago.

Callanish and Maen Achwyfan can be seen as examples of a process known today. There is a searching in music, poetry, writing, art and architecture to express and communicate deep spiritual experiences reflecting the wonder and mystery of life itself. Scientists and theologians alike search out this mystery but it is as unknowable today as it was for the people of Callanish. It remains an unending exploration as each new generation experiences the mystery and responds in praise, worship and humble acceptance.

This book explores aspects of art, as expressed by the peoples of the islands, in the 500 years leading up to the time of Maen Achwyfan, commonly known as the early medieval period and sometimes as the 'Dark Ages'. Much of this art relates to the emergence of Christianity, a religion that speaks of a personal God known through the life and teaching of a man called Jesus, who lived 2000 years ago. Jesus was a Jew and he shared the rich religious teaching and understanding of the God of the Jews: a God of creation. Christians acknowledge Jesus as 'the Christ' – a saviour or messiah – and respond to the mystery in their lives as 'of God'. Jesus died by crucifixion on a cross and now 'lives', for Christians, by physical or experiential resurrection, as part of a triune God. So it is that a cross is the most powerful and enduring symbol of Christianity. It is a symbol that is identified with many intangible aspects of life common to all mankind. In crucifixion the cross is identified with suffering and in resurrection it is identified with hope. In sharing the Jewish faith Christians see God as creator of all things and all creation as being sacred.

PATTERNS IN SCIENCE AND ART

The use of geometry in early medieval art is truly remarkable. This art has survived in illuminated manuscripts, elaborate stone carvings and in a wide range of metal artefacts. Patterns, created by a combination of motifs, notably spirals, key patterns, interlacing and zoomorphic and vegetal forms, create complex and intriguing images that give an insight into the genius of the artists who created them. They range from highly ordered patterns, regimented in military arrays, to seemingly chaotic designs.

The motifs and component parts of this art have their origins in the art of earlier cultures. Most scholars acknowledge that the abstract motifs had deep spiritual, emotional and possibly political significance for the people. No single group, tribe, nation or culture can rightly claim to 'own' this art. Equally, one cannot assume that motifs, styles, forms and patterns meant the same to successive artists, patrons, tribes or nation states. The meaning of the motifs has not survived to the present day and there is only the creative imagination of contemporary writers to suggest what the meaning might be. For this reason exploration of the symbolic aspects of the patterns, and the sense of mystery and wonder arising from this symbolism, is not a major theme in this book.

Patterns, created from abstract and semi-abstract motifs, were often combined with a variety of other images, reflecting religious and political aspects of contemporary life, and with inscriptions in a variety of forms – Latin, Ogam and Runic. These give additional insights into the beliefs, spiritual experiences and cultures of the people. They also illuminate the meaning of the art and provide information about technical aspects of the work. They have been the subject of extensive research but are also outside the scope of this book.

We turn to the sense of mystery and wonder to be found in the intrinsic aspects of abstract and semi-abstract patterns, totally distinct from any real or imagined symbolic meaning or, indeed, from the beauty of the work as a whole. This resonates with the sense of wonder that scientists experience when observing and searching out the meaning of the brilliant patterns of the natural world. Light and electron microscopes reveal wonderful patterns in natural and synthetic materials and telescopes reveal endless patterns in the sky. These patterns tell exciting stories when they are interpreted and understood. Part of the process of understanding involves being able to recognise and describe the patterns.

Take, for example, the pattern of waves created when a pebble is thrown into a mill pond, or the seemingly random imprints of birds feeding on freshly washed sand, or the ordered arrays of soldiers on a parade ground, or the ever-expanding river-like patterns on the leaves of trees and the petals of flowers. Each pattern is intrinsically fascinating and contains large amounts of information. The amount of information that is revealed depends on many subjective factors including the skill, knowledge and experience of the observer as well as the methods and tools of observation. At the end of the day, in science as in art, 'beauty (and understanding) is in the eye (and mind) of the beholder'.

Another aspect of patterns, particularly important in scientific studies, is that there is usually information at different scales of observation. Thus, from a distance, the soldiers on the parade ground are identical and the patterns they produce consist of regular rows of repeat units. The quality of the parade is judged by the straightness of the lines and the absence of regions of irregularity. Closer to, it seems that all the soldiers have exactly the same uniform but there are differences in the way the uniforms are decorated, with stripes, insignia and ribbons. Even closer, the regular patterns, evident from a distance, have been lost completely and each soldier has unique facial characteristics.

There is a subtle tension between order and chaos – of patterns that at one scale can be described by simple rules of repetition and symmetry and at another do not show any apparent signs of organisation or order. For scientists the most interesting aspect of patterns is in exploring the way that the internal order of things, revealed by the patterns, relates to the external behaviour or appearance of things.

Diamonds are crystals that consist of highly ordered arrays of carbon atoms. The beauty of diamonds depends on how accurately the facets are cut parallel to planes of atoms in the crystal and the perfection of the arrangement of the atoms themselves. Tiny defects in the organisation of the atoms result in the scattering of light and loss of brilliance. Like diamonds, steel also has a highly ordered array of atoms but the steel technologist has fashioned the internal order so that it contains a very high density of defects, making steel both strong and tough. A similar story can be told in almost every branch of science.

Unravelling the way that patterns in the art of early medieval times have been formed and modified is intrinsically intriguing and fascinating. It offers insights into the art and the artists (and their life and times) and enriches the appreciation of the art as a whole. In his book *The Meaning of Art*, Herbert Read (1931) quotes Lamprecht, a German historian of art, on the subject of early medieval art: 'Fantastically confused patterns are thus evolved, whose puzzle asks to be unravelled, whose convolutions seem alternatively to seek and avoid each other, whose component parts, endowed as it were with sensibility, captivate sight and sense in passionately vital movement'.

THE BACKGROUND STORY

Early medieval art is set in a time of many cultural, artistic, religious and political developments. It draws on a wealth of art stretching back thousands of years. The migration of peoples, the establishment of kingdoms and the spread of Christianity influenced it. The national boundaries of countries in the twenty-first century are a poor basis for discussing the development and origin of this art. However, there is no escape from using the present geographical boundaries of England, Ireland, Scotland and Wales in describing the distribution and movement of peoples in earlier times. Nevertheless, it must be recognised that these peoples had many different ethnic origins and interacted by trade, war and migration with peoples from all over Europe and beyond. It is not helpful to think in terms of a pure indigenous art, for early medieval art is a rich soup of the art and crafts of many peoples.

The story of the peoples who inhabited these islands is a complex one and is still being explored by archaeologists. The writings of historians and archaeologists in the past provide clear evidence that there is no 'absolute chronological framework' that can be used for early medieval art. The 'background story' in this section is not intended as a rigorous account of events. It merely serves to provide a context for discussing the development of the geometric aspects of the art of this period.

We can imagine that, as the great ice sheet retreated northwards about 12,000 years ago, the early inhabitants spread throughout the islands and more and more people arrived from mainland Europe. Slowly these people changed from hunter-gatherers to farmers. Their tools and weapons became more sophisticated as stone was replaced by bronze and eventually by iron. The example of Callanish suggests that these peoples had a deep sense of things outside and beyond themselves.

Aspects of Celtic culture came with the movement of peoples from Central Europe, leading to new lifestyles and religious beliefs. The Celts decorated their metalwork, ornaments and stone carvings with an abstract art. Roman armies arrived in AD 43 and spread out from the south-east corner of England, reaching the Grampians in Scotland by AD 84. Although they built the Antonine wall in 139, and had some military stations north of this wall, the Romans never occupied the Scottish Highlands or Ireland. It is said that they gave the name *Picti* (Picts or 'painted ones') to the tribes who resisted their advance in north-east Scotland. On the outer fringes, particularly in Scotland, Ireland and the northern parts of Wales, where the Roman influence was developed least, the tribal communities retained many of their own traditions.

The Romans brought a new way of life as evidenced by the artefacts and buildings that still remain. They built a strong urban-based culture and created a network of roads connecting towns and military stations which formed the basis of a political and organisational system. This was fundamentally different from the tribal systems of the earlier peoples. Christianity came through Roman connections. St Patrick and St Ninian, who were trained within the Roman tradition, are the best known of the 'missionaries' who took Christianity to Ireland and Scotland.

By 410, economic and political troubles at home and aggressive attacks by invaders forced the Romans to leave Britain. Also at this time there were migrations from Ireland to the western parts of Britain. According to Bede's *Ecclesiastical History*, settlement by Angles, Saxons and Jutes, who were basically Germanic peoples, some with Scandinavian connections, was encouraged by the native Britons. Much of Roman civilisation crumbled. Assimilation of pagan peoples, with their own cultures, lifestyles and art, led to a decline in the fragile Christian presence that had grown up during the Roman occupation. Only in the outer parts of the islands was there the opportunity for the growth of strong Christian communities. Here monasteries were founded and eventually flourished to become centres of learning, prayer and missionary work. Within the monasteries, particularly in Ireland, scriptoria were established, dedicated to producing manuscripts to be used in worship and study. Missionary activities spread out from Ireland to the western parts of Scotland and Europe.

Anglo-Saxon expansion continued on the mainland throughout the fifth to eighth centuries with the formation of strong and powerful kingdoms, notably those in Northumbria, Mercia, East Anglia, Kent and Wessex. Northumbrian expansion into Scotland was halted by the Picts, at the Battle of Nechtansmere, at the end of the seventh century. Expansion westwards was halted, in the late eighth century, close to a line which became Offa's Dyke along the borders of Wales. Parts of north-east Wales were occupied by Anglo-Saxons after the eighth century. This was a time of many battles; Anglo-Saxon kings fought each other, and the emergent kingdoms in the Celtic-influenced regions fought among themselves and with their neighbours.

The events leading to the Synod of Whitby in 664, as described by Bede, are central to the history of this time and to an understanding of the influence of cultures and lifestyles on early medieval art. By this time the ethnic mixture of the peoples of the islands had changed many times and each new invasion and migration had transformed and enriched the heritage of the people resulting in links with peoples from many parts of the known world. Ostensibly, the Synod of Whitby was mainly about the date of Easter used by the two main sections of the church (Celtic and Roman). In reality, it was about power and authority in church governance, for two different approaches had developed, one in the fringes, including Ireland, and the other in the central mainland of Britain.

Columba, who died in 597, was one of many missionaries, dedicated to a strict regime of prayer, religious study and self-denial, nurtured in strong monastic traditions in Ireland. Missionaries left Ireland for Britain and the continent of Europe. Columba brought a new wave of Christianity to the Scoti in Dalriada, a kingdom in the west of Scotland formed by the migration of people from the north of Ireland (the Scoti) at the end of the Roman period and the Picts in north-east Scotland.

It was in 563, at the age of 42, that Columba went to Iona, an island off the coast of Mull in Scotland, and founded a monastery. So the monastic tradition that had developed in Ireland and to a lesser extent in Wales was now encouraged in Scotland. This influence spread into England when Oswald became king of Anglo-Saxon Northumbria. He had experienced monastic Christianity in Ireland and in 635 encouraged Aiden from Iona to found a monastery at Lindisfarne on Holy Island, off the coast of Northumbria, a few miles from the royal fortress at Bamborough. Oswald died in 642.

Oswald's brother and successor, King Oswy, married into the traditions of Roman Christianity. It was this influence that led to the Synod of Whitby. Thus, at the time when monastic traditions were developing and spreading, Augustine arrived in Britain from Rome in 596–97, with the authority of Pope Gregory I, to preach Christianity to pagan Anglo-Saxons. He established a cathedral church at Canterbury and thereby introduced artefacts, works of art and manuscripts from Rome. The Anglo-Saxon kings were strongly influenced by Aethelbert, King of Kent, who married a Christian Gaulish princess. Another important Anglo-Saxon king was Raedwald, of East Anglia, who died in 624 and was probably buried at Sutton Hoo. The kings eventually accepted the Roman Episcopal approach to church governance based on the structures of the old Roman province of Britain.

Leaders of the two groups of churches met at Whitby in 664 and eventually agreed to accept the Roman date for Easter and other Roman practices. Notwithstanding this, the spread of Roman influence around the kingdoms of the islands was a slow process and there were pockets of resistance in the Celtic lands for centuries.

The decisions at Whitby were particularly relevant to the situation in the monastery at Lindisfarne. Following Whitby, the Columban monks led by Bishop Colman, who could not agree to the changes, left Lindisfarne along with some Anglo-Saxon monks. Those who stayed retained much of the inspiration of Columban monastic traditions. Cuthbert (634–87), an Anglo-Saxon saint, entered monastic life as a youth in 651. As Bishop of Lindisfarne he belonged to the post-Whitby Northumbrian church and took an active part in the diocesan organisation. Strong links with Rome developed and visits to Rome and other countries resulted in the foundation of important monasteries, such as Monkwearmouth and Jarrow, and the acquisition of relics, icons, vestments, textiles, sacred vessels and precious books. Thus at Lindisfarne, at the time of the production of the Lindisfarne Gospels in c. 715, there was a rich mixture of traditions influenced by Anglo-Saxon, Roman, Celtic and Mediterranean art.

Everything changed again with the arrival of the Vikings. Having developed navigation, ship-building and rigging skills, many Scandinavian people with new cultures, traditions and gods arrived on the coasts of these islands. First recorded in 793, with the destruction of Lindisfarne, there followed attacks on Iona in 794 and on many other places, marking the start of what is now called the Viking Age. Later, Orkney and Shetland became Norse colonies followed by the entire Hebridean Islands, the Isle of Man and parts of the mainland.

Another wave of Vikings (Danes) arrived on the east coast of England around the middle of the ninth century. They established powerful new kingdoms that took control of large parts of England from the Anglo-Saxons and established the Danelaw. For nearly two centuries the boundaries between the lands under the control of the Vikings and the Anglo-Saxons changed before the arrival of William (the Conqueror) in 1066. The Vikings introduced new styles of art that had a strong influence on the art of the earlier peoples.

ORIGINS AND AVAILABILITY OF EARLY MEDIEVAL ART

Each work of art can be seen as an individual response to a sense of wonder and mystery. And yet artists work, almost invariably, within a framework of support that provides resources and finance. Most early medieval art still surviving today is the product of metal and stone workshops and scriptoria under the patronage of tribal chiefs, kings and monasteries. The art had a function clearly identified in the work that has survived.

Illuminated manuscripts were mainly copies of books of the Bible, particularly the Gospels, and served in worship and in missionary activities. The great Gospel books, such as Durrow, Lindisfarne and Kells, provided a central focus for ceremony and worship. The quality of these works testifies to a great sense of dedication, commitment and adoration. Like manuscripts, stone carvings were almost invariably linked to religious activity. The great majority have a strong Christian emphasis, providing grave-markers, tombstones, central points for worship and monuments of commemoration. Art on metalwork was linked to a much wider range of uses and spans pre-Christian and Christian times. Ornamented metalwork as diverse as vessels, reliquaries, weapons, decorative ware and jewellery has been found.

With a succession of invasions and tribal wars it is not surprising that only a limited amount of art has survived in the islands. In the centuries following the Dark Ages there were periods, as during the Reformation, when much was destroyed. However, a significant number of manuscripts have survived. Few are undamaged and complete. Books are relatively small, so they were hidden easily and readily transported. Vellum, paints and inks age only slowly, providing they are kept dry and are protected from sunlight and the ravages of insects and animals. Stone monuments were difficult to transport and usually remained *in situ* open to all weathers. Many carvings have been severely eroded by wind and rain. Others have been broken, dispersed and used elsewhere as building materials. Completely undamaged stones are rare. In recent times dedicated local historians, antiquarians and archaeologists have carefully reassembled many stone monuments.

Metal artefacts were readily stolen, melted down and reused. The main sources of metal artefacts are pagan Anglo-Saxon cemeteries, such as Sutton Hoo in Suffolk, and hoards such as those at St Ninian's Isle in the Shetland islands and Donore in Co. Meath, Ireland. Some hoards are a direct result of people attempting to protect their valuables from marauding and pillaging tribes. The majority are linked with burials. The richest treasures were in the graves of great pagan chieftains and kings, reflecting their wealth and power. Some graves contained all manner of artefacts. The bodies of the dead were adorned with jewellery and opulent wares. Metals, particularly iron, are subject to corrosion. In the harsh environment of watery graves few iron artefacts survived. Bronze is more resistant and the noble metals, silver and gold, more so. Some fine gold jewellery, richly decorated with coloured glasses and precious stones, has been recovered in excellent condition.

Manuscripts, stones and metalwork offer many clues as to their date and provenance but there are few, if any, absolutes. Commonality of style and use of motifs indicates that there was extensive overlap between artists working in different media. Studies of these features provide evidence for the development of the art. But accurate dating has proved exceptionally difficult and has often been frustrated by subjective factors, leading to considerable debate, argument and disagreement among archaeologists and historians.

Although accurate dating is not particularly important for the study and appreciation of the geometric aspects of the art, some general indication of date and provenance is of interest. The dates and origins of manuscripts examined in this book are taken from J.G.G. Alexander's book, *Insular manuscripts: 6th to 9th centuries* (1978). This book includes details of all the relevant Insular manuscripts and a selection of black and white and coloured photographic reproductions of these works. For an analysis of the Insular manuscripts, with a comprehensive treatment of the historical context, see Henderson (1987). The word 'Insular' implies that the manuscripts (and, where relevant, other works of art) belong stylistically to early medieval art created in Britain and Ireland.

Some dates are accepted more or less universally and these provide useful fixed points. Thus, it is widely acknowledged that Mound 1 at Sutton Hoo, possibly the grave of Raedwald, can be dated to c. 625 on the basis of the evidence of coins found in the burial site. It follows that all the art found in this burial mound pre-dates this. Similarly, there is agreement about the dates of the Synod of Whitby in 664, the production of the Lindisfarne Gospels in c. 715, and the first Viking raids on Lindisfarne in 793.

In the next chapter, brief reference is made to the development of geometric art using the metalwork of Sutton Hoo, mainly attributed to Anglo-Saxon workshops, as a starting point. Manuscript art is concentrated in a period of about 200 years from the middle of the seventh century, 50 years after Sutton Hoo, and is closely linked to monasteries founded in Iona, Lindisfarne and on the continent of Europe by missionaries from Ireland. The evidence from stone carvings is spread over a much longer period and stretches to the eleventh century. It embraces a wide range of cultural influences – Celtic, Pictish, Anglo-Saxon – and includes the later Viking migrations, particularly in the Isle of Man and northern England.

The detail of the ornamentation on stone carvings is particularly interesting because it provides one way of relating art created in different media. Since the vast majority of stone monuments are linked to Christian traditions, the symbol of the cross becomes a central feature. Christianity led to the establishment of monasteries with scriptoria and workshops. They were the power-houses of early medieval art, a major source of links with other cultures and countries, and the origin of a new vocabulary of symbolism, most uniquely represented by the cross.

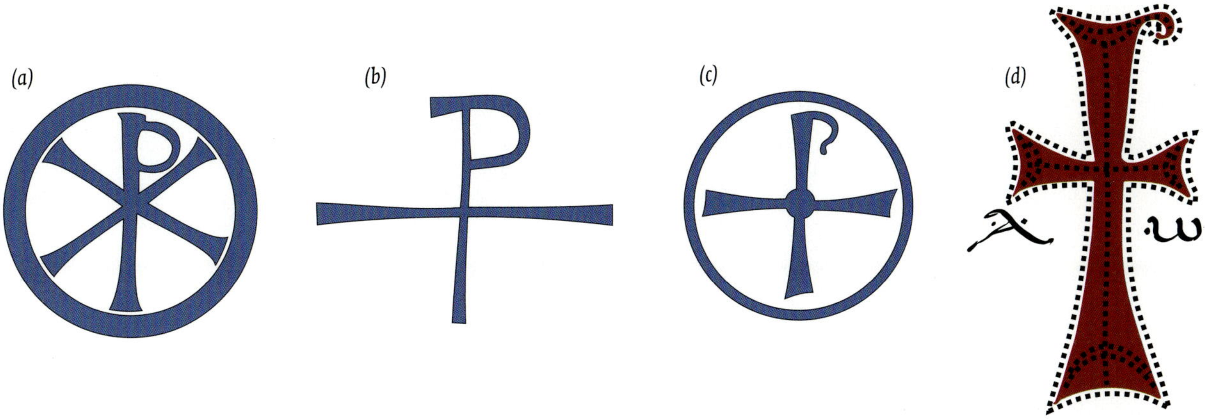

Figure 1.3
Early examples of simple crosses developed from the Chi-Rho monogram. (a) Conventional arrangement of monogram on a sarcophagus in the Vatican dated c. AD 340. (b) Incised cross at Penmachno, Gwynedd, Wales, 5th to 6th C. (c) Incised cross at Kirkmadrine, Galloway, Scotland, a few miles from Whithorn, site of St. Ninian's monastery, 5th to 6th C. (d) Decorated cross in a severely damaged Gospel book (Codex Usserianus Primus) now in Trinity College, Dublin, early 7th C.

The progressive development in the skills and techniques associated with the creation of geometric art is admirably demonstrated by the way the cross is represented in stone carvings. The first crosses were simple shapes incised on unshaped pieces of stone. In later years superb three-dimensional carvings were produced. Classification of stone monuments is often based on the degree of sophistication used by stonemasons. There are many simple and elegant crosses on stones and in manuscripts and there are hundreds of different primary shapes of crosses, each having some symbolic association. Two early examples of rough stones incised with simple crosses, both accompanied by Latin inscriptions, are illustrated in Figs. 1.3b and c. The shape of these crosses evolved from the Chi-Rho (XP) monogram (Fig. 1.3a), X and P being the first two letters of the title 'Christ' in Greek. In Figs. 1.3b and c, X has been rotated transforming the monogram into a cross with a loop at the top. Figure 1.3d is an example of the same form of cross in an early manuscript, probably produced in Ireland. Enclosing a cross in a circle, as in the Kirkmadrine cross in Fig. 1.3c, may be an early form of the so-called Celtic cross that is still widely used on gravestones.

The evolution of the shape of the cross motif is a separate story which is not developed here. However, the ornamentation of the cross is one of the major features of early medieval art and it is used throughout this book to link the work of artists in stone with those working in other media. Inevitably, emphasis on the cross means that some aspects of the art are overlooked; nevertheless the fundamental geometric features can be treated comprehensively using this approach.

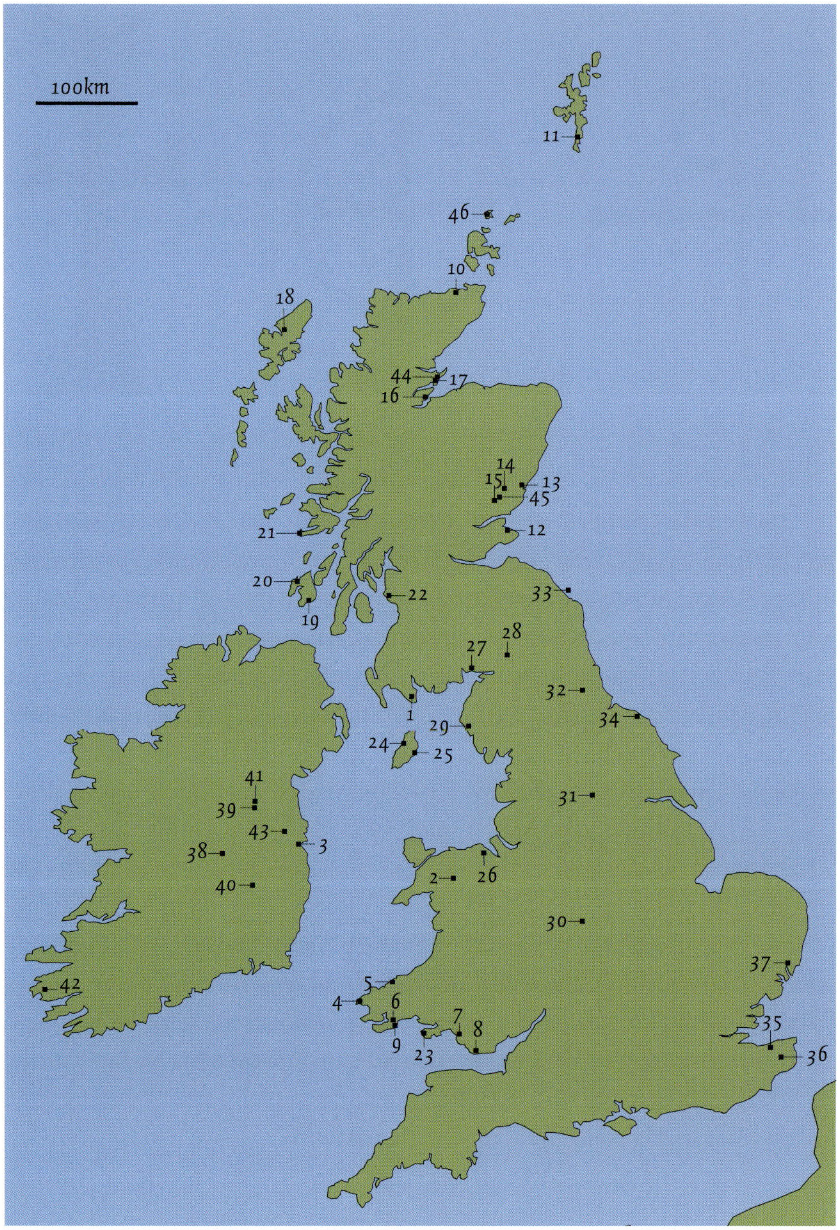

Figure 1.4
Distribution of the sites of monuments referred to in this book.

1 Kirkmadrine
2 Penmachno
3 Dublin
4 St Davids
5 Nevern
6 Carew
8 Margam
9 Llantwit Major
10 Thurso
11 St Ninian's Isle
12 St Andrew's
13 Montrose
14 Aberlemno
15 Meigle
16 Rosemarkie
17 Nigg
18 Callanish
19 Kildalton
20 Kilnave
21 Iona
22 Hunterston
23 Llangenydd
24 Kirk Michael
25 Lonan, Groundle
26 Whitford
27 Ruthwell
28 Bewcastle
29 Gosforth
30 Lichfield
31 Leeds
32 Durham
33 Lindisfarne
34 Whitby
35 Faversham
36 Kingston
37 Sutton Hoo
38 Durrow
39 Kells
40 Castledermot
41 Donore, Moynalty
42 Cloon Lough, Kerry
43 Lagore
44 Shandwick
45 Glamis
46 Westray

RECORDING AND VIEWING EARLY MEDIEVAL ART

Early medieval art has been found in all corners of the islands. All the sites referred to in this book are shown in Fig. 1.4. Table 1 (pp.34–35) is a summary of some of the main sources of books that include photographic copies of the art. Nowadays, original manuscripts are kept in libraries under stringent security conditions in carefully controlled environments. The

Books of Durrow and Kells are in the Library of Trinity College, Dublin, and the Lindisfarne Gospels are in the British Library in London. Direct access is exceptionally difficult but there are some superb, photographically produced facsimile editions available in special collections in other libraries. These can be accessed without too much difficulty. The facsimile editions often include authoritative commentaries describing many aspects of the work. More popular accounts of some of the Gospel books, which include selected colour reproductions, are available. Because of the close links that existed between monasteries in Ireland, Iona and Lindisfarne, widely recognised as important sources of the inspiration for all the manuscripts of this period, they are often referred to as Hiberno-Saxon or Insular manuscripts.

Metal artefacts are held in museums. Photographic records of the artefacts are available in a number of sources. For major finds, as at Sutton Hoo and St Ninian's Isle, there are substantial archaeologically oriented publications with numerous photographs of the discoveries. In recent years there have been a number of major exhibitions, promoted by the national museums of England, Ireland, Scotland and Wales, devoted to the metalwork of the early medieval period. Full colour catalogues were produced for these exhibitions. They provide an important record of many outstanding artefacts.

Most of the monumental stones remain at, or close to, their original sites in fields, churchyards, churches and local museums. These are often in remote places but they are readily accessible and can be visited freely. It is one of the joys of exploring geometric art to visit these quiet places and reflect on the ways of the people who inspired the art. The progressive deterioration of stone monuments exposed to wind and rain has resulted in a number of approaches to preservation, including moving them into nearby churches, enclosing them in glass cases and making full-size replicas that are then displayed in museums. Many monuments remain exposed to the elements and deterioration continues. Photographic records are available in corpora of monumental stones with descriptive notes and commentaries.

Before the development of photography archaeologists and others recorded the art with drawings and paintings. An outstanding example of this approach can be found in the work of J. O. Westwood (1868), which includes complete reproductions of some of the superb carpet pages in the Books of Durrow, Lindisfarne, Kells and others. Inevitably, the quality falls short of the original. The efforts of early archaeologists to record the patterns on stone monuments were far less successful, partly because these had to be drawn, in difficult conditions, in fields and churchyards.

Art historical studies require very accurate recording of patterns and styles. This is particularly difficult with damaged and eroded stone monuments. Many archaeologists have used brass rubbing techniques to reproduce the details. Modern techniques of illustration combine the use of photographic analysis and direct observation. There are some fine illustrations, from the work of a contemporary archaeological illustrator, I. G. Scott, in *Pictish Symbol Stones* (1999).

Graphical recording, and to a lesser extent photography, have limitations because there is a strong subjective element involved. The observer 'sees' what he or she recognises and understands and seeks to reproduce it. Nevertheless, the act of drawing does involve some 'unravelling' of the patterns and in the process one gains insights into the approach used by the original artists and craftspeople. George Bain (1951), whose work is discussed in the next section, used the maxim 'Theory may inform but Practice convinces' as a guiding principle of his approach to reproducing Celtic art. Similarly, in the Preface to his book, which includes a large number of his drawings of stone crosses, W. G. Collingwood (1927) observed, 'Line-drawings rather than photographs are given because they show the facts of design disentangled from the accidents of wear and tear'.

Even more understanding is gained when the art can be produced from first principles. Knowledge of the geometric factors that underpin the art removes some of the subjective aspects of recording by drawing. There is a world of difference between an accurate drawing that simply reproduces another image and a drawing created using the approach of the original artist. This approach also goes beyond the best photographic record, for 'what one can draw, from first principles, one can also understand'. This, of course, does not replace or compete with the original. One will never cease to wonder at the creative brilliance of the artists of the Dark Ages and the incredible skills of its craftspeople.

UNDERSTANDING ART AND GEOMETRY

A natural starting point for pursuing the geometric aspects of early medieval art is George Bain's sketch book *Celtic Art: The Methods of Construction* (1951). This work was first published in 1945 as a series of booklets and has been continuously in print since 1972. Bain based his work on extensive studies of what he referred to as 'the great intellectual artists and craftsmen of the Pictish nation, who produced the great art of the cross-slab stones of East Pictland and their counterparts in the Books of Durrow, Kells and Lindisfarne, the Tara Brooch, the Ardagh Chalice and other masterpieces of the Celtic jewellers' art'. Although this suggests that he neglected the contributions of non-Celtic peoples it is clear from his book that he recognised that the art had roots in many cultures beyond the narrow bounds implied by the title *Celtic Art*.

Bain was an artist and a teacher. His outstanding contribution was to provide an understanding of the way the patterns were constructed, giving his students the tools to create their own designs using the principles derived from his studies. A natural end result of a study of Bain's book is a design for an artefact to be crafted in materials of one's choice. After his death in 1968 the family of George Bain presented his drawings, and examples of his work, to the Groam House Museum in Rosemarkie, near Inverness in north-east Scotland. The museum is a centre of Pictish work and is most celebrated for the Rosemarkie stone (see Chapter 3) which takes a central place. The curator, Susan Seright, has written an appreciation of the life and work of Bain, *George Bain – Master of Celtic Art* (1997). It is worth noting that there are those who find Bain's book difficult to follow. Many other elementary guides to the creation of designs characteristic of 'Celtic art' are now available.

Bain saw his approach to the development of patterns in Celtic art as 'mathematical'. There are indeed some challenging mathematical problems associated with the patterns but Bain's description gives a rather mistaken view of what is involved and the approach that he used. The formation of patterns requires some skills in conventional geometry of the kind one learns in the first few years of secondary school. It is a skill not given to everyone. With Bain's book one can spend many fascinating hours and days and years unravelling patterns and even more time attempting to produce original designs that follow the rules evident in the patterns used by the original artists.

Regular and irregular

The concept of 'rules' and 'principles' in relation to art requires some explanation. Thus, for example, one of the most common motifs in Insular art is interlacing, also referred to as interlace. A simple interlacing pattern, set in a rectangular panel, is shown in Fig. 1.5a. The pattern follows a number of rules that may be said to be characteristic of regular interlacing. These are summarised as follows: (i) the cords of the interlacing cross over and under at each successive intersection, (ii) the orientations of the cords

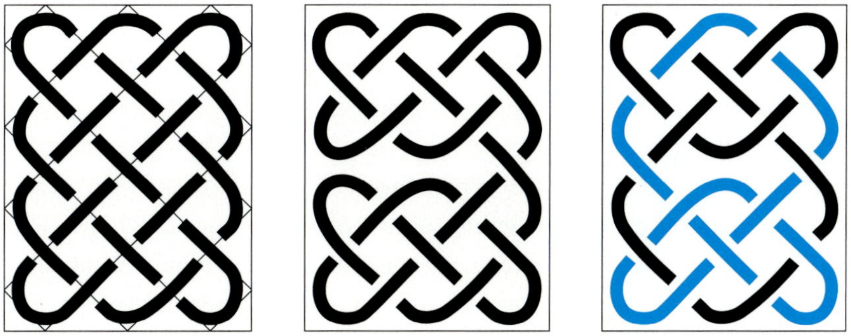

Figure 1.5
Panels ornamented with simple interlacing patterns.

(a) *(b)* *(c)*

follow a simple grid produced by two sets of equal-spaced parallel lines, (iii) the spacing of the cords is uniform, and (iv) the whole pattern is produced from a single unbroken and continuous cord. A whole series of closely similar patterns can be drawn obeying all these rules. An example is shown in Fig. 1.5b. The example in Fig. 1.5c has two independent cords and thereby does not satisfy rule (iv) above.

A pattern, comparable to Fig. 1.5a, occurs in one of the panels of the Maen Achwyfan cross at Whitford (Fig. 1.2) as illustrated in Fig. 1.6. It is apparent immediately that here all the above rules have been broken. The edges of the stone have been damaged so it is not possible to determine the arrangement of the loops at the sides of the panel. Even so, it is clear that the interlacing pattern on the cross does not follow a regular grid and is formed from many unconnected cords. The design has a beauty and fascination of its own but it has broken the rules set by the interlacing in Fig. 1.5.

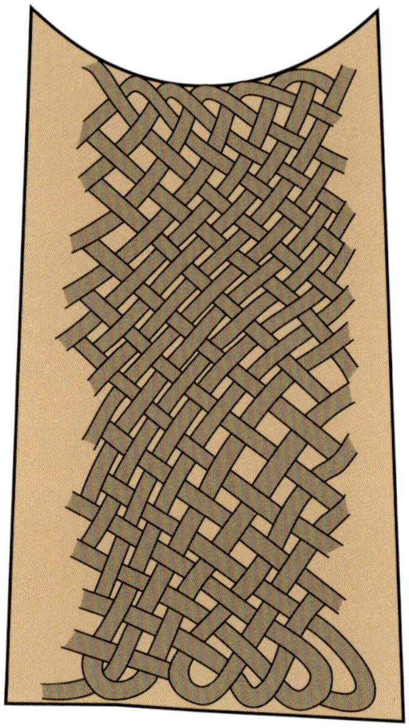

Figure 1.6
Illustration of design of interlacing in a panel on the east-facing side of Maen Achwyfan, Whitford. The edges of the panel are damaged so it is not possible to complete the detail.

If one asks the question, implied by this approach, 'What are the rules and who decided what they were?', one is drawn inevitably to the work of the artists and craftsmen who produced the Insular manuscripts and the Pictish cross-slabs. Although many of the motifs have their origins in designs produced by much earlier peoples, the art displayed in these manuscripts and stones undoubtedly reached a high-water mark of achievement and creative skill.

Bain drew much of his inspiration, for the interpretation of the patterns, from the earlier work of J. Romilly Allen. The book by Allen and Anderson, *The Early Christian Monuments of Scotland* (1903), represents probably the most influential contribution ever produced to an understanding of the methods of construction of geometric art of this period. It remains, to this day, a most valuable source of reference, used widely by archaeologists and art historians. Inevitably, there are numerous references to this work in the present book.

There is no direct evidence that a set of rules ever existed – except the circumstantial evidence of the work itself. Some scholars have suggested that pattern books were produced, and circulated, for use by other artists. One suspects that the underlying principles – the geometric rules – were taught and instilled in scriptoria and workshops over many decades. How exciting it would have been to tiptoe into the scriptorium at Lindisfarne to watch the work in progress! One can only guess at how the master craftsmen and artists assembled teams to support their work.

Procedures

Searching for the rules is an exciting journey of exploration and discovery for, as alluded to earlier, the patterns are intrinsically attractive and beautiful. The temptation to dismiss them as dull and monotonous must be avoided. Even seemingly perfectly symmetrical patterns are never truly so. The theme of the next two chapters is a description of the underlying framework of the designs and the rules that underpin the development of the intricate patterns.

Most of the illustrations in this book were developed from first principles without recourse to routine copying. Naturally, they reproduce the work of the original artists and craftspeople. A limited amount of conventional copying and tracing has been used. By drawing the patterns from first principles one discovers the skills needed to produce them and obtains an insight into the imagination and creativity of the artists. My drawing board is a computer screen and my drawing instruments the tools provided in a graphics software package that allows the manipulation of 'pen' and 'brush' in much the same way as in conventional graphic art using pen and brush, straight-edge and compasses. I have relied, almost entirely, on a vector-based programme. This approach has a number of technical benefits over conventional methods but it is essentially the same as in the original works of art, drawn out on wax, slate, bone, wood or wet clay, before being transferred to vellum, metal or stone. Many of the drawings, particularly those involving spirals and zoomorphic motifs, require some 'freehand' drawing because the shapes do not follow rigorous geometric forms. These were also produced by vector-based computer drawing using the equivalent of conventional tracing and sketching to define the overall shape.

In exploring the grids used by the original artists, and seeking ways of reproducing the patterns, I have diverged from the conventional facsimile approach. The emphasis is on communicating the patterns rather than producing an exact copy. In any case photographs do this so much better. However, throughout the book I have followed closely the patterns as they were drawn and sculpted including fascinating deviations. Lines that the artist clearly intended to be straight are drawn straight. Details, such as the width of lines and the distribution of colours, have not been reproduced precisely. This sometimes results in a different aesthetic effect. It would be quite wrong to attempt to reproduce the imprint of time and age that has made the patterns on these ancient documents, stones and metal artefacts so wonderful.

In the final paragraphs of her seminal book, *Irish Art in the Early Christian Period (to 800 AD)* (1965), Henry discusses the use of mechanical aids, by which she was referring to the geometric approach, used by artists to create their designs, observing that 'they are tools to be used to best effect, his [the artist's] role being to combine the patterns which help him to produce and make a work of art out of that inert material. Of these tools his mind must remain master.' In this way she signalled the value of the geometric approach but offered an important warning about the pitfalls of following this approach too rigorously. However, it is important to recognise that rules must be learnt and understood before they can be distorted.

Medium	Location	Sources
General	Anglo-Saxon	Wilson, D. M. (1984), *Anglo-Saxon Art: From the Seventh Century to the Norman Conquest*, London, Thames and Hudson
Metalwork (general)	Anglo-Saxon	Webster, L. and Backhouse, J. (eds) (1991), *The Making of England: Anglo-Saxon Art and Culture AD 600–900*, London, British Museum
	Celtic	Youngs, S. (ed.) (1989) *'The Work of Angels': Masterpieces of Celtic Metalwork 6th to 9th Centuries AD*, London, British Museum
Metalwork (hoards)	Sutton Hoo	Bruce-Mitford, R. and others (1975–83), *The Sutton Hoo Ship-Burial* (3 vols), London, British Museum Publications
		Bruce-Mitford, R. (1979), *The Sutton Hoo Ship-Burial: A Handbook by Rupert Bruce-Mitford*, London, British Museum Publications
	St Ninian's Isle	Small, A., Thomas, C. and Wilson, D. M. (1973), *St Ninian's Isle and its Treasures* (2 vols), London, Oxford University Press
Manuscripts	Insular: general	Alexander, J. G. G. (1978), *Insular Manuscripts 6th to 9th Centuries*, London, Harvey Miller
		Henderson, G. (1987), *From Durrow to Kells: The Insular Gospel-Books, 650–800*, London, Thames and Hudson
		Henry, F. (1965), *Irish Art in the Early Christian Period (to 800 AD)*, London, Methuen

Table 1

A selection of primary sources of photographs of early medieval art

Medium	**Location**	**Sources**
Manuscripts (by location)	Lindisfarne	Backhouse, J. (1981), *The Lindisfarne Gospels*, London, Phaidon Press
		Kendrick, T. D. (1956–60), *Evangelorium Quattuor Codex Lindisfarnensis* (2 vols), Olten, Switzerland, Urs Graf-Verlag
	Durrow	Luce, A. A. (1960), *Evangelorium Quattuor Durmachensis (The Book of Durrow)* (2 vols), Olten, Switzerland, Urs Graf-Verlag
	Kells	Brown, P. (1980), *The Book of Kells*, London, Thames and Hudson
		Henry, F. (1974), *The Book of Kells: Reproductions from the Manuscript at Trinity College Dublin*, London, Thames and Hudson
	Wales	Nash-Williams, V. E. (1950), *The Early Christian Monuments of Wales*, Cardiff, University of Wales Press
	Ireland	Henry, F. (1965), *Irish Art in the Early Christian Period (to 800 AD)*, London, Methuen
		Henry, F. (1967), *Irish Art during the Viking Invasions (800–1020 AD)*, London, Methuen
	Isle of Man	Kermode, P. M. C. (1907), *Manx Crosses*, London, Bembrose and Sons. A facsimile edition has been published by Pinkfoot Press.

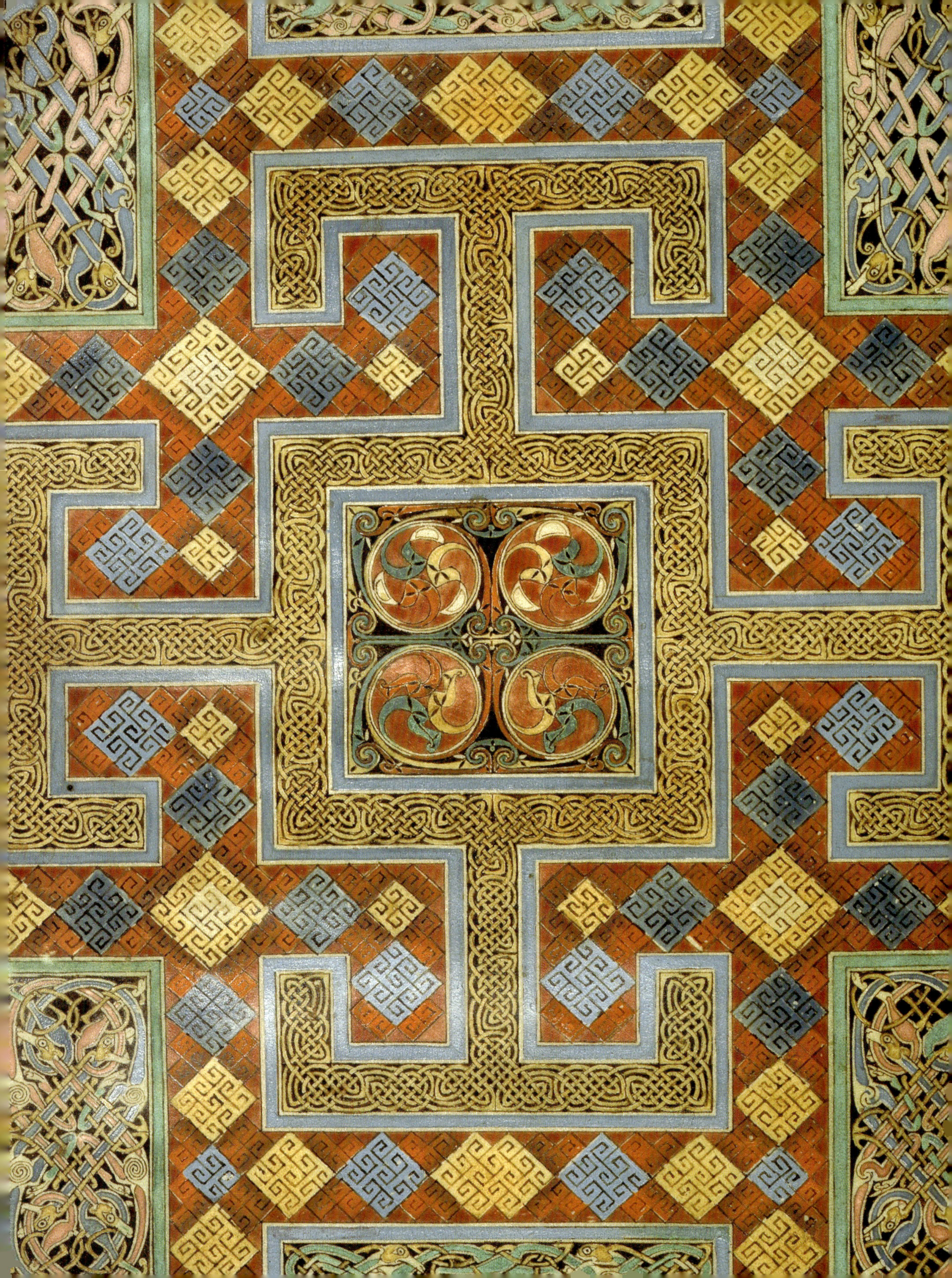

2

Panels and layout

IMPORTANCE OF PANELS

One of the most characteristic features of geometric art, common to manuscripts, stone monuments and metalwork, is the display of complex patterns in separate panels. The design of each panel is distinct and often unrelated to the design of adjacent panels except in a rather general way. Some of the main features of the panel approach are explored in Chapters 3 and 4 along with the methods used by artists and draughtsmen to create exotic and fascinating images.

In the first part of this chapter the construction and design of the layout of one of the magnificent cross-carpet pages of the Lindisfarne Gospel Book (Fig. 2.1) is described. The whole page is made up of panels ornamented with interlacing, spiral, key, and zoomorphic motifs. The shape and distribution of the panels is based on a grid of squares created with compasses and straight-edge using simple geometric procedures.

In general, the shapes of panels are not restricted to squares and rectangles. Any shape of panel is possible. Thus, in the centre of the carpet page in Fig. 2.1 there is a cross-shaped panel decorated with very fine interlacing. The outline of this equal-armed cross follows the square grid of the overall design. An early example of the use of a grid approach for the layout of panels is shown in Fig. 2.2 from the *Diatessaron*, a sixteenth-century Persian copy of the Gospel harmony of Tatian produced in the second century. Circular panels are also common and were often used in metalwork. Two classical metalwork examples, the Kingston brooch and the Donore disc, are used to introduce some of the geometric methods that are involved. Examples of the use of irregularly shaped panels to decorate initial letters, canon tables and more complex crosses are included in Chapter 3.

Careful investigative work, particularly by Bruce-Mitford at the British Museum in relation to the Lindisfarne Gospels, has shown how the primary grids were marked out on vellum using very fine prick marks (see Kendrick, 1956–60). The detail is remarkable. Even more remarkable is the way that secondary and tertiary grids were produced to provide the layout for the motif

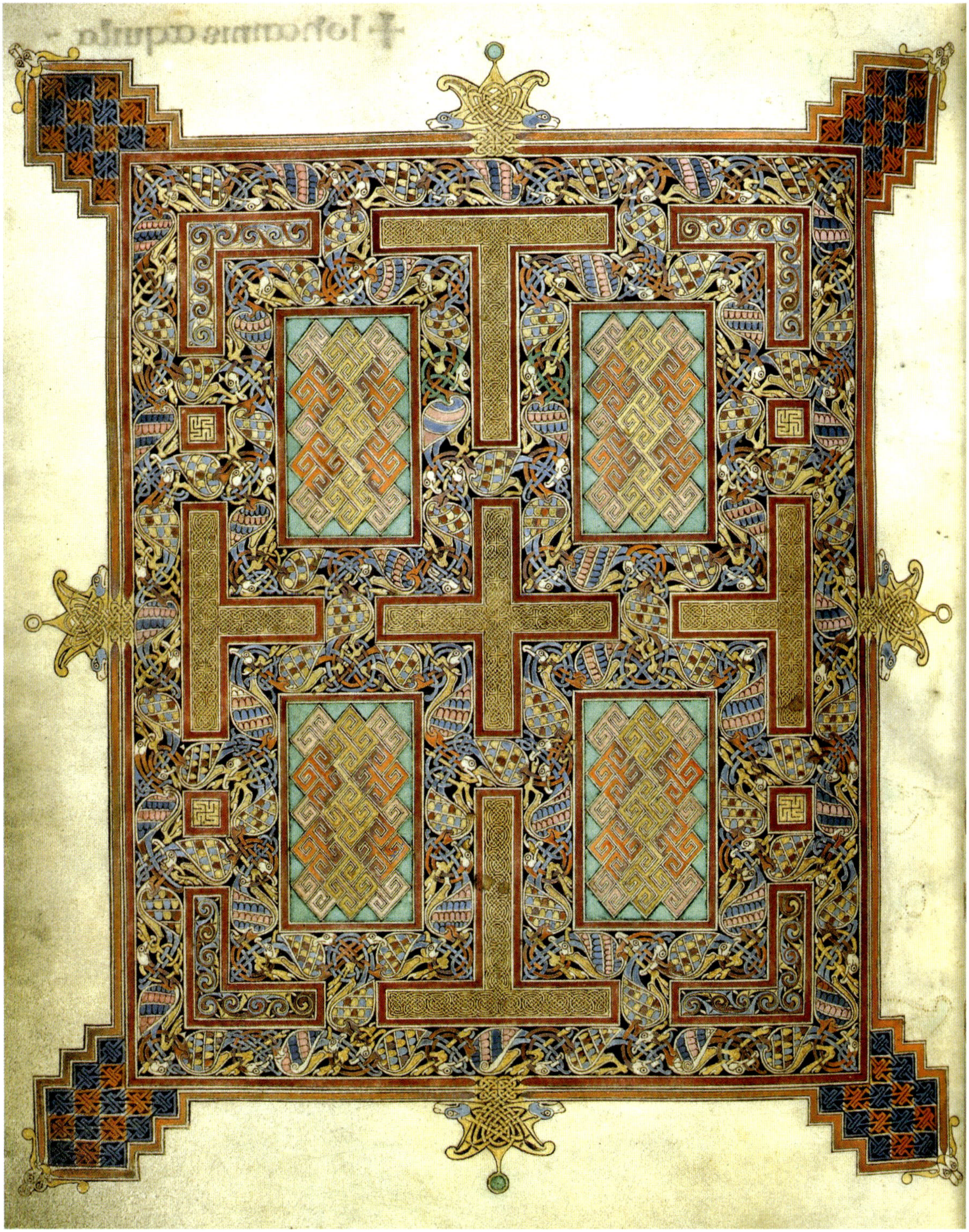

Figure 2.1

Photograph of cross-carpet page f. 210v of Lindisfarne Gospels (by permission of British Library). Each page of the Gospel book measures 340 mm by 240 mm.

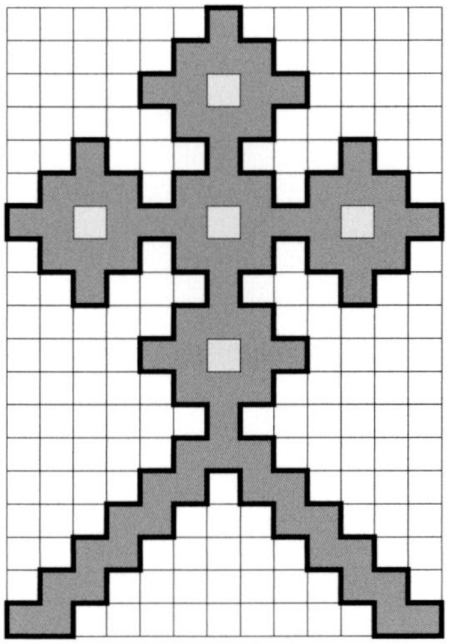

Figure 2.2
Cross-shaped panel formed from a grid of squares 13-by-19 based on a cross-carpet page in the Persian Diatessaron. *For details see* Nordenfalk *(1968, 1977).*

designs inside the panels. Examination of the reverse side of the vellum, behind the central cross in Fig. 2.1, revealed a network of prick marks that was used to create a grid for the interlacing pattern and, thereby, determine the orientation and distribution of the cords in the interlacing. There can be little doubt that similar methods were used in the layout and design of stone monuments. As an example, the construction of the patterns on one face of the Rosemarkie stone is included in Chapter 3. This demonstrates how the layout of panels is determined from the primary grid and the way that the distribution of motifs in the panels is based on secondary and tertiary grids, related to the primary grid.

Another remarkable feature of the art is the way that motifs are arranged to completely fill the panels irrespective of their shape. This is attributable to two main features of the work: first, the close correlation between the primary, secondary and tertiary grids and, secondly, the flexible use of motifs. These ideas are developed in Chapter 3.

At the end of this chapter there is a discussion of some issues that are generally referred to as 'style'. They have only secondary relevance to geometric aspects and rules. However, they are important for art historians and archaeologists concerned with understanding the development of art and the historical context of the work. Although the basic geometric aspects are common to all media, the appearance of the art is influenced by the individual 'styles' of the craftsmen, the choice of motifs, the way that motifs are represented, and the materials and techniques available.

LAYING OUT PRIMARY AND SECONDARY GRIDS

Book of Lindisfarne cross-carpet page, folio 210v

The Lindisfarne Gospels, now in the British Library, provide an excellent guide to most of the principles that determine the geometric aspects of early medieval art. Produced in the monastery at Lindisfarne, the Gospel book survived raiding visits by the Vikings in the ninth and tenth centuries. For many years it was kept in Durham Cathedral. A limited-edition facsimile of the book, *Evangelium Quattuor Codex Lindisfarnensis*, was published in two volumes in 1956 and 1960. This work has excellent photographic colour reproductions and many detailed and authoritative essays on various aspects of the book. The essays by Bruce-Mitford are particularly important in the context of geometric art. There is a good introductory commentary on the Gospels by Backhouse (1981). See also Brown (2003).

According to the evidence of the colophon, part of which is copied below, the Lindisfarne Gospels were produced in about 698:

Eadfrith, Bishop of the Lindisfarne Church, originally wrote this book for God and for Saint Cuthbert and – jointly – for all the saints whose relics are in the Island. And Ethelwald, Bishop of the Lindisfarne islanders, impressed it on the outside and covered it – as he well knew how to do. And Billfrith, the anchorite, forged the ornaments which are on it on the outside and adorned it with gold and with gems and also with gilded-over silver – pure metal. And Aldred, unworthy and most miserable priest, glossed it in English between the lines with the help of God and Saint Cuthbert.

This colophon was written in Latin about 250 years after the production of the manuscript and is widely held to be authoritative. Experts seem to agree that Eadfrith, who was bishop of the monastery at Lindisfarne on Holy Island, was the main 'scribe and illuminator' of the manuscript. The work is of monumental proportions, involving many skills and techniques. It seems most likely that, in the scriptorium at Lindisfarne, Eadfrith worked with a team of craftspeople, skilled in the preparation of vellums, inks and paints, and assisted by novices, apprentices and other artists in the design and execution of the work. Each page was produced individually before binding.

Folio 210v (Fig. 2.1) introduces the Gospel according to St John. It is one of the finest examples of a cross-carpet page in all of the Gospel books. The layout of f. 210v is shown in Fig. 2.3. The detail is based on the photograph in Fig. 2.1 augmented by reference to the full-colour facsimile edition of the Gospels. The image in Fig. 2.1 is somewhat distorted because the photograph was taken of the open book and the inner binding has resulted in some of the dimensions being foreshortened. In producing the layout diagram it was assumed that the original drawing was symmetrical and undistorted. The pages of the Gospel book are about 240 mm by 340 mm.

The reverse side of f. 210v is also reproduced in the facsimile edition as f. 209r. This page is almost blank, without script or illustration. As mentioned previously it reveals many of the markings that were used in the creation of f. 210v. The pricks and marking-out lines can be used to explore the way that the artist mapped out the design.

Grid arrangements

The design of the rectangular area marked by the two diagonal lines in Fig. 2.3 is based on a grid of orthogonal, equal-spaced lines that form a set of squares 15 by 19. The position and shape of the panels are shown by the shaded regions. Each panel has a border, and a characteristic design, based on the primary motifs – interlacing, key, spiral and zoomorphic. In Fig. 2.3 panels with similar motifs are shaded to the same density. With an odd number of squares on each side of the grid, the panel in the centre of the page forms an equal-armed cross, five squares by five squares. The cross is

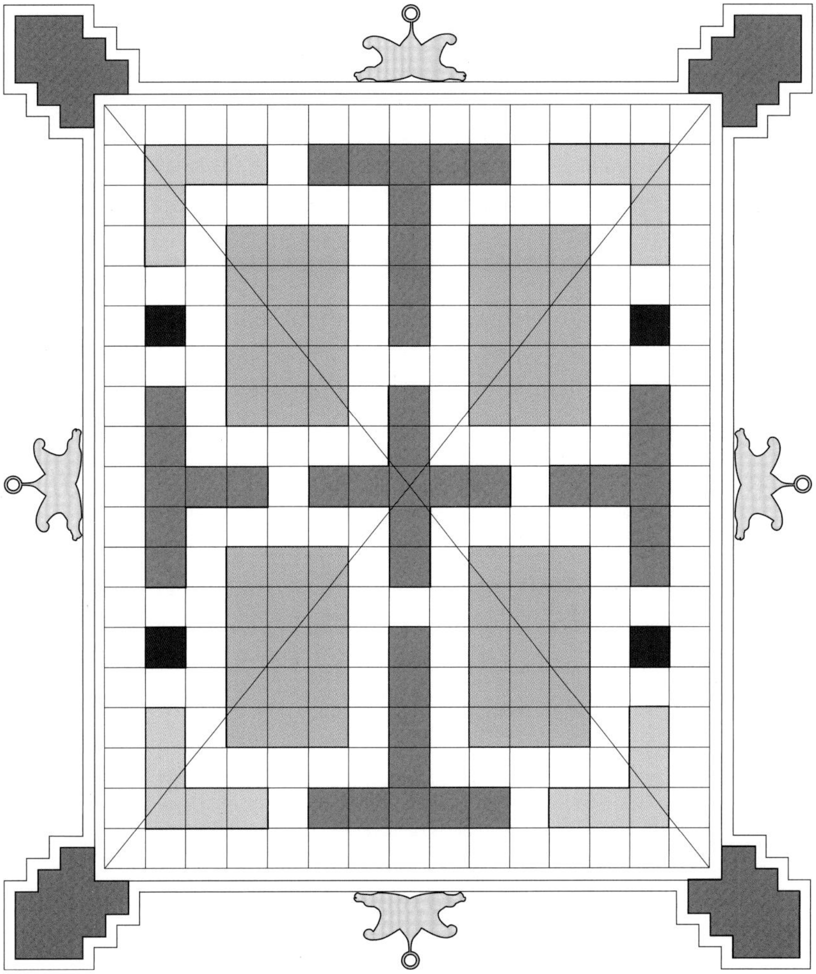

Figure 2.3
Outline grid of cross-carpet page f. 210v of Lindisfarne Gospels showing distribution of panels ornamented with different motifs.

decorated with an interlacing pattern. A similar pattern was used to decorate the T-shaped panels that are shaded in the same density as the central cross. The four rectangular panels, three squares by five squares, are ornamented with a key pattern and the L-shaped corner panels have a spiral design. There are four 'single-square' panels with a swastika motif.

The panels appear to be set on a background pattern rather like a set of paintings displayed on a wall with decorated wallpaper. However, this is not a true or accurate description. The 'background' to the panels is effectively another panel, having a zoomorphic design that fills precisely the squares of the grid between the main panels. In other words the main panels do not overlay the zoomorphic designs. The birds of the zoomorphic pattern are organised and oriented in a very precise fashion – their position, orientation and plumage have close similarities to the distribution of soldiers in a military tattoo carrying out a complex, but ordered, manoeuvre. The ornamentation of the border is also in the form of panels. The corner finials of the main frame have a border around a key pattern and the centre of each side of the frame has an interlaced zoomorphic pattern.

The primary grid provides a framework for the description of the designs of the individual panels that make up the cross-carpet page. Within each panel there is a secondary grid that determines the form of the pattern. In some panels a tertiary grid is used. The identification of these grid structures lies at the heart of developing the geometric designs. Eventually, as the scale of the pattern becomes even finer, there is a degree of randomness in the designs. This is attributable to a number of factors such as the personal whims and mischief of the artist, mistakes in execution, and the fineness of the detail that extends beyond the resolution of the artists' tools and the medium of the work.

Cross-shaped panel ornamented with interlacing, f. 210v

The equal-armed cross with its border (Fig. 2.4) occupies nine squares of the primary grid and forms only a small part of the overall design. Its shape and form derive directly from the primary grid. The pricks evident on the reverse side of the vellum (f. 209r) reveal the grid used to produce the interlacing pattern. As illustrated in Fig. 2.5 they form a network of squares with sides

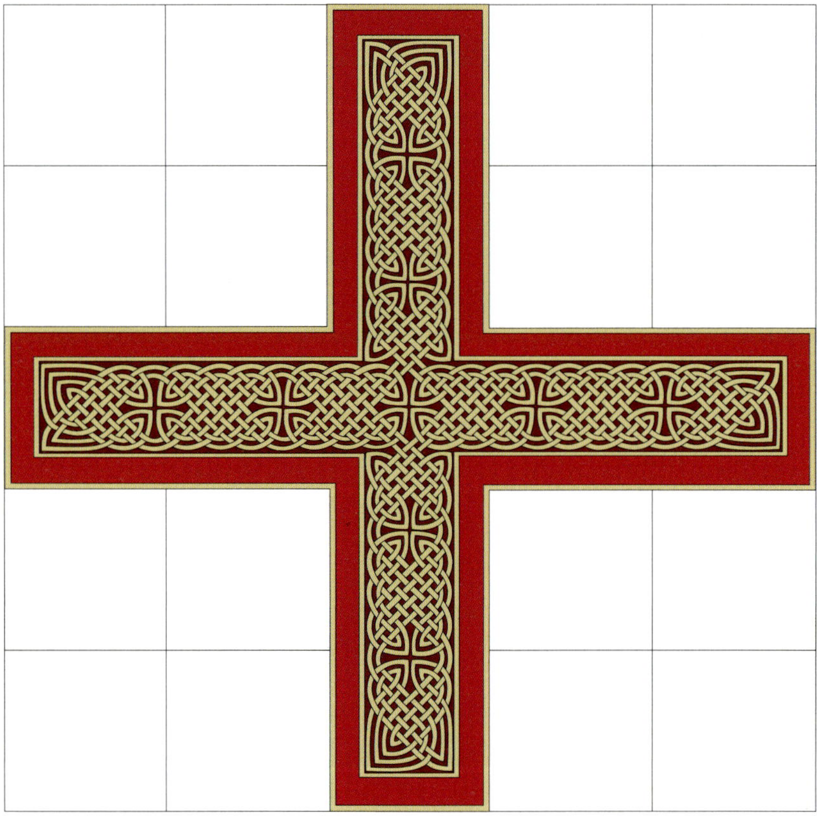

Figure 2.4
Cross-shaped panel, ornamented with interlacing from f. 210v of Lindisfarne Gospels. Length of sides of each square of the five-by-five grid is about 12.5 mm.

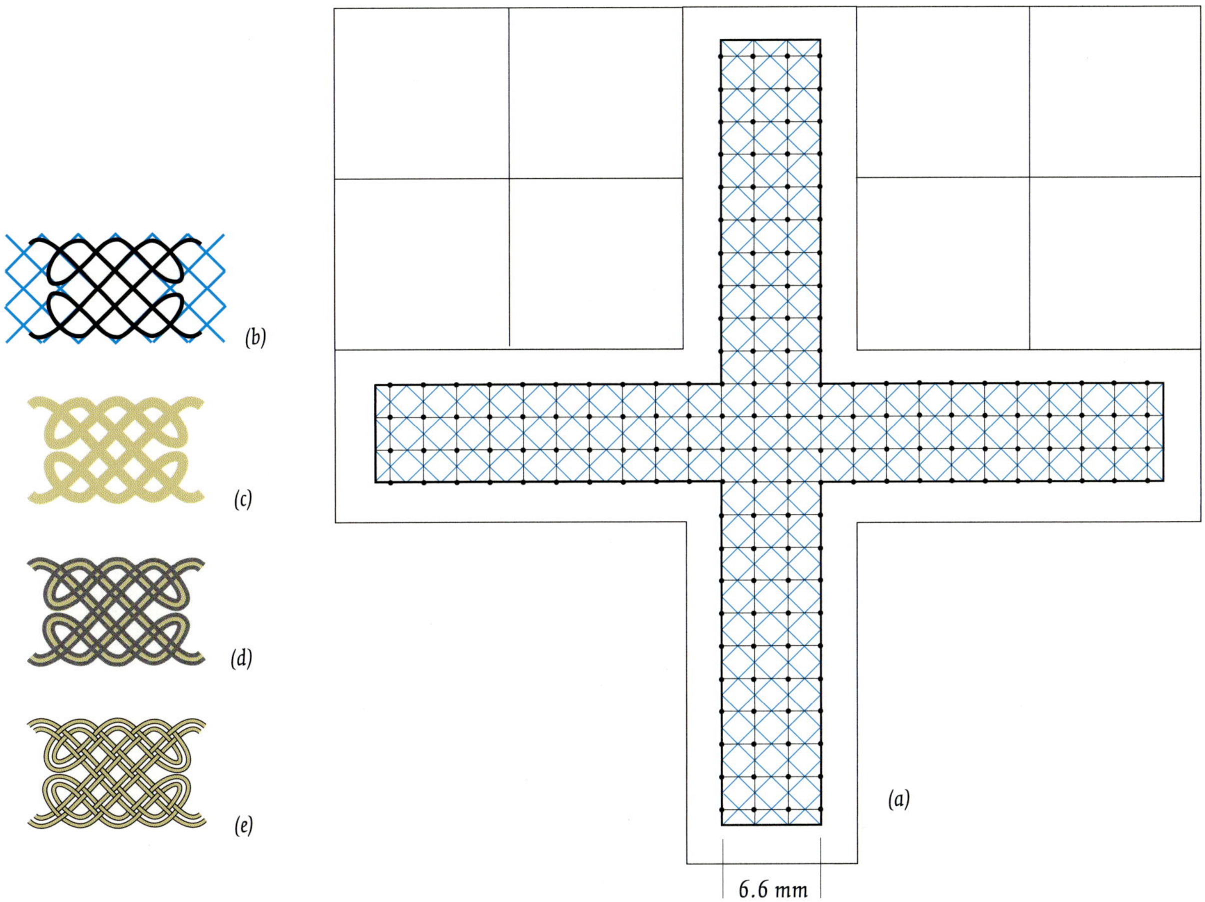

Figure 2.5
Method of construction of the interlacing in the cross-shaped panel shown in Fig. 2.4. The black dots show the positions of prick-marks visible on reverse side of the vellum.

2.2 mm long. The vertical and horizontal lines, joining the pricks at the corners of the squares of the grid, are also apparent on the reverse side of the vellum. This square grid was used to produce an even finer square grid oriented at 45° to the first grid. The cords of the interlacing pattern follow this finer grid.

More details of the construction of interlacing patterns are given in Chapter 4. It is sufficient here to record the drawing sequence used to produce the final pattern in Fig. 2.4. This is illustrated in Fig. 2.5. The position of the pricks and the secondary and tertiary square grids are shown in Fig. 2.5a. In Fig. 2.5b the lines of the finer grid, oriented at 45° to the first grid, have been widened and a simple interlacing design drawn by following the lines of this grid. The lines of this pattern were then widened into cords or bands (Fig. 2.5c) and the sides of the cords highlighted, as in Fig. 2.5d. The final structure of the interlacing was obtained by outlining the sides of the new lines and interlacing the individual sub-cords (Fig. 2.5e). The unit pattern in Fig. 2.5e is repeated six times in the cross-shaped panel (Fig. 2.4). These, with the addition of six modified units, form the final interlacing

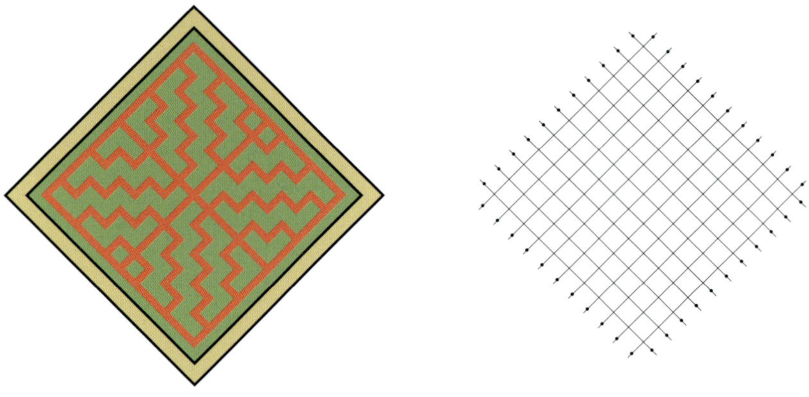

(a) (b)

Figure 2.6
Simple square panel with a step pattern, part of the initial page f. 211v in the Lindisfarne Gospels. (a) Pattern formed by following grid lines. (b) 10-by-10 square grid marked out by pricks clearly visible on the reverse side of the vellum.

pattern. There are 56 under-and-over intersections in each unit pattern and nearly 600 intersections in the whole pattern. The dimensions of the square grid, 12.5 mm square, in Fig. 2.4 give a striking impression of the fineness of the detail in the pattern and the skills of the artist.

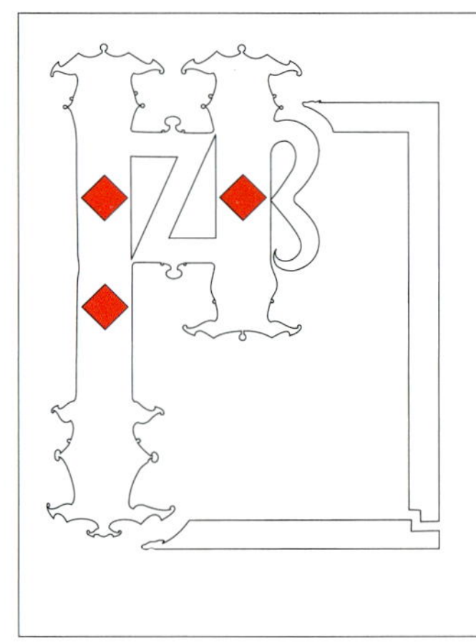

Figure 2.7
Outline of initial page f. 211v at beginning of St John's Gospel in Lindisfarne Gospels showing position and size of square panels in Fig. 2.6.

Book of Lindisfarne initial letter page, f. 211v

This page offers another simple example of the use of pricks and very fine-scale grids. It follows immediately after f. 210v and has an initial letter with numerous panels richly ornamented with motif designs, a single human face, and the first few words of St John's Gospel 'In the beginning was the word ... ' written in Latin. It includes three small slightly distorted square panels, 15 mm by 15 mm, ornamented with step patterns (Fig. 2.6a). An outline of the design of the page, with the position of the panels shaded red, is shown in Fig. 2.7. The pricks on the reverse side of this panel reveal a 10-by-10 square grid (Fig. 2.7b). Remarkably, the lines of the grid are only 1.5 mm apart. Following the lines of the grid created the simple and elegant step pattern in Fig. 2.6a.

GEOMETRIC METHODS

Simple methods in geometry

The main tools or instruments used for setting out designs are compasses and straight-edge. There is no need for the measurement of length or angle. The application of the ideas and principles of scaling mean that geometric procedures can be applied on large and small-scale outlines and patterns. The artists of early medieval times had the benefit of hundreds of years of Egyptian, Greek and Roman art and architecture in which the use of compasses and straight-edge had been developed and refined to a high level. There is endless potential for creating shapes of all kinds using these two simple instruments.

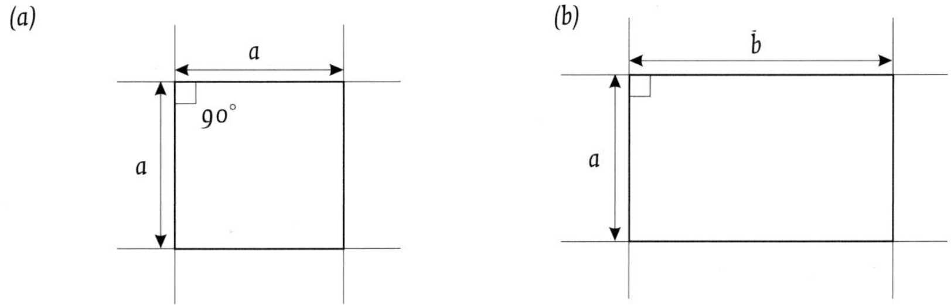

Figure 2.8
Square and rectangle formed by intersection of two sets of equal-spaced parallel straight lines.

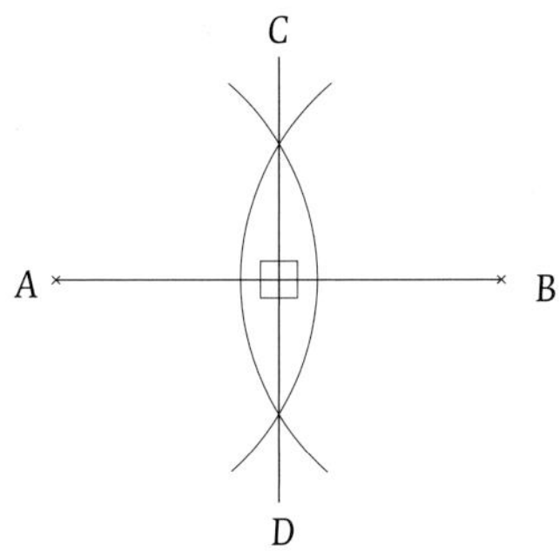

Figure 2.9
Method of dividing line AB into two equal parts. Line CD is at right angles (orthogonal or normal) to AB.

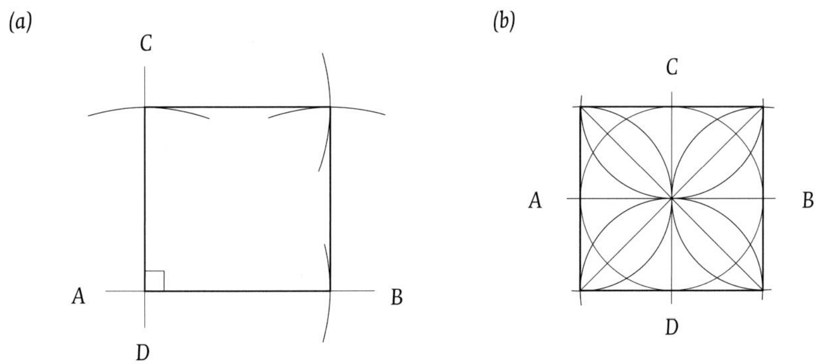

Figure 2.10
Two methods of constructing squares. In both the first step is forming a right angle at intersection of AB and CD. The second step in (b) is drawing a circle centred at the intersection.

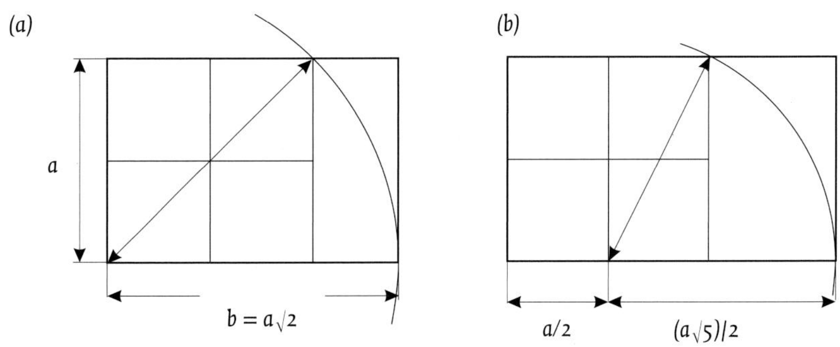

Figure 2.11
Construction of rectangles with fixed a/b ratios. (a) $a/b = 1/\sqrt{2} = 0.7071...$, *(b)* $a/b = 2/(1 + \sqrt{5}) = 0.6180...$

The underlying principles are those of elementary geometry. The starting point for most designs is either a square or a rectangle (Fig. 2.8) constructed from two sets of lines intersecting at right angles. Drawing a right angle and dividing a straight line into two equal parts is achieved using compasses and straight-edge as illustrated in Fig. 2.9. Similarly, a square is produced, by the constructions shown in Fig. 2.10, without the need for a set-square or protractor.

There are many ways of producing rectangles with precise values for the ratio of the lengths of the two sides (a/b). Two simple examples are illustrated in Fig. 2.11. In Fig. 2.11a the length of the longer side b is equal to the length of the diagonal of the square. From the theorem of Pythagoras, relating the lengths of the sides of a right-angled triangle to each other, it follows that $b^2 = a^2+a^2$ so that $b = (2a^2)^{1/2}$. The ratio of the lengths of the sides $a/b = 1/2^{1/2}$, also written as $1/\sqrt{2}$, which is an irrational number, 0.7071... Similarly, for the construction in Fig. 2.11b, the length of the longer side $b = a/2+(a^2+a^2/4)^{1/2}$. For this rectangle $a/b = 2/(1+\sqrt{5})$ which is also an irrational number, 0.6180...

Irrational numbers are not commensurate with ordinary quantities such as natural numbers. This means, in simple terms, that they cannot be written precisely. They can be written in decimal terms to a given approximation whereas, in principle, by using geometric constructions the ratios are produced exactly. The two examples of rectangles shown in Fig. 2.11 have been called 'true measures'. In particular, the rectangle with $a/b = 2/(1+\sqrt{5})$ is called the golden section, or golden ratio, which has long been regarded as one of the keys to the mysteries of art. In art, architecture and other forms, use of the golden section creates a sense of harmony that is aesthetically pleasing.

Geometric constructions are used to form grids of equally spaced lines. The construction in Fig. 2.9 divides the line AB into two equal lengths and this can be repeated successively. Alternatively, a grid is formed by the use of compasses to step out equal intervals along two intersecting lines. Figure 2.12 illustrates a simple procedure for dividing a line of fixed length AB into a given number of equal lengths (say six). A second line AC is drawn at an angle to AB and, using compasses, six equal distances of arbitrary length are marked along AC. Line AB is then divided into six equal lengths by drawing a set of lines parallel to BC intersecting AB.

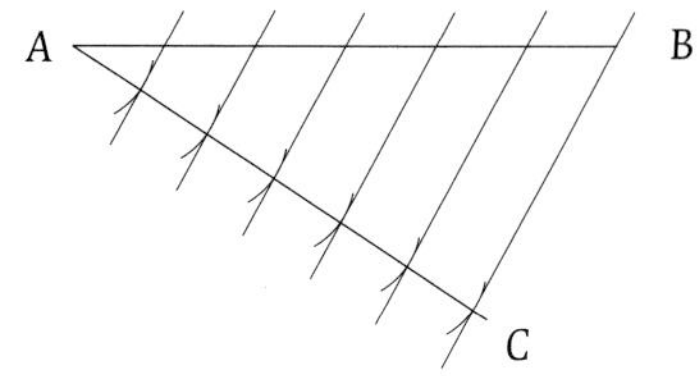

Figure 2.12
Method of dividing a line AB into six equal lengths using compasses and straight-edge.

The overall shape of a design is determined largely by practical and aesthetic factors such as the size and shape of the manuscript page or the block of stone. Many examples of layouts are included in this book. Each face of the Rosemarkie stone is ornamented with panels of different shapes and sizes but the individual panels have been designed using a well-defined, geometrically constructed grid. The central cross panel is based on a square grid that has been formed from a square by dividing the sides into nine equal parts. Every detail of the rest of the design, including the equal-armed cross, conforms to this grid. The cross-carpet page f. 210v of the Lindisfarne Gospels, described earlier, is also based on a square grid. The external rectangular form, excluding the border, is produced with 15 squares on the short sides and 19 squares on the long sides so that $a/b = 15/19 = 0.7894...$

Book of Lindisfarne cross-carpet page, f. 2v

In his book *The Earliest Irish and English Bookarts: Visual and Poetic Forms before AD 1000* (1994), Stevick develops an approach to the layout of manuscripts that gives particular emphasis to geometric constructions. He identified numerous ratios for rectangles (a/b) and related the ratios in 'bookart' with those found in the structure of poems written in the same historical period. This approach was applied to illuminated pages in many works including the Gospel books of Kells, Lindisfarne and Durrow. Numerous ingenious constructions were illustrated. However, the work is overly complicated and insufficient emphasis is given, in determining the basis for the overall layout, to the interaction between large-scale geometric constructions and the detailed fine-scale geometric features of the ornamentation. Some examples of the constructions used by Stevick to describe the distribution of panels and other features of the design are not adequate.

The layout of Lindisfarne f. 2v provides a good example of the need to include fine-scale geometric parameters in the interpretation of the approach used by the artist in achieving the overall design. The outline of the cross-carpet page f. 2v, containing a six-square cross, is shown in Fig. 2.13. The original artwork is distorted, presumably as a result of changes in the shape of the vellum owing to ageing and the effects of dampness. This makes accurate dimensioning of the original work impossible. In spite of these difficulties Stevick showed that the shape of the outer frame can be matched closely to that formed by two rectangles, each with a ratio $a/b = 2/(1+\sqrt{5})$, equivalent to the golden section, sharing a common long side. This shape is formed by combining two rectangles, using the construction in Fig. 2.11b for the golden section, or alternatively, by the construction in Fig. 2.14. Since BC $= (a\sqrt{5}/2 - a/2) = a(\sqrt{5} - 1)/2$ it follows that $BC/AB = (\sqrt{5} - 1)/2$ which can be shown to be equal to $2/(1+\sqrt{5})$, the golden ratio. The rectangle forming the outer frame has $a/b = 1/(\sqrt{5} - 1) = 0.8090...$

The shape and position of the cross within the inner border or frame depends on two factors, related only loosely to the shape of the outer border: first, the symmetrical position of the cross in the inner frame and, secondly, the tessellated diagonal fret or key pattern design used to ornament the cross. The position of the cross is based on the construction in Fig. 2.13a.

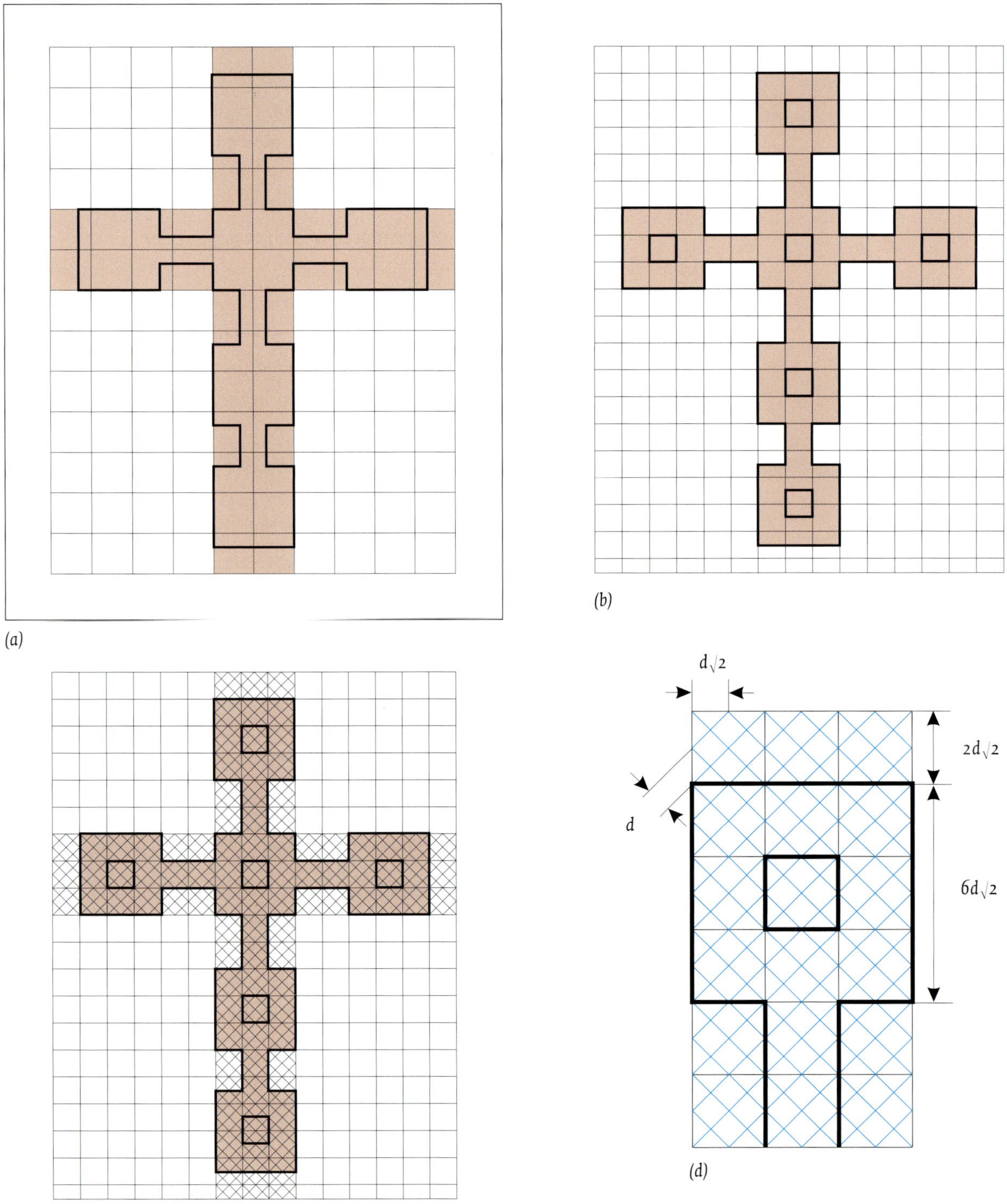

Figure 2.13

Primary and secondary grids used in the layout of the cross and the key pattern ornamenting the cross in Lindisfarne cross-carpet page f. 2v: (a) primary grid with inner and outer frame, (b) alternative primary grid in inner frame, (c) secondary grid used for ornamenting the cross, (d) detail of (c).

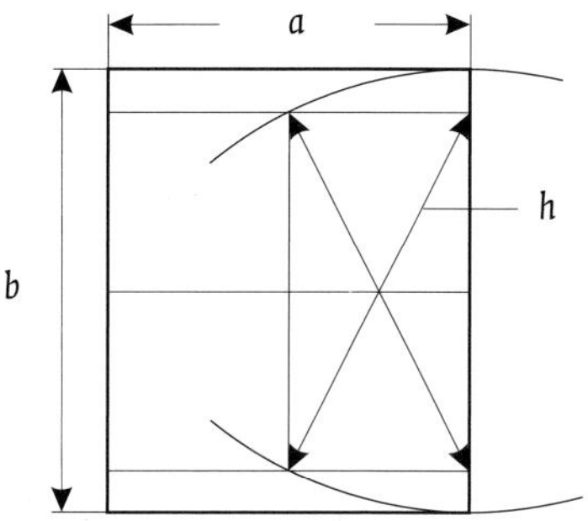

$b=\sqrt{((a/2)^2+a^2)} = (a\sqrt{5})/2$

Figure 2.14
A geometric construction for the outer frame of Lindisfarne f. 2v. Note $AB/BC=a/[(a/2)^2+a^2)^{1/2}-a/2]=2/(\sqrt{5}-1)$ *which is the golden ratio.*

This shows a square grid, with ten squares along the short sides of the rectangle forming the inside of the border and 13 squares on the long sides, so that for the inner frame $a/b = 10/13 = 0.7692...$ The size of the six squares of the cross is two squares by two squares of this grid and the cross is located in two orthogonal x-bands. However, the positions of the squares of the cross do not coincide with the squares of the grid. The shape of the cross is formed with a different grid (Fig. 2.13b) with 15 squares on the short side and 19.5 squares on the long side. The key pattern, in each square of the cross, is formed on an even finer square grid set at 45° to the primary grid and the main axes of the cross (Fig. 2.13c). It is described in detail in Chapter 5.

When the fine secondary grid is extended throughout the cross it becomes clear that the dimensions of the cross, with squares and connecting sections, are determined by the dimensions of this grid pattern. The length of the sides of the squares of the cross is equivalent to six diagonal lengths of the secondary grid ($6d\sqrt{2}$), where d is the length of the sides of the squares in the secondary grid (Fig. 2.13d). Each of the four sections connecting the five upper squares of the cross is four diagonals long ($4d\sqrt{2}$) and two diagonals wide ($2d\sqrt{2}$). The section connecting the two lower squares is three diagonals long ($3d\sqrt{2}$) and two diagonals wide ($2d\sqrt{2}$). Similarly, the spacing between the ends of the arms of the cross and the boundary of the inner border is two diagonals ($2d\sqrt{2}$) so that the cross is centred within the frame. In this way the artist has integrated the shape of the overall frame, based on a simple geometric construction, with the fine grid structure required to produce the shape of the cross and the fine detail of the key pattern.

Book of Lindisfarne cross-carpet page, f. 138v

The example above demonstrates how a fine grid provides the framework for the key pattern ornamentation in the inside of the cross and also defines the proportions and details of the cross as a whole. A closely similar construction is used in f. 138v of the same Gospel book (Fig. 2.15). A simple key pattern, based on square-sided spirals, is used to decorate the space around the cross. Fig. 2.16 shows that the length of the diagonals of the secondary grid determines the outline of the cross. The central rectangular panel of this design is described in some detail in Chapter 4 to illustrate spiral motifs. Although the central panel appears square it is actually rectangular and the angle subtended by the diagonals is 92.6°. This is a direct result of the shape and proportions of the underlying grid.

The layout of panels in f. 138v is based on a primary grid of rectangles with $AB/AC = 1.045$ (Fig. 2.16). There are 13 rectangles along the short sides of the inner frame and 17 along the long sides. It follows that the ratio a/b of the inside frame is $13 \times 1.045/17 = 0.799...$ This is close to the shape of the

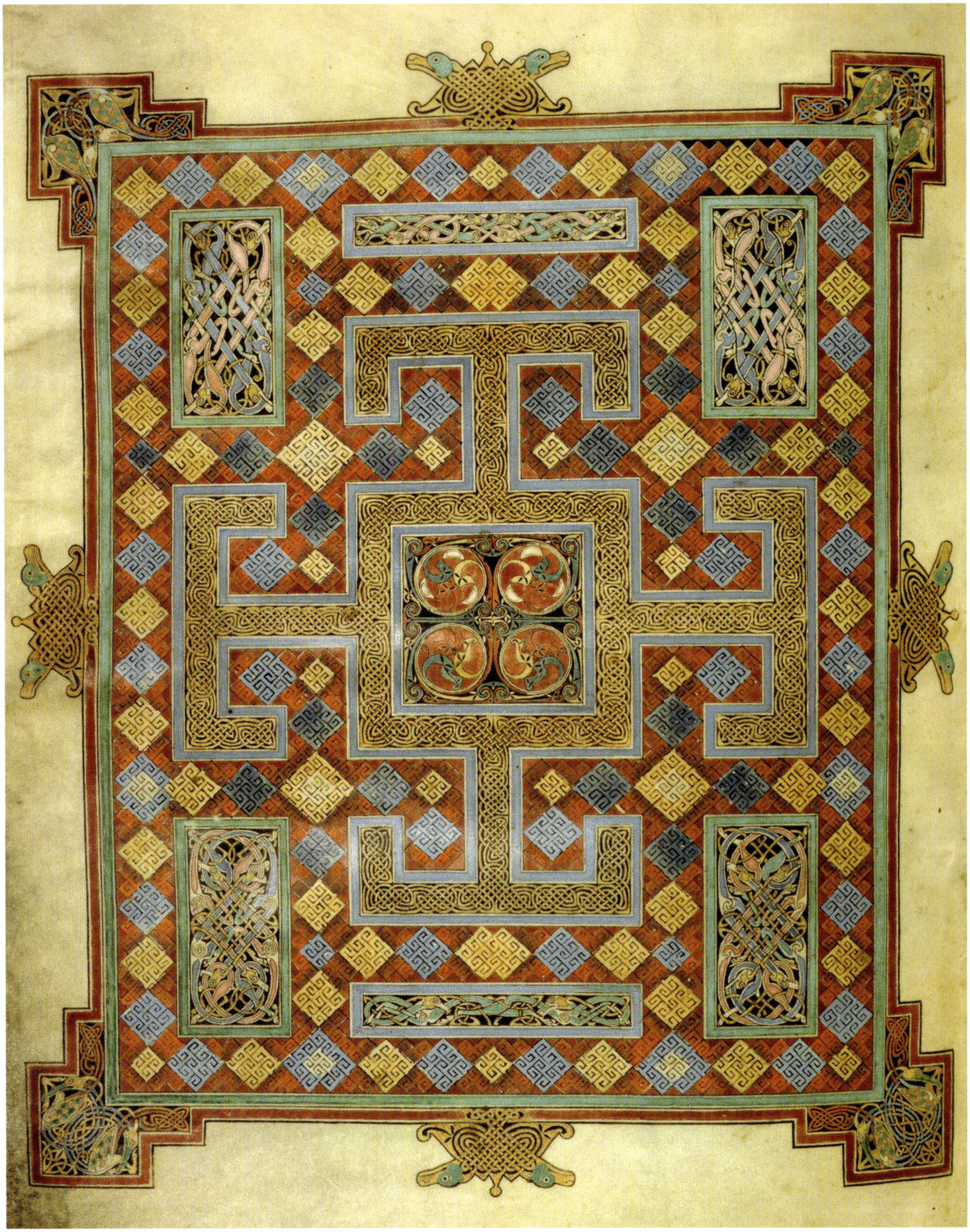

Figure 2.15
Photograph of cross-carpet page f. 138v of Lindisfarne Gospels (by permission of British Library).

Figure 2.16
Layout of cross-carpet page f. 138v of Lindisfarne Gospels showing the secondary diagonal grid that forms the basic framework for the external shape of the cross and surrounding panels and for the key pattern around the panels. Outer frame is not included.

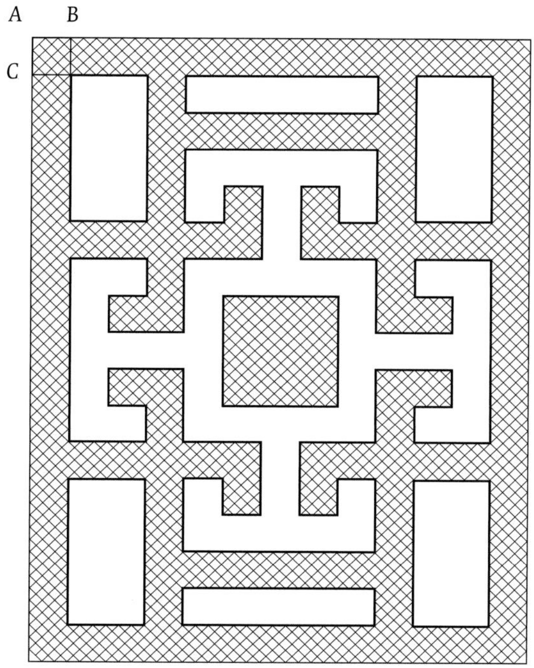

comparable frame of f. 2v, where $a/b = 0.769...$, but the ratio is sufficiently different for it not to have been produced by the same geometric construction. The sides of each rectangle of the primary grid are divided into three to form a secondary grid at about 45°, so there are 39 divisions on the short sides and 51 divisions on the long sides. This is in agreement with the observation of pricks on the reverse side of the vellum which revealed 51 divisions on the long sides. For further details see Bruce-Mitford in Kendrick (1956–60). Note that the ratio AB/AC of the primary grid is the same as that of the central panel of the cross. Because the grid is rectangular, rather than square, the unusually shaped cross is not equal-armed.

It is interesting to note that the approach to layout described in this section for f. 2v and f. 138v is not the same as that used by Stevick (1994) but is similar to the approach adopted by Guilmain (1985) in two papers on the Lindisfarne Gospels.

Shrinkage and distortion

Of all the media used for early medieval art that survive today, vellum is most likely to have been subject to changes in shape during the hundreds of years since the work was created. An apocryphal story about the Book of Durrow illustrates this. It is said that the book was believed to be endowed with spiritual and healing powers so that, in the seventeenth century, when a herd of cattle contracted a disease, the book was dipped into the drinking water to cure the animals.

The vellum of the Lindisfarne Gospels is calf-skin, a natural material. It has a fine inner texture which is far from homogeneous or isotropic. In preparing the skin for use it would have been cleaned, stretched and dried. Inevitably, changes in humidity and, in particular, dipping in water would result in changes in shape that, because the material is not homogeneous, are not uniform.

Mention has been made earlier of evidence for distortion of f. 2v and one might argue, without serious justification, that the rectangular grid of f. 138v is also the result of distortion and that the grid was originally square. There is no satisfactory way of clarifying this type of issue. In contrast, the distortion of f. 2v is non-uniform so that the overall layout is now a distorted rectangle. There can be little doubt that the artist started with a perfectly aligned and regular grid that has become distorted with age.

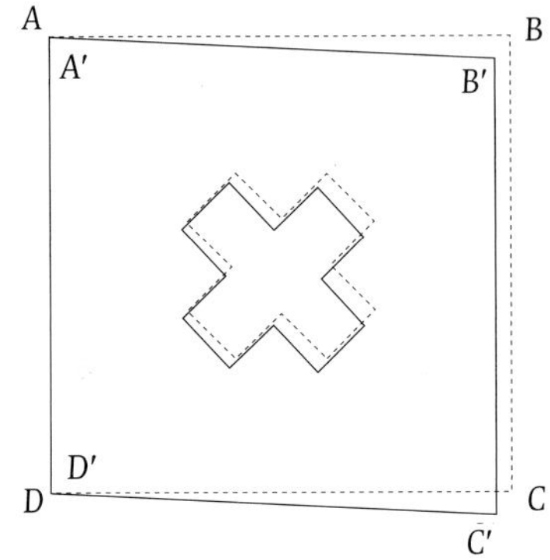

Figure 2.17
Distortion of f. 248r of Book of Durrow owing to ageing and water damage. ABCD is a square in the undistorted page and A′B′C′D′ is the distorted square.

One of the best examples of distortion, which can also be used to determine the nature of the distortion, is cross-carpet page f. 248r of the Book of Durrow. The ornamentation of this page is used in Chapter 5 to illustrate embedded crosses. Many of the pages of the Book of Durrow show evidence of distortion and water damage as well as mechanical damage by wear and tear. It seems reasonable to assume that the original ornamentation of f. 248r was set in a rectangle and that each of the 28 equal-armed crosses, set in the diagonal trellis, was truly symmetrical. With this, and an assumption that the distortion of the page is approximately uniform, it is possible to determine the extent of distortion from the deformation necessary to change a true rectangle to the 'distorted' rectangle and the symmetrical crosses to distorted crosses. These simple ideas are illustrated in Fig. 2.17 with reference to f. 248r (see Fig. 5.32). The approximate 'square' A′B′C′D′ represents a feature that was a true square ABCD in the original pattern. The deformation required to change the shape of the true square ABCD to A′B′C′D′ represents the distortion of the page as a result of humidity and ageing. The change in shape, indicated in Fig. 2.17, involves shear and shrinkage (described technically as an in-plane shear of about 2.7° and a dilational shrinkage strain of about 0.03 or 3%).

Donore disc No. 1 and the Kingston brooch

Some emphasis has been given to the layout procedures used by the artist of the Lindisfarne Gospels because they are relatively simple and straightforward, as well as being disciplined and formal. Artists working on other manuscripts and in other media undoubtedly used similar procedures. These methods are used throughout this book to develop illustrations from first principles. As indicated earlier, the methods are applicable at different scales and levels of detail. The disciplined approach of the early illustrators is

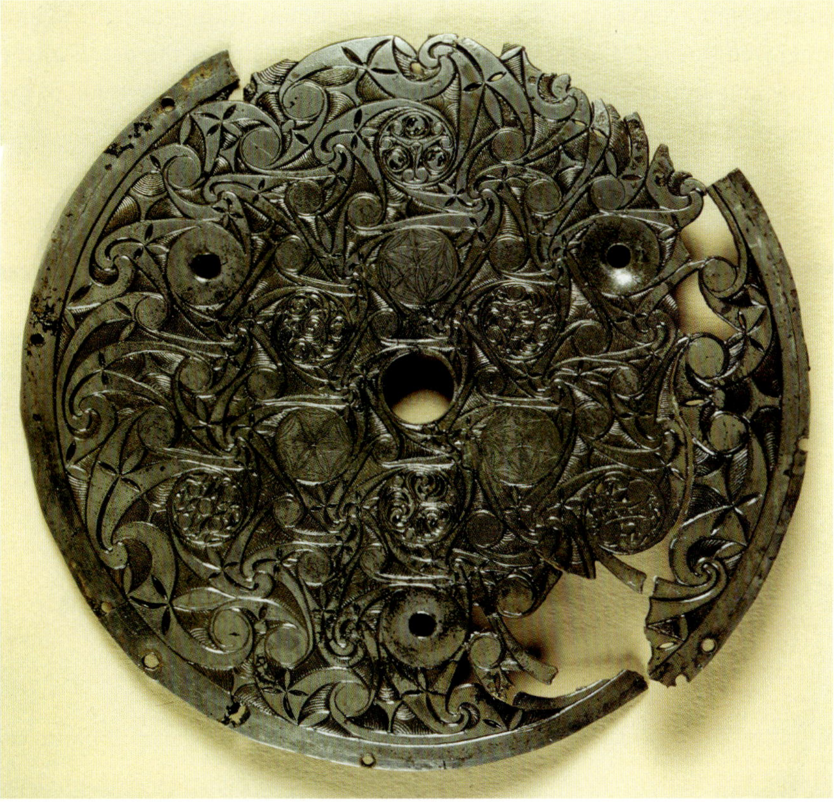

Figure 2.18
Photograph of Donore disc No. 1 (by permission of National Museum of Ireland).

not so evident in much of the later work although the underlying principles must have been applied.

It is often argued on the basis of evidence from ornamented metalwork, as in the treasures from the royal burial at Sutton Hoo, that marking out procedures were used and understood long before the Gospel books were written and illuminated. Indeed reference has been made already to the contributions of Egyptians, Greeks and Romans. The contribution of metalsmiths is very important and two examples are used to illustrate some grid architectures and geometric constructions not yet considered. They apply equally to manuscripts and stone carvings. The use of metalwork examples at this stage also provides an introduction to some concepts relating to 'styles', considered in the next section.

Donore disc No. 1 (Fig. 2.18) was part of a hoard of early medieval metalwork found in a riverbank in 1984 in Co. Meath, Ireland. It is now in the National Museum of Ireland, Dublin. The disc is damaged and incomplete, so an element of interpretation and reconstruction is required in describing the ornamentation. The emphasis here is on the layout of the design. This has been unravelled by Ryan (1995) who dates the work as late seventh or early eighth century. The 131.3 mm diameter disc is made of cast and beaten bronze coated with tin. The ornamentation was incised and engraved through the tin coating. Figure 2.19 illustrates the detail of the ornamentation on a small section of the disc and gives an impression of the quality of the work.

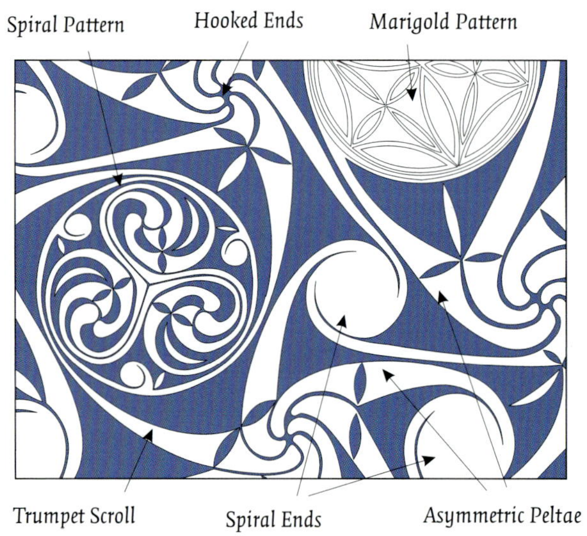

Figure 2.19
Detail of ornamentation on part of Donore disc No. 1.

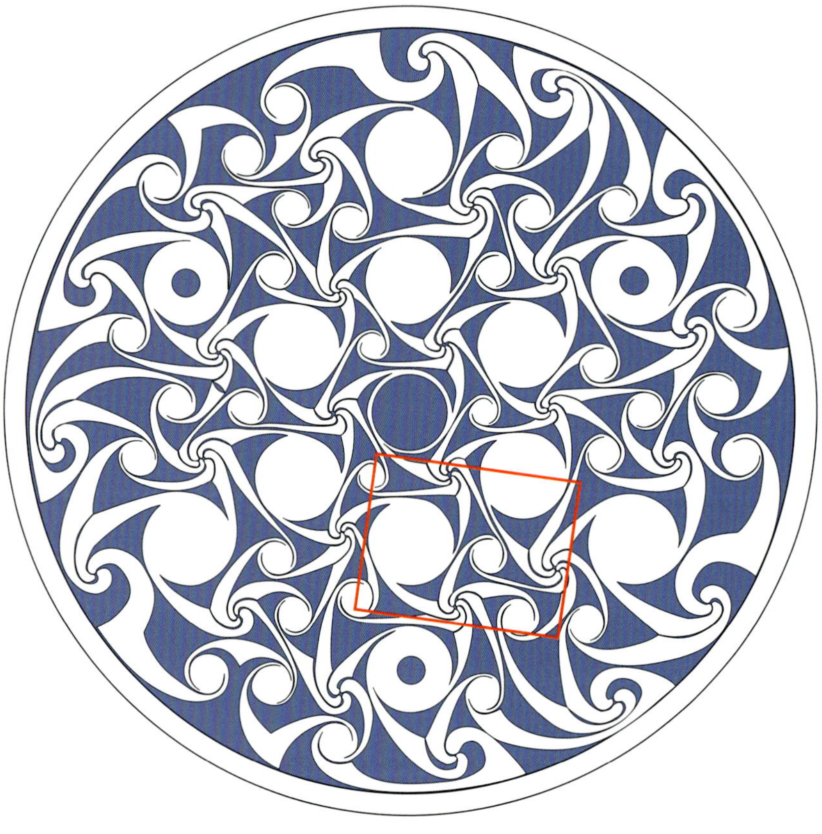

Figure 2.20
Outline layout of linked spirals on Donore disc No. 1.

A simplified diagram of the overall layout is shown in Fig. 2.20. Ryan refers to the design as 'a field of trumpet scrolls, which form asymmetrical peltae linked by hooked or spiral endings'. At one level the design can be considered as a single panel with an array of spiral motifs. However, each of the large open roundels is effectively another panel ornamented with either fine spirals or marigold motifs. In his work Ryan proposed that the layout of the primary grid was based on a hexagonal network produced by a geometric construction involving extensive compass work (Fig. 2.21). There is ample evidence for the use of compasses from the prick marks that remain on the surface of the disc. Much of the fine detail of the ornamentation of the roundels also involved the use of compasses. Circles as small as 1 mm radius were engraved on the surface.

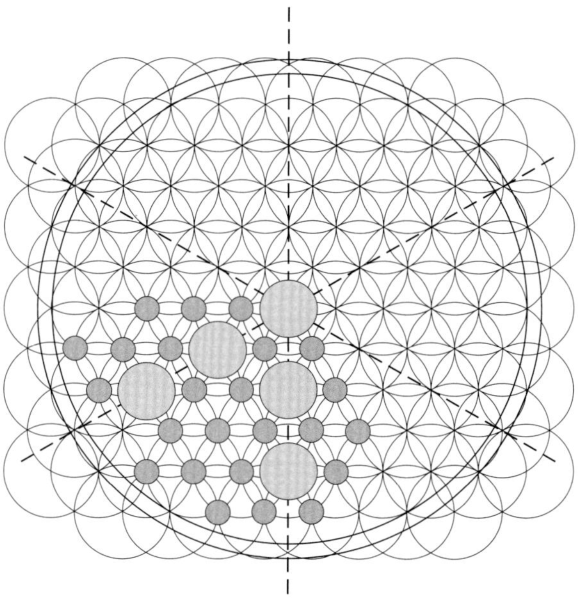

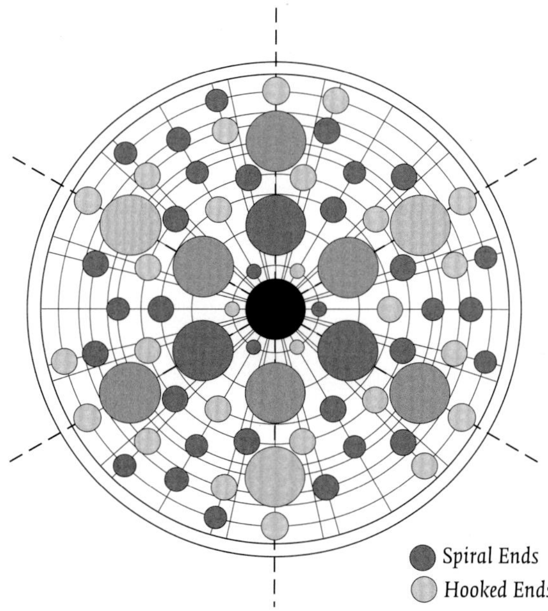

Figure 2.21
Hexagonal network proposed by Ryan (1995) as the basis of the grid used for the ornamentation of Donore disc No. 1.

Figure 2.22
A possible polar grid for the ornamentation of Donore disc No. 1.

The hexagonal network of Fig. 2.21 is perfectly adequate but it seems more likely that the artist used a polar grid of concentric circles and radial lines (Fig. 2.22). The centres of the spirals lie at the intersections of the two sets of lines. The large roundels lie on six radial lines at 60° to each other and the centres of the small spirals lie on other radial lines at 30° to the main radial lines and also at arbitrary angles.

Drawing polar grids with radial lines at specific angles involves dividing a circle into well-defined segments. This is achieved using geometric constructions without the use of a protractor to measure the angles. The methods date to the time of Pythagoras. To illustrate them, an even more fascinating piece of ornamentation, evident on the Kingston brooch, is considered. The brooch is contemporary with other pieces of jewellery, ornamented in a similar manner, found in the Sutton Hoo burial, indicating that it was produced in the late sixth or early seventh centuries in southern England. It is one of the finest examples of Anglo-Saxon jewellery.

The brooch (Fig. 2.23) was recovered from a grave on Kingston Down in Kent in the eighteenth century and is now in Liverpool Museum. More details of the brooch are recorded in Webster and Backhouse (1991). For a description of some of the technical aspects involved in making composite disc brooches see Pinder (1995). The brooch consists of a solid silver disc, 85.5 mm in diameter, covered by a thin sheet of gold. It is ornamented with gold cloisonné with the cells filled with inlays of garnets, coloured glasses, white shells, millefiori and filigree panels. The brooch is in good condition although there is some evidence of damage and loss of inlays. An outline of the main features of the pattern (Fig. 2.24) indicates that it was designed using a polar grid.

The first stage in making this brooch was setting out the main outline, shown by the black lines in Fig. 2.24, by soldering thin rectangular-section gold wire on to the thin sheet of gold. The spaces, or cloisons, created by this outline were then filled with: (i) thin pieces of gold foil, stamped with a fine waffle or chequer-board pattern, overlaid with thin slices of polished garnet, blue glass or

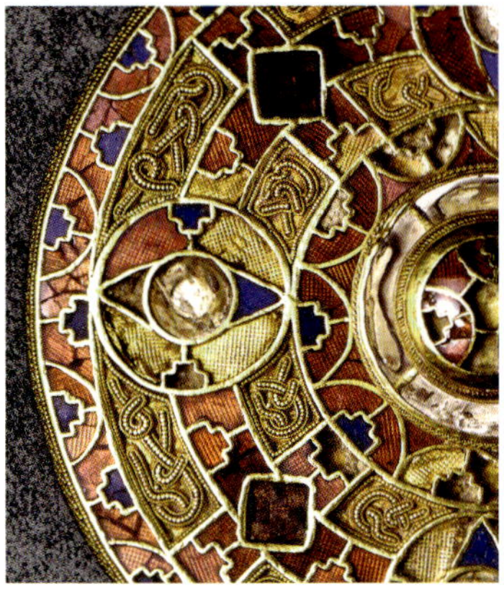

Figure 2.23
Photograph of Kingston brooch (by permission of the Trustees, National Museums, Liverpool).

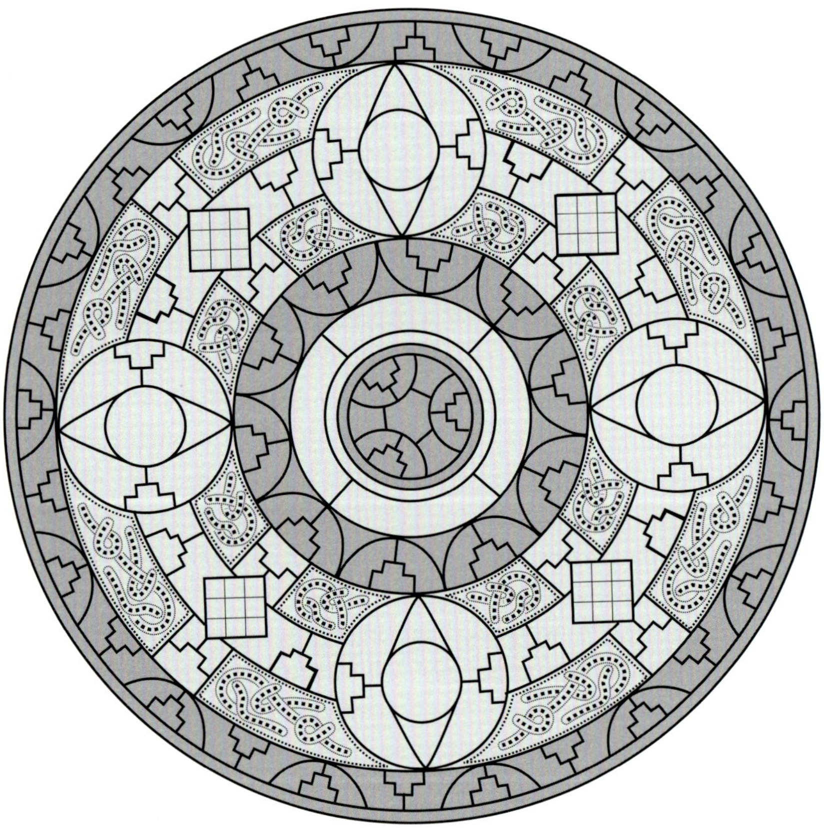

Figure 2.24
Layout of cloisons and zones of different symmetry on Kingston brooch.

white shell (garnet is red and transparent so the waffle pattern of the foil shows through to brilliant effect); (ii) thin slices of millefiori cut normal to the drawing direction of the millefiori rods; and (iii) filigree produced by soldering beaded gold wire onto a gold foil to produce a zoomorphic motif with a border of finer beaded wire. A beaded and twisted gold wire was used to decorate some of the circles and the outer border of the brooch.

Anticipating the discussion of symmetry and repetition in Chapter 4, it can be seen that the overall design of the brooch has no symmetry. However, there are five zones, as indicated by the shading in Fig. 2.24, each displaying a high level of symmetry. The combination of elements, with differing symmetry, produces a fascinating and intriguing effect not easily unravelled. The design is based on a series of approximately equal-spaced concentric circles marked out by the gold wire boundaries of the cloisonné. The central region or zone has triangular, threefold symmetry and is surrounded by a zone with white shell inlay that has fourfold symmetry. The third zone has tenfold symmetry and is decorated with semi-circles and step-patterns that are repeated ten times. The fourth zone contains three rings with step and zoomorphic motifs, squares filled with millefiori, and roundels. The pattern has fourfold symmetry. The zoomorphic motifs reflect each other across diametric lines. Finally, in the outer zone, the step and semi-circular pattern is repeated 14 times.

To create the grid for this pattern the artist used compasses for the concentric circles and then had to divide the circular space successively into three, four, ten, four and fourteen equal segments. Geometric constructions to divide a circle into three or four equal segments are relatively simple (Fig. 2.25). The triangle in Fig. 2.25a is produced by marking out distances, equal to the radius of the circle, around the circumference of the circle. The square in Fig. 2.25b is produced by drawing two lines at right angles through the centre of the circle. The construction of five and ten equal segments is complicated and producing fourteen equal segments is impossible except by trial and error methods. Note that $360/14 = 51.4571...$ which is an irrational number.

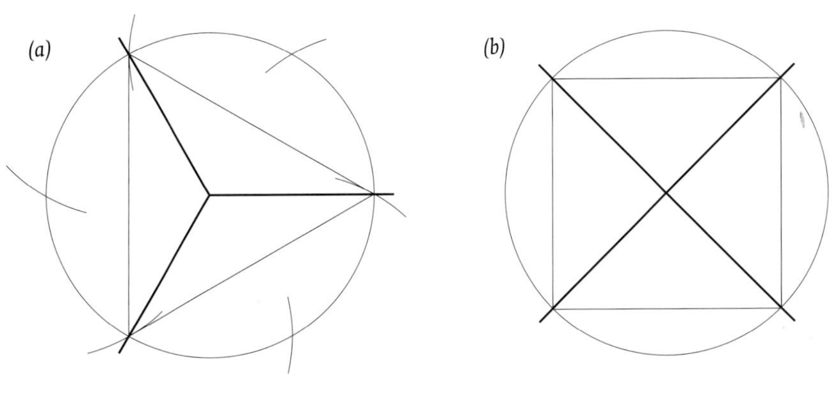

Figure 2.25
Methods for dividing a circle into (a) three and (b) four equal segments.

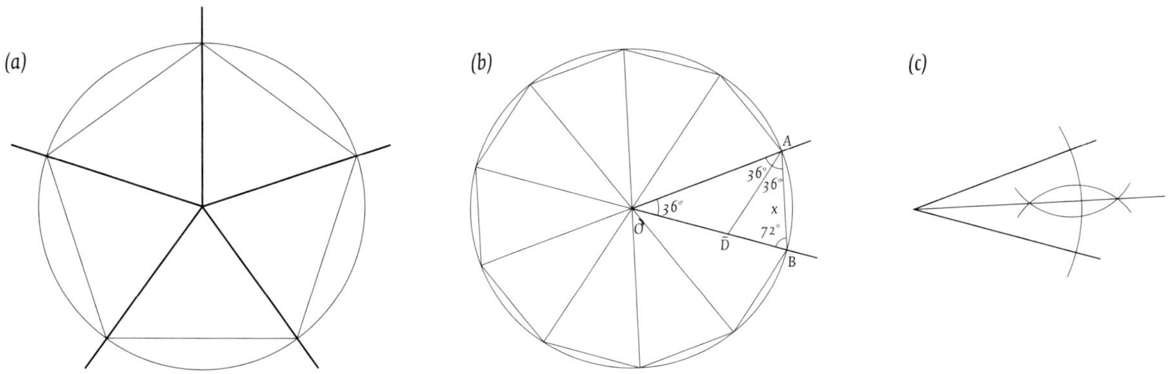

Figure 2.26
Geometric construction that provides a method for dividing a circle into five equal segments.

Dividing a circle into five equal segments presents the same problems as drawing a regular pentagon. The angle between each radial direction, 360°/5 = 72°, is readily measured with a protractor. There are a number of approximate methods of doing this without a protractor using only a straight-edge and compasses. A precise method of construction comes from the Greeks and is based on a simple mathematical principle that relates to the golden section and, in particular, to the ratio $(\sqrt{5}-1)/2$. For completeness, the method can be summarised as follows. Suppose a circle of unit diameter is divided (hypothetically) into ten equal segments to produce a regular decagon (Fig. 2.26a). The angle AOB in each segment is 360°/10 = 36°. AOB is an isosceles triangle with angle OAB = angle ABO = 72°. Angle OAB is bisected, using the same type of construction as that used to divide a line into two equal parts (Fig. 2.26b), to obtain D. Since OAB and ADB are similar triangles $1/x = x/1\text{-}x$. Solving this equation gives $x = (\sqrt{5}-1)/2$. Thus the ratio of the length x = AB to the radius of the circle OB, which is set at unity, is $(\sqrt{5}-1)/2$, the golden ratio. Regular decagons and pentagons are produced by following the construction for $(\sqrt{5}-1)$ in Fig. 2.14. Another geometric method for constructing a regular pentagon is illustrated in Chapter 8 (Fig. 8.1).

Although the principles of construction of the design of circular panels do not involve measurement of specific angles it is interesting to note that the geometric methods illustrated in Figs. 2.25 and 2.26 can be used to construct angles of 90°, 72° and 60° which can then be divided geometrically to 45°, 36° and 30°, and so on. Addition and subtraction of these angles produce many other angles.

MATTERS OF STYLE

Metals, manuscripts and stones

The approach to the descriptions of the ornament on metalwork objects, such as the Donore disc and the Kingston brooch, as presented in Figs. 2.20

and 2.24, is indistinguishable from that of manuscripts. In reality these figures are two-dimensional representations of what are essentially three-dimensional artefacts. The Donore disc is a shallow disc with the ornament on the convex side and the Kingston brooch has a central domed boss and domed satellite bosses in the four roundels. The appearance of the ornament on these artefacts is dependent also on the surface topography created by the metalworker. This is particularly so for the Donore disc in which the design is achieved entirely by incising and engraving without the use of coloured gems and glasses. Similar observations can be made with respect to stone carvings. The question arises as to whether or not this leads to any fundamental distinction between the designs of geometric art as displayed on metals, manuscripts and stones. Apart from some distinctly three-dimensional stone carvings, referred to briefly in the last section of this chapter, one can conclude that there are no significant differences.

However, the medium has a significant effect on the qualities of the art and on the way that artists and craftsmen create patterns and motifs. These issues relate to the subject of style which has been defined by Speake (1980) as 'the conventions, qualities, and expressions of an individual or group which make up the art of any particular time or place'. It is subjective and a particular style may be given different names by different scholars. This topic is considered later in this section by reference to the way that interlacing motifs are represented. The medium also affects what can be achieved, most particularly in relation to the amount of detail that can be shown.

A quite separate aspect influencing appearance, particularly important to art historians and archaeologists, is the way that individual artists and schools of art represented their work. Thus, even a simple motif can be represented in many different ways. There is also evidence for the progressive evolution of styles that leads eventually to debasement, distortion and metamorphosis as described in Chapter 7.

Materials and methods

Manuscripts were produced on vellum, which has a very fine surface texture. Marking out the grid and the main features of the design was achieved using the equivalent of pencils and pricks as described earlier. In this way the field to be ornamented was divided into areas or spaces by partition lines, most of which were highlighted as dark lines. Each part or division was given a single colour, with no shading or diffusion of colours, using dyes and paints. This is a characteristic of heraldic design. Exceptionally fine and detailed patterns were possible and the resolution was dependent on the fineness of the pencils and brushes. In the limit it was possible to create designs using brushes with single hairs. The work of the Book of Kells is elegant testimony to the skill of the illuminator. There is ample evidence for work as fine as 0.1 mm, which is close to the maximum resolution of the eye unaided by magnifying lenses.

The work of stonemasons developed progressively in the period AD 500 to 1000 from simple patterns incised on rough-hewn stone to sophisticated three-dimensional carvings with intricate designs. Representation of the Christian cross evolved from a simple, often elegant outline to superb cross-slabs, typified by the Rosemarkie stone, and the ornamented crosses found in all the countries of the islands. These different forms are used as a basis for classifying sculpture, as exemplified by the work of Allen and Anderson (1903).

The geometric art of cross-slabs and crosses is essentially the same as in manuscripts in that it is based on panels ornamented with motifs. The choice of motif varies significantly from region to region and is also used in classification. Thus, for example, there is an emphasis on vegetal vine motifs on Northumbrian crosses and on interlacing and key patterns on Welsh stones.

There is fragmentary evidence that some carved stones were originally painted. This would have made it possible to achieve colour effects similar to those in manuscripts. The paintwork has seldom survived and so the features of the patterns are revealed by the partition lines and possibly by the use of carving texture in the spaces separated by partition lines. Partition lines take many forms (Fig. 2.27) and have a three-dimensional character so that the patterns are revealed by changes in shadow contrast. Researchers use light directed at a small angle to the surface to reveal the maximum amount of detail. Take, for example, the carving on the Nigg stone, now inside the church at Nigg, a tiny village about 30 km north of Inverness in north-east Scotland (Fig. 2.28). The cross-slab is set in a sump that allows visitors to view all aspects of the cross. In the afternoon, sunlight from a nearby window slants across the stone, revealing intricate carving on this splendid example of Pictish sculpture dating back to the early ninth century.

The fineness of detail depends on the skill of the sculptor, the quality of the tools and, quite fundamentally, on the qualities of the stone being carved. Maximum detail is achieved in fine-grained sedimentary rocks, free from pronounced laminated microstructures. These rocks are relatively soft and isotropic so that fine detail can be carved and splitting avoided. The disadvantage of these rocks is that they weather rapidly. Strongly laminated rocks are unsuitable for relief carving because they split easily. Rock is difficult to transport so that, in general, stonemasons had to use locally acquired stone. However, there are some examples of stone being transported over considerable distances.

The properties of metals have a profound effect on what can be achieved. Most of the artefacts that have survived are made from either alloys of copper, notably bronze as in the Donore disc, or noble metals – gold and silver – as

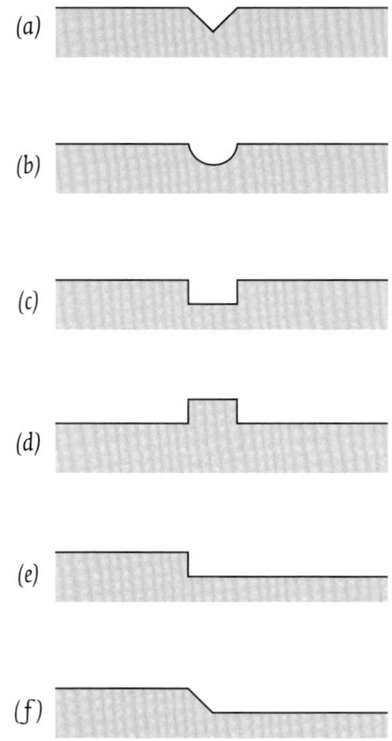

Figure 2.27
Schematic of typical sections through partition lines on stone carvings.

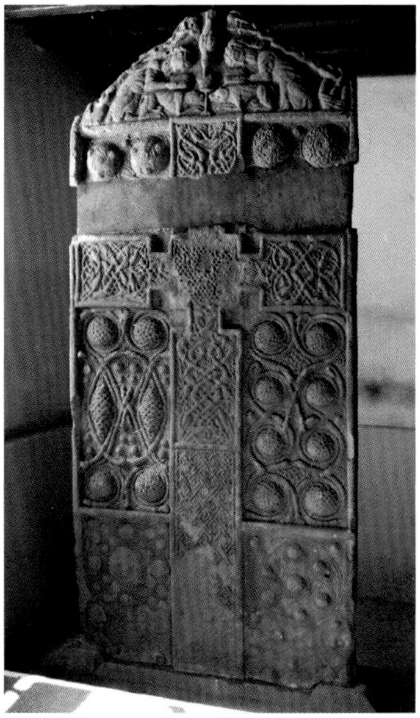

Figure 2.28
Magnificent cross-slab at Nigg in Scotland photographed in afternoon sunlight.

in the Kingston brooch, primarily because they resist corrosion. Well-annealed gold and silver are very soft, particularly when they are pure. It is possible to produce exceptionally thin foils and very fine wires of these metals to use for very detailed ornamental work. Bronze is much harder but it is suitable for engraving and chip carving as demonstrated to great effect in the Donore disc. Metal artefacts were fashioned to their primary shapes by casting and mechanical working treatments, such as forging and stamping, to produce flat and curved surfaces for detailed ornamentation.

Figure 2.29
Schematic of typical sections through partition lines on metal artefacts.

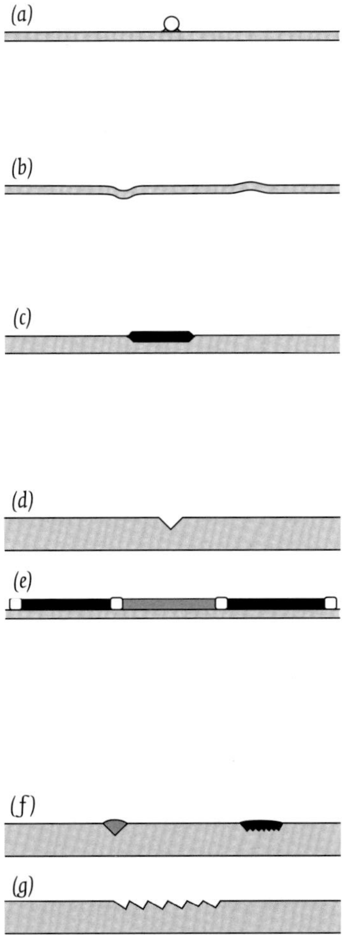

A wide range of metalworking techniques was available to the early craftsmen and jewellers allowing them to achieve both topographical and colour distinction. The same ideas about the division of fields based on partition lines apply as in manuscripts and stone carvings. The main techniques are illustrated in Fig. 2.29 and are summarised as follows:

(a) *Filigree.* Very fine wires or rows of minute granules of gold are soldered to a thin sheet or solid block of gold to form partition lines or create zoomorphic images. Various types of wire are used including unbeaded, beaded, twisted, plaited and knitted strands.

(b) *Repoussé.* Positive and negative relief is produced by hammering or punching from the underside of a sheet of material to create partition lines. The impressions may be continuous or dotted. Pointillé is a special case of repoussé and consists of a stippled array of small punch marks.

(c) *Niello and damascene.* In niello an impression is made on the surface that is filled with a black compound of sulphur, silver, lead or copper. In damascene the impression, usually formed by etching, is filled with another metal of contrasting colour. In both methods the boundaries of the inlaid material represent the partition lines in the design.

(d) *Incise.* The surface is cut with a sharp tool.

(e) *Cloisonné.* Square section wire is soldered to a sheet or block of metal to form the partition lines of the field. The cloisonné cells (cloisons or spaces) created by these outlines, are filled with coloured glasses and enamels or thin slices of precious stones, shells, and millefiori. As noted in the description of the Kingston brooch, a very thin sheet of gold with a waffle pattern (diapered gold foil) may be used underneath transparent inlays to achieve added brilliance.

(f) *Champlevé.* Grooves are cut in the metal surface and filled with coloured glasses and enamels.

(g) *Chip carving.* Surface texture is produced by a sharp tool usually as sets of straight or curved parallel lines and sometimes as a pattern of fine dots. Different surface textures are used to distinguish different areas of a field. The boundaries between different textures may be partition lines. The same surface texture is produced by the 'lost wax' type of casting.

Interlacing

A fundamental rule of interlacing is that the cords, also called straps, strands and ribbons, follow a rigorous under-and-over sequence at each and every crossing point. In geometric terms the under-and-over sequences are independent of medium and style. However, medium and style have a significant effect on the appearance of interlacing. Many approaches are used to represent the under-and-over sequences in two-dimensional paintings on manuscripts and in the quasi-three-dimensional patterns on stone and metalwork. Even within a single manuscript the same interlacing pattern may appear in many styles or categories; Bruce-Mitford (see Kendrick, 1956–60) identified seven categories of interlacing in the Lindisfarne Gospels.

The three main styles of interlacing used in manuscripts, stone and metalwork are illustrated in Fig. 2.30 using a simple four-cord interlacing design. The appearance created by these is related to the techniques described above. In Fig. 2.30a the pattern is made up of a series of dots, often shown in manuscripts as a row of red dots. Exactly the same pattern is achieved in metals when rows of fine granules are soldered to the surface of the base metal or a row of dots is punched on the surface. The single line shown in Fig. 2.30b is readily produced by fine pens on manuscripts and by incising metals and stones. The same effect can be produced with fine metal wires soldered to the surface. By far the most common style is achieved when the lines are broadened into bands as in Fig. 2.30c. The width of the band influences the appearance and is a matter of style. Narrow bands produce an open lattice effect and broad bands fill the space so that in the limit the bands touch each other leaving no background space. In manuscripts the edges of the cords are usually highlighted with dark ink or paint and the band itself is given a different colour from the background. Wide cords are carved in stone as illustrated schematically in Fig. 2.27c and d. Many of the techniques illustrated in Fig. 2.29 have been used to create wide bands in the ornamentation of metals. A wide variety of styles have been used. Thus, for example, the ornamentation on some of the interlaced bodies of the zoomorphs on the great gold belt-buckle found in the Sutton Hoo burial (illustrated later in Fig. 3.1b) are formed from bands with a ladder-like effect created from two thin nielloed grooves on each side of a row of rectangular dots, also formed by niello.

Continuous cords of interlacing can be followed throughout an interlacing design. In some work, as in Fig. 2.4, all the cords or bands have the same colour. Alternatively, individual cords may be given the same colour with other cords having different colours. In other work the colour of a cord varies from one part of the design to another within the same interlacing pattern. These are matters of artistic choice and convention and also apply to the way that cords are treated in stone carvings and metalwork.

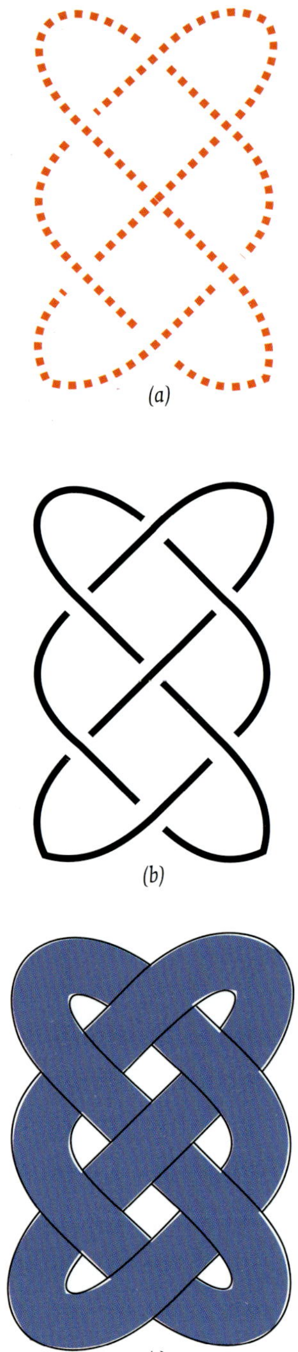

(a) (b) (c)

Figure 2.30
Styles of interlacing.

Zoomorphic design

The matters of style identified by the discussion of interlacing apply equally to key patterns and spiral motifs because all these patterns are created by dividing the field with partition lines and illuminating the spaces created with different colours or textures. Issues of style are more complex in zoomorphic motifs. This subject takes us far beyond the geometric approach. It is the source of extensive work by art historians and archaeologists; development of zoomorphic styles provides a rich resource for the study of the evolution of art and culture.

Many zoomorphic designs involve complex interlacing of legs, wings, tongues, beaks and bodies with strict adherence to the rules of interlacing. It is in the way that the animals are represented in a semi-naturalistic form that the issue of styles is important. Take, for example, the zoomorphic motifs on the Kingston brooch shown in Figs. 2.23 and 2.24. A casual observer is unlikely to identify the filigree patterns with any form of animal but the specialist will recognise this as Anglo-Saxon 'Style II', derived from earlier Germanic/Scandinavian styles, and originally called 'Salin Style II'; a metalwork style widely used on high-quality jewellery. The absence of detail in the zoomorphs on the brooch arises, in part, from the scale of the work and the limits of resolution possible with filigree work. At this scale the beaded gold wires are too coarse to be shaped to give greater detail. Zoomorphic ornamentation in manuscript art usually has more detail, as demonstrated in Fig. 2.1 from the Lindisfarne Gospels, because the effective resolution of the techniques, in relation to the dimensions of the space being illuminated, is greater. Nevertheless, even with the capacity for providing greater detail, the zoomorphs are almost invariably semi-naturalistic. Various strategies have been developed to classify the different forms of zoomorph into a series of styles. For an authoritative account of the styles of Anglo-Saxon animal art see Speake (1980).

OTHER TOPICS

More matters of style

So 'matters of style' provide a basic resource for art historians and archaeologists. They have a bearing on the place and time of the art and can be used to address questions such as at which monastery, scriptorium or workshop was the art created? Who influenced the style of the art? Why was the art created – was it in praise of God or to propagate the Gospel or for the adornment and glorification of a great leader? These topics have to be left behind. The role of the individual artist and craftsperson, whose artistic creativity was superimposed on the practices and traditions of the scriptorium and workshop, must not be forgotten. Each had their own style, strongly conditioned by the medium, art form, tradition and the wishes of patrons. This, in turn, affected the quality of the work, the motifs used, the amount of time spent in production and the amount of detail that was included. An artist with exceptional skills and imagination may create a style that others might wish to emulate, or that a particular patron would like to see used. The tension between originality and conformity must have been as great in early medieval times as it is today, although the pressures to conform might have been different.

There is an important constraint relating to the art of the possible. When one has seen a particular approach or technique applied successfully there is a strong incentive to follow. Innovative approaches are set against the pressures of tradition and continuity that relate, in part, to the learning and training processes – the apprentice follows the master. Thus there is always the possibility of evolution (or metamorphosis) and one can speak of styles evolving. Styles evolved at different rates and in different ways in different workshops and scriptoria. The interchange of knowledge and experience, supported and encouraged by the migration of artists and craftsmen, reduced the possibility of complete fragmentation.

It is interesting to speculate on the prospect of a progressive development of the geometric approach to art, particularly in the context of the apparent lack of geometric discipline in some of the later works. However, there is no evidence for the introduction of new geometric concepts during the period AD 500–1000. Any changes in the art must be attributed either to deliberate changes of style or to different and changing levels of ability in using geometric methods.

Tracing the source of inspiration: Sutton Hoo – Durrow – Lindisfarne

In the massive volume of explanatory material that accompanies the facsimile volume of the Lindisfarne Gospels there are some superb colour photographs of artefacts from the Sutton Hoo burial. They include jewellery and hanging bowl escutcheons that display a wide range of motifs, including step, interlacing, zoomorphic and spiral, so providing unequivocal evidence for the existence of these art forms at and before the time of the burial. The dating of the many burial mounds at Sutton Hoo has been the subject of much archaeological research. Precise dating is very difficult. Recent studies suggest that all the mound burials belong to the years around AD 600. It is widely believed that Mound 1 is the final resting place of Raedwald, King of East Anglia, who died in AD 625. Analysis of the works of art suggests that the burials include contributions from Germanic, Scandinavian and Celtic cultures. Bruce-Mitford (see Kendrick, 1956–60) emphasised the importance of recognising that later developments in the art were made on the basis of earlier work. Thus, to paraphrase him: 'No one who studies artefacts of Sutton Hoo need be surprised at the artistic phenomenon of the Lindisfarne Gospels... it is all there in essence, or in embryo, between 50 and 70 years earlier in the Sutton Hoo burial. How often it is repeated – correctly – that the roots of Hiberno-Saxon ornamentation in manuscripts and sculpture are in the metalwork of the preceding period.'

Bruce-Mitford offers many detailed comparisons relating to the style and form of motifs and layout that support his view that 'it is all there in embryo'. To take just one example, he illustrates six examples of the use of the procession of interlocked animals as a decorative feature. Three of these are shown in Fig. 2.31. The first example (Fig. 2.31a) is from the hinged shoulder-clasps found at Sutton Hoo. The clasps are made of gold and ornamented with cloisonné. The pattern on the clasp has a layout resembling a carpet page in manuscripts. The central panel has an array of equal-armed crosses set out in cloisonné with the cloisons filled with garnets and millefiori. A border of processing animals, also made using a form of cloisonné with either garnet or deep red glass over stamped gold foil filling the cloisons, surrounds this. The eyes of the animals are of an opaque pale blue glass. Note that the border shown in Fig. 2.31a is represented as a continuous procession of animals whereas on the actual work there are only three animals contained in a border panel. The animals have a similar, Style II, appearance to those on the Kingston brooch but the jeweller has used a completely different technique. Because the shoulder clasp is quite small the amount of detail is very limited, particularly since each piece of garnet or glass had to be cut and polished before being fitted into a cloison. The animals have no hind legs and the bodies of successive animals are interlaced.

The same form of decoration is used in a carpet page (f. 192v) at the beginning of St John's Gospel in the Book of Durrow (Fig. 2.31b). Here, processions of animals form a border around a large roundel filled with a circular interlacing pattern. This is the only animal form used in the decorative design of Durrow. In an early facsimile edition of the Insular manuscripts, Robinson (1908) suggests that these animals are dogs resembling Irish wolfhounds. This is, of course, a natural conclusion for those who attribute the production of the Book of Durrow to Ireland. Alexander (1978) dates Durrow to AD 675. Processions of animals are used widely in the decoration of the initial letter pages of the Lindisfarne Gospels. The example in Fig. 2.31c is from f. 27r at the beginning of St Matthew's Gospel. The layout of this page is similar to that of f. 211r illustrated in Fig. 2.7. The procession of animals fills a narrow border at the bottom of the page. This procession is shown at a similar scale to the Sutton Hoo example. The techniques available to the illuminator of manuscripts have a much higher resolution than those of the metalworker; there is considerably more detail in this example with extensive interlacing of the legs, tails, necks and bodies of the animals. The sequences of colouring of the animals in the Durrow and Lindisfarne examples, shown in Fig. 2.31, correspond to those used by the original artists.

There seems little doubt, even from these isolated examples, that the artists of Durrow and Lindisfarne have extended the approach of the earlier workers in metal to their own medium. The conclusion, widely drawn, that Durrow preceded Lindisfarne follows because the style of the former is less sophisticated and represents an earlier extension of the art of metalwork.

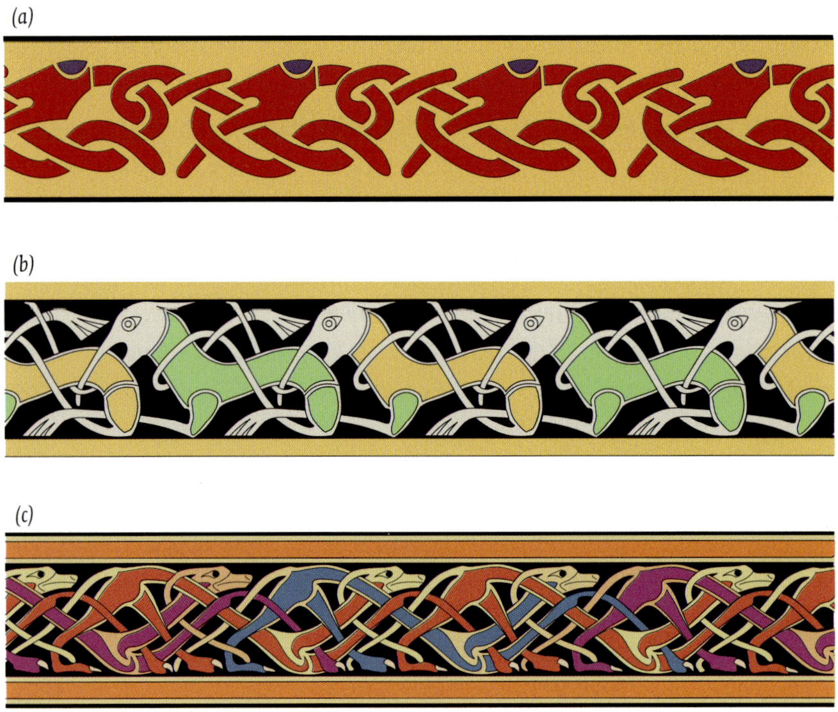

Figure 2.31
Borders of processing animals. (a) Ornamented gold shoulder clasps from the Sutton Hoo burial (full width 8 mm). (b) Border of cross-carpet page f. 192v in Book of Durrow (full width 23 mm). (c) Frame of initial page f. 27r in Lindisfarne Gospels (full width 17.5 mm).

However, there is no intention here to offer any serious conclusions about the chronology of these works of art. They stand alone. There are numerous scholarly works on this subject reflecting a significant measure of disagreement: see, for example, the papers in *Ireland and Insular Art* (Ryan 1987), and in particular the introductory paper by Nordenfalk. An observation by Luce (1960), in the Preface to the facsimile of the Book of Durrow (*Evangeliorum Quattuor Durmachensis*), gives a flavour of the debate: 'I have not stated that the Book of Durrow was written in Ireland; an ancient manuscript deserves to be handled... with scholarly caution and reserve...

[However,] I ought to add that the prima facie probabilities are so strongly in favour of Irish origin of the codex that the onus probandi lies fairly and squarely on the shoulders of those who think it is of English origin'. Needless to say, not everyone will agree. There are those who now see it as a product of Iona and others who think it is Anglo-Saxon and was written at Lindisfarne.

An example of the application of stylistic argument to evaluating the provenance of artefacts and other works can be found in an essay by Wilson (1973) on the St Ninian's Isle hoard. The hoard of 28 pieces of ornamented silver, including a hanging bowl and many penannular brooches, was discovered in 1958 on St Ninian's Isle, a tiny island off the west coast of the southern end of Shetland. From a comparison with art of Ireland, Pictland, Northumbria and Mercia it seems likely that the treasures were buried about AD 800. They are generally regarded as examples of Pictish metalwork though some influences were coming from Anglo-Saxon England. It is fascinating to speculate on the story of the treasure. Will the details of how it was accumulated and why it was buried ever be known?

There are many other matters that relate to the provenance and chronology of manuscripts, stones and metalwork. These include palaeography, composition of alloys, type and composition of paints and dyes, and language of text, as well as the social and political events surrounding them. All these have diagnostic qualities – again only marginally relevant to the exploration of the geometric aspects.

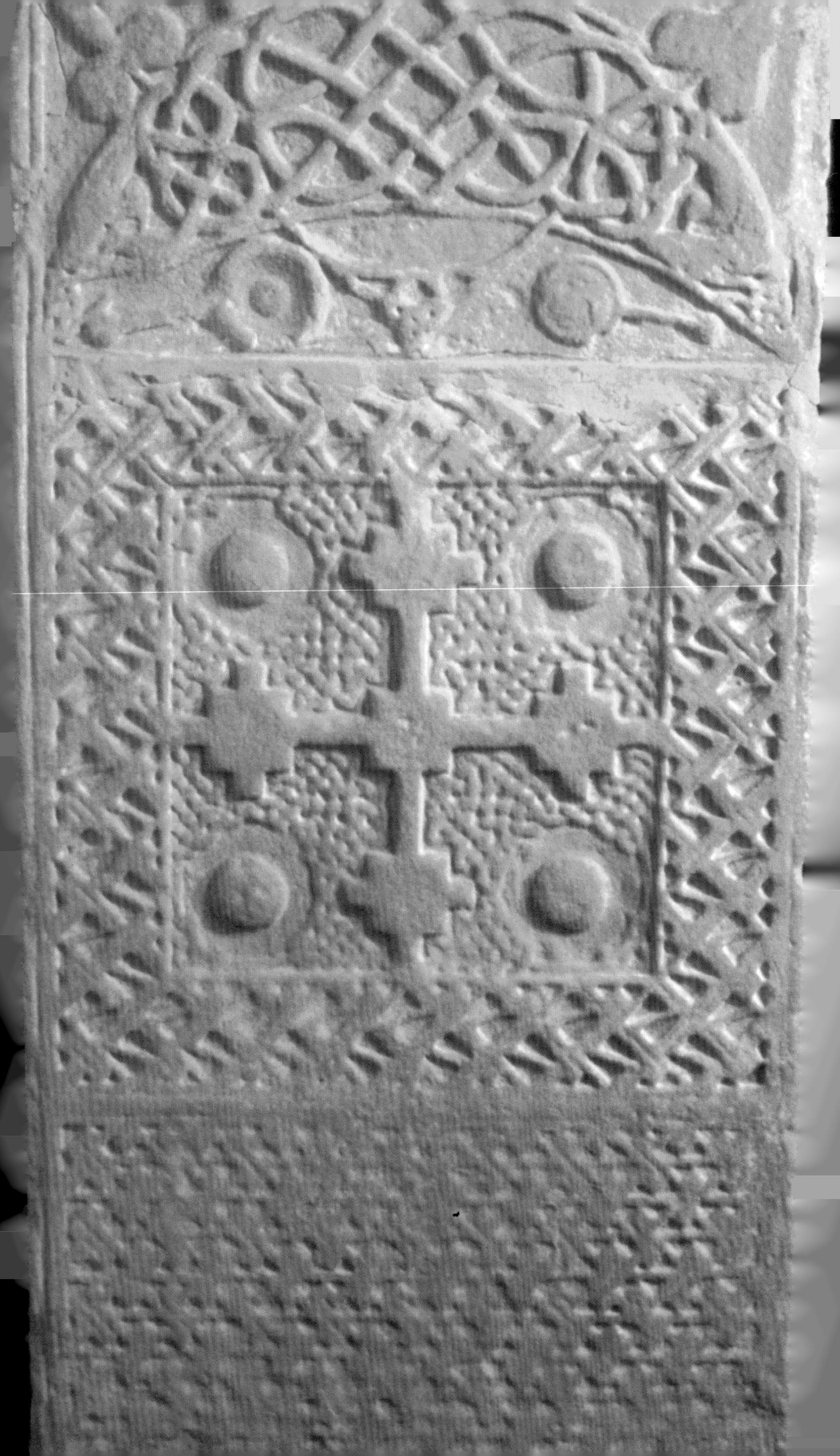

3
Panels and motifs

SINGLE PANELS

In the previous chapter the emphasis was on geometric approaches to layout and design. Using f. 210v of the Lindisfarne Gospels it was shown how grids were used to set out the shape and distribution of panels to form an elaborately decorated cross-carpet page. The account in this chapter illustrates the way that, for each panel, geometric methods can be used to create complex patterns from well-defined motifs.

Since each panel is related only partly to the whole it can be treated as an independent and isolated piece of work. Clearly the whole is much greater than the sum of the parts but each panel has an intrinsic quality of its own and can be illustrated without reference to other panels. The beauty of single panels is highlighted in the first part of this chapter with four single-panel examples from metalwork. These are taken from small pieces of jewellery and escutcheons where composite designs, based on many panels, are inappropriate. Later in the chapter consideration is given to designs of individual panels within a composite design. The approach is applicable equally to stone carvings, manuscripts and metalwork. Examples are included from all these media.

The four examples illustrated in Fig. 3.1 are from different sources and display a range of motifs, styles and techniques. The design in Fig. 3.1a has threefold symmetry and is used on a gold pendant found at Faversham in Kent. The pendant is now in the British Museum and is attributed to Anglo-

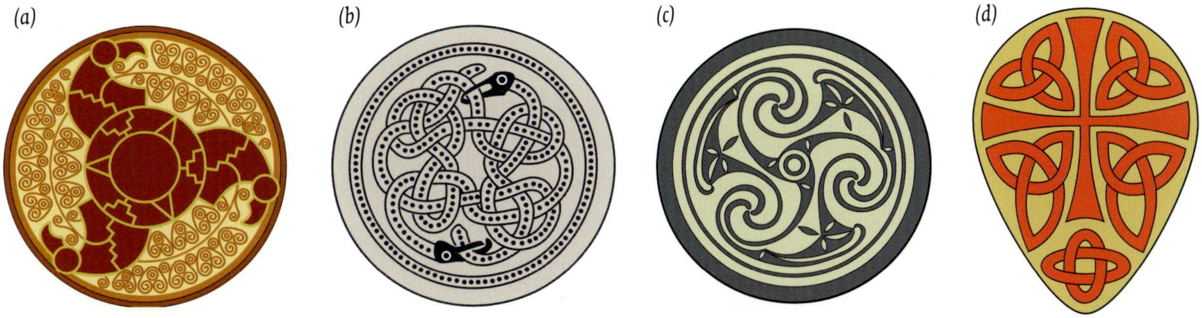

Figure 3.1
Examples of metal artefacts with single panels. (a) Gold pendant with cloisonné and filigree ornamentation from Faversham, Kent, England (diameter 37 mm). (b) Tongue-plate of gold buckle found in the Sutton Hoo burial with niello ornamentation (diameter 29 mm). (c) Bronze disc brooch from Lagore Crannog, Co. Meath, Ireland ornamented with champlevé enamel (diameter 20 mm). (d) Bronze hanging bowl escutcheon from Whitby, England also ornamented with champlevé enamel (width 56 mm).

Saxon workmanship of the seventh century. The three birds' heads and central ring are formed from cloisonné with garnet inlays. The spaces around the cloisonné are richly decorated with beaded gold wire filigree in tightly coiled spirals and the rim has gold wire in a herringbone or plaited pattern. The inlay from the central circular cloison has been lost but is shown as a garnet inlay in Fig. 3.1a. The pattern in Fig. 3.1b is from the tongue-plate of the gold belt-buckle found in Sutton Hoo Burial Mound 1, so it is of a similar period to the Faversham pendant. It is also in the British Museum. The design is crafted in niello and consists of two interlaced and knotted serpents. Both these Anglo-Saxon examples are described in *The Making of England: Anglo-Saxon Art and Culture AD 600–900* (Webster and Backhouse, 1991).

The other examples in Fig. 3.1 are made of a copper alloy, probably bronze. They are decorated with champlevé enamel. The spiral pattern in Fig. 3.1c is from a disc brooch found at Lagore Crannog in County Meath, Ireland. It is now in the National Museum of Ireland and is dated to the seventh or eighth century. It forms the central feature of a simple rimmed disc about 70 mm in diameter and was decorated on a separate octagonal-shaped plate attached to the main disc. The spiral triskele design is raised above a red enamelled background. It is described in *The Work of Angels* (Youngs, 1989).

The simple cross separating four triquetra knots, illustrated in Fig. 3.1d, was used to decorate an escutcheon on a hanging bowl. Bruce-Mitford (1987) describes a wide range of escutcheons and uses them as the basis for a discussion of the development of metalwork in the islands. The example shown in Fig. 3.1d was found at Whitby in northern England. A photograph of the escutcheon is included in a detailed report of the archaeological discoveries at the monastery by Peers and Radford (1943). The escutcheon is damaged and the interlacing has some mistakes. These have been corrected in the illustration in Fig. 3.1d. The cross and interlacing are decorated with red enamel with a background of yellow enamel.

COMPOSITE PANEL DESIGN: LINDISFARNE GOSPELS

Geometric methods must have been used, to a greater or lesser extent, to design and construct the spiral, key, interlacing and zoomorphic motifs in the 'single panels' illustrated in Fig. 3.1. A possible exception is the arrangement of the writhing serpents in Fig. 3.1b although, even here, compasses were used to draw the circles for the niello ornamentation around the serpents.

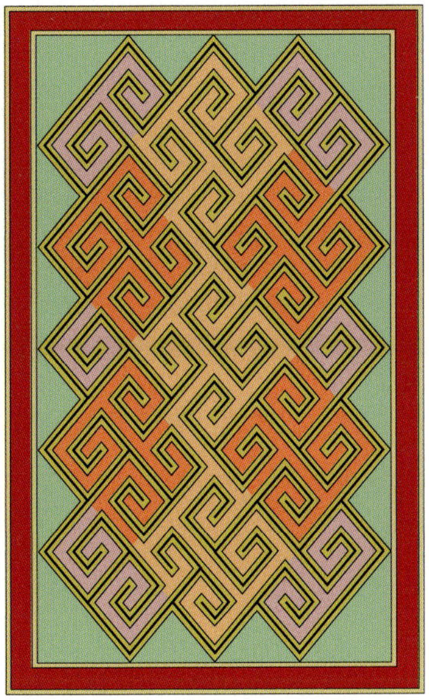

Figure 3.2
Rectangular panel decorated with key pattern based on straight-sided spirals, from Lindisfarne Gospels, f. 210v (width 37 mm).

The prick-marks in Lindisfarne f. 210v (Fig. 2.1) provide unambiguous evidence that geometric methods were used. The geometric order and discipline evident in the Lindisfarne Gospels is sometimes used to criticise it for being over-formalised and rigid. However, in seeking to understand the approach used by the artist one discovers that designs, which at first sight appear highly ordered, contain many fascinating features. In this section each panel of f. 210v is considered separately. The panels are independent of each other except that they all conform to the primary grid (Fig. 2.3).

Rectangular panels with key motif

The key patterns, formed from straight-sided spirals, in the four rectangular panels of f. 210v are both simple and mysterious (Fig. 3.2). The designs resemble complex mazes and labyrinths. The pattern in each panel is based on a grid of two sets of equal-spaced lines lying at ±40° to the long axis of the panel (Fig. 3.3a). The rectangle inside the border is divided into four equal parts in the horizontal direction and six in the vertical direction. Obviously, the number of divisions and the width of the border determine the angle of the grid lines. This angle is close to the angle of the diagonals shown on the primary grid (Fig. 2.3) which lie at ±38.3° to the vertical axis, although the secondary grid inside the panel is unrelated to the primary grid.

The remarkable feature of the pattern is the arrangement of the straight-sided spirals within the panel. Although there are some constraints, associated with the boundaries, there are many possible arrangements. Two of the panels have the same arrangement (top left and bottom right) but the other two panels have different arrangements. The panel shown in Fig. 3.3 is from the bottom left-hand corner of the page.

The nature of the variability of the arrangement of spirals becomes clear when one attempts to reproduce the pattern without using direct tracing methods. The first stage in drawing the pattern is to recognise that the grid lines in the panel divide the space, inside the border, into units filled by straight-sided spirals. To illustrate the approach, consider first a grid of equal-spaced orthogonal lines with straight-sided spirals in a square grid. This grid is further divided to form a finer, tertiary grid, on which the spirals are drawn by unit movements with the sequence 1:1:2:2:3:3:3 (Fig. 3.3b). The spiral provides the basic unit for the pattern and can be oriented in eight different positions depending on the starting point and the direction of rotation (Fig. 3.3c). Orientations (i) to (iv) are formed by a clockwise rotation of the spiral (inside to outside) and are related to each other by rotations of 90°. Similarly, orientations (v) to (viii) are formed by anti-clockwise rotations and are also related to each other by 90° rotations. The pattern is built up by joining these units. Different patterns are achieved by selecting different

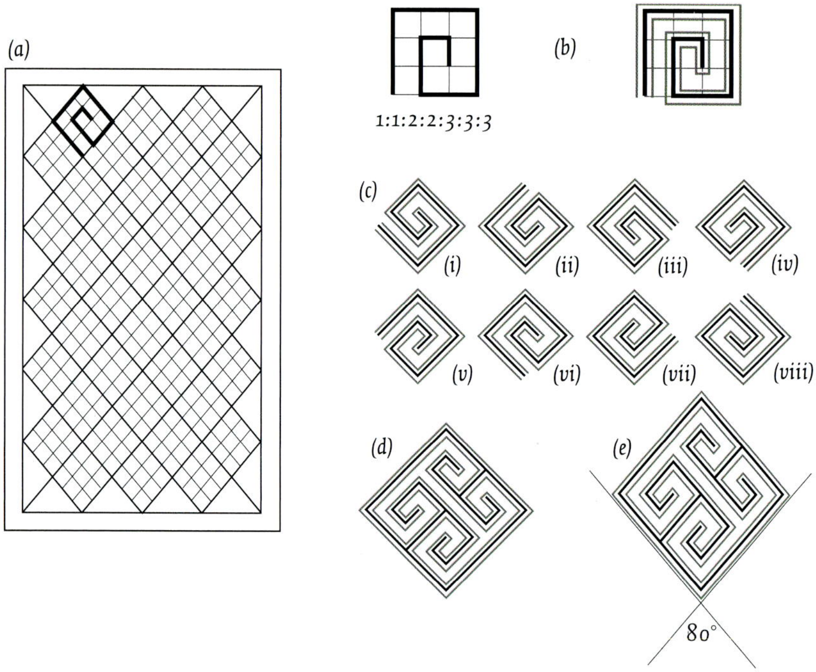

Figure 3.3
Method of construction of rectangular panel in Fig. 3.2. (a) Secondary and tertiary grids. (b) Sequence of steps to produce the basic straight-sided spiral. (c) Eight configurations of basic spiral. (d) Simple pattern formed by combining four spirals with different configurations. (e) Change of shape of pattern in (d) so that grid lines intersect at 80°.

variants of the same basic unit. An example of a simple pattern formed from four units, (i), (ii), (vi) and (vii), is shown in Fig. 3.3d.

In reality, the key patterns in the rectangular panels of f. 210v are based on a grid formed by lines at ±40° to the long axis of the rectangle. The procedure for creating the key pattern is the same using a tertiary grid also set at ±40°. In computer drawing a change from an orthogonal ±45°, or diagonal square grid, to a ±40° grid is achieved by a shape transformation involving changing the scales in the horizontal and vertical directions. The result of such a transformation applied to the four-unit pattern in Fig. 3.3d is shown in Fig. 3.3e. The panel in Fig. 3.2 has seven of the eight variants of the basic units in the final design. To draw the panel the individual units were combined according to the sequence used in the manuscript and then the grid angles were changed as described above. Clearly, the seventh- and eighth-century artists did not follow this particular drawing sequence but, in principle, the approach must have been closely similar. The coarse and fine grid lines, as illustrated earlier in Fig. 3.3a, with the grid lines at ±40°, would have been used to construct the key pattern. The angle is a natural consequence of the choice of grid spacing and width of the border and would not have been measured. The pattern of spirals would then have been mapped on to the grid, as illustrated in the corner of the diagram in Fig. 3.3a. The detailed artistic work would have followed naturally once the basic patterns had been established.

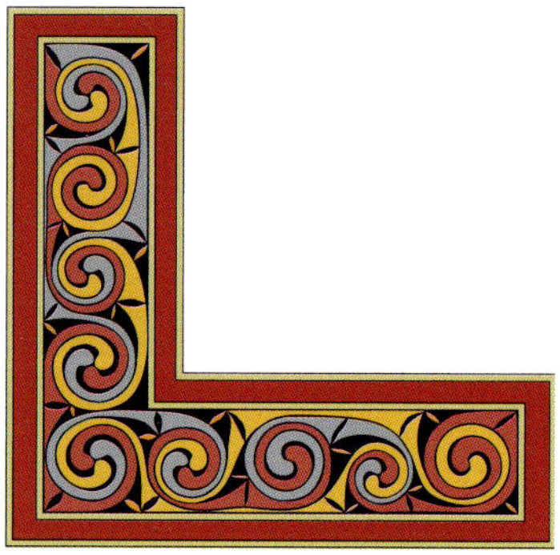

Figure 3.4
L-shaped panel decorated with spirals, from Lindisfarne Gospels, f. 210v (width 37 mm).

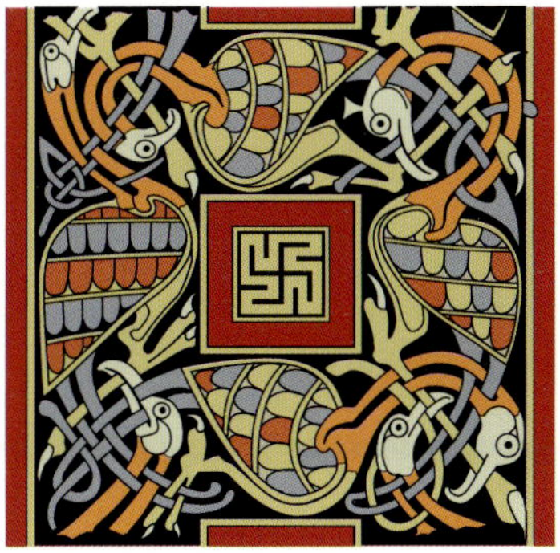

Figure 3.5
Part of the zoomorphic panel that forms a background feature for the other panels, from Lindisfarne Gospels, f. 210v (width, not including borders, 37 mm).

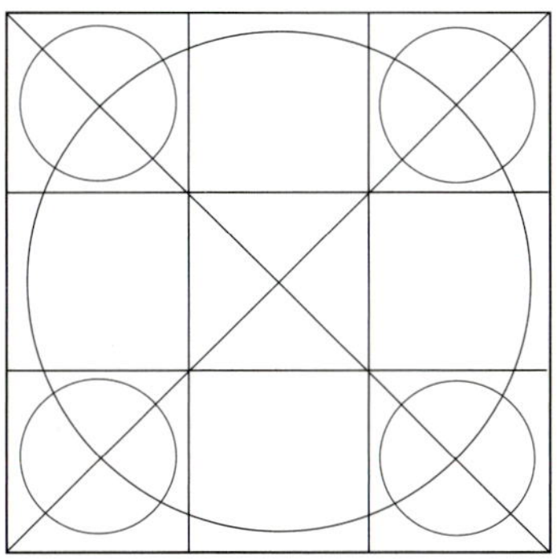

Figure 3.6
Simple outline grid and construction lines for zoomorphic panel in Fig. 3.5.

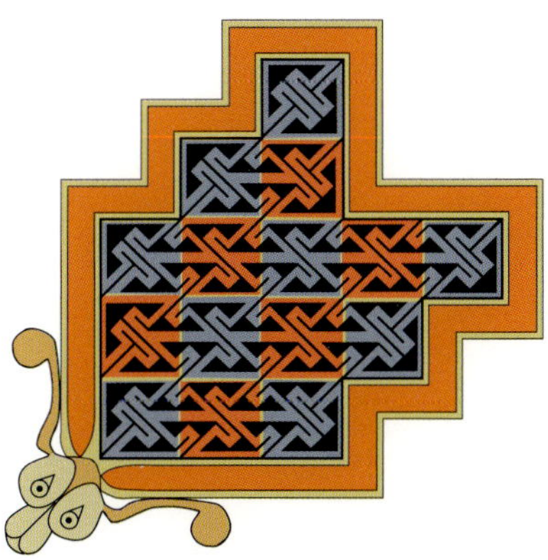

Figure 3.7
Corner finial panel with key pattern, from Lindisfarne Gospels, f. 210v.

The approach to the design described in this section is similar to that used by Bain in *Celtic Art* (1951) and is one of the patterns (No. 970) illustrated in Allen and Anderson (1903). Bruce-Mitford (see Kendrick, 1956–60) has an identical construction and observed that he produced the grid before even seeing the work of Bain or Allen and Anderson, presumably on the basis of the prick-marks. The detail relating to the organisation of the straight-sided spirals described here was not considered by any of these scholars.

The colours used in Fig. 3.2 are close to those in the original manuscript. The main pattern is set in a green background. The artist used different colours to highlight parts of the overall pattern. With a few small exceptions these additional colourings have a symmetrical distribution and are the same in all four panels. They add further mystery to this remarkable pattern.

L-shaped panels with spiral motifs

The four L-shaped panels are decorated with relatively simple spiral patterns. The patterns are not identical but all have the same arrangement, consisting of five equal-spaced spirals aligned vertically and five spirals aligned horizontally. The colour sequence in one of the corners is different from the other three. There is a mixture of two- and three-coil spirals that rotate in clockwise and anti-clockwise directions. The way that the spirals are linked and the treatment of the trumpet ends that join the coils of adjacent spirals is described in Chapter 4. The example illustrated in Fig. 3.4 is from the bottom left-hand corner of the carpet page.

Zoomorphic design forming a background panel

As mentioned earlier, the panels on the carpet page are surrounded by a zoomorphic pattern that is, essentially, a panel in itself. This idea is illustrated in Fig. 3.5, which is taken from the upper left-hand corner of the page in Fig. 2.1. The pattern is based on a set of nine primary grid squares. The central square is decorated with a clockwise swastika surrounded by a conventional border. Prick-marks on the vellum show that the swastika was constructed from a six-by-six square grid. Four birds, with beaks similar to cormorants, a familiar bird on Holy Island, and the feet and claws of raptors decorate the eight squares around the central square. The bodies of the birds lie in alternate squares. Three of the birds have multi-coloured plumage and one has two-colour plumage. These distinctions are relevant to the way that birds of different plumage are distributed throughout the panel, as described in Chapter 5. The distribution of the birds in the primary grid and the shape of their legs, neck and plumage follow the construction lines sketched in Fig. 3.6.

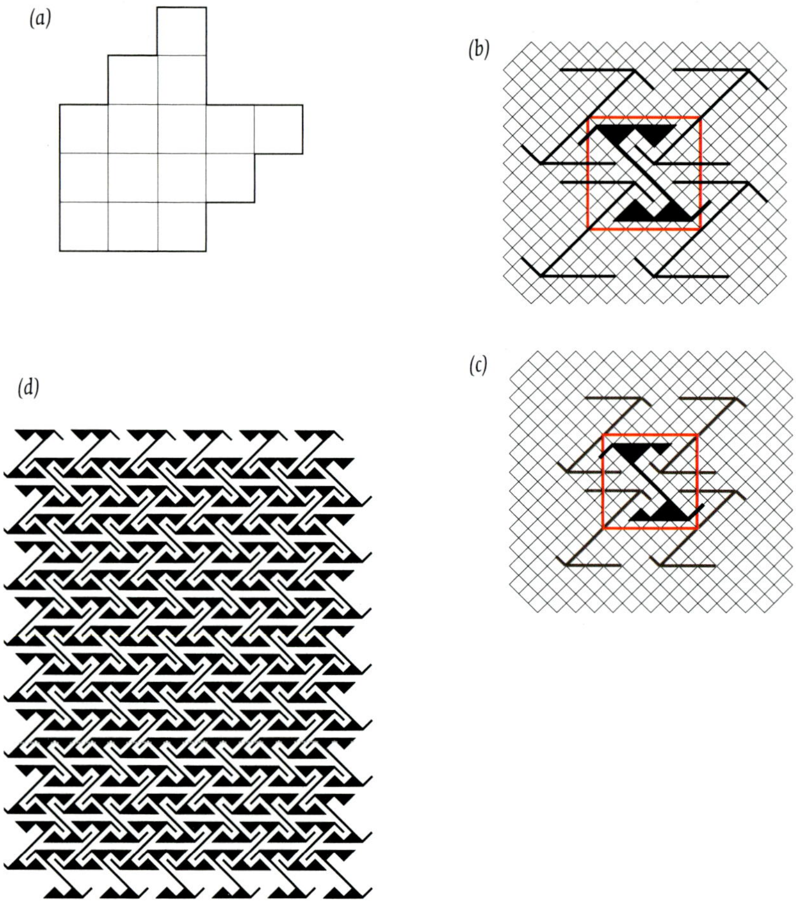

Figure 3.8
Methods of construction of key pattern in panel shown in Fig. 3.7. (a) Primary grid. (b) Unit key pattern for Fig. 3.7 on secondary grid. (c) Similar key pattern to (b). (d) Continuous key pattern formed using basic unit in (b).

Corner finial panels with key motif

The corner panel in Fig. 3.7 is from the bottom left-hand corner of the carpet page. It is shown as a closed panel although, on the actual page, part of the outer border extends around the whole of the design. The corner of the panel is ornamented with a zoomorphic design resembling a dog. The inner panel has a simple square grid (Fig. 3.8a) and this determines the dimensions of the key pattern. The basic elements of this pattern are illustrated in Fig. 3.8b to d; more details are given in Chapter 4. Each square of the grid is divided into a finer square grid at 45° to the main grid. The finer grid divides the edges of each side of the main grid into six equal parts. The arrangement of the primary motif of the key pattern is shown in the square in Fig. 3.8b. It is formed by a Z-shaped pattern 4:10:4 with additional ends, two diagonal units long, at 45°. The ornamentation and distribution of the primary motifs is also shown in Fig. 3.8b. The key pattern is achieved by combining the individual squares to produce a continuous array, as shown in Fig. 3.8d. The irregularly shaped corner panels are decorated in a similar way with simple

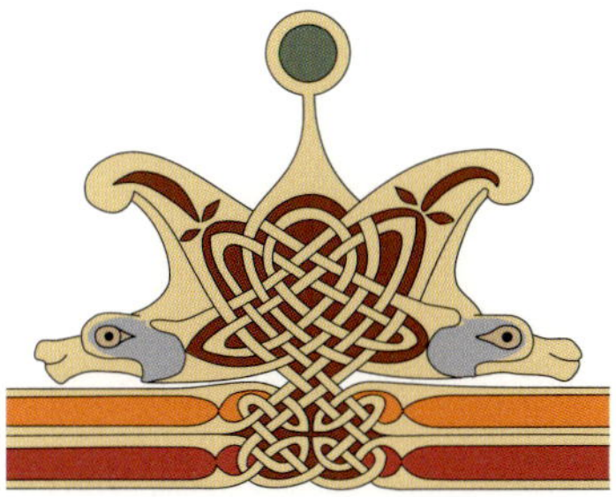

Figure 3.9
Interlacing zoomorphic design of side finials, from Lindisfarne Gospels, f.210v.

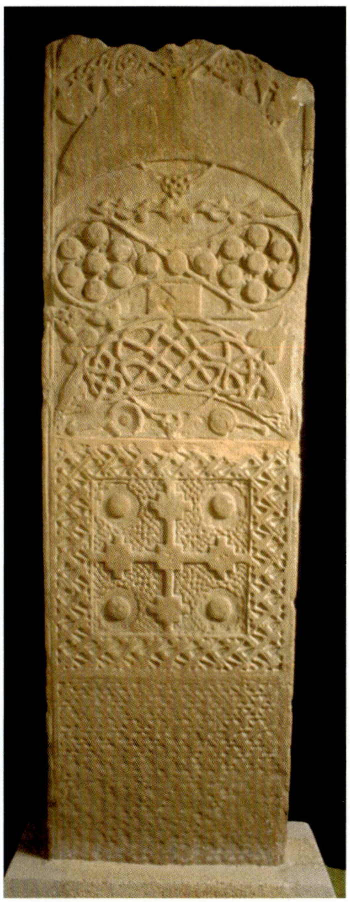

Figure 3.10
Photograph of Rosemarkie No.1, a Pictish cross-slab in the Groam House Museum (by permission of Directors of Groam House Museum).

modifications to the basic motifs at the internal and external corners of the pattern. Superimposed on the key pattern is a two-colour square pattern.

The pattern in Fig. 3.8d is illustrated in Bain (1951) and in Allen and Anderson (1903). The appearance of the pattern depends on the relative thickness of the different coloured lines. A similar pattern, also based on a square net, is achieved with a Z-shaped motif formed by a 3:8:3 sequence, as illustrated in Fig. 3.8c. There are only a limited number of sequences that meet the space-filling requirements of this type of key pattern.

Side finial with interlacing motif

Although not strictly panels, the finials in the centre of the sides of the page have a simple and elegant design, as shown in Fig. 3.9. The pattern is integrated into the border of the main design with interlacing. The pattern of interlacing differs from one edge of the frame to the next. The main ornamentation is in harmony with the animals at the corner finials and shows a simple interlaced zoomorphic design.

COMPOSITE PANEL DESIGN: ROSEMARKIE STONE

The Rosemarkie stone is a Pictish cross-slab which is now in the Groam House Museum in Rosemarkie. The museum also houses work associated with George Bain including original drawings, printed materials, textiles, photographs and craft work. The main feature of the museum, which is devoted to Pictish themes, is a collection of 15 carved Pictish stones all originating in Rosemarkie. The cross-slab (Fig 3.10) is the pride of the collection and is illustrated in many books and on websites relating to Pictish art and history. Allen and Anderson (1903) refer to the cross-slab as Rosemarkie No. 1. The stone is dated to the eighth or ninth century.

The Rosemarkie stone is featured in Bain (1951). The interpretation of the patterns on the stone has been advanced by the recent archaeological drawings of Scott (see RCAHMS, 1999). The drawings are the most accurate available and faithfully record much of the topography of the stone surface that has been badly damaged and eroded by misuse and weathering. Scott's drawings have been used as a basis for the description and design of the panels in this section. The extent to which Scott used his interpretative skills in representing the topography is not entirely clear.

Layout of panels

The monument was carved from sandstone. It is 2.59 m high and is set in a concrete base that hides some of the carving on the bottom of the stone. The shape of the stone and the arrangement of the panels are shown in Fig. 3.11. All four sides of the stone have been carved with intricate designs. The two broad faces (A and C in Fig. 3.11) taper outwards towards the top. According to Scott's drawings the taper is slightly different on the two faces but overall it is about 1.3° on each side, making a total included angle of 2.6°. The result of the taper is that the large panels are not strictly square or rectangular. For the purposes of representing the patterns the taper has been ignored. The narrow faces (B and D) have closely parallel edges. The top of the slab has been broken off and lost so one can only surmise as to the actual shape of the original stone. The distribution of patterns suggests that the original shape was as represented in Scott's drawing. The shaded region in Fig. 3.11 represents the broken part of the stone.

There is a cross on both of the main faces of the stone. In this section emphasis is given to the arrangement of panels on face C. The main feature

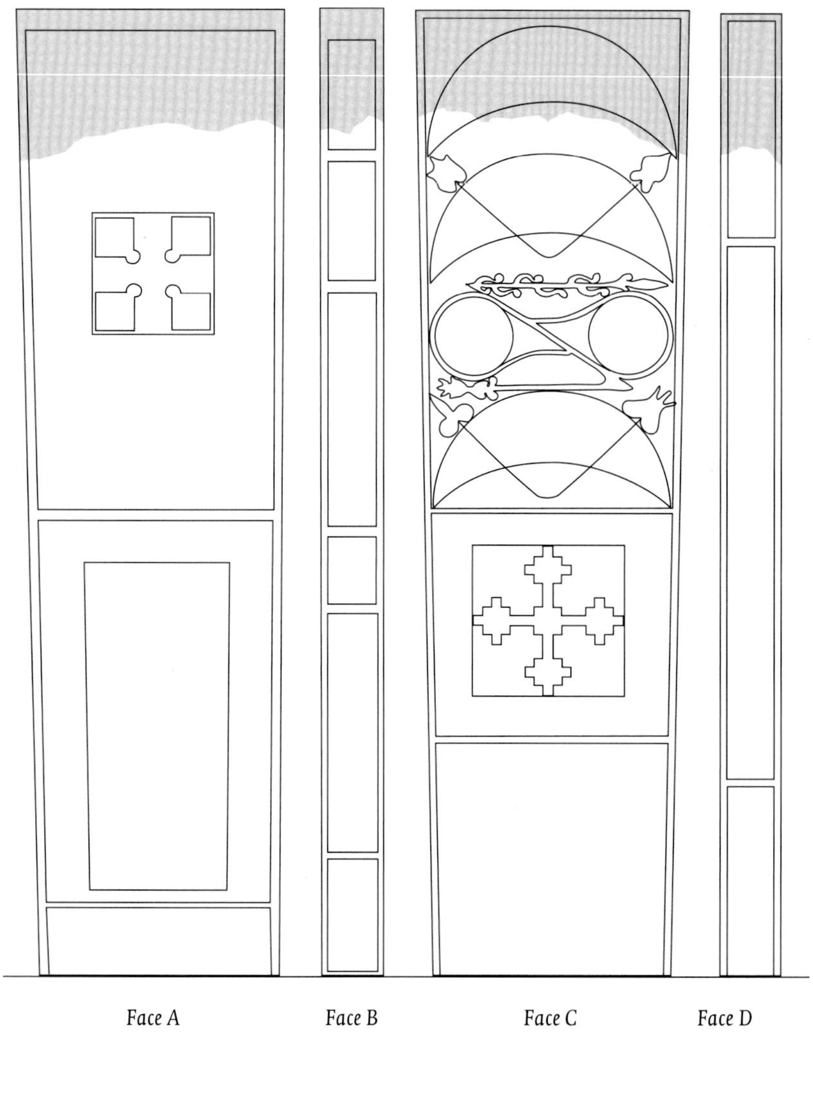

Figure 3.11
Outline of distribution of panels on four sides of Rosemarkie No. 1 cross-slab.

is a square panel with a magnificent equal-armed cross surrounded by interlacing and key patterns. In addition, there are three crescent-shaped panels with V-shaped rods. The crescent and V-shaped rod symbol is one of nearly 50 symbols that appear on Pictish stones. Their origin is unknown and their meaning has defied interpretation, although the symbols were almost certainly related to some aspect of Pictish identity or had some religious meaning for the people. One of the most authoritative accounts of these stones can be found in Henderson (1967). Details of all the Pictish stones and their symbols are given in RCAHMS (1999), referred to above. In their seminal work Allen and Anderson (1903) divided the monuments of Scotland into three groups: Class I, rough-cut standing stones with little ornamentation or decoration other than incised symbols; Class II, stones or monuments with symbols and ornament carved in relief; and Class III, stones or monuments with heavily carved geometric art without any symbols. Rosemarkie No. 1 is in Class II.

Other Pictish symbols on face C include a comb and two mirrors, not shown in Fig. 3.11, and the prominent double-disc and Z-shaped rod that separates two of the crescent-shaped panels. The discs are treated as separate circular panels. The bottom square panel on face C has a fine key pattern similar to the pattern in the corner panels of the Lindisfarne cross-carpet page f. 210v (Figs. 3.7 and 3.8).

It is important to recognise that to illustrate three-dimensional (monochrome) patterns carved on stone as two-dimensional images some interpretation is essential. Exact comparisons are not always possible. It seems likely, from archaeological evidence, that in earlier times some of the stones were painted. Presumably the colours available were similar to those used in manuscripts and in metalwork. Colours are used here to enhance the detail but they cannot be justified by evidence. These issues and problems associated with loss of detail owing to damage and erosion mean that, whereas many of the patterns in manuscripts can be obtained by tracing and copying, the representation of the patterns on carved stones is more difficult and obscure. A stronger element of interpretation is involved and successful drawing and reproduction require a deeper knowledge and understanding of the principles used in design. It is here that the work of Allen and Anderson is so important.

As mentioned in Chapter 2, in order to compare the designs in manuscripts with those on sculptured stones and metalwork the same style of representation has been used throughout the book. Three-dimensional carvings are shown in two dimensions using fine black lines to separate areas in the pattern that, in manuscripts, would be shown in different colours.

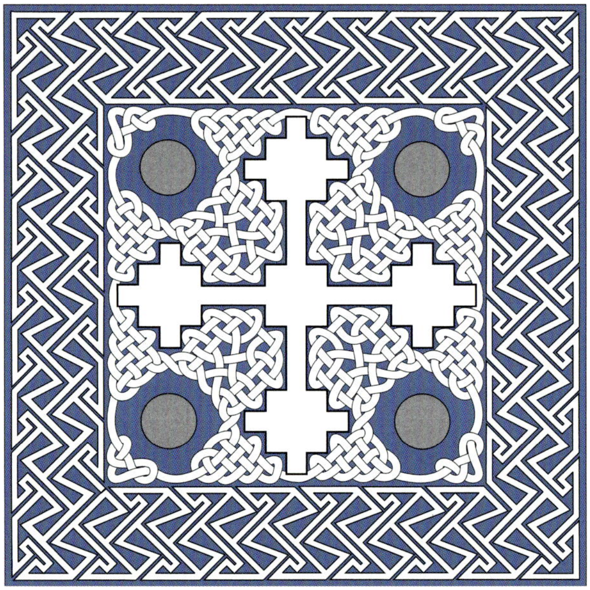

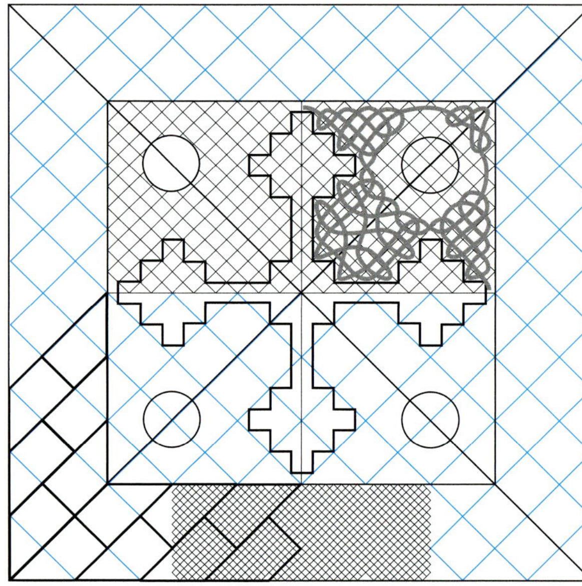

Figure 3.12
Central cross-panel on Rosemarkie No. 1 cross-slab.

Figure 3.13
Primary, secondary and tertiary grids used in constructing the interlacing and key patterns on the central cross-panel of Rosemarkie No. 1.

Cross-panel decorated with interlacing and key patterns

It is not immediately obvious that the exciting and intricate design in Fig. 3.12 is formed in a single panel. The central region with the cross, surrounded by interlacing, seems to be set in an unrelated border of key pattern. Yet the panel was undoubtedly designed as a whole. How did the design develop? A sketch in Allen and Anderson (1903) sets out the basic pattern and Bain, in *Celtic Art* (1951), has highlighted some of the features of the pattern by superimposing his drawing on a photograph. The appearance of the stone in photographs varies depending on the direction of illumination because the pattern is produced in three dimensions. Scott's drawing is the most reliable but it emphasises actual topographical detail rather than the geometric aspects of the design.

The most effective way to discover how the pattern is constructed is to attempt to create it from first principles using sketches, drawings and photographs. These show that the edges of the square panel are divided into nine equal parts. The basic or primary grid for the design consists of two sets of equal-spaced lines at $\pm 45°$ to the sides of the square, as shown in Fig. 3.13. With this grid it becomes clear that the inner square of the panel is related directly to the primary grid and that the roundels are centred at the intersection of lines of the grid. For detail in the inner square the artist has used a secondary grid that divides each square of the primary grid into nine equal squares. The shape and dimensions of the equal-armed cross are formed by joining intersection points of the secondary grid. The interlacing pattern is also based on the secondary grid in a similar way to the interlacing patterns described in relation to Fig. 2.5.

The key pattern surrounding the inner square also follows the primary grid. The grid divides the space into a series of tiles (marked by thick lines in the left-hand corner of Fig. 3.13). These tiles provide a unit pattern for the overall key pattern design. The detail in these units is obtained by a further refinement of the primary grid that divides each square of the grid into 64 equal-sized squares. The method of producing the unit structures is shown in Fig. 3.14. The initial key pattern is drawn following the lines of the tertiary grid (Fig. 3.14a and b). This line is then broadened to produce the desired effect, as in Fig. 3.14c and d. Combining these unit structures or cells produces the key pattern border round the inner square. Two types, or

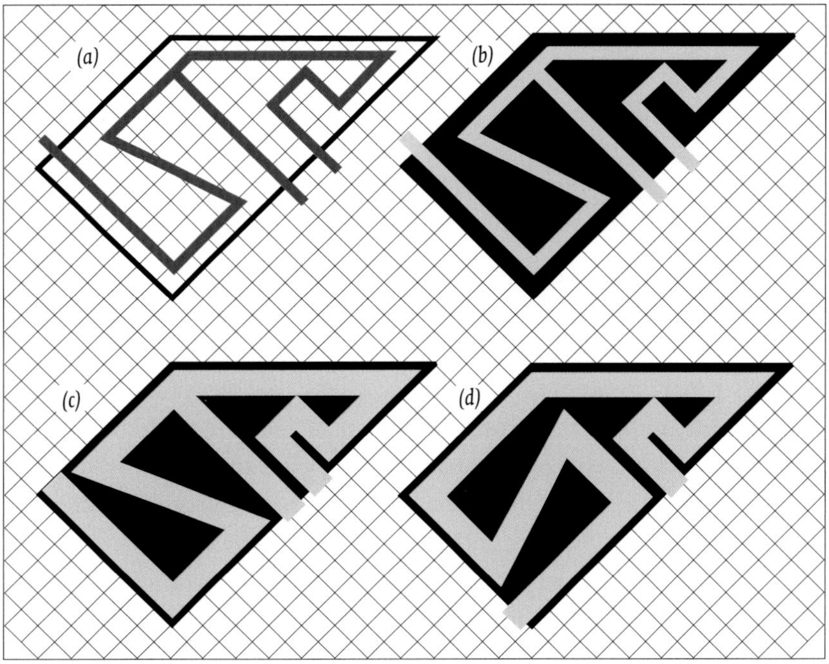

Figure 3.14
Method of constructing the key pattern on the central cross-panel of Rosemarkie No. 1.

designs, of unit cell are required for this panel. The cell shown in Fig. 3.14c is used in the top and bottom of the border and the cell in Fig. 3.14d is used in the sides of the border. Each cell is used in two mirror-related orientations (see Chapter 4) to achieve the final pattern.

In mapping the interlacing patterns Scott's interpretation has been used in most cases. The rather awkward interlacing arrangements in the corners of the square are as drawn by Scott even though more pleasing patterns are possible. The overall design of the interlacing in each quadrant is not identical. The two top quadrants match each other and are related by a 90° rotation. The two bottom quadrants are the same and are similarly related. Differences in interlacing sequences are a common feature of these designs and add interest and mystery to them.

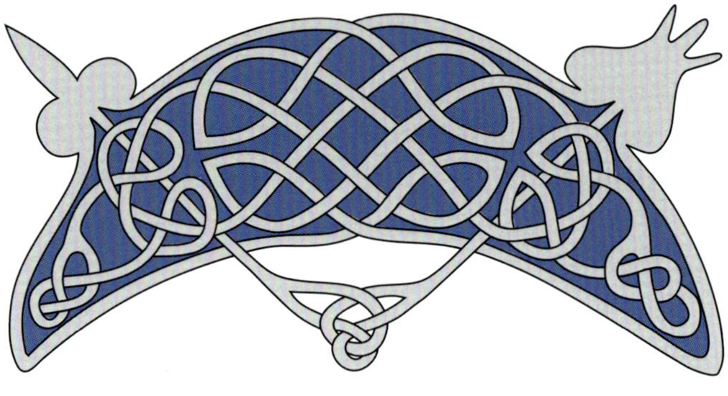

Figure 3.15
Design of lower crescent and V-shaped rod on Rosemarkie No. 1 as used in the logo of the Groam House Museum in Rosemarkie.

As noted earlier the panel is not exactly square because the cross-slab tapers outwards towards the top. This adds to the complexity of the design. One can only wonder how the eighth-century sculptors achieved this. The identification of an underlying grid, which is the basis for the details in the design, provides a way of producing the design when the panel is not square. As before, each side of the panel is divided into nine equal parts and a grid produced in the same way.

Groam House Museum logo

The crescent-shaped panel, complete with V-shaped rod (usually referred to as a crescent and V-rod Pictish symbol), in the centre of the stone just above the cross-panel is used by the museum as a logo. The design in the crescent incorporates the V-shaped rod and has an interlacing pattern. The full pattern is not clear because of damage; the logo is a simplified version. The arrangement of the interlacing is unambiguous in the centre of the crescent but in the corner regions it is far from clear and has defied any worthwhile interpretation. Scott's drawing suggests that there may be an element of zoomorphic design in the corners with the heads of beasts, possibly snakes or serpents, pointing downwards into the tips of the crescent.

Comparison with Scott's drawing shows that the museum design is somewhat different to the one on the stone. For our purposes it is sufficient to use the pattern used by the museum as shown in Fig. 3.15. The pattern breaks some of the rules of simple interlacing – it is not fully interlaced, there are cords with loose ends, and there are cords that branch, or bifurcate, into two cords.

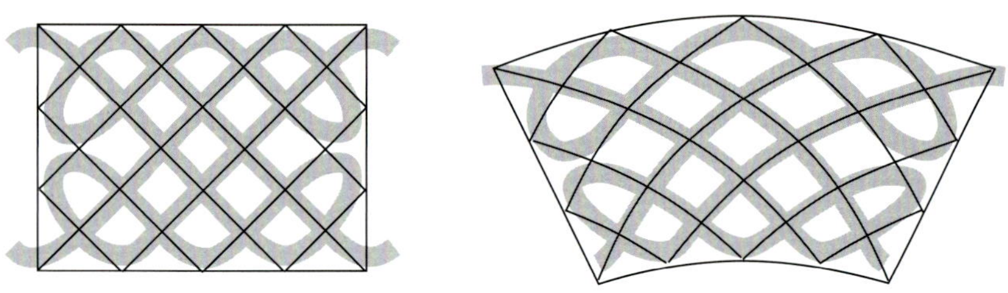

(a) *(b)*

Figure 3.16
Method of changing shape of interlacing design as used in Groam House Museum logo.

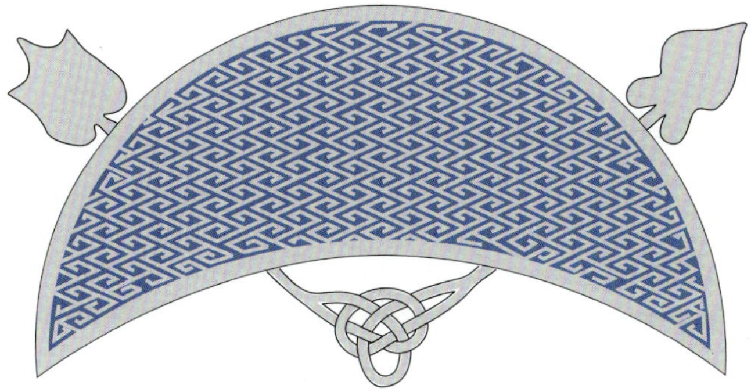

Figure 3.17
Design of upper crescent with V-shaped rod on Rosemarkie No. 1.

The interlacing pattern in the centre of the crescent is the same as the unit pattern identified in Lindisfarne f. 210v (Fig. 2.5). To fit the space in the crescent, between the two sides of the V-shaped rod, the unit pattern has been changed slightly without changing the interlacing sequences. This is illustrated in Fig. 3.16. Fig. 3.16a shows the unit interlacing pattern in a square grid. Modifying the grid, as shown in Fig. 3.16b, changes the shape of the unit pattern.

Top crescent and V-rod panel

The details in this pattern, shown in Fig. 3.17, are based on Scott's drawing. There is some uncertainty about the shape of the terminals on the V-shaped rod. The ones illustrated here were added for completeness only. The crescent is filled with a key pattern similar to that in Lindisfarne f. 210v illustrated in Figs. 3.7 and 3.8, with some important differences. It is based

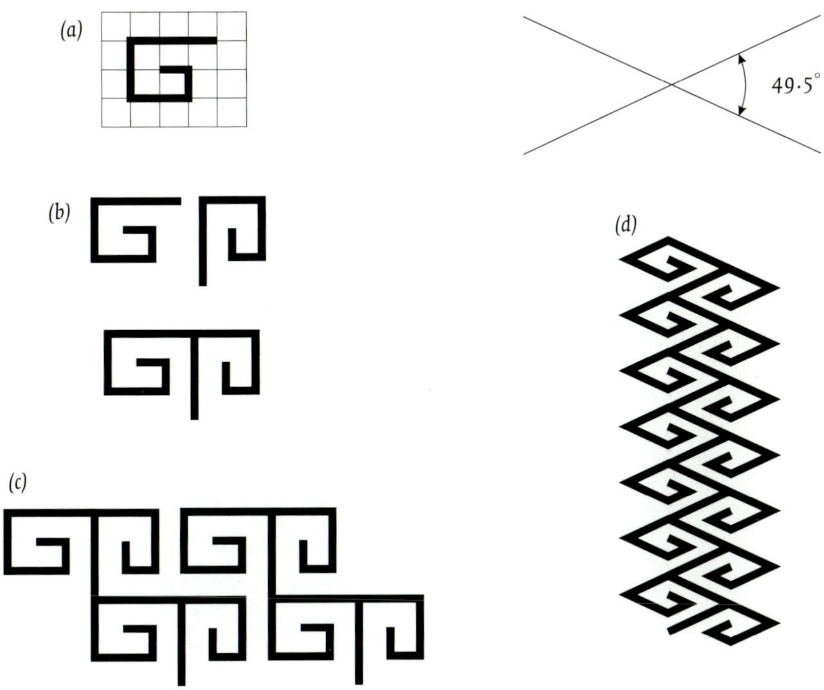

Figure 3.18
Method of constructing key pattern used to ornament the crescent shown in Fig. 3.17. (a) Basic, straight-sided, square spiral. (b) Unit key pattern. (c) Formation of continuous key pattern from unit key pattern. (d) Transformation of continuous pattern from a grid intersecting at 90° to a grid intersecting at 49.5° after a rotation of 45°.

on a grid of two sets of equal-spaced lines at 49.5° to each other. The sequence used in producing the design is summarised in Fig. 3.18.

A unit-square spiral was drawn in a square grid with a clockwise sequence 1:1:2:2:3, as shown in Fig. 3.18a. This was combined with a second spiral, after rotation and reflection, and joined to form the basic unit for the design (Fig. 3.18b). Adding the units sequentially, as shown in Fig. 3.18c, produced a pattern consisting of a continuous array of basic units. In the crescent there are eight units along the centre, arranged vertically, and six units on each side, arranged horizontally. The whole array, produced by the procedure in Fig. 3.18c, was rotated 45° so that the sides of the square were symmetrical about the vertical axis and then distorted to change the angle between the edges from 90° to 49.5° (Fig. 3.18d). Around the edges of the crescent the shapes of the individual units were modified to produce a pleasing effect in the final design.

(a)

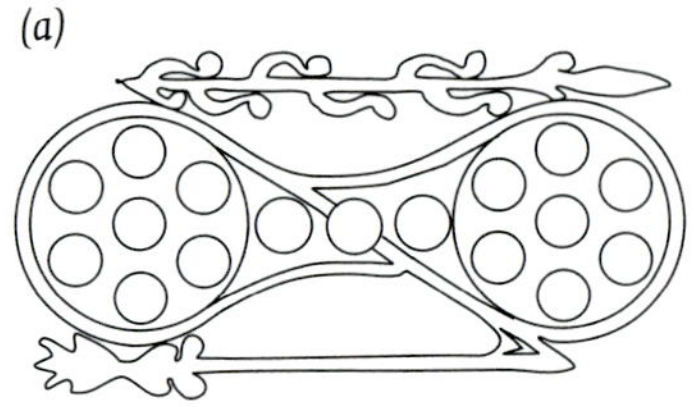

(b)

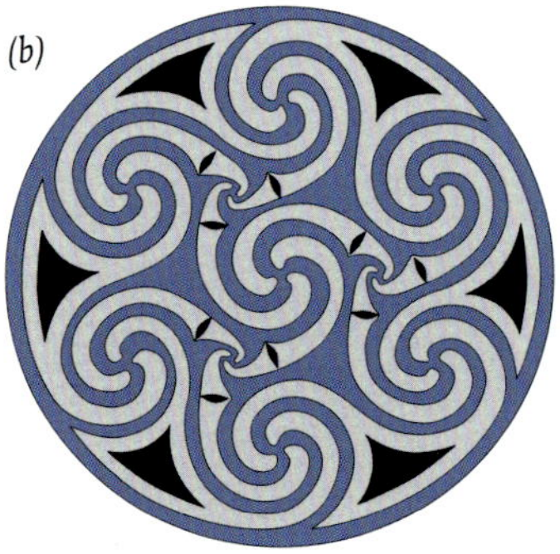

Figure 3.19
Design of double-disc and Z-shaped rod panel on Rosemarkie No. 1: (a) outline, (b) spiral pattern based on a suggestion by Bain.

Double-disc and Z-shaped rod panel

The photograph of the Rosemarkie stone in Fig. 3.10 shows that each disc of the double-disc and Z-shaped rod symbol contains seven roundels in a hexagonal array. The decoration of the panels is far from clear. There is evidence in Scott's drawing for some form of spiral pattern. Bain, in *Celtic Art* (1951), goes further and highlights, on a photograph of the stone, a full spiral pattern. In Fig. 3.19 each disc is treated as a separate panel. The design in Fig. 3.19b is an interpretation based on Bain's drawing.

The roundels in the discs are actually small bosses and they stand proud of the background surface. This makes interpretation even more problematical. Patterns formed on 'three-dimensional' curved surfaces occur many times on sculptured stones and are referred to briefly in Chapter 6.

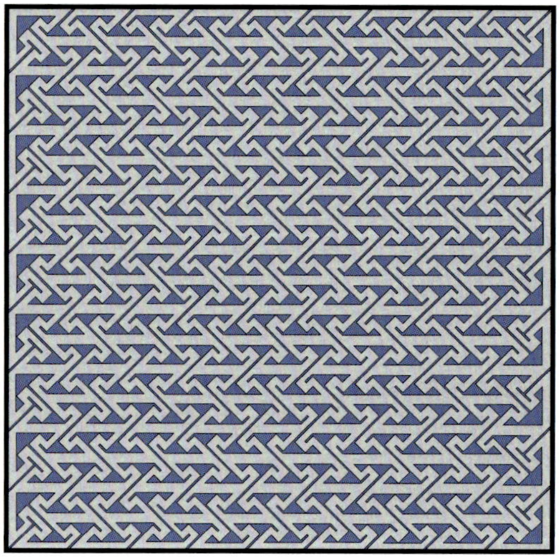

Figure 3.20
Design of key pattern in square panel on Rosemarkie No. 1.

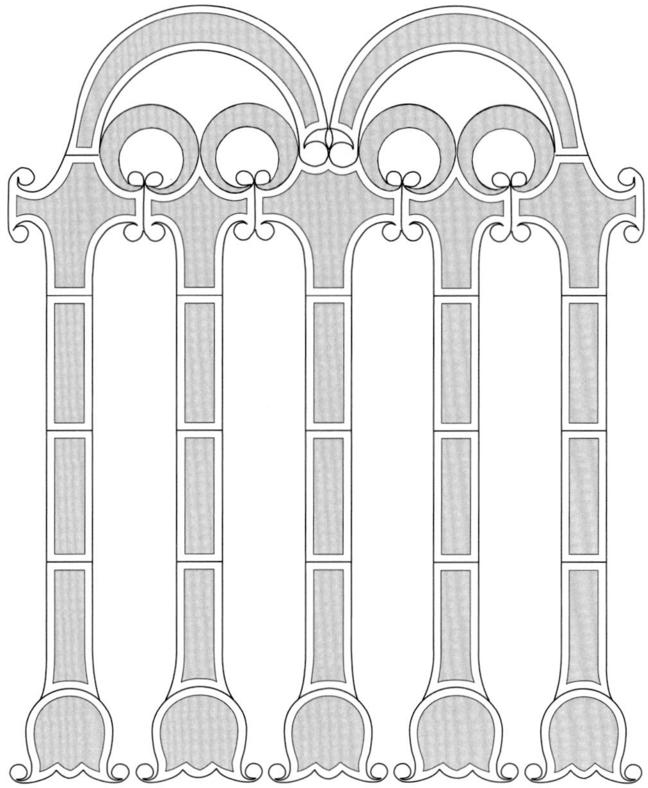

Figure 3.21
Outline of canon table f. 12 in St Petersburg Gospel book showing distribution of panels.

Key pattern square panel

The design of this panel, illustrated in Fig. 3.20, is essentially the same as for the corner key panel in Lindisfarne f. 210v shown in Fig. 3.7. The only difference is that the square unit cell is based on the 3:8:3 sequence shown in Fig. 3.8c rather than the 4:10:4 sequence shown in Fig. 3.8b. As mentioned previously, both of these sequences allow the formation of a pattern based on a square grid. The panel in the illustration has the same nine by nine primary square grid as the cross-panel. It is also not perfectly square because the sides of the stone have a slight taper.

The panel is badly eroded so one has to use a significant amount of interpretation in representing the pattern. Bain has sketched a pattern for part of the panel on a photograph of the stone whereas Scott has relied on interpretation and seems to have used a mixture of the 3:8:3 and 4:10:4 sequences, which is, of course, highly unlikely to have been used by the original artist.

These examples from the Lindisfarne Gospels and the Rosemarkie stone have been treated in a closely similar way. In both, the panel approach is well established. Many of the motifs are common to both works of art. The medium of the art and the crafts required to create them are profoundly

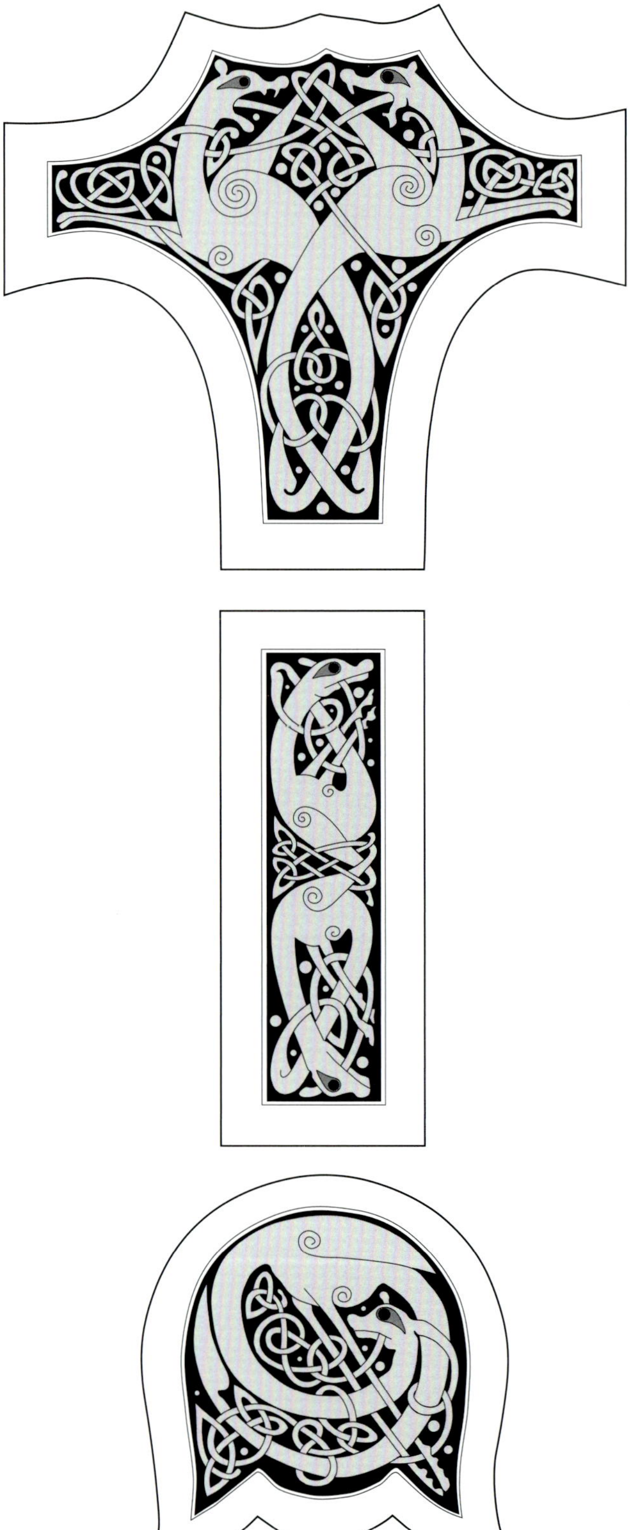

Figure 3.22
Zoomorphic designs in top, middle and bottom panels of central column of canon table f. 12 of St Petersburg Gospel book.

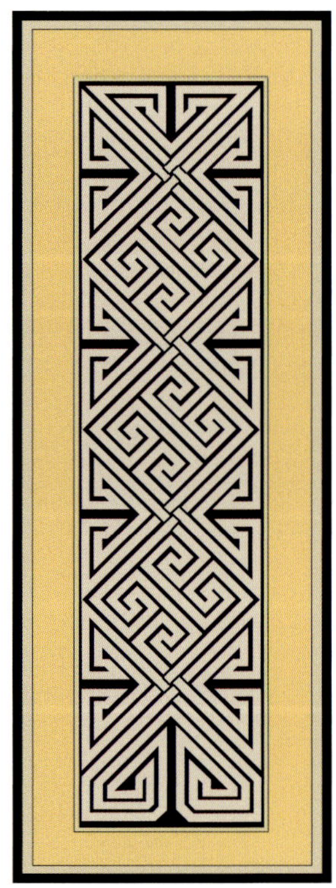

Figure 3.23
Key pattern design in one panel in central column of canon table f. 12 of St Petersburg Gospel book.

different and yet there is no avoiding the conclusion that the creative artistic work is of the same genre. In both examples there is extensive evidence for the use of grids for displaying motifs in panels. This is a theme that is developed further in the next chapter. In the remaining sections of this chapter other examples of panel designs are used to demonstrate that the approach was widely used in manuscripts and in metalwork.

COMPOSITE PANEL DESIGN: CANON TABLE, ST PETERSBURG GOSPEL BOOK

Canon tables are a familiar feature at the beginning of Insular Gospels and many other gospel writings. Alexander (1978) describes a canon table as 'A concordance table of references to passages occurring in one or in two or more of the four Gospels compiled by Eusebius of Caesarea in the fourth century and usually arranged in columns under arches'. The St Petersburg Gospel book is held in the State Public Library, St Petersburg, reference Cod.F.v.I.8. It is attributed by Alexander to the late eighth century and is claimed by him to have been written and illuminated at Lindisfarne. This example is based on the illustration in the frontispiece of Alexander's book. The columns and arches are decorated with panels using similar designs and motifs to those in other Insular manuscripts.

An outline of canon table f. 12 is illustrated in Fig. 3.21. In the photographic reproduction in Alexander's book the columns are bent and distorted, presumably as a result of changes in the shape of the vellum after the work was completed. The outline is equivalent to the primary grid used to illustrate the design of the carpet page and the sculptured stone in previous sections. In producing this outline it has been assumed that, in the original design, the columns were straight and vertical and the arches to the columns were symmetrical.

The canon table is decorated with 31 separate panels, shown as shaded areas in the outline drawing. The designs in the panels have a range of zoomorphic, interlacing, key and spiral patterns. There is some symmetry in the distribution of these motifs, but the decoration in each panel is unique. Spirals are used to ornament the top and bottom of the columns. Five panels in the central column have been selected to illustrate some of the designs that have been used.

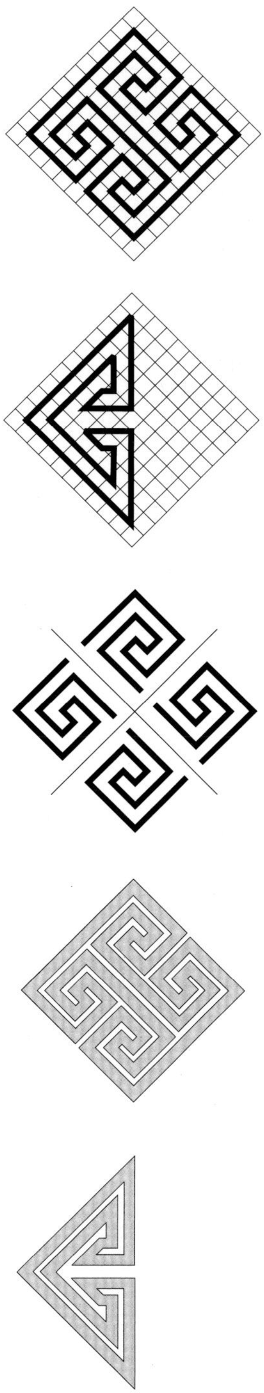

Figure 3.24
Method of construction of key pattern design in Fig. 3.23.

Zoomorphic designs

In the central column, the top, middle and bottom panels have zoomorphic designs as illustrated in Fig. 3.22. The animals are beasts of some kind, which are severely distorted and unworldly, with intricate interlacing adornments. The interlacing is of high quality and the most remarkable feature is the way that the artist has achieved patterns that fill the irregularly shaped panels uniformly. The panels are coloured in mild shades of blue, yellow and red. They are illustrated in monotone to bring out the pattern more clearly. There is some symmetry in the distribution and form of the animals in the two top panels but the symmetry breaks down at finer scales.

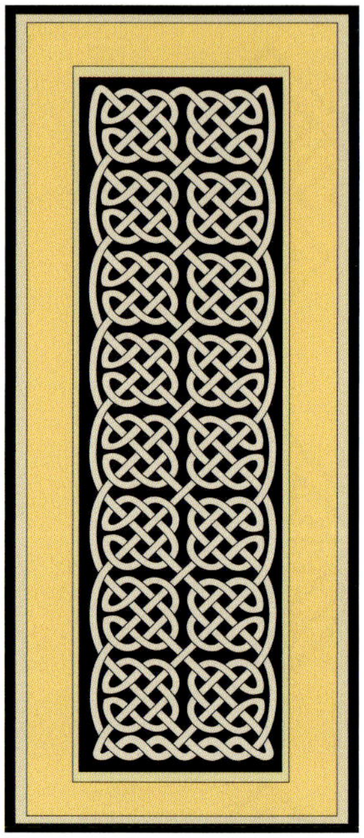

Figure 3.25
Interlacing pattern design in one panel in central column of canon table f. 12 of St Petersburg Gospel book.

Other panels

The elegant key pattern in Fig. 3.23 is based on a simple grid of squares and diagonals; it was constructed by combining multiples of the two units shown in Fig. 3.24. Each of these units is a composite of basic units. Modifications to the design are required at the bottom of the panel because the shape of the panel does not match exactly the square grid.

The interlacing panel in Fig. 3.25 has the same primary grid as the key panel. There are some adjustments to the design at the bottom of the panel. The pattern is made up of 16 simple interlacing units constructed on a finer grid (Fig. 3.26). The units lie in two columns of eight. The individual units in the left-hand column are related to those in the right-hand column by a 180° rotation.

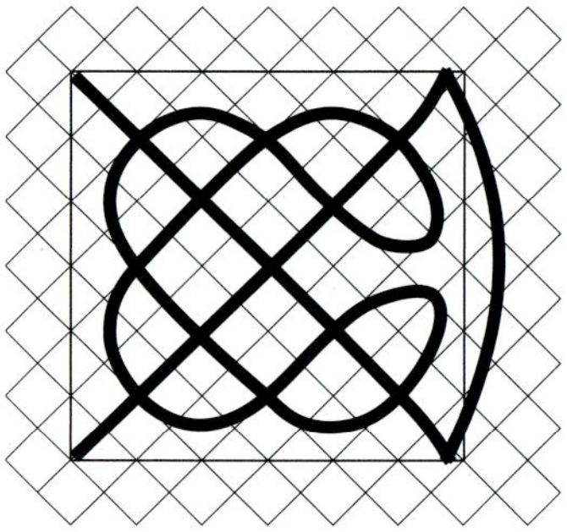

Figure 3.26
Method of construction of interlacing pattern design in Fig. 3.25.

INITIAL LETTERS: ST GALL GOSPEL BOOK AND BOOK OF KELLS

Two examples are used to illustrate the panel approach in ornamenting initial letters. They were chosen, in part, because they span a range of skills and styles. The XPI letters, shown in outline in Fig. 3.27, are from the St Gall Gospel book. St Gall was born in Ireland in the middle of the sixth century and went with St Columbanus to St Gall in Switzerland where they formed a cell and eventually a monastery. The Gospel book (Cod. 51) is in Stiftsbibliothek in St Gallen, Switzerland. According to Alexander (1978) it was produced in Ireland in the second half of the eighth century. The initial letters are decorated with panels, both inside and outside the letters, with a strong emphasis on spiral patterns. The geometric details are consistent with other works but the quality is relatively poor. Compared with the equivalent letters in the Book of Kells (monogram page f. 34r) both the quality and style are inferior. Nevertheless, the St Gall Gospels provide evidence that the geometric approach to ornamentation was used in scriptoria other than the well-known ones associated with the Gospel books of Lindisfarne and Kells.

The outline of the XPI letters in the Book of Kells (see Fig. 3.28), which post-dates the St Gall Gospels, is very similar to that in Fig. 3.27. Even here the difference in style and flair is evident. But it is in the ornamentation that

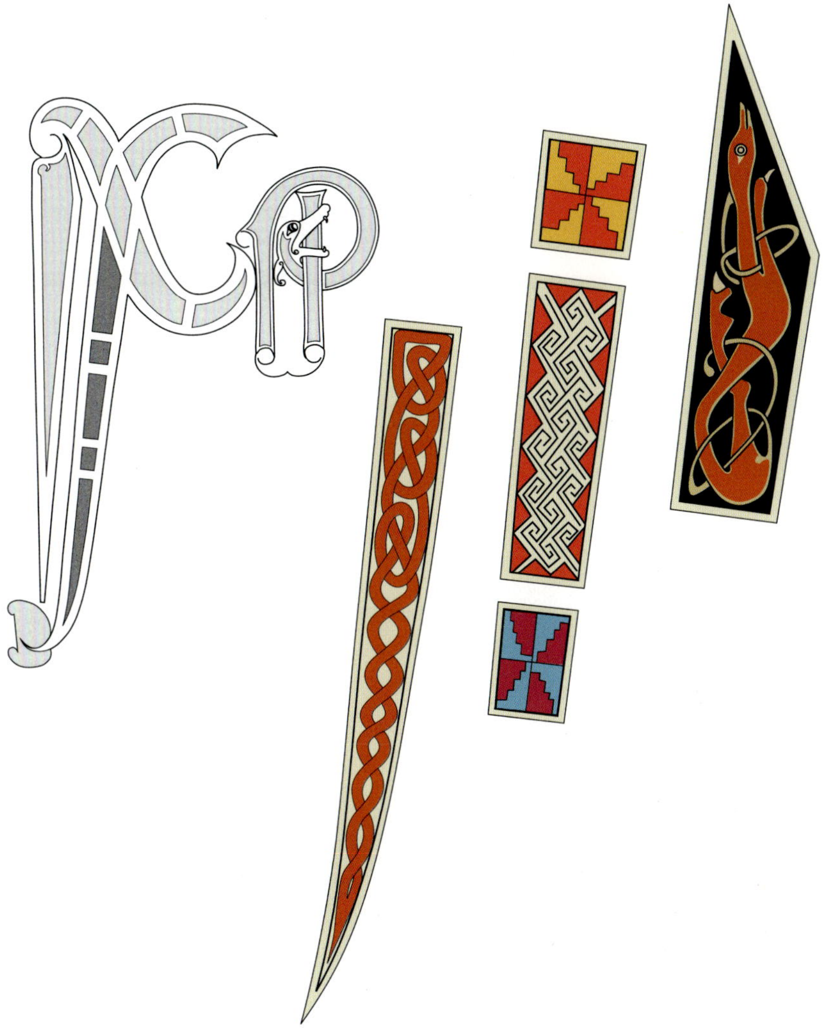

Figure 3.27
Outline and details of five panels ornamenting the XPI letters of Matthew 1:18 in St Gall Gospels.

the difference in quality is so marked. Sullivan (1920) quotes Westwood, who described the XPI monogram page in the Book of Kells as 'the most elaborate specimen of calligraphy which was perhaps ever executed', and also quotes Brunn, who observed that the page surpassed as a piece of decoration '...anything to be met with in any other written book. It is a page to discourage even the most accomplished and most enthusiastic modern draughtsmen...'

The complexity of the ornamentation in the Book of Kells makes it difficult to use it for illustration although the panel approach still applies. Some examples of individual panels are included in later chapters of this book. To provide a brief insight into the quality of the work the second example in this section is a simple initial letter from the Book of Kells.

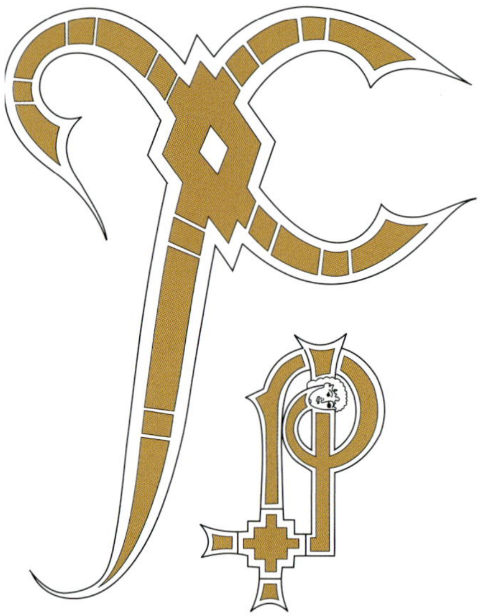

Figure 3.28
Outline of XPI letters of Matthew 1:18 in Book of Kells.

XPI monogram from Gospel book of St Gall

The XPI monogram page contains some words of the gospel according to St Matthew 1:18, '*XPI (Christi) autem generatio*' – the birth of Jesus Christ. There is a black and white photographic copy of this page in Alexander's book (1978). A fine collection of hand-drawn facsimiles of manuscript pages was published, in colour, by Westwood (1868). It includes a complete drawing of the monogram. He used direct tracing to reproduce the patterns but the quality of this work, though impressive, cannot be relied on for accuracy of detail. Some of the apparent 'mistakes' in the facsimile can be attributed to 'corrections' to the original made by Westwood to follow more accurately the

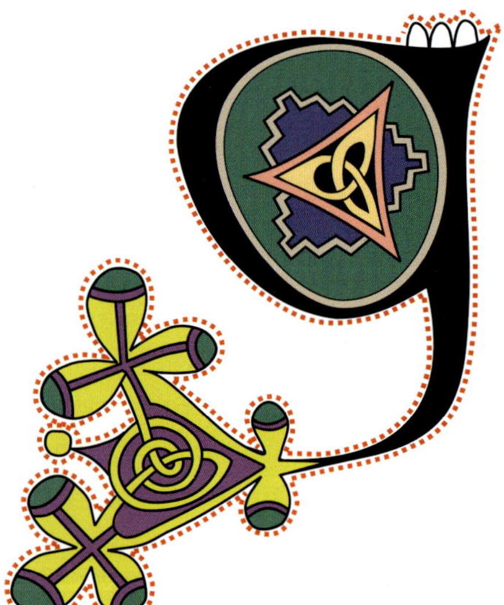

Figure 3.29
Initial letter Q from Book of Kells.

'rules' of geometric art. Many must be regarded as 'mistakes'. The colours in Fig. 3.27 are similar to those used by Westwood but they cannot be relied on as accurate reproductions of the actual manuscript.

In Fig. 3.27 the designs of a selection of panels, shown in a darker shade in the outline drawing, are illustrated. They include interlacing, step, zoomorphic and key patterns. The shape of the panels is determined by the outline of the XPI letters. This makes filling the panels more complicated than for regularly shaped panels. The key pattern panel illustrates the complications as well as the absence of real quality in the artistic work. The panel is not rectilinear so that there are immediate problems in fitting a pattern, based on a regular grid, into a space that tapers along its length. The key pattern in the Gospel book is very irregular and is even more irregular in Westwood's work. This can be attributed, in part, to the artist's attempt to make the pattern fill the space. The illustration in Fig. 3.27 reproduces the pattern in the Gospel book. Later, in Chapter 4, the reconstruction of the pattern, so that it matches the qualities displayed by the artists of the Lindisfarne Gospels, is illustrated. The maze pattern is similar to the rectangular panels in Lindisfarne f. 210v but the straight-sided spirals are not properly aligned and there is a selection of different spiral sequences.

Initial letter from Book of Kells

The simple and elegant initial letter Q from the Book of Kells (Fig. 3.29) is one of a selection of initial and compound letters illustrated in Sullivan (1920). The closed part of the letter, with a triqetra knot and step pattern, acts as a panel, as does the spiral interlacing at the tail of the Q. The contrast between the quality and style of this simple letter and that of the work of the artist of the St Gall Gospel is remarkable. In the genealogical section of the Book of Kells the letter Q is ornamented in numerous different ways, demonstrating the creative skills of the artist. The style throughout is more free-flowing and yet the construction of the motifs is underpinned by geometric constraints and rules.

COMPOSITE PANEL DESIGN: HUNTERSTON BROOCH

The Hunterston brooch (Fig. 3.30), like the equally celebrated Tara brooch, has many characteristics of Anglo-Saxon jewellery produced in south-east England in the first half of the seventh century. It was discovered in 1830 on a beach near Hunterston, West Kilbride, Ayrshire in south-west Scotland. It was probably made towards the end of the seventh century or early in the eighth century. It has been suggested that it was produced by an Anglo-Saxon

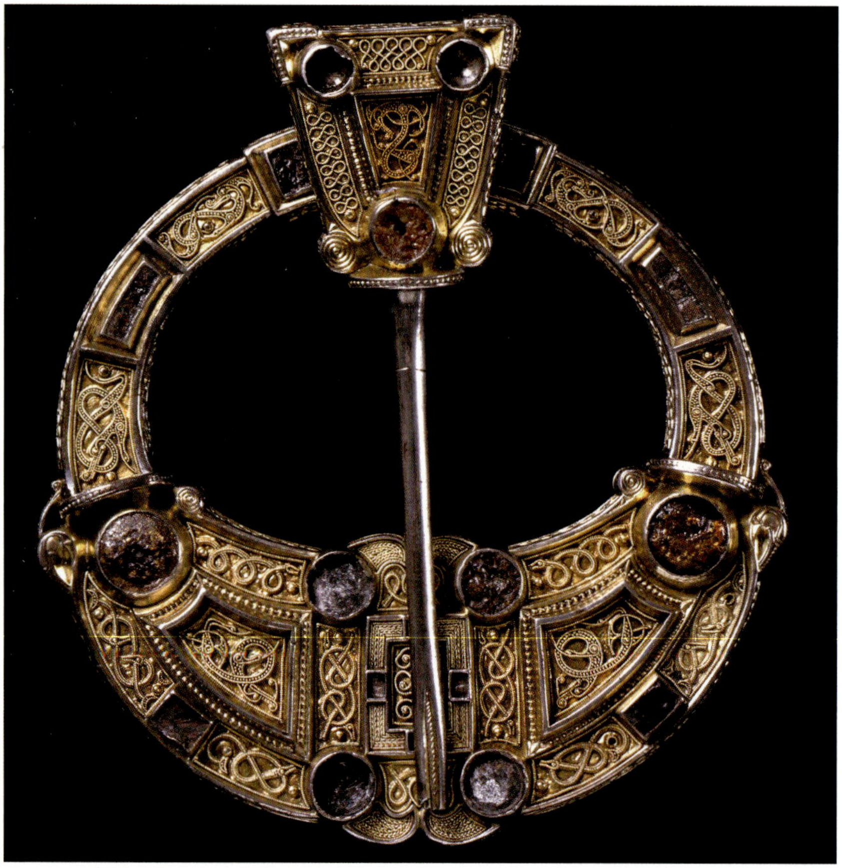

Figure 3.30
Photograph of Hunterston brooch. Diameter of brooch is 122 mm (by permission of the Trustees of the National Museums of Scotland).

artist for a Celtic patron. The brooch is now displayed in the National Museums of Scotland in Edinburgh.

Technically, the brooch is described as pseudo-penannular, meaning that it is a penannular brooch without an opening. It is made of solid silver and decorated with gold and silver filigree and amber studs. There is an excellent colour photograph of the brooch in Douane (1996). It was included in the '*Work of Angels*' exhibition at the British Museum in 1989 (see Youngs, 1989). The most detailed description of the brooch is by Stevenson (1974). Some geometric aspects of the design are described by Whitfield (1999).

An outline of the design of the brooch and panels is shown in Fig. 3.31. The brooch pin, which is also decorated with panels and filigree, has been omitted for clarity. The layout of the panels, shown in light grey, is based on a series of circles. The arms of the brooch are joined by a composite panel, with a cross motif, suggesting a Christian influence. There are five basic types of filigree ornamentation in the panels. The majority are either beasts with ribbon-like bodies or interlaced serpents. Two examples are illustrated in Fig. 3.31. The detail of the metalwork is closely similar to that described briefly in Chapter 2, particularly in connection with the Kingston brooch.

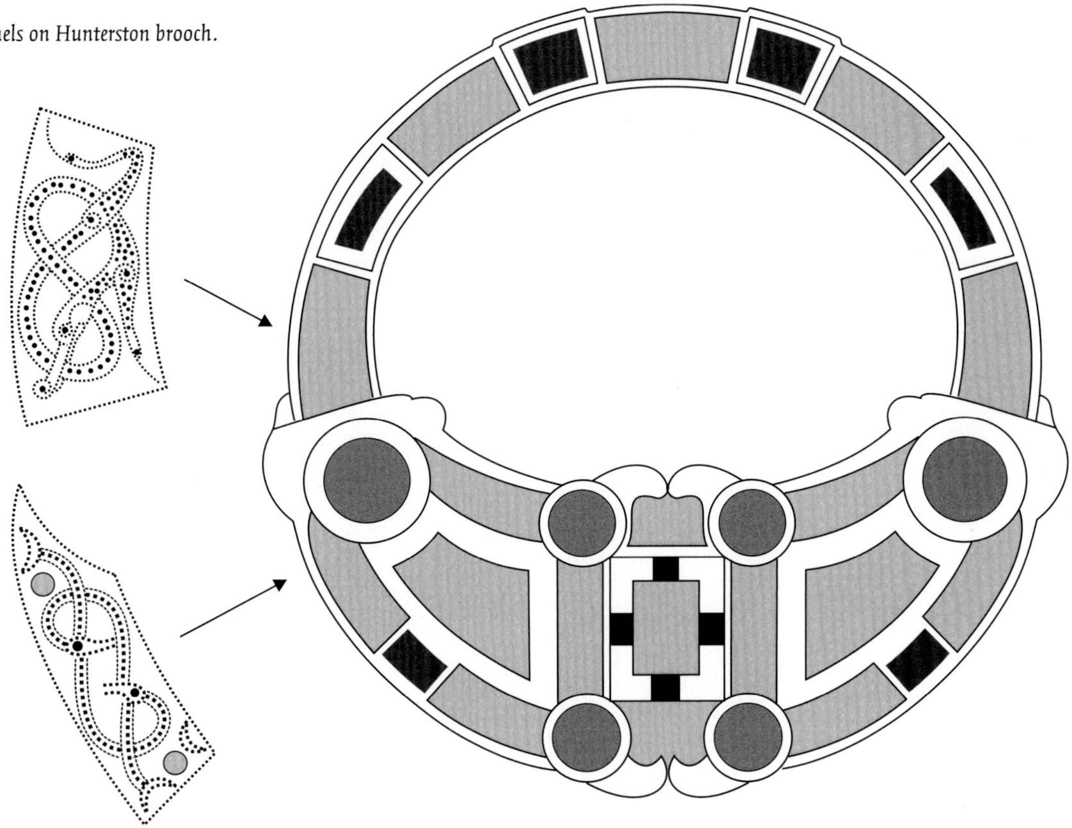

Figure 3.31
Layout of panels on Hunterston brooch.

There are close parallels with many of the beasts in the Lindisfarne Gospels, such as, for example, the procession of beasts illustrated in Fig. 2.31c. The serpents, beasts and other filigree patterns are displayed symmetrically about a vertical axis through the centre of the brooch and they are almost mirror-related.

The approach to panel layout in the Hunterston brooch is consistent with the methods used for other contemporary works of art in stone and in manuscripts described in this chapter. The geometric approach to design is used throughout and there is extensive overlap in the use of motifs in different media. The work described in this chapter spans over 200 years and derives its inspiration from many cultural sources, particularly the peoples whose roots lie in Anglo-Saxon and Celtic, including Pictish, traditions.

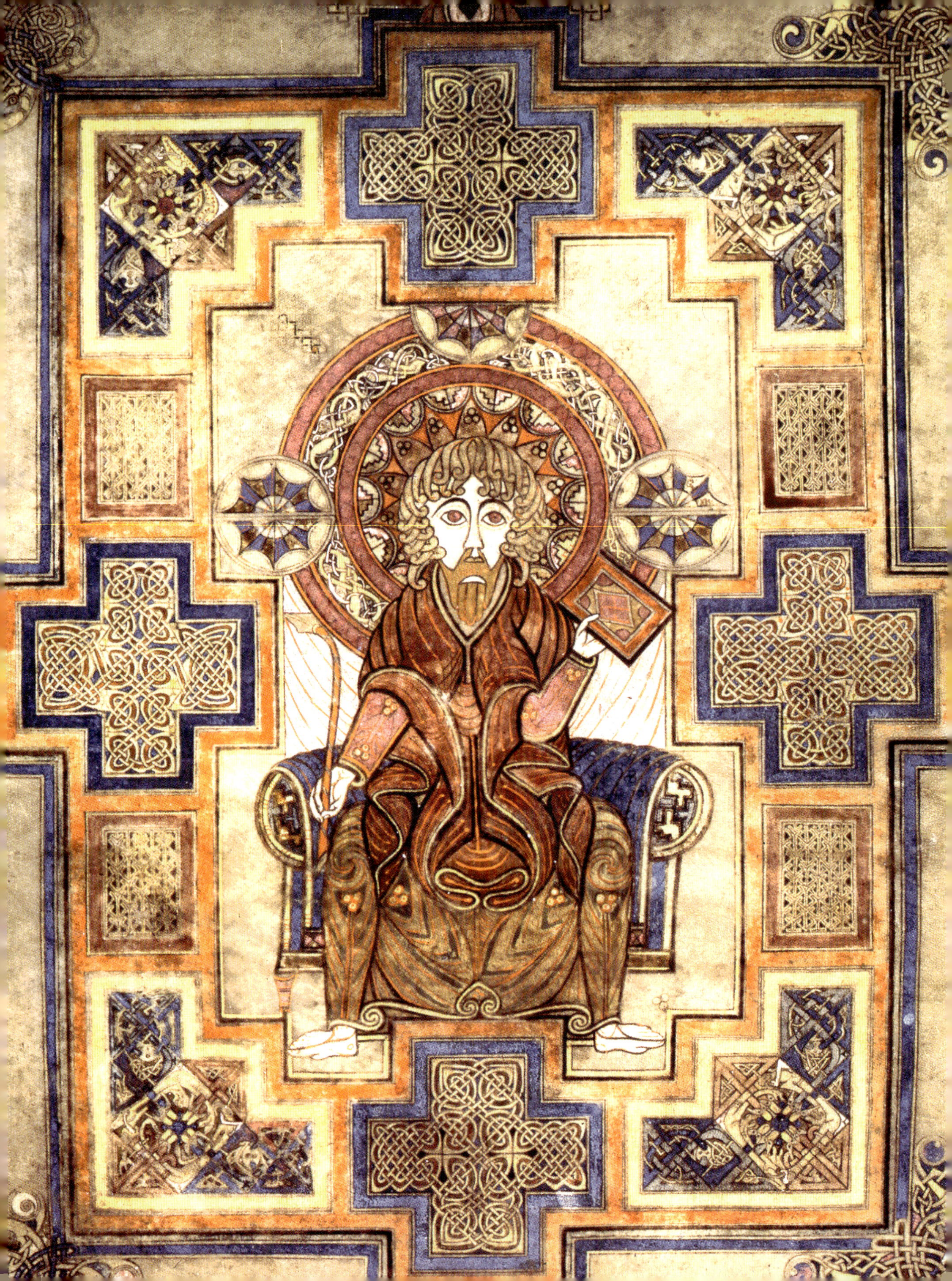

4
Rules and geometry

A SIMPLE CROSS: ULBSTER STONE

In the previous chapter it was shown that one of the key features of the geometric art of the early medieval period was the ornamentation of panels. In this chapter the emphasis is on the rules developed by early artists which were applied in stone, metal and manuscript art. The starting point is a simple and remarkable cross that is carved in light relief on a sandstone slab now known as the Ulbster stone. One face of the stone is illustrated in Fig. 4.1. The two-metre high monument, originally from an ancient burial-ground at Ulbster, a village 11 km south of Wick on the Caithness coast in northern Scotland, is now in the entrance of Thurso Museum on the north coast of Scotland.

The face illustrated in Fig. 4.1 has a cross and eight Pictish symbols. Our primary interest is in the equal-armed cross but the presence of the symbols must not be overlooked. The stone has rough-hewn edges and two flat faces, each inscribed with a cross and Pictish symbols. The face shown in Fig. 4.1 is referred to as the 'back face' by Allen and Anderson (1903) and has the simpler design of the two faces. According to Allen and Anderson's classification, the Ulbster stone stands close to the transition between Class I and Class II, having both incised Pictish symbols and a cross, but is best included in Class II. The most common symbol, the crescent with V-shaped rod, appears at the top of the back face of the Ulbster stone

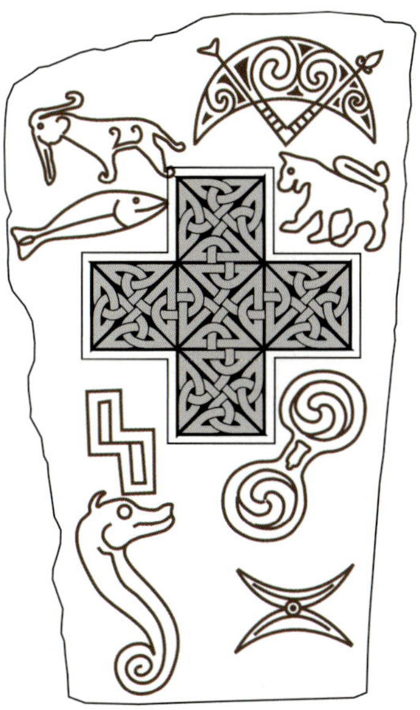

Figure 4.1
Back face of Ulbster stone with a cross, decorated with interlacing, surrounded by Pictish symbols.

The Ulbster stone gives a clear indication that the spiritual and religious emotions associated with these Pictish symbols were held alongside those engendered by the new message of Christianity, symbolised by the cross. There can be little doubt that the crosses on both faces of the stone were carved before the Pictish symbols because of the way that the symbols are distributed randomly around the cross.

The symbols illustrated in Fig. 4.1 were drawn using a photograph taken of the stone in 1999. The stone is severely worn and the fine detail cannot be relied on. The symbols had been incised on the flat faces of the stone with little evidence of three-dimensional sculptural work, although some of the detail on the cross shows that the under-and-over features of the interlacing have been highlighted. The illustrations in Allen and Anderson show more detail. They date from the late nineteenth century when the stone was probably less worn. Some of the detail on the front face of the stone has been destroyed by a crudely carved inscription 'The Ulbster Stone' in Gothic lettering.

The equal-armed cross on the back face is not as geometrically precise as in the illustration in Fig. 4.1. Nevertheless the quality is consistent with other work of this period. The interlacing pattern is readily constructed without the use of tracing. It is represented in colour using the same approach as in the manuscripts and in the manner adopted for the Rosemarkie stone in the previous chapter. In the next section the cross on the Ulbster stone is used to introduce some ideas about the development of patterns.

SYMMETRY AND REPETITION: TRANSLATION, ROTATION AND REFLECTION

Simple concepts of symmetry and repetition provide useful tools for the description of geometric art and, in particular, the external shape and the ornamentation of crosses. These concepts are widely used in the science of crystallography to describe the external form of crystals and the inner organisation of the atoms within crystals. The principles are also applied in other disciplines such as architecture and design. However, whereas crystalline order and architectural detail are described in three-dimensional space, the description of geometric patterns is largely restricted to two dimensions. This section provides a brief introduction to some of the ideas of symmetry and repetition without adopting the rigorous mathematical definitions necessary in crystallography. A more thorough and rigorous treatment can be found in Stevens (1981). The real enthusiast is referred to Shubnikov and Koptsik (1974).

As mentioned before, it is interesting to note that Bain (1951) describes his approach as mathematical, but it isn't clear what he means. Although an understanding of geometry is essential for interpreting and constructing the patterns of Insular art the level required is well within the grasp of anyone who has been to secondary school. Mathematicians looking at these patterns are challenged to describe them in the context of disciplines such as fractal geometry, topology and crystallography, but these matters do not need to concern us in this book. The geometric approach to art reaches a refined and elegant form in Islamic art (see, for example, El-Said and Parman, 1976), but even here the level of mathematics required is only modest. The geometric art of Escher, described in a splendid book by Schattschneider (1990), is of a different kind and involves more complex geometric concepts.

Figure 4.2
Illustration of symmetry elements in a simple equal-armed cross and other geometric figures.

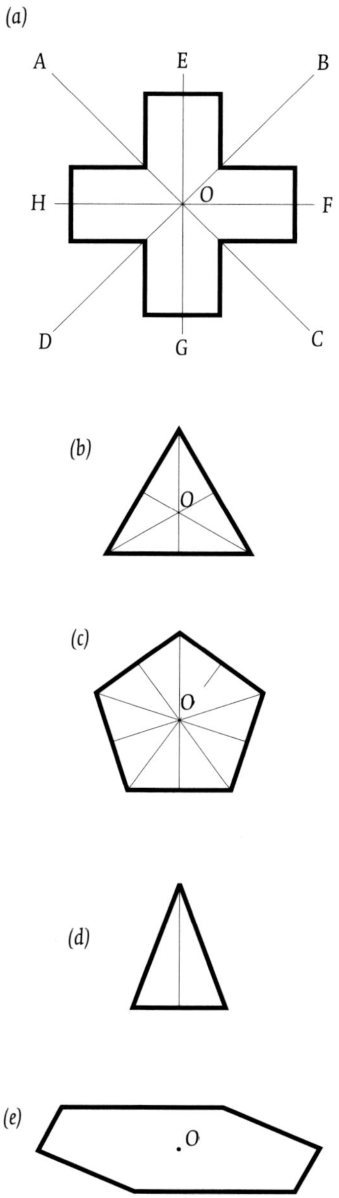

As with Islamic art, there are few records of the way that artists designed and created the masterpieces of geometric Insular art. Clearly they used straight-edges and compasses to set out the primary and secondary grid lines but there are few records of the way they developed the principles of geometry required to produce them. One can only guess at the way the geometric rules were used and transmitted from one generation of artists to the next.

Proceeding by way of example, some simple ideas associated with symmetry and repetition are introduced. The outline of the equal-armed cross in Fig. 4.1 has a high degree of symmetry, as is shown in Fig. 4.2a. An imaginary line drawn through the centre of the cross at O, at right angles to the plane of the paper (sometimes expressed as *normal* to the plane of the paper) is an axis of fourfold symmetry. Because the cross is a two-dimensional image the axis can be replaced by a point so that O, in Fig. 4.2a, becomes a fourfold rotation point. By rotating the cross about this point it is possible to find four positions where the cross appears the same in relation to its position on the page. These positions are 90° apart. Similarly, the equilateral triangle in Fig. 4.2b has a threefold rotation point at O with three equivalent positions 120° apart and the regular pentagon in Fig. 4.2c has a fivefold rotation point at O with five equivalent positions 72° apart. The irregular hexagon in Fig. 4.2e has a twofold rotation axis at O.

Another important feature of symmetry is the occurrence of mirror reflections. When a flat mirror is placed along a line, such as AC in Fig. 4.2a, at right angles to the plane of the paper, a cross is observed when the half image of the cross, not hidden by the mirror, is viewed from one side of the mirror. AC represents the trace of the mirror plane. It is called a mirror line. All of the fine lines in Fig. 4.2(a-d) are mirror lines; the cross has four such lines and the isosceles triangle in Fig. 4.2d has only one. Although the irregular hexagon in Fig. 4.2e has a twofold rotation point there are no mirror lines. The symmetry properties, such as rotation points and mirror lines, of any given shape are referred to collectively as symmetry elements or a symmetry group. Only three symmetry operations are used in this work – translation, rotation and reflection. Reflection can be divided into two distinct operations: first, a simple mirror reflection as described above, and, secondly, a translation reflection in which the motifs in a pattern are related to each other by a mirror reflection combined with a displacement.

The cross on the Ulbster stone, ornamented with interlacing, has a lower level of symmetry than the cross in Fig. 4.2a without the ornamentation. There is only one axis of symmetry for the ornamented cross, which corresponds to a fourfold rotation point in the centre of the cross at a position equivalent to O in Fig. 4.2a. The other symmetry elements in

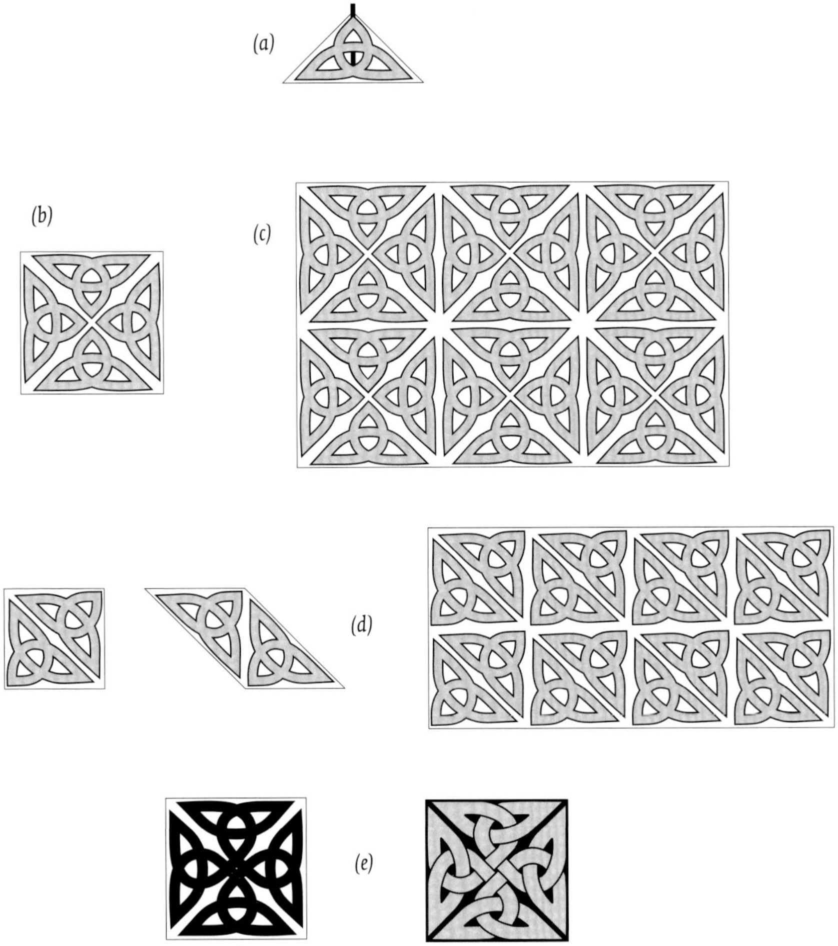

Figure 4.3
Development of patterns. (a) Triquetra knot in a right-angled isosceles triangle. (b) Unit cell or repeat unit formed from four triquetra knots. (c) Pattern formed by repetition and translation of repeat unit in (b). (d) Repeat units based on two triquetra knots forming an alternative pattern of knots. (e) Formation of an interlaced repeat unit from four triquetra knots.

Fig. 4.2a are broken by the interlacing sequence. To understand this, and to introduce the concept of repeat units, the formation of the interlacing pattern is considered.

The basic unit of the interlaced pattern in Fig. 4.1 is a triquetra knot set in a right-angled isosceles triangle (Fig. 4.3a). At this stage the knot is shown without any interlacing of the cord so that this simple motif has a single mirror line of symmetry. When the cords are interlaced the symmetry of the outline remains but the symmetry of the pattern as a whole is lost. Four of these basic units can be arranged to form a square (Fig. 4.3b) that has the same symmetry elements as the simple equal-armed cross. Placing these squares side-by-side to form a two-dimensional array produces a continuous pattern (Fig. 4.3c). Arranging two basic units to form a smaller square (Fig. 4.3d) forms an alternate pattern, using the same primary motif. Following the language of crystallography, the repeat unit is called a unit cell. To form the pattern in Fig. 4.3b the repeat unit consists of four basic motif units and

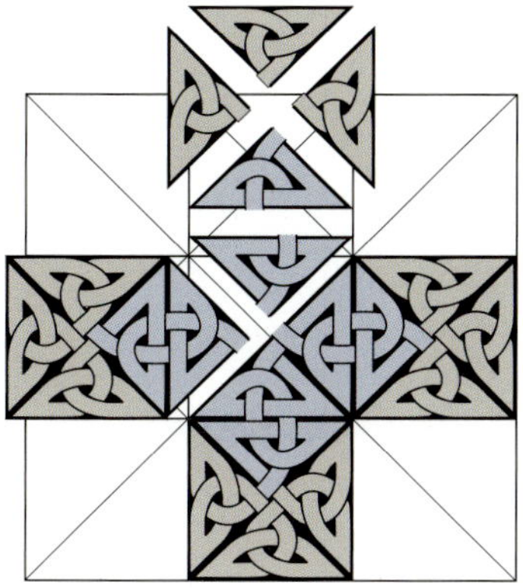

Figure 4.4
Development of interlacing pattern on the cross on back face of the Ulbster stone.

for the pattern in Fig. 4.3d the repeat unit consists of two basic motifs. The repeat unit for producing the continuous pattern in Fig 4.3d can be either a square or a parallelogram. The successive reproduction and displacement of repeat units is the basis of translation.

The interlacing design in Fig. 4.1 consists of a single, continuous and unbroken cord. The first stage in producing this design is to combine the four triquetra knots in the repeat unit shown in Fig. 4.3b by breaking and rejoining the knots (Fig. 4.3e). Five of these groupings are then combined to form the cross and further breaking and rejoining of the individual cords produces the final construction of the interlacing ornamentation, as illustrated in Fig. 4.4.

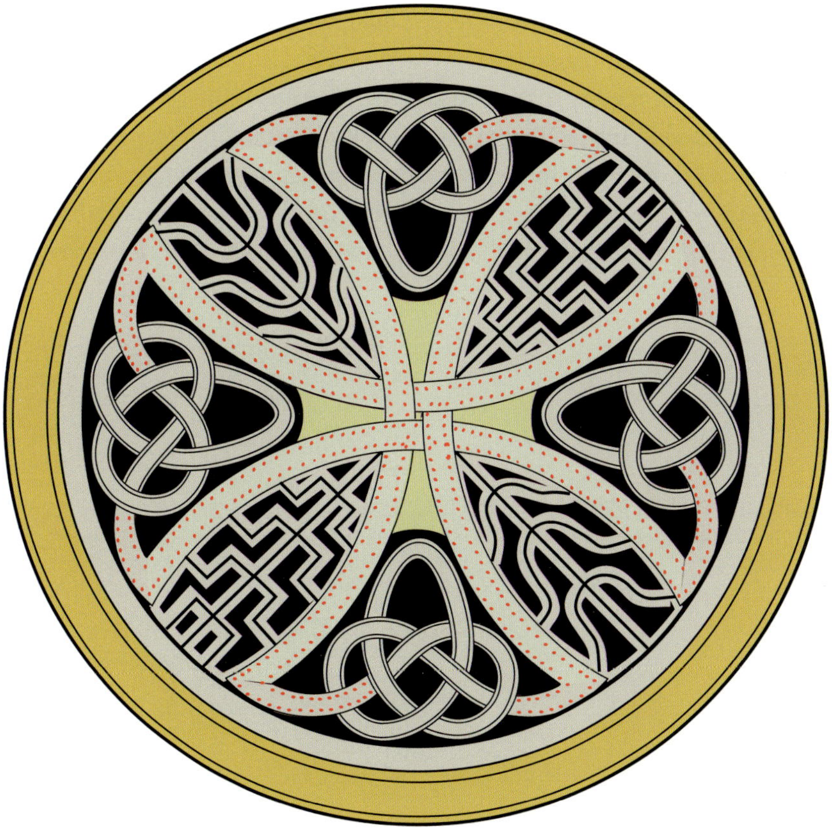

Figure 4.5
Splayed-armed cross in central medallion of f. 85v of Book of Durrow. Diameter of outer ring is 37 mm.

A completely different equal-armed cross with similar though not identical symmetry properties is shown in Fig. 4.5. It provides a good example of the way that the level of symmetry decreases as the complexity of the detail and the scale of observation increase. The cross, sometimes referred to as a cross of arcs, is in the central medallion of a cross-carpet page in the Book of Durrow. This early Gospel book (c. AD 650–75) is in

Trinity College Old Library in Dublin and is displayed as part of the splendid Book of Kells exhibition *'Turning Darkness into Light'*. A fine facsimile edition of the book is available (see Luce, 1960). Cross-carpet page f. 85v of the Book of Durrow is ornamented with 15 linked medallions (Fig. 4.6). The cross is in the central medallion and is illustrated in Fig. 4.5 without the linking cords. Some of the marking-out lines, used in drawing the pattern, are shown in Fig. 4.7. The cross has splayed ends that form an interlacing pattern integral with the arms. Considering only the cross there is a single fourfold rotation point as in the cross on the Ulbster stone. Each of the straight and curved step patterns between the arms of the cross has single mirror-line symmetry. Taken as a whole the design has no mirror lines and only one twofold rotation point at the centre of the cross. Note that the arms of the cross are decorated with a single row of fine red dots, which is a common feature of decoration in Insular manuscripts.

The use of symmetry to understand the structure of interlacing and other patterns is readily applied to the examples described in Chapters 2 and 3. For example, there are many interesting aspects of symmetry and repeat units in the design of the interlacing on the cross on f. 210v of the Lindisfarne Gospels (Fig. 2.4). Many of the symmetry properties of patterns are not

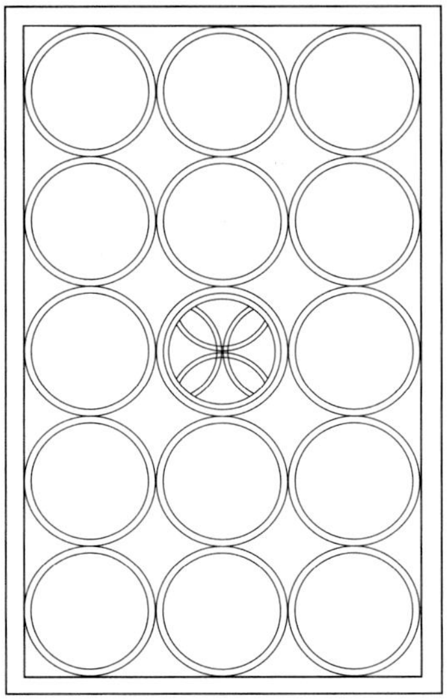

Figure 4.6
Layout of medallions and central splayed cross on f. 85v of Book of Durrow.

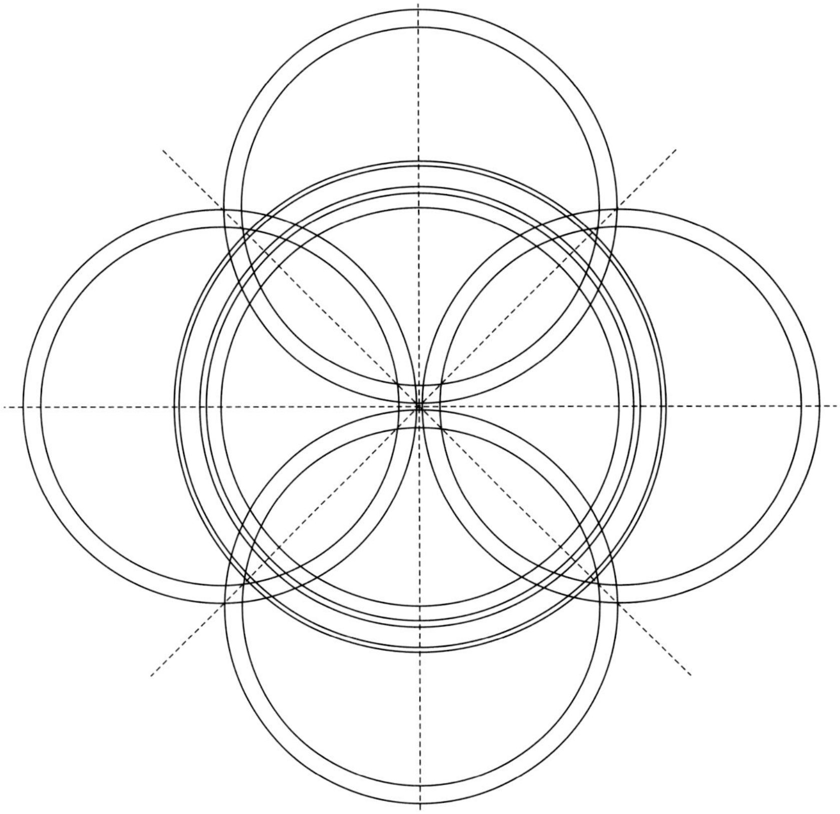

Figure 4.7
Lines used in construction of splayed-armed cross illustrated in Fig. 4.5.

always obvious and not everyone is able to recognise them. Nevertheless, the approach to pattern construction based on an understanding of symmetry is very important and provides a powerful tool in design.

This section concludes with an example of a handsome cross that has been ornamented by reproducing a repeat unit throughout the cross by translations without rotation or reflection. The shape of the repeat unit determines the shape and dimensions of the cross. The repeat unit is identical to the key pattern used in the corner finials of Lindisfarne f. 210v (Figs. 3.7 and 3.8b). It is also closely similar to the repeat unit used in the bottom panel of the Rosemarkie stone (Figs. 3.20 and 3.8c). The cross, illustrated in Fig. 4.8, is the main feature of the cross-carpet page f. 126v in the Schloss-Harburg Gospel book. The manuscript, Cod. I.2.4.2, is now in

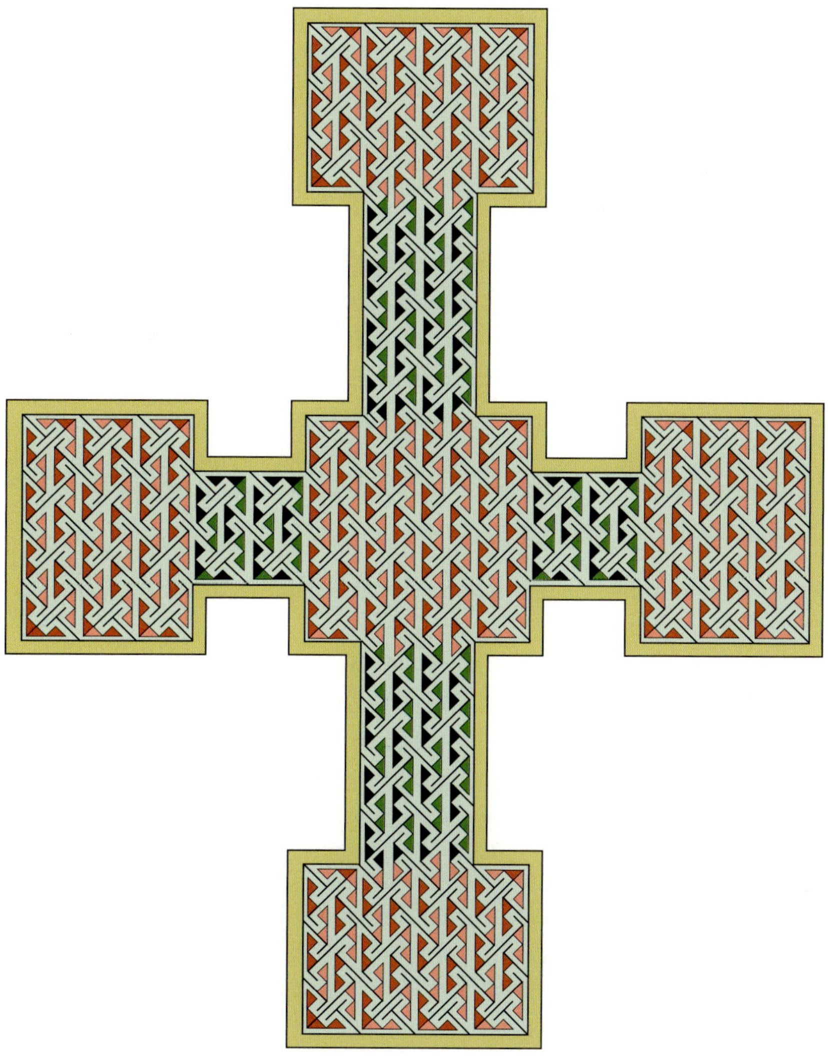

Figure 4.8
Cross decorated with a key pattern in f. 126v of Schloss-Harburg Gospel book.

the Universitätsbibliothek in Augsburg. According to Alexander (1978), it was produced in Echternach early in the eighth century.

The design of the page, including the border, is based on a 16-by-20 square grid (Fig. 4.9). The panels, between the arms of the cross, are ornamented with a different key pattern and there is a border of interlacing, one square wide, on the outside. Further ornamentation is achieved by the use of different colours in the arms and ends of the cross. As with the cross in the *Diatessaron* (Fig. 2.2), the cross is formed by following the primary grid lines. The arms of the cross, without the border, are two squares wide and the rectangular ends are formed by a three-by-four array of grid squares. Each square of the grid, inside the boundaries of the cross, is filled with the same repeat unit except for the corners where modifications are made for aesthetic reasons.

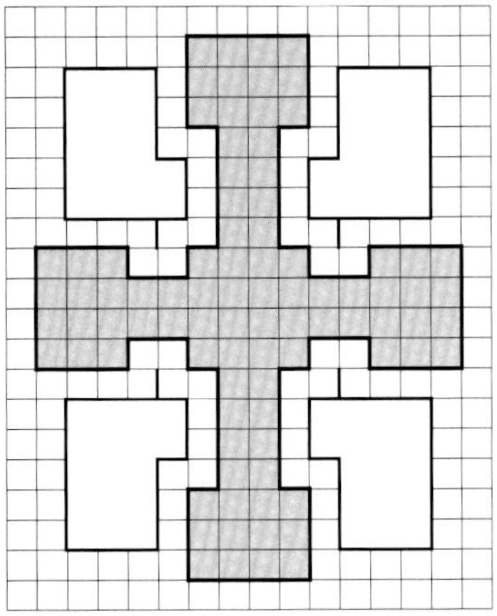

Figure 4.9
Grid used to construct the layout of the cross-carpet page f. 126v of Schloss-Harburg Gospel Book.

KEY PATTERNS

In his book, Nordenfalk likens the interplay of motifs in the ornamentation of Insular art to an orchestra:

> *Just as in an orchestra, there are three main classes of instruments – string, wind and percussion – so here we can distinguish three main classes of ornament. These are the interlacing, curvilinear and rectilinear patterns. And just as in an orchestra there are different types of string, wind and percussion instruments, so each of the three main classes of ornament is divisible into various fixed types of pattern. Within rectilinear ornament there are the check, step and key patterns and the diagonal fret. Curvilinear decoration comprises circles, spirals, whirls and trumpet patterns. As to the various types of interlacing, they are defined either by the dimensions of their 'strings', or by the fact that they are either single, double or triple.* (1977)

He sees zoomorphic designs, and presumably patterns involving plants, as a special form of interlacing.

In the next three sections this simple classification is followed, although there is some confusion in the literature about the names given to the motifs in each of the groups. This is particularly true in relation to the words 'fret' and 'key', which are often used interchangeably. According to Allen and Anderson (1903) the expression 'key pattern'

> *is a convenient way to describe certain geometric designs composed of straight lines, or, more strictly speaking, narrow straight bars making successive angular bends and interlocked with other similar bars, but leaving a space or background between the bars thus resembling the L- or T-shaped slots in an ordinary key to allow it to pass the wards of the lock.*

Later they observe that another name for a key pattern is a Greek fret. For convenience 'key pattern' is used here, in a similar way to Allen and Anderson, as a generic description of motifs and patterns made up of straight lines. Many of these patterns have been illustrated earlier in describing the ornamentation of panels. Thus, there are step patterns in Figs. 2.6 and 3.27, diagonal patterns, resembling conventional Greek fret patterns, in Figs. 3.2, 3.17, 3.23 and 3.27, and zigzag patterns in Figs. 3.7, 3.9 and 4.8. Many other examples are included in later chapters.

There is no limit to the number of possible key patterns and little prospect of recording all the ones that have been used in ornamentation. Numerous examples are illustrated in Bain (1951) and in Allen and Anderson (1903). These works also include various approaches to constructing key patterns. All rely on the use of a grid or lattice that forms the basis for arranging the motifs in a two-dimensional array. These approaches are essentially the same as those used in creating the key patterns in the illustrations listed above, but this may not be immediately obvious. As an example consider the method used by Allen and Anderson to produce the zigzag key pattern (No. 974) which is used in the cross in Fig. 4.8. The starting point is a simple grid (Fig. 4.10a) that is changed to a diagonal grid (Fig. 4.10b) by rotation. The positions of the motifs are mapped on this grid (Fig. 4.10c). Every line in Fig.

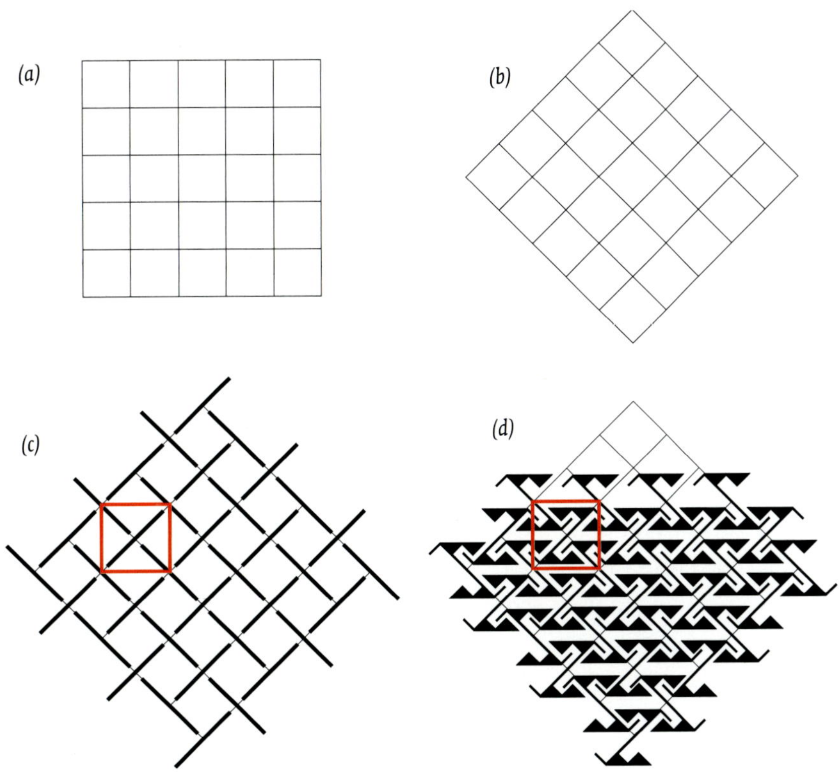

Figure 4.10
Approach used by Allen and Anderson to produce a zigzag key pattern. (a) Simple square grid. (b) Square grid rotated 45° to produce a diagonal grid. (c) Layout of lines on grid that define the positions of zigzag motifs. (d) Completed key pattern with a square unit cell or repeat unit outlined.

4.10c is then elaborated to produce an interlocking key pattern. This pattern can be extended indefinitely in two-dimensional space (Fig. 4.10d) and only needs modification at the boundaries of a panel. The square cell in Fig. 4.10d marks the repeat unit for this pattern. The duplication and translation of this repeat unit produces the final pattern. The importance of emphasising the repeat unit is that in constructing the design one needs to have a smaller grid to create the repeat unit accurately. Two different square repeat units for zigzag key patterns, formed on smaller grids, have been illustrated already in Fig. 3.8. This precisely defined repeat unit can then be used to construct the pattern using the diagonal grid of Fig. 4.10b.

A whole series of key patterns are formed using different repeat units and arranging them, by rotation, reflection and translation using the diagonal grid of Fig. 4.10b. In this section emphasis is given to three aspects of key patterns: first, the development of a multitude of patterns derived from the classical Greek fret pattern; secondly, using an example of a type of key pattern not previously illustrated, the need for flexibility in applying the principles of reflection, translation and rotation; and thirdly, the application of ideas about key patterns even when the lines are not all straight.

Greek frets

Border patterns, such as those shown in Fig. 4.11, are a common feature of the decoration of Greek earthenware artefacts of the fifth century BC and are still widely used today in ornamentation in buildings and for house decoration to give a sense of the classical. Most borders are formed by the repetition and translation of a simple pattern or repeat unit, in a linear one-dimensional array (linear translation). The formation of a repeat unit in a square grid is illustrated in Fig. 4.11a and b. The repeat unit in Fig. 4.11c consists of two-coil straight-sided square spirals each with a 1:2:3:4:5:6 sequence of right-angled bends. The width or thickness of the bands is a matter of taste but often, as in this diagram, the space between the bands is the same as the width of the bands themselves. Combining repeat units in a linear array produces the border in Fig. 4.11e. The repeat unit in Fig. 4.11d and the border in Fig. 4.11f are exactly the same design as in Fig. 4.11c and e respectively with a reversal of colours. They are said to be complementary. The spirals in Fig. 4.11c expand in an anti-clockwise direction from the inside. The border in Fig. 4.11g consists of clockwise and anti-clockwise spirals alternating in pairs separated by a diagonal cross motif.

Any number of sequences may be used in forming the spirals. The repeat unit in the border of Fig. 4.11h consists of two anti-clockwise spirals with a 1:2:3:4:5:6:7 sequence and the border in Fig. 4.11i is exactly the same, but the sequence is 1:2:3. The complement of Fig. 4.11i, with the colours reversed, is

Figure 4.11
Simple border patterns based on a Greek fret.

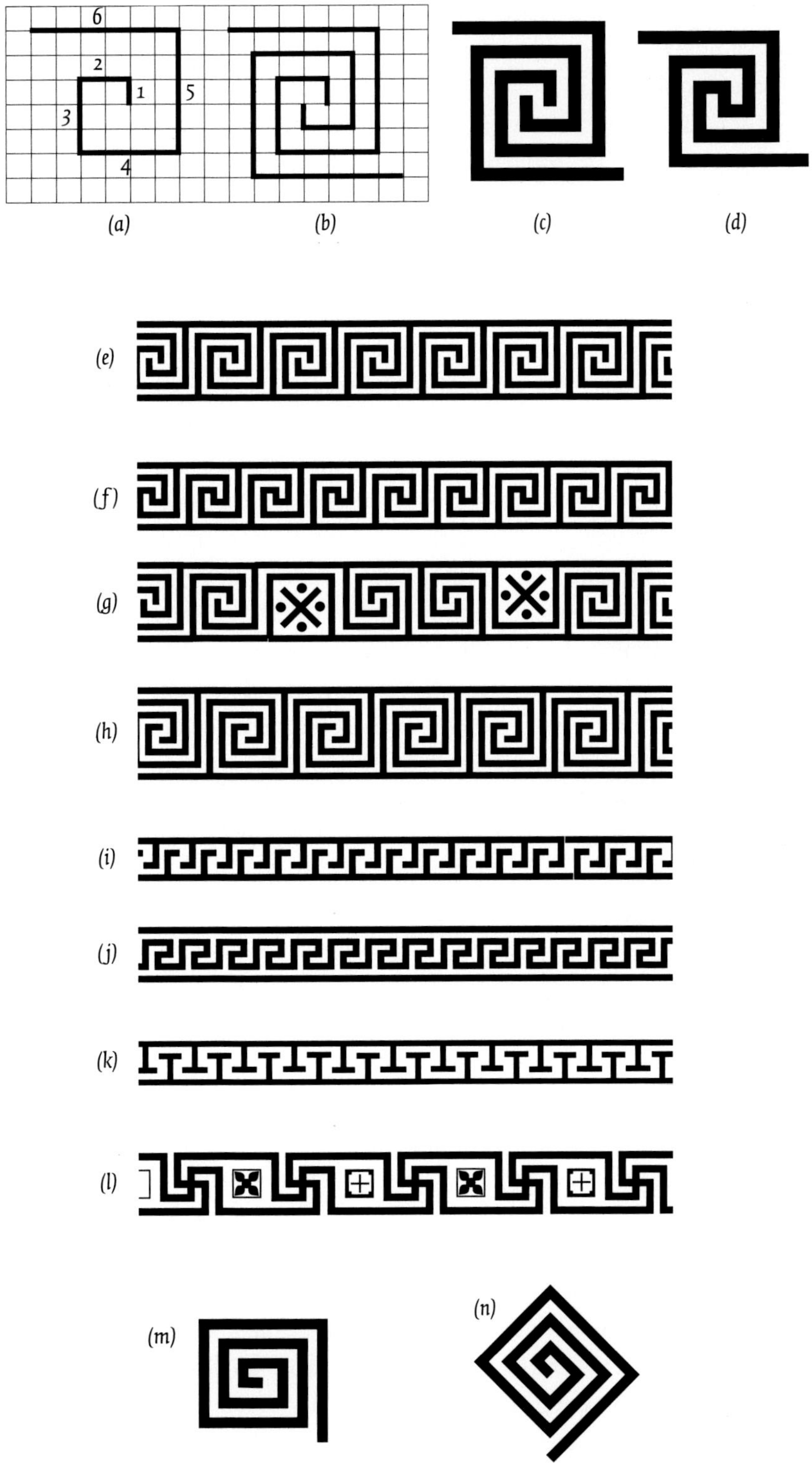

Fig. 4.11j. The example in Fig. 4.11k is based on two alternating T-motifs and the example in Fig. 4.11l has a series of four square-sided spirals, separated by other motifs.

There are many examples in Insular art of the use of Greek fret patterns without rotation of the principal directions. A simple example is the swastika figure in the centre of the zoomorphic pattern from f. 210v of the Lindisfarne Gospels, shown in Fig. 3.5. Other examples are illustrated in later chapters. An important development in the use of the Greek fret is the rotation of the primary motifs so that the sides of the straight-sided spirals are at an angle, usually about 45°, to the principal directions of the main design, such as the sides of the panels. The method of construction of patterns using this approach was described in Chapter 3 in relation to the labyrinth panel in Lindisfarne f. 210v (Figs. 3.2 and 3.3). Here the primary motif is a single-coil spiral formed in a conventional square grid with a sequence of bends 1:1:2:2:3:3:4:4:5:5:6 ... (Fig. 4.11m and n). The pattern is formed by repetition and translation of the primary motif in two directions, with rotation and mirror reflection, rather than by linear translation, as in border patterns. Additional changes are achieved by transforming the square grid into an array of parallelograms. Single-coil spirals are also used in the ornamentation of the upper crescent of the Rosemarkie stone (Figs. 3.17 and 3.18). A double-coil spiral (Fig. 4.11d) is used in the panel of the St Petersburg Gospel book shown in Fig. 3.23.

Flexible use of repeat units

The elegant cross in Fig. 4.12a is from the Macdurnan Gospel book, which is now in the library of Lambeth Palace, the official home of the Archbishop of Canterbury in London. Maelbrigt Macdurnan was Abbot of Armagh towards the end of the ninth century. According to Alexander (1978), the Gospel book was produced in the second half of the ninth century in Ireland. This is about 50 years after the Book of Kells and 150 years after the Lindisfarne Gospels. The illumination of the Macdurnan Gospels is restricted to four Evangelist portraits, the introductory cross page (f. 1v) and initial letters for the Gospels. The cross on f. 1v (Fig. 4.12b) divides the page into quadrants that contain the Evangelist symbols: man (Matthew, Homo), eagle (John, Aquila), calf (Luke, Vitulus) and lion (Mark, Leo).

Although Alexander finds the illumination of the Macdurnan Gospels of fine quality, the artwork associated with the cross falls short of the quality of Kells and Lindisfarne. However, it does have some interesting features suggesting that the style has evolved from an earlier, more rigorously geometric style, particularly that associated with Lindisfarne. It is not clear whether or not this arises from poor setting-out work or a deliberate

Figure 4.12
Macdurnan Gospel book, f. 1v.
(a) Photograph (by permission of Lambeth Palace Library, MS.1370).
(b) Ornamentation of the cross (overleaf).

(a)

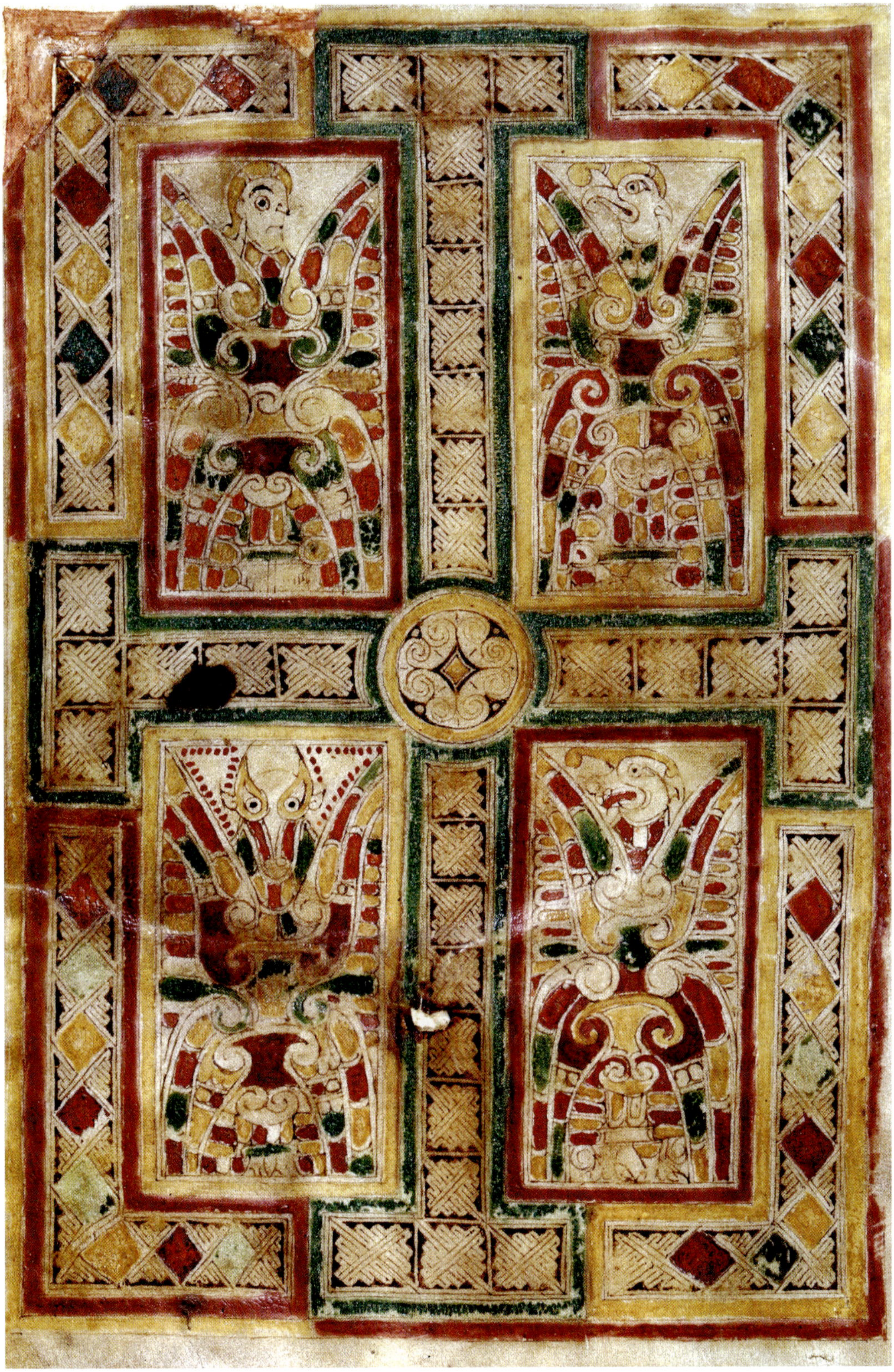

(b)

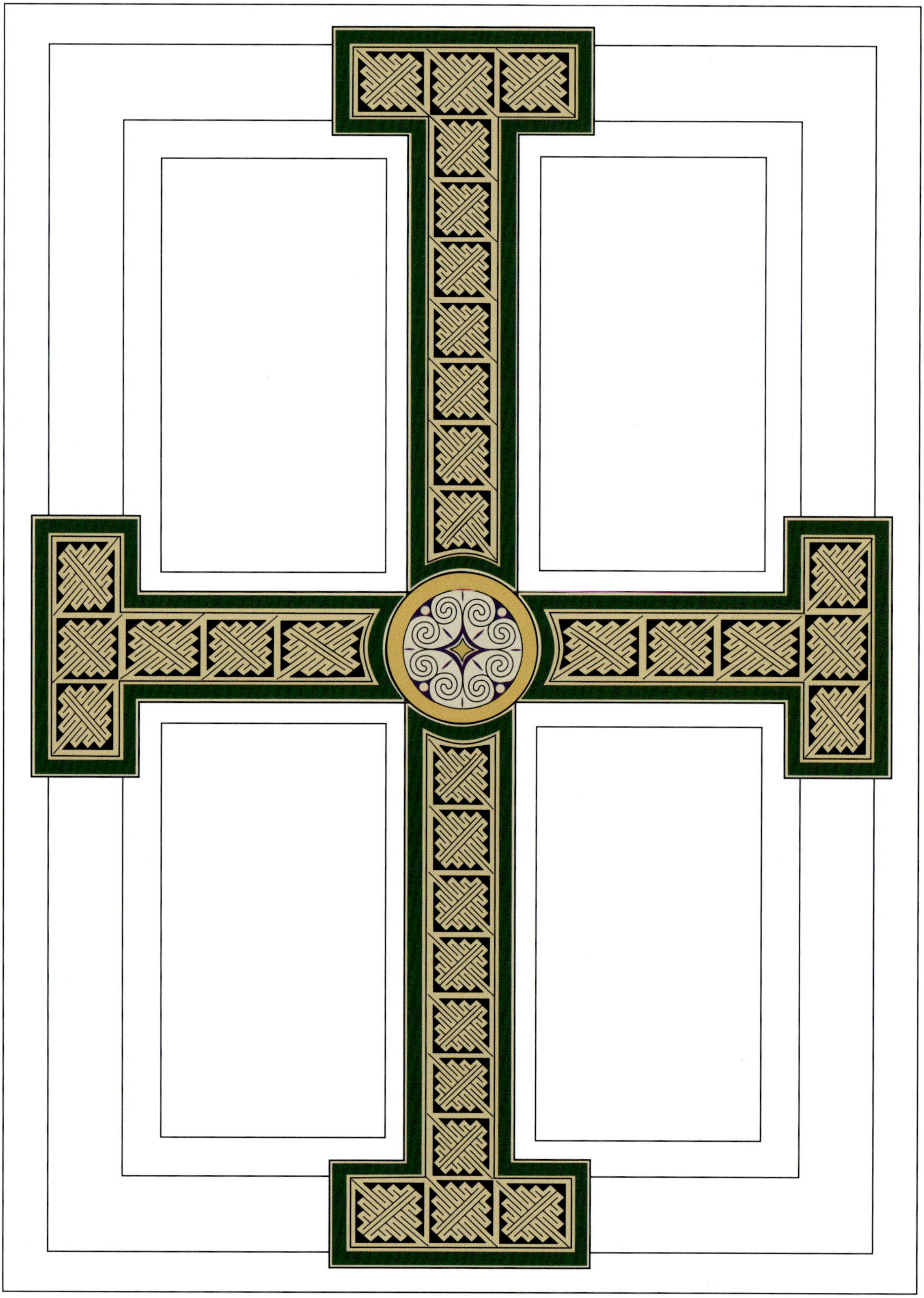

evolution of style. In any event the artist has had to use some ingenuity to produce this design.

The design of the page is based on a 24-by-34 square grid (Fig. 4.13a). The Evangelist symbols fit comfortably in panels in the space around the cross. The arms and ends of the cross, without the green border, are two squares wide. They are decorated with a diagonal key pattern (Fig. 4.13b) that Allen and Anderson refer to as a stem line with branches. In its simple form it is based on a square grid with all the lines in the pattern at 45° to the grid lines so that the diagonal lines are at 90° to each other. This pattern forms the basic repeat unit for the ornamentation of the cross. The intriguing aspect of the design is that the repeat unit is smaller than the two-by-two square units of the primary grid because a secondary border (Fig. 4.13c) surrounds it. To fit the repeat unit to the arms of the cross, and accommodate the necessary changes in border, the shape of the repeat unit has been changed.

The changes are achieved by either 'stretching' or 'shrinking' the repeat unit. A repeat unit, stretched in the horizontal direction, is shown in Fig. 4.13d. The internal arrangement of the key pattern is unchanged but it is drawn on a grid of rectangles rather than squares. The diagonals are no longer at 90°. In Fig. 4.13d the angle between the diagonals is 74°. In the ornamentation of the cross in Fig. 4.12 the angle ranges from 72° to 94°. It is

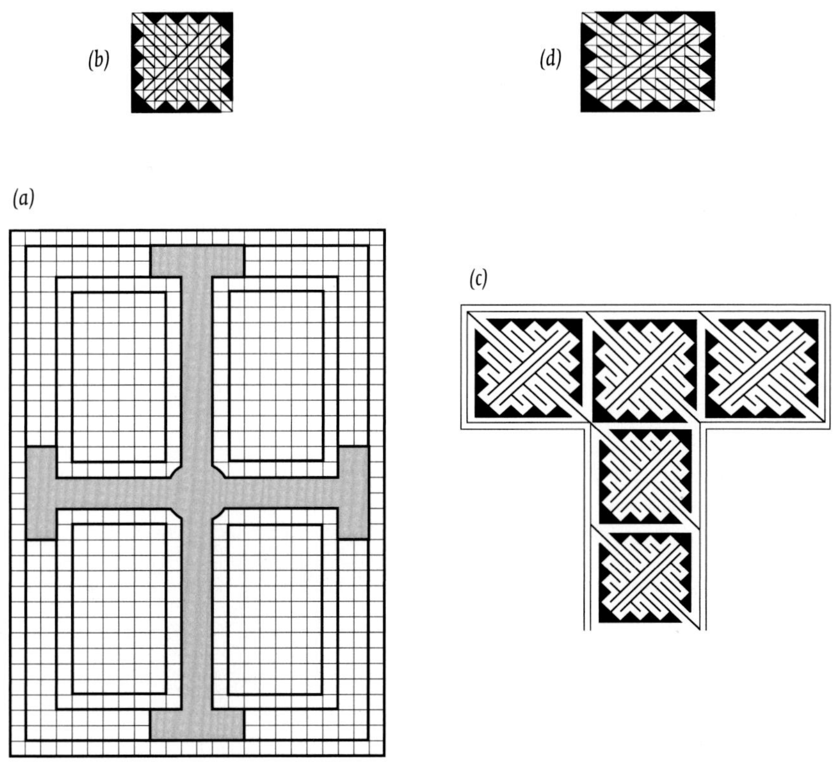

Figure 4.13
Method of construction of the stem line with branches key pattern on the cross in Fig. 4.12. (a) Primary grid. (b) Repeat unit of key pattern formed in a square secondary grid. (c) Layout of repeat units in the primary grid. (d) Repeat unit of key pattern on a rectangular secondary grid.

impossible to know how conscious the original artist was of the subtle details of the design. It seems unlikely that the rather rigorous approach described here was used. Nevertheless, it is clear that by allowing a degree of flexibility in the application of a repeat unit or motif the artist has achieved an aesthetically pleasing result. Note that the orientations of the diagonals of the repeat units in the horizontal arms of the cross are mirror images of those in the vertical arms about a mirror line parallel to the long axis.

Key patterns using curvilinear designs

The concept of forming motifs and repeat units by drawing the lines on a grid can be applied to grids that are not based on a simple square grid. Suppose that the square grid of Fig. 4.14a is replaced by a grid of concentric circles and radial lines as in Fig. 4.14b (a polar grid). The same sequence of displacements can be used to form the pattern on the polar grid as on the square grid. The single-coil square spiral of the Greek fret (Fig. 4.11m), produced by a sequence 1:1:2:2:3:3:4:4:5:6:6, has been drawn on the polar grid in Fig. 4.14c along with two other key patterns. Similarly, the alternating

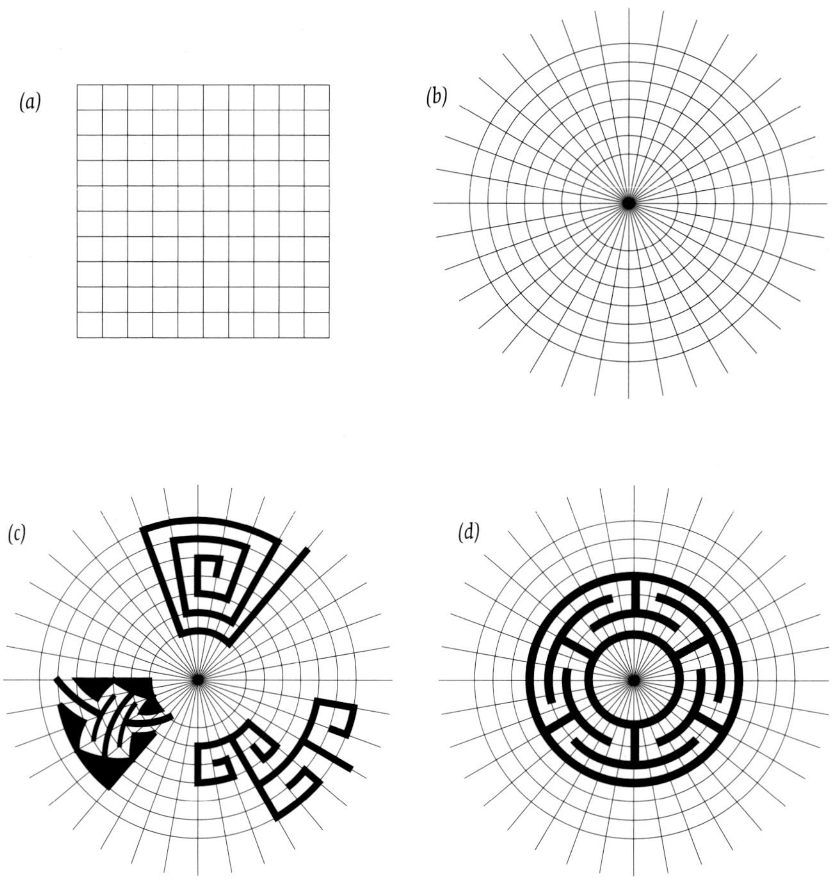

Figure 4.14
Construction of key patterns on polar grids. (a) Square grid. (b) Polar grid. (c and d) Key patterns.

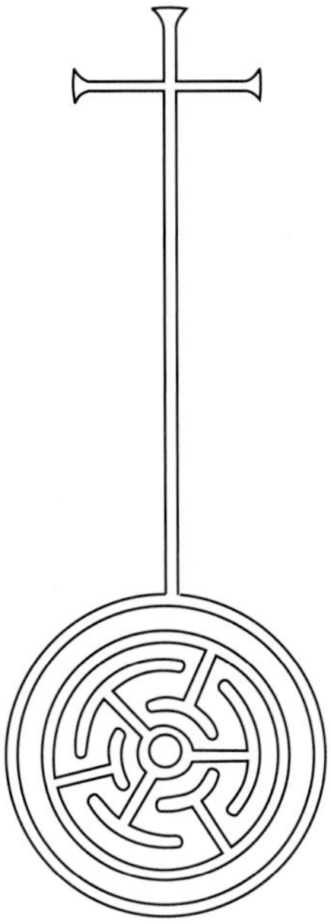

Figure 4.15
Cross formed from a Greek fret on a polar grid incised on a stone slab in Cloon Lough, Kerry, Ireland.

T-motif pattern of Fig. 4.11k is shown on a polar grid in Fig. 4.14d. This design is used for a simple cross that is incised on a stone slab in Cloon Lough in Kerry, Ireland (Fig. 4.15). The circular fret pattern in Fig. 4.14d has an axis of threefold symmetry so that the pattern is repeated every 120° rotation about the centre of the polar grid. The pattern in the Cloon Lough cross is not so perfect, primarily because the radial arms are not exactly 120° apart. A slightly more complicated example, from the Book of Kells (f. 32r), is illustrated in Chapter 5 in the section on embedded crosses.

In principle, any two sets of lines forming a grid can be used in the design of a key pattern. In this way it is possible to fit patterns into irregularly shaped panels, as in the example of the modified Greek fret pattern used in the ornamentation of the initial XPI letter of the St Gall Gospels shown in Fig. 3.27. A reconstruction of this panel design is shown in Fig. 4.16 on a regular square grid and on a distorted diamond-shaped grid. Essentially, the pattern is the same in both illustrations. Note that in the context of the previous discussion, relating to the use of Greek frets, the artist of the St Gall Gospels has used two different motifs, equivalent to the complementary designs in Fig. 4.11c and d.

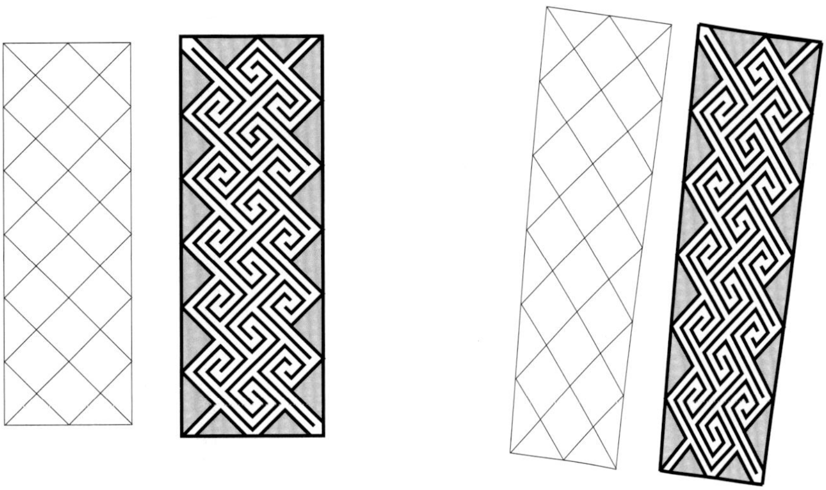

Figure 4.16
Reconstruction of key pattern, based on a Greek fret, by changing the shape of the grid.

SPIRAL PATTERNS

The spiral motif was used in decorative art by early civilisations as far apart as the deserts of Peru and the islands of New Guinea. Examples dating back to the Stone Age are to be found in Ireland, notably in the burial mound at Newgrange and on Westray in the Orkney Islands. However, it seems likely that the development of spirals in Insular art derives from the influence of late Celtic and Iron Age art. In Anglo-Saxon metalwork spiral ornamentation first appears in plant motifs. There are many interpretations of the meaning of the spiral symbol reflecting mystical and religious experiences. Spirals are found in many naturally occurring phenomena such as whirlpools, tornadoes, plant and shell forms, and even in cracking patterns.

There are many different forms of spiral. The spirals on many shells closely resemble logarithmic spirals (Fig. 4.17a) and differ significantly from most of the spirals found in geometric art. The distinction is an important one and has a bearing on the way that spirals are represented or treated in art. The logarithmic spiral is best described by the mathematical equation $r = e^{a\theta}$ which can also be written as $\log r = a\theta$, where r and θ are the polar co-ordinates of any point on the line and a is a constant (see Fig. 4.17b). The most significant feature of this spiral is the progressive expansion of the line as it moves outwards. Conversely, as it moves inwards the spiral becomes a tighter and tighter. The logarithmic spiral has no beginning and no ending. In contrast, the radial separation between successive circuits of the spirals in most Insular art is constant (Fig. 4.18) and the equation of the spiral is $r = a\theta$. This is the spiral of Archimedes. For convenience it is called here an equal-spacing spiral. This is the spiral that is formed when a piece of rope or a metal wire is coiled tightly on a flat surface.

In mathematical terms the line of a spiral has no thickness. For spirals in art the thickness of the line determines the appearance of the design. Consider the four single-coil equal-spacing spirals in Fig. 4.18. Since the spacing between successive circuits is constant the thickened line eventually touches along the full length of the spiral (Fig. 4.18d). This is in contrast to the corresponding sequence in a logarithmic spiral. When the width or thickness of the line or band in an equal-spacing spiral is the same as that of the gap, as in Fig. 4.18b, it is not clear which is the spiral – is it the white band or the black band? In a sense this is a pointless question but the

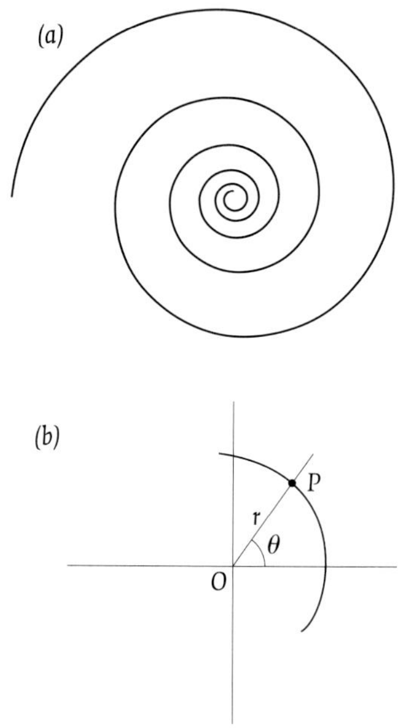

Figure 4.17
(a) Logarithmic spiral. (b) Polar co-ordinates: the position of any point P on the curved line is specified by the angle θ and the distance r (θ and r are the polar co-ordinates of P).

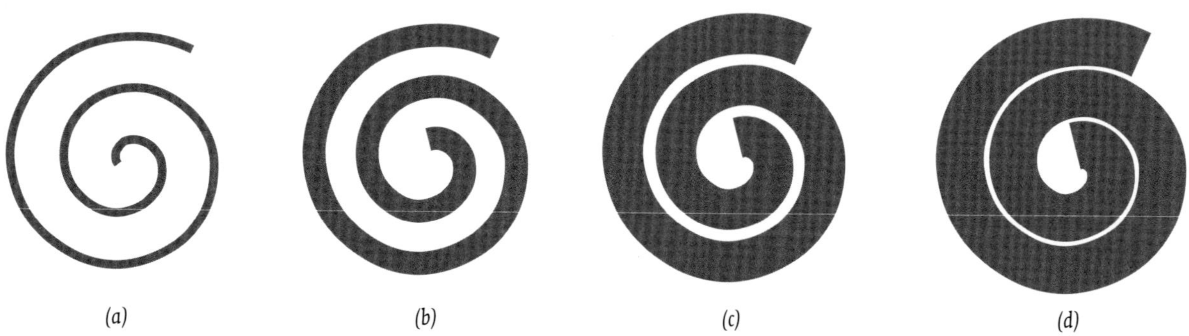

Figure 4.18
Equal-spacing spiral showing the effect of line or cord thickness on appearance.

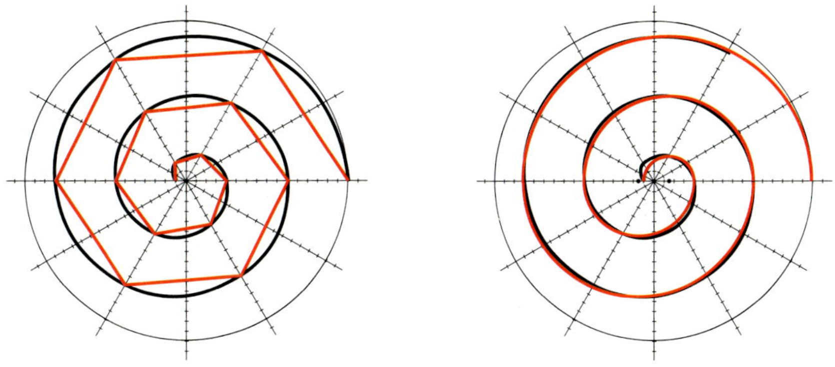

Figure 4.19
Methods of drawing equal-spacing spirals.

distinction is very important when consideration is given to combining spirals to form continuous patterns.

There are many methods of drawing spirals. By far the most accurate is to use the mathematical equations of the spiral but this approach is not accessible to most artists and was certainly not the approach used by early artists. It seems likely that many of the spirals were drawn freehand by artists with a steady hand and a good eye. An equal-spacing spiral can be sketched using the approach illustrated in Fig. 4.19a. The method is closely analogous to that used to produce the square-sided spirals described in the previous section (see Fig. 4.11). The first stage is the production of a polar net with equal-spaced divisions on the radial lines. A spiral with straight sides is produced by joining points on the radial lines so that they move outwards the same amount for each unit of angular rotation. In the diagram the unit of angular rotation is 60°. The lines are then smoothed into a curved spiral that passes through the same points on the radial lines as the straight-sided spiral. A closer representation to the final spiral is produced when the straight-sided spiral is drawn connecting points at 30° rotations. In the limit, as the unit of angular rotation approaches zero, the line becomes a smooth continuous spiral. The smoothed curve is shown in Fig. 4.19a superimposed on the straight-sided curve. Alternatively, a spiral is produced using compasses as shown in Fig. 4.19b. A series of semi-circles, with the point of the compasses placed alternately at the positions marked by the two dots, are drawn with radii determined so that each semi-circle connects with the previous one. The shape of the final spiral produced by this method, shown in red, is close to the smoothed spiral produced by the previous method, shown in black.

Whatever the method used by the Insular artists to produce spirals it is possible to describe how these artists developed patterns from arrays of spirals. Spirals can be drawn as a single coil, as in Fig. 4.20a, and in multiples of coils: two, three, four and so on, as in Fig. 4.20b to d. The double-coil

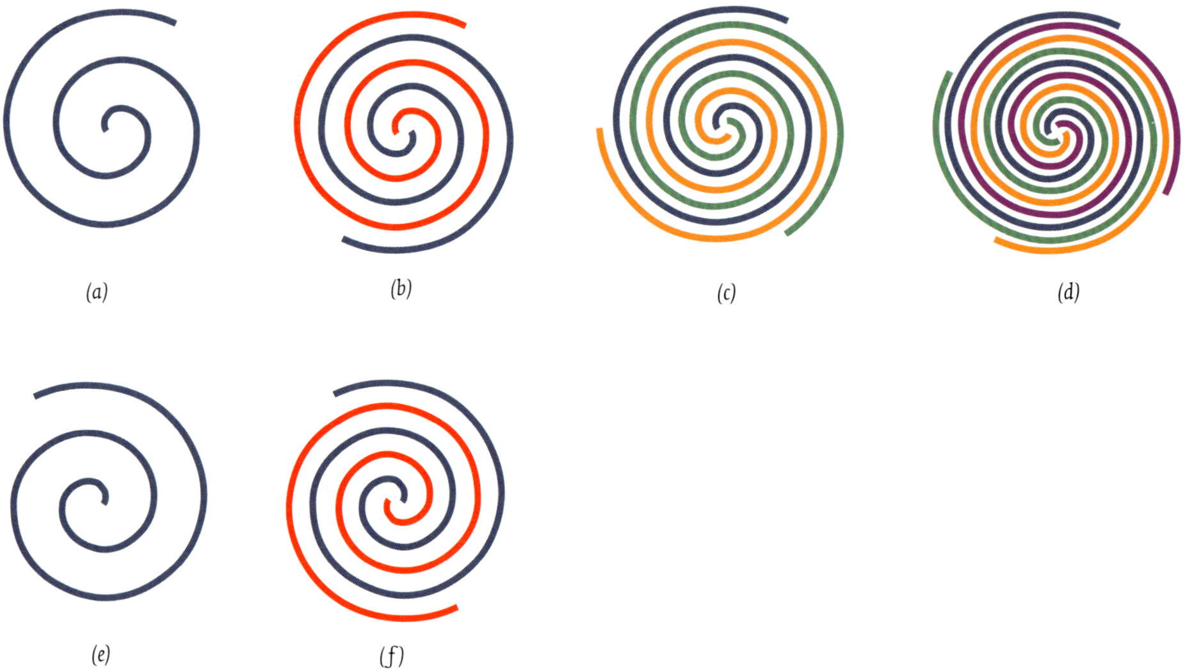

spiral (Fig. 4.20b) is formed by duplicating the single coil and rotating it 180°. Similarly, the triple-coil spiral is formed by duplication and rotations of 120°. The direction of a spiral, starting from the inside and following the path of the spiral outwards, may be clockwise or anti-clockwise. Within a multi-coil spiral the direction of the coils is the same. The centres of spirals are treated in many different ways. An appreciation of the range of possibilities may be obtained from the three examples shown in Fig. 4.21 for triple-coil spirals. In

Figure 4.20
Single- and multi-coil spirals, clockwise (a-d) and anti-clockwise (e-f).

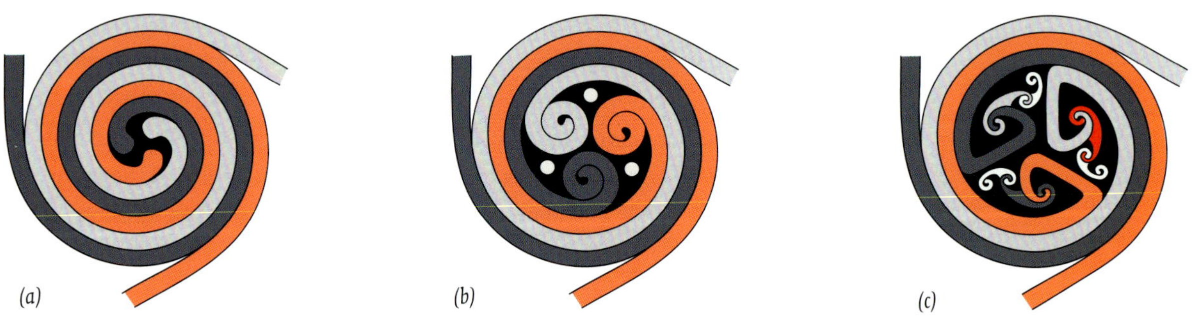

the facsimile edition of the Lindisfarne Gospels (Kendrick 1956–60) there is a whole page of illustrations (p. 208) of the centres of spirals used in the ornamentation of the Gospels.

Figure 4.21
Examples of ornamentation of centres of three-coil spirals.

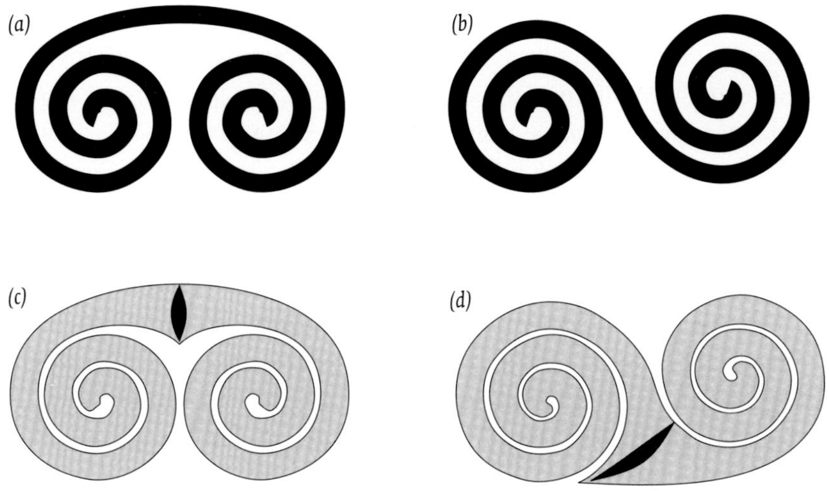

Figure 4.22
C- and S-shaped connections with and without trumpet shapes.

The outsides of individual coils of spirals are joined, almost invariably, to other spirals. A clockwise spiral is joined to an anti-clockwise spiral by a C-shaped connection (Fig. 4.22a) and two spirals of the same rotational direction are joined by S-shaped connections (Fig. 4.22b). The individual coils expand out tangentially from the spiral (Fig. 4.21). A common artistic feature is the expansion of the width of the coil to form a trumpet as in Figs. 4.22c-d. From these simple ideas about joining spirals it follows that a one-coil spiral is linked or joined to only one spiral, a two-coil spiral is linked to two spirals and so on. An example of a three-coil spiral linked to three one-coil spirals by C-shaped connections is shown in Fig. 4.23. The arrangement of two spirals of opposite rotation (Figs. 4.22a and c) is sometimes referred to as a *pelta* because it resembles the shape of a shield used in ancient armour.

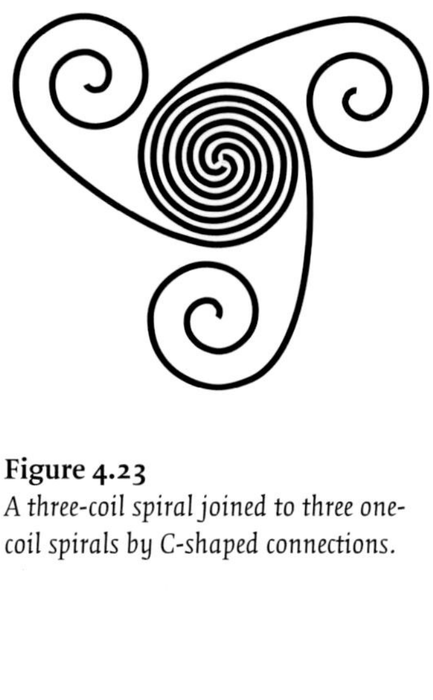

Figure 4.23
A three-coil spiral joined to three one-coil spirals by C-shaped connections.

It is possible to produce exciting patterns by combining spirals in different arrangements. The distribution of the spirals may be random or ordered. The spiral ornamentation of the L-shaped panel in the cross-carpet page of the Lindisfarne Gospels illustrated in Fig. 3.4 is somewhat between these two extremes. The pattern consists of a series of two- and three-coil spirals that are alternately clockwise and anti-clockwise. They are joined by simple and complicated C-shaped trumpet connections. The spirals are aligned in the panel but there is little evidence of any significant symmetry. This example also highlights the issue of the colouring of spirals. In the illustration in Fig. 3.4, each coil of the spiral is bounded by a thin black line and has a single colour. In most cases a connecting spiral has the same colour but in some cases the colour changes from one coil to the next. This simple rule applies in most manuscript art but is of little consequence in stone carvings and metalwork. There are examples in manuscript art where the colour changes within a single coil but it is far from clear whether or not this was intended as an artistic feature or was a consequence of lack of precision in the artwork. There is a simple ordered arrangement of spirals in the centre of the Macdurnan cross, shown in Fig. 4.12. Eight two-coil spirals are arranged in a circle and are joined by C-shaped connections. This array of interlinked peltae has a high level of symmetry with a fourfold rotation point and four mirror lines. An identical arrangement of spirals occurs on an escutcheon on a small hanging bowl found in the Sutton Hoo burial.

Random spiral pattern in St Gall Gospels cross-carpet page

The layout of the cross-carpet page, identified as Cod. 51, p. 6 (cat. 44) in the St Gall Gospels (see Chapter 3), is similar to that of the cross-carpet page of the Lindisfarne Gospels f. 210v illustrated in Fig. 2.2. A square grid 26 by 34 was used. The arms of the central cross are two squares wide, ten squares across and twelve squares long. The cross is ornamented with an array of spirals (Fig. 4.24) and is surrounded by panels ornamented with interlacing, key, zoomorphic and step motifs. The spirals are distributed randomly and the whole pattern appears somewhat chaotic. Many different forms of spirals and connections have been used. The drawing in Fig. 4.24 is based on a full-size black and white photograph in Alexander (1978) with additional evidence from the coloured lithograph by Westwood (1868). The resolution

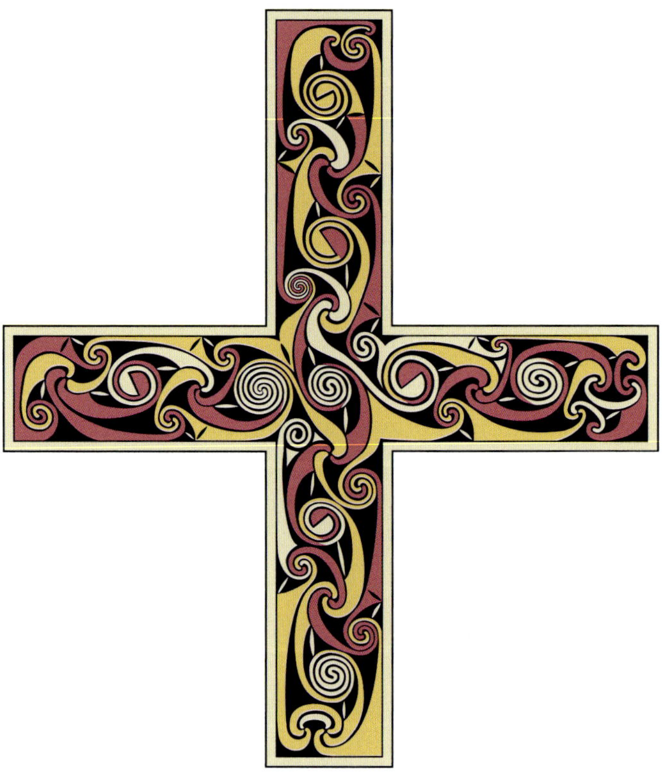

Figure 4.24
Cross in St Gall Gospel book ornamented with a random spiral pattern.

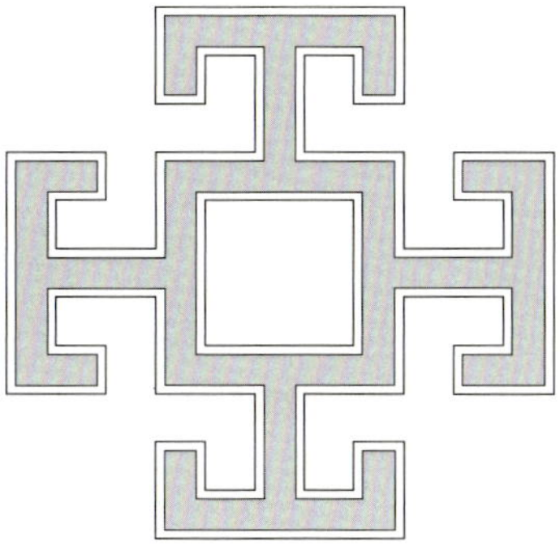

Figure 4.25
Shape of central cross on f. 138v of Lindisfarne Gospels.

of the photograph is not sufficient to establish unambiguously all the details of the design. The drawing in Fig. 4.24 was produced on the assumption that the artist followed the rules for spiral formation and connection outlined above. Thus, in the initial stages the pattern was drawn by mapping out the position of the spirals without additional ornamentation and then completed by following the rules and adopting the style of early artists. This example demonstrates that by using spirals of different sizes it is possible to achieve the space-filling qualities characteristic of Insular art. No attempt has been made to reproduce the many irregular features, such as the distorted spirals, or the actual colours of the original. The emphasis has been on representing the details of the pattern.

Ordered spiral pattern in Lindisfarne Gospels cross-carpet page f. 138v

The layout of this cross-carpet page, which introduces the Gospel according to St Luke in the Lindisfarne Gospels, has been described previously (see Fig. 2.16). The outline of the cross in the centre of the page is illustrated in Fig. 4.25. As mentioned previously, the central panel is a rectangle rather than a square as a direct result of the dimensions of the grid used to compose the whole page. The panel is ornamented with a regular spiral pattern and the arms of the cross are ornamented with a fine interlacing

Figure 4.26
Ordered spiral ornamentation in central panel of cross on f. 138v of Lindisfarne Gospels.

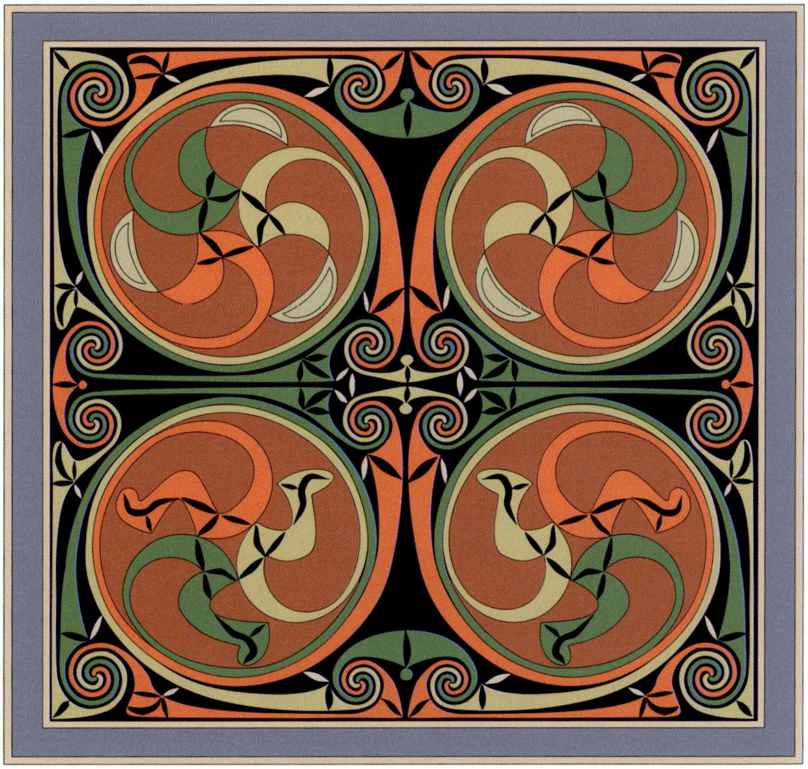

similar to that in the arms of the cross in f. 210v in the Lindisfarne Gospels, shown in Fig. 2.4.

The regular spiral pattern in the central panel has many symmetrical features (Fig. 4.26). In the four quadrants there are large three-coil spirals, each joined to three three-coil spirals in the corners of the quadrants by C-type trumpet connections. These three-coiled spirals are joined to each other by C- and S-type trumpet connections. Two different designs are used in the ornamentation of the centres of the large spirals. The two top quadrants are related to each other by a mirror reflection, and similarly the two bottom quadrants. The pattern obeys all the rules for the design of spiral patterns described earlier and each spiral is self-coloured. The construction of the design in the centres of the large spirals is based on a series of arcs of circles produced using compasses, as illustrated in Fig. 4.27. The main factor in the construction of this design is the identification of threefold symmetry so that the space is divided into three equal segments. In his studies, Bruce-Mitford (see Kendrick, 1956–60) identified pricks in the original manuscript corresponding to the position of some of the compass points. The details in Fig. 4.27 resemble those adopted by Bruce-Mitford but they are not exactly the same.

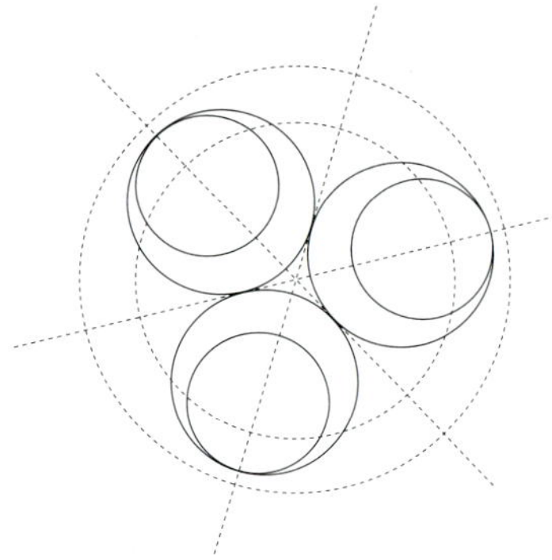

Figure 4.27
Details of construction of one of the spiral centres in Fig. 4.26.

Ordered arrays of spirals on stone crosses

The simple design in Fig. 4.28 illustrates the way that spirals, with different numbers of coils, are joined in an ordered and regular way. The panel is from one side of the base of a stone cross, found on the site of a monastery at Castledermot in Kildare, Ireland. The monastery was founded in 812 so the cross post-dates this. There is a black and white photograph of the stone in

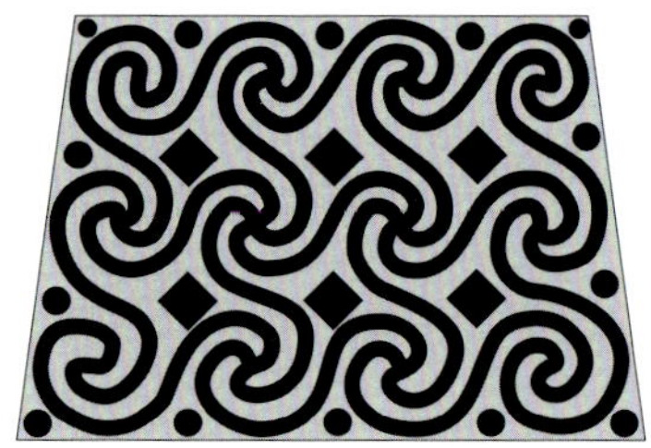

Figure 4.28
Ordered arrays of spirals on the base of a stone cross at Castledermot, Kildare, Ireland.

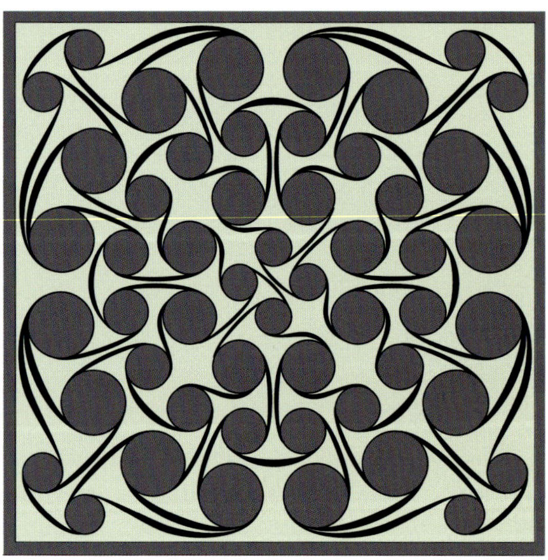

Figure 4.29
Arrangement of spirals on one panel of the Shandwick stone in north-east Scotland.

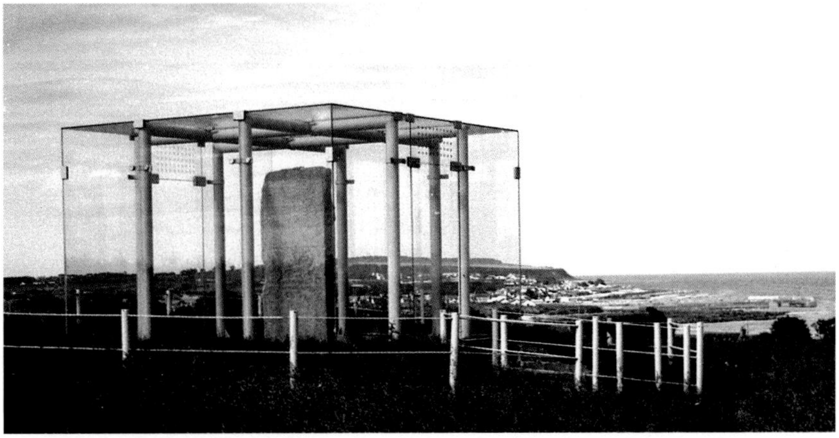

Figure 4.30
Photograph of Shandwick stone in Scotland showing the metal-framed glass enclosure that protects the stone from weathering.

Henry (1967). The base forms a truncated pyramid so that the panel is a regular trapezium rather than a rectangle. The face of the base, illustrated in Fig. 4.28, is ornamented with twelve spirals arranged on a 'distorted' square lattice. The two-coil spirals in the corners of the panel have two nearest neighbours to which they are joined. Similarly, the six three-coil spirals, between the corner spirals, have three nearest neighbours and the two four-coil spirals, in the centre of the panel, have four nearest neighbours. The spirals are anti-clockwise (inside to outside) and are joined by S-shaped connections. The faces of the cross are decorated with biblical scenes that are described in some detail by Henry.

A more sophisticated regular spiral pattern, illustrated in schematic form in Fig. 4.29, was carved on one of the panels of the Shandwick stone cross. The cross stands on a small hill overlooking Balintore in the north-east of Scotland, north of Inverness, and is protected by a giant metal-framed glass shelter (Fig. 4.30). There is an excellent photograph of the cross in RCAHMS (1999) and there are many drawings of it in Allen and Anderson (1903). On the front face there is spiral work against a background of angels, beasts, and panels of interlacing. The reverse side bears a double-disc symbol, a hunting scene and panels of interlacing and spirals. The drawing in Fig. 4.29 is from the reverse side and the pattern is No. 1079 in Allen and Anderson.

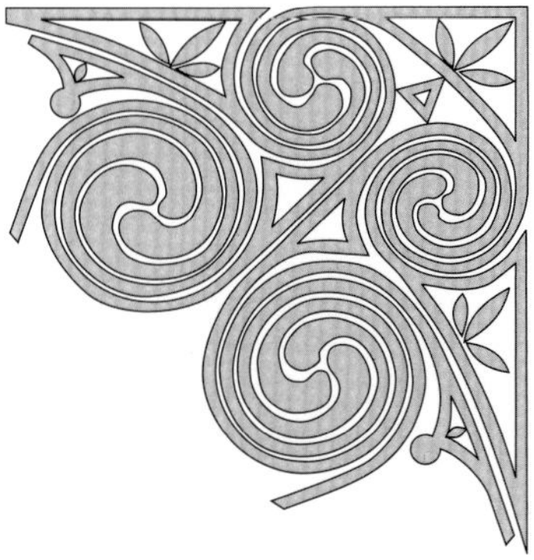

Figure 4.31
Detail of one corner of spiral panel on Shandwick stone.

Each closed circle in Fig. 4.29 represents a three-coil spiral. The outline design shows that the pattern consists of five concentric rings of equal-spaced spirals resembling the swirling dresses in a highly disciplined and choreographed dance. There are four spirals in the inner ring, eight spirals in the next ring, and so on. In each ring the spirals alternate between clockwise and anti-clockwise orientations. Each spiral is linked to three other spirals by C- and S-shaped connections. The outer ring is only partially formed but, even here, each spiral in the ring is connected to three other spirals. Some idea of the detail of the carving on this magnificent stone is evident in

Fig. 4.31, which illustrates the way that four spirals, in one corner of the square panel, are joined. There is a mirror line at 45° to the sides of the square through the top right-hand corner.

Triskele and the Aberlemno stone cross

There is a special spiral configuration in the centre of a stone cross at Aberlemno. This upright cross-slab, designated Aberlemno No. 2 by Allen and Anderson, stands outside the church in the little village of Aberlemno in mid-Scotland near Forfar. The stone is of considerable interest for a number of reasons and is described in more detail in Chapter 5. The circular panel (Fig. 4.32) has a spiral pattern consisting of three interconnected triskele (Fig. 4.33) surrounded by six three-coil spirals linked by S-shaped connections. The resultant design illustrates the most efficient way of filling space with equal-sized spirals in a close-packed configuration. All the spirals rotate in a clockwise direction.

The construction of this design is best understood by recognising the symmetrical features. The pattern as a whole has a threefold rotation point at the centre and each triskele has a threefold rotation point. The pattern can be built up by arranging triads of three-coil spirals in such a way that they are related by rotations of 120°, and then combining them to form a triskele. Thereafter the triskeles are combined and the completion of the design follows. Bain (1951) also emphasised the importance of recognising the way that a triskele is formed but provided a rather different approach. He included examples of two attempts to illustrate this pattern that had been published before his own work. They are poor imitations and emphasise the difficulties of reproduction. Bain's comments on these attempts tell us something about Bain himself as well as about the difficulties of drawing spirals: 'These examples show the gross travesties of Pictish Art in Publications by supposed authorities that have been for the past fifty years the only source of information for students and others in the libraries of every university and centre of Art Education in the civilised world'.

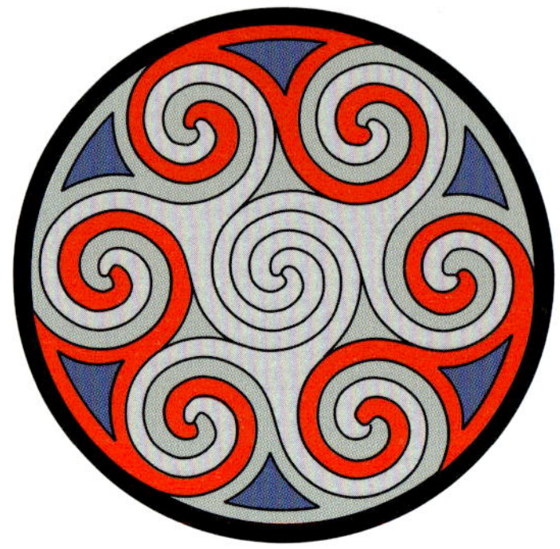

Figure 4.32
Triskele-based spiral pattern in centre of cross on Aberlemno No. 2 cross-slab.

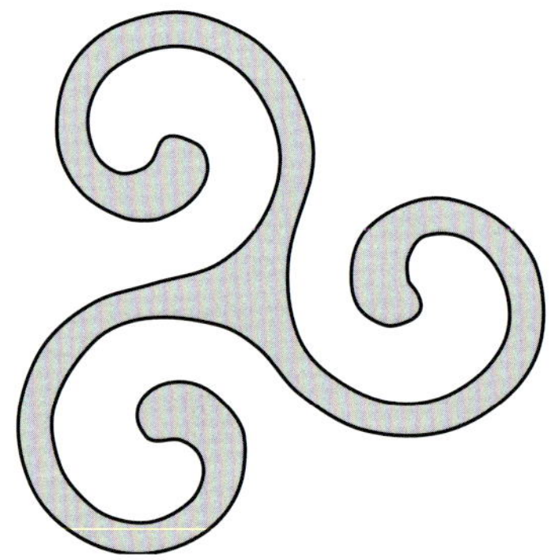

Figure 4.33
Triskele formed by combining three clockwise spirals.

INTERLACING PATTERNS

Under-and-over junctions

The origin of interlacing patterns in Insular manuscripts and on stone carvings dates back to the earliest times of artistic representation and was probably inspired by the primitive crafts of weaving, rope-work, basketry, net-making and braiding. The patterns consist of continuously curving cords interconnected by under-and-over junctions. To the earliest peoples and even

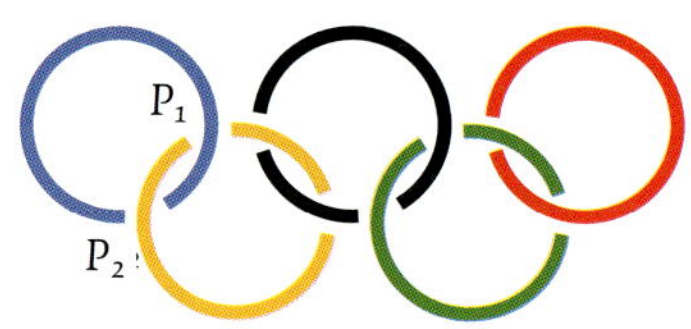

Figure 4.34
Intersecting rings with alternate under-and-over passes at intersections.

for people today, these unbroken cords speak of infinity and everlasting or unending dimensions. In the art of the seventh to ninth centuries the quality of the interlacing patterns reached a high level of perfection. Some insights into the way that the early artists devised and constructed these elegant patterns are developed in this section.

One of the basic principles of interlacing design, as used by the Insular artists, is the strict adherence to the under-and-over principle. More formally, when following a curve in a fixed direction the line makes a succession of under-and-over passes which alternate regularly throughout the whole curve. The principle can be understood by considering the combination of five closed loops in the motif of the Olympic Games (Fig. 4.34). If the loops merely overlap each other they are unconnected and are free to move independently. If the loops interlock they cannot be separated without breaking them. When they are represented as a two-dimensional drawing, the loops appear to go under and over each other alternately. Thus the blue loop goes over the yellow loop at P_1 and under the same loop at P_2, and so on. Fig. 4.35a shows three interlocking loops with alternate under-and-over junctions. Consider what happens to the sequence when the black loop is introduced with under-and-over junctions, as in Fig. 4.35b. The red loop still goes over the green loop at P_1 and under at P_2, but it also goes over the black loop at P_3 that is immediately adjacent to P_1. There are now two over passes next to each other so this pattern breaks the under-and-over rule. The correct sequence is restored by changing the under-and-over passes successively starting at any point in the network (Fig. 4.35c). Note that the red loop now goes over the

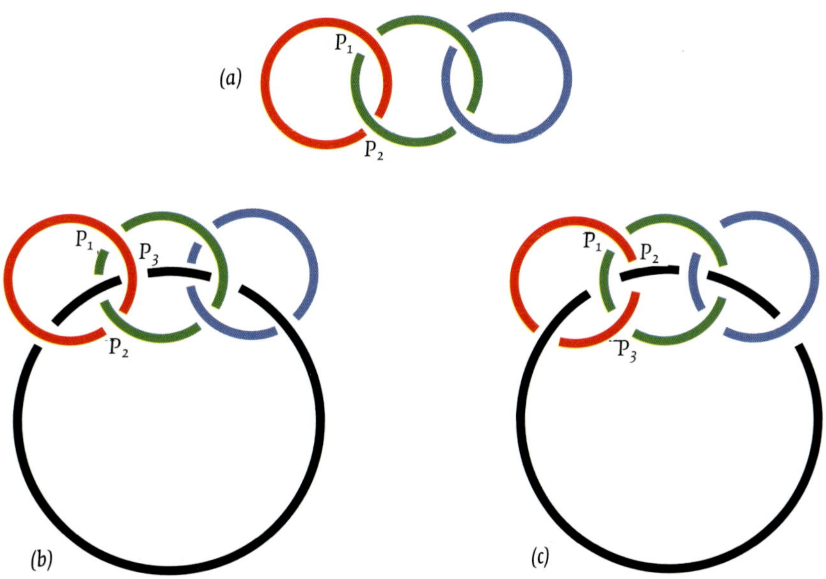

Figure 4.35
Effect of introducing another loop on the under-and-over sequence.

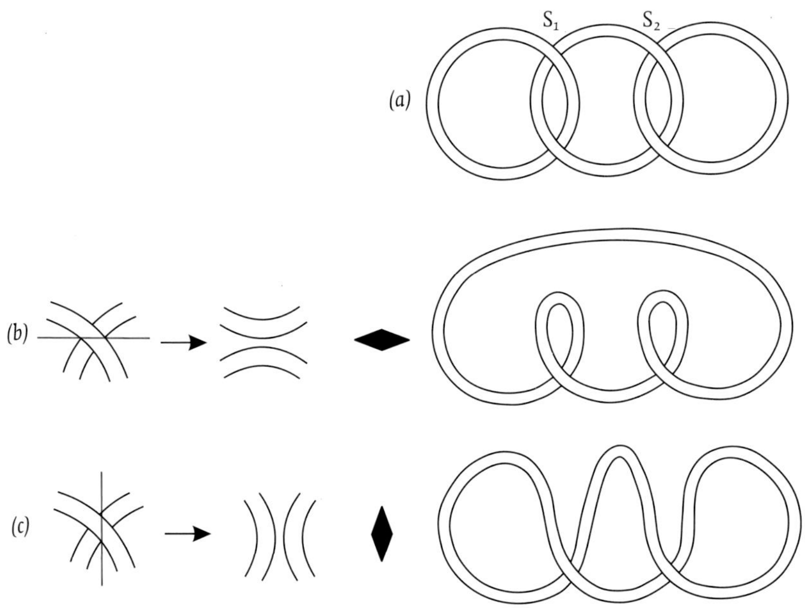

Figure 4.36
Breaking and joining at junctions to form continuous loops.

green loop at both P_1 and P_2. This simple demonstration highlights a very important aspect in constructing interlacing designs – the pattern of the cords must be completed before introducing interlacing sequences.

Another important principle in interlacing design is the concept of continuous paths. This subject is treated in more detail in Chapter 7 in relation to the great cross at Old Lonan in the Isle of Man. The basic ideas are relevant to all stages of interlacing design and can be understood in simple terms. With few exceptions, interlacing patterns are made up of closed loops. In some designs it is clear that the artist has made subtle changes to ensure that the whole pattern is one continuous cord or loop. Changing a set of multiple continuous cords into a continuous cord involves breaking and joining as illustrated in Fig. 4.36. Here, three interlocking cords are transformed into a single cord by breaking and rejoining at two intersections, such as those marked S_1 and S_2. The final shape of the cord depends on the way the broken loops are rejoined. There are always two possible configurations at each intersection as shown on the left-hand side of Fig. 4.36. Two possible shapes are shown on the right-hand side. Although these appear to be different they are essentially the same. By treating them as flexible cords each shape can be 'unravelled' to form a single open loop.

The three interlocking loops in Fig. 4.37 are also transformed into a single cord by breaking and rejoining at two intersections. The designs in Fig. 4.37b and c are achieved by choosing different breaking and rejoining options. They are essentially the same continuous loop; both can be transformed into the triquetra knot shown in Fig. 4.37d by unravelling.

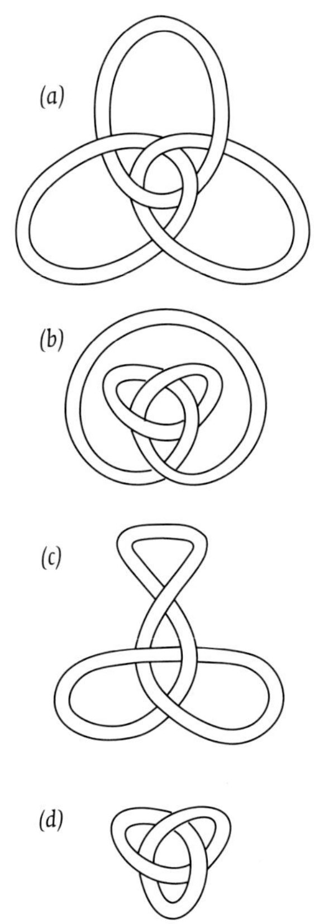

Figure 4.37
Forming a triquetra knot.

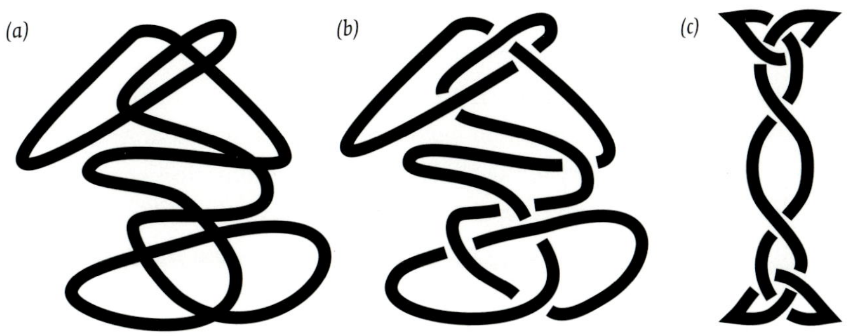

Figure 4.38
Interlacing a continuous strand and changing it into a regular shape.

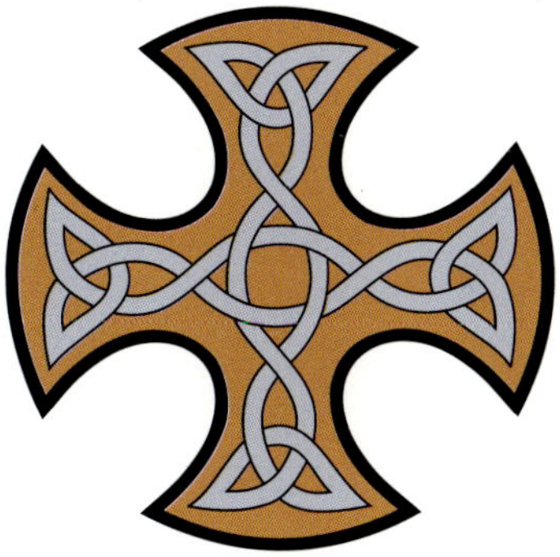

Figure 4.39
Cross on a stone cross-slab at St Brynach's church, Nevern, Wales.

This is the same knot that is used in the design of the cross on the Ulbster stone described at the beginning of this chapter. The principle underlying the formation of a continuous cord from a set of multiple cords can be expressed in more general terms as follows: any set of n continuous cords are transformed into a single cord by breaking and rejoining $(n-1)$ intersections providing all the cords in the set are involved.

Unlike the single cords in Fig. 4.36, those in Fig. 4.37 cannot be unravelled to produce an open loop. This rather trivial example provides an introduction to the formal definition of a knot as used by mathematicians in a branch of mathematics called topology. A simple loop is called an unknot and a continuous cord that cannot be unravelled is called a knot. Topology offers insights into understanding the complex interlacing designs of the Insular artists and an awareness of the importance of under-and-over sequences. A taste of the mathematical approach can be found in Cromwell (1993). The paper offers a brief introduction to knot theory but concentrates mainly on the use of symmetry concepts to describe interlacing borders. Fortunately, there is no need to develop the subject in so much detail to follow the development of interlacing designs.

Any continuous loop or cord can be transformed into a fully interlaced network of under-and-over junctions that satisfy the rules mentioned above. The tangle in Fig. 4.38a represents a single closed loop without interlacing. The procedure for drawing an interlacing pattern involves creating either an under- or an over-pass at an intersection and then making under-and-over passes at all the other intersections sequentially (Fig. 4.38b). If the cords are flexible it is possible to reshape this irregular pattern into two of the arms of a simple interlacing cross without changing any of the under- or over-passes, or breaking the closed loop (Fig. 4.38c). This interlacing pattern is used to ornament the cross head of the stone cross at St Brynach's church in Nevern in Pembrokeshire, Wales (Fig. 4.39). The pattern is used on the colourful embroidered pew-kneelers inside the church.

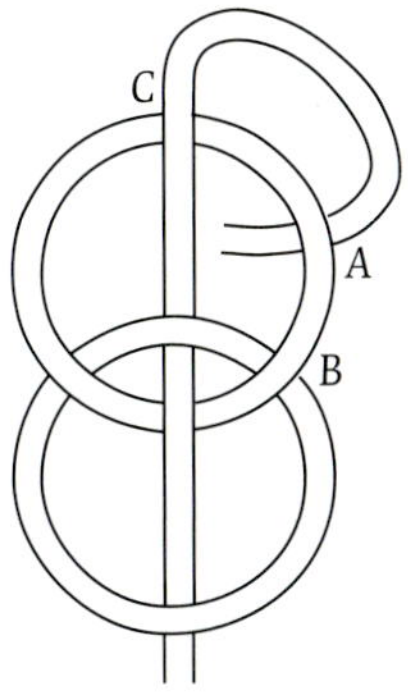

Figure 4.40
Breaking the under-and-over interlacing rule.

There is one source for an apparent breakdown of the under-and-over rule, other than poor workmanship, that may occur in designs with non-continuous strands. This is particularly relevant in zoomorphic designs where tails, necks, legs, wings and head-feathers are interlaced. An example can be found in Chapter 5 in the zoomorphic ornamentation of the cross-carpet page in the Lichfield Gospels. The problem is illustrated in schematic form in Fig. 4.40. Here two loops are interlaced with a cord that ends inside one of the loops. It is impossible to complete a fully alternating under-and-over sequence because there will always be two consecutive under- or over-passes in part of the interlacing, as at A and B.

Interlacing multiple-cord strands to form border designs

With these general ideas about interlacing the designs used by the Insular artists can now be considered. Allen (see Allen and Anderson, 1903) produced over 600 drawings of different interlacing designs based on his studies of stones and manuscripts of the seventh to ninth centuries. He also catalogued the locations where these designs were used on Pictish stones and, to a lesser extent, in the Insular manuscripts. Although, as demonstrated in the next chapter, some of the designs are complex, the underlying geometric principles are relatively simple. The starting point, as with all regular patterns, and to a lesser extent with irregular patterns, is a network of intersecting lines. The most straightforward patterns are those derived from plaiting or braiding. A set of strands, cords or strips forms a continuously intertwining plait or braid. The set may contain any number of cords and innumerable sequences of twists and weaves may be used to produce different types of plait. The plaiting sequence is represented in two dimensions using the under-and-over convention introduced above. To illustrate the approach, and the way that subsequent breaking and rejoining at intersections leads to an ever-increasing variety of patterns, consider a simple six-cord plait. (Note that plaits with an even number of cords are symmetrical and those with an odd number of cords are asymmetrical.)

The cords in Fig. 4.41a are drawn on a square grid with each cord identified by a different colour. The smoothed curves in Fig. 4.41b are a two-dimensional representation of a bundle of six cords that has been twisted without interlacing. Interlacing the cords produces the pattern shown in Fig. 4.41c. Alternate under- and over-passes have been made at every intersection. Note that there is no requirement in conventional plaiting or braiding for the under-and-over sequence to be over single cords but it appears to be an absolute rule in Insular art.

Allen's work showed how different patterns are produced from a fully interlaced plait (as in Fig. 4.41c) by breaking and rejoining cord

Figure 4.41
Development of interlacing border designs in a six-strand plait by breaking and joining intersections.

(a) (b) (c) (d) (e) (f) (g)

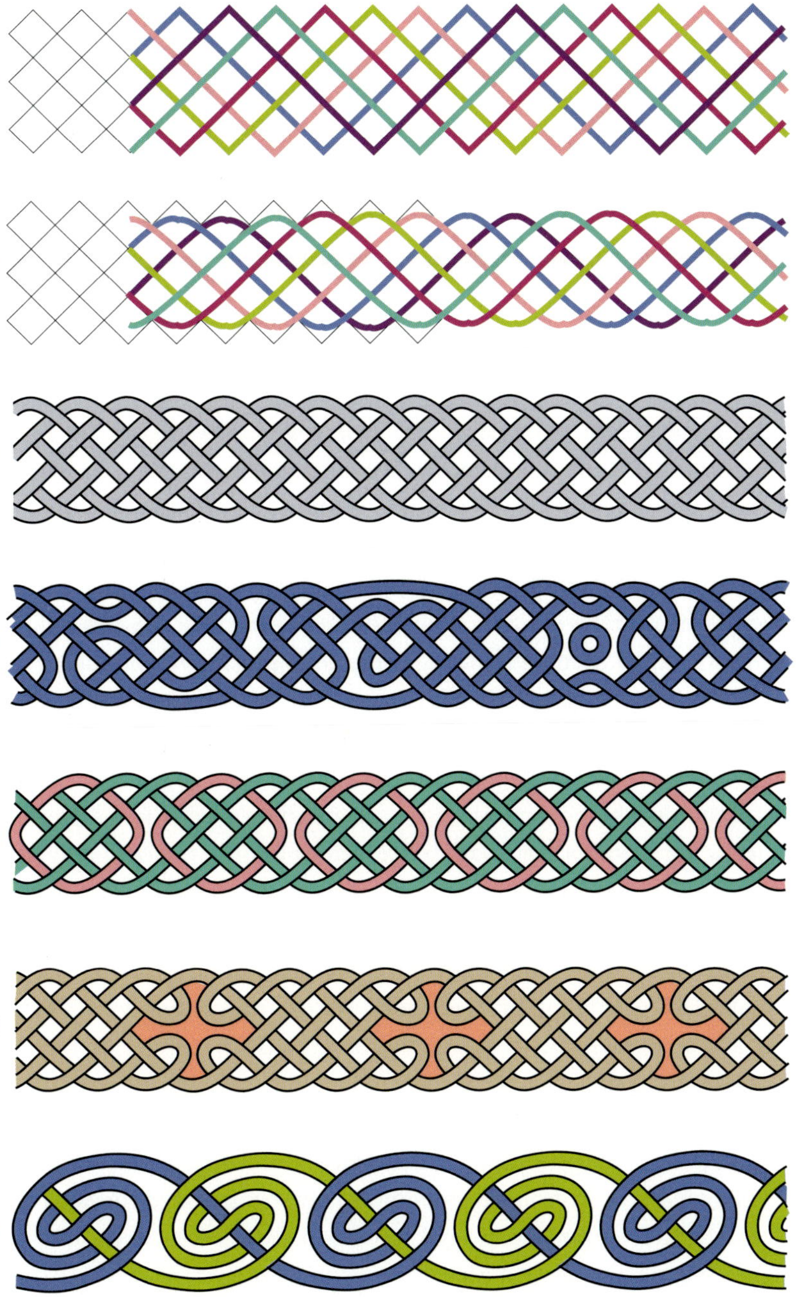

intersections. As illustrated in Fig. 4.36, there are always two configurations of the cords after a breaking and rejoining process. The choice has a strong influence on the final pattern.

Breaking and rejoining a fully interlaced plait at intersection points chosen at random forms the irregular pattern in Fig. 4.41d. Breaking and

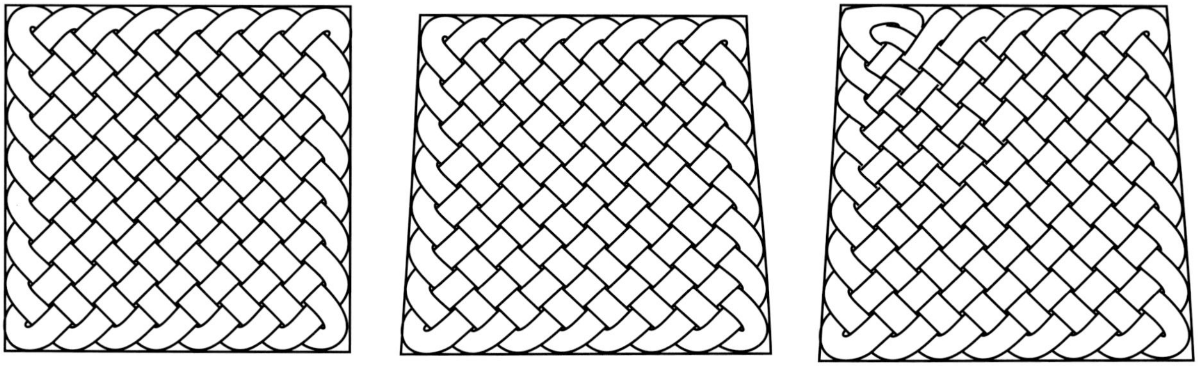

(a) (b) (c)

Figure 4.42
Panels ornamented with interlacing. (a) Square panel with a sixteen-strand plait. (b) Tapered panel with sixteen-strand plait. (c) Interlacing design used on Samson cross, Llantwit Major, Wales.

rejoining in an ordered manner creates the other three patterns in Fig. 4.41. Patterns of this kind were used widely in ornamenting the borders of pages in Insular manuscripts and to a lesser extent in the ornamentation of stone crosses. The best example is the cross on the Lindisfarne cross-carpet page used in Chapter 2 to illustrate the panel approach to design (see Figs. 2.4 and 2.5). The basic unit in this design is similar to that shown in Fig. 4.41f. A similar unit is used on the Rosemarkie stone. There is no specific requirement that the initial pattern (Fig. 4.41a) is based on a square net. Any network of lines can be used. The development of the approach to non-square grids is illustrated in Fig. 3.16. Many, more complex, examples are described elsewhere in this book.

Although the borders in Fig. 4.41 are shown with loose ends these interlacing patterns are invariably closed by joining the cords together in various ways. Borders decorated with these patterns are essentially panels. Indeed there are many examples of panels, particularly on stone monuments, ornamented with a simple multi-cord interlaced braid with the ends of the braid folded over to form closed cords. The example in Fig. 4.42 is based on the Samson cross-slab in St Illtud's church, Llantwit Major, in the Vale of Glamorgan, Wales. This is a free-standing pillar, without its original cross-head, and it is ornamented with a range of panels and motifs. The panel in Fig. 4.42 is basically a simple interlaced sixteen-cord plait with the loose ends folded over. In reality the design is more complicated for two reasons. First, the panel is not square, and second, in the top left-hand corner of the panel the simple 16-cord plait reduces to a 14-cord plait. One can only surmise about the source of this second complication but it seems likely that it relates to an attempt by the artist or sculptor to accommodate the interlacing pattern to the taper in the stone shaft.

The vast number of possible interlacing patterns makes classification, for the purposes of archaeological research and analysis, rather difficult. Several attempts have been made to produce a simple classification, following Allen and Anderson's monumental work. Cramp (1991) produced one such classification that was originally developed by Adcock for an MPhil thesis (1974). The approach is based on identifying the different elements of interlacing border designs and the way that these elements are related to each other. An alternative approach, which provides a method of describing precisely the interlacing configuration of all patterns in multiple continuous cords, is introduced in Fig. 4.43 using a simple six-cord plait. It is based on the methods used by Allen and Anderson and is applied to a more complicated example, the Llangenydd stone, in Chapter 7.

The regular six-cord plait in Fig. 4.41c is reproduced in Fig. 4.43a. Each cord extends the full length of the plait. Fine horizontal lines, numbered 1 to 27, mark the crossover points or 'intersections'. On odd-numbered lines there are two intersections and on even-numbered lines there are three intersections. The interlacing pattern is formed by a series of break-and-join sequences (Fig. 4.43b). The diamond-shaped markings define both the position and orientation of the break-and-joins. A break-and-join normal (n) to the axis of

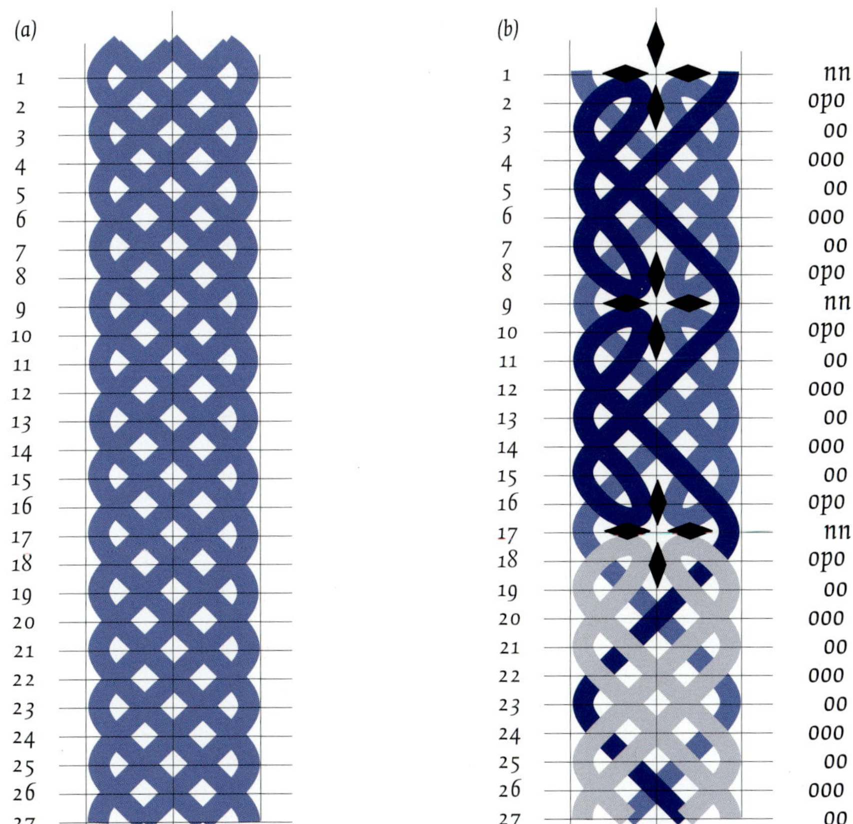

six cord twisted plait

[nn/opo/oo/ooo/oo/ooo/oo/opo]

p is a break – join parallel to twisted plait
n is a break – join normal to twisted plait
r is a repeat, the full border pattern is formed by repeating the initial sequence

Figure 4.43
Construction of an interlacing border by a sequence of break-and-joins in six-cord twisted strand.

the plait is shown as a diamond pointing at right angles to the plait and a break-and-join parallel (p) to the plait as a diamond parallel to the plait. An intersection without a break-and-join is referred to as (o). The interlacing pattern in Fig. 4.43b is formed by the sequence of break-and-joins represented on the right-hand side of the diagram. The whole pattern is defined precisely as a six-cord plait [nn/opo/oo/ooo/oo/ooo/oo/opo]$_r$ where r means that the sequence is repeated. Similarly, the border in Fig. 4.41e is defined as a six-cord plait [ono/oo/ooo/oo]$_r$ and part of the irregular design in Fig. 4.41d as a six-cord plait [no/ooo/op/ooo/oo/poo/poo/ooo/on/ooo/ oo/ooo/no/pop/oo/oop ...].

Book of Kells:
examples of cross-shaped panels ornamented with interlacing

Many more sophisticated and interesting interlacing decorations are to be found in Insular manuscripts and on Pictish stones. Some of these are

(a)

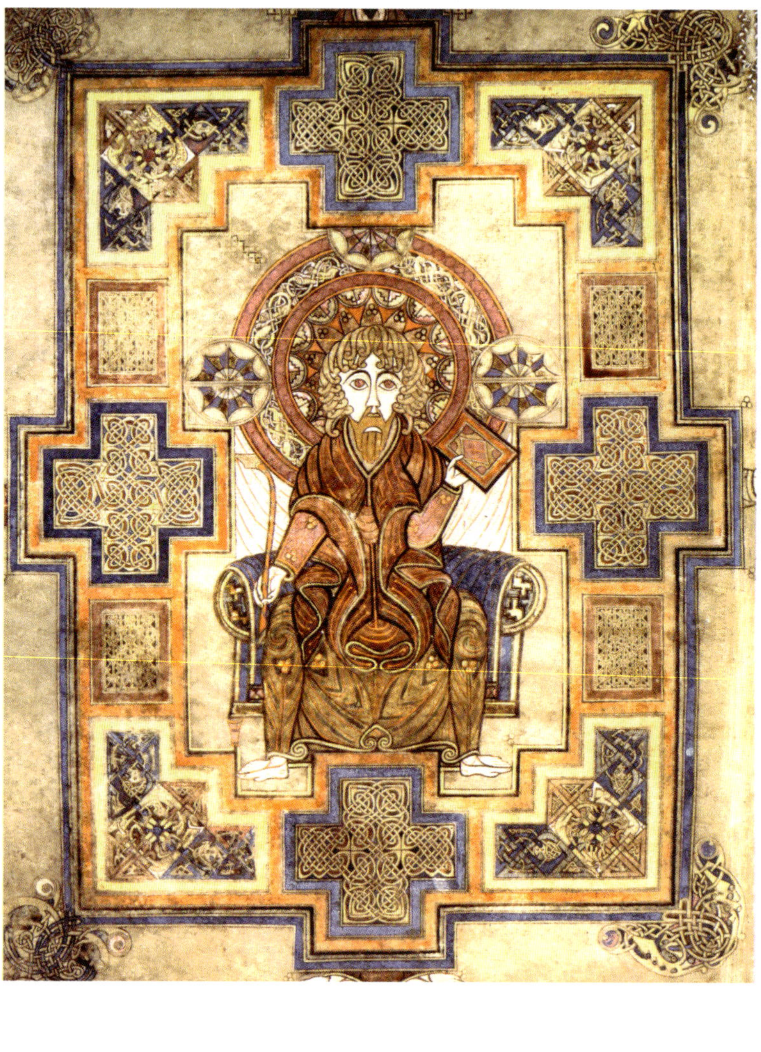

Figure 4.44
St John's portrait page f. 291v of Book of Kells.
(a) Photograph (by permission of the Board of Trinity College Dublin).
(b) Layout showing the distribution of crosses (opposite).

included in the next chapter. This section ends with two fine examples from the Book of Kells. Both relate to cross-shaped panels that form only a small part of richly ornamented pages. They highlight some ideas about interlacing, only touched upon in this section, such as (1) the way that regular interlacing designs are developed to fill panels with an irregular shape, (2) the use of differently shaped grids to map out the positions of the cords, (3) the development of different interlacing sequences from the same grid, and (4) the importance of mapping out the position of the cords before completing the interlacing sequencing.

There are four crosses in the border around the portrait of St John, f. 291v of the Book of Kells (Fig. 4.44a). The formal layout of this page, which measures 330 mm by 250 mm, is shown in Fig. 4.44b. All the crosses are the same shape and size with the long dimension parallel to the border. The crosses in the side borders are oriented at 90° to those at the top and bottom. Each cross is filled

(b)

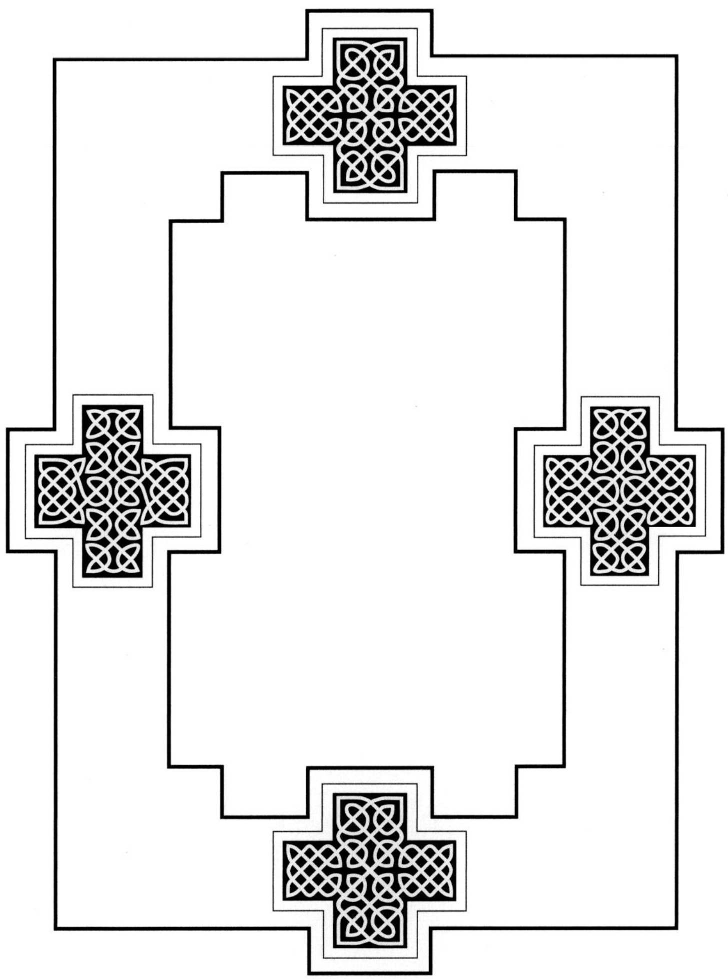

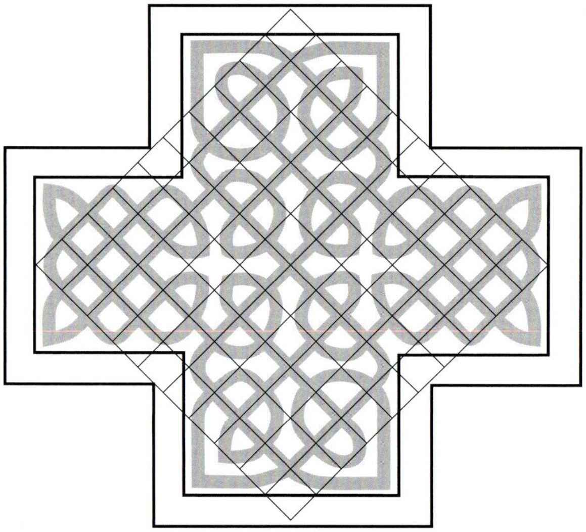

Figure 4.45
Interlacing design developed from a square grid (see Fig. 4.44).

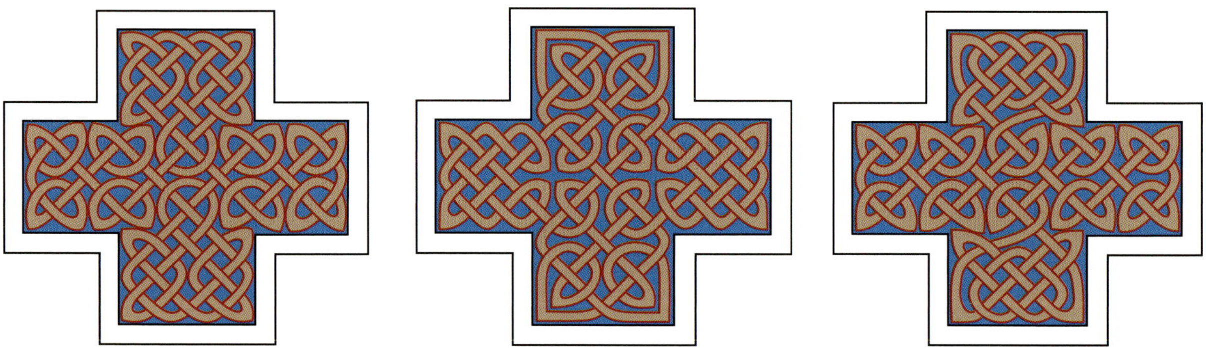

Figure 4.46
Three different interlacing designs used to ornament the four crosses on St John's portrait page f. 291v of Book of Kells.

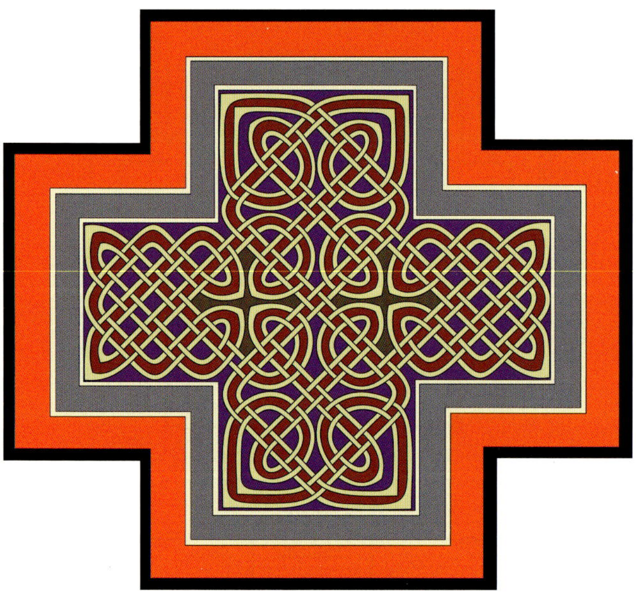

Figure 4.47
Detail of fine-scale interlacing used on the four crosses on St John's portrait page f. 291v of Book of Kells.

with an interlacing pattern based on a square grid oriented at 45° to the edges of the border (Fig. 4.45). There are three different interlacing designs in the crosses. The crosses at the top and bottom have the same design whereas the two crosses at the sides have different designs. The three outline designs in Fig. 4.46 were produced, with the same grid, by changing the orientation and distribution of breaking and rejoining points, using the same approach as that described for the interlacing borders in Fig. 4.41.

The fine detail of the interlacing design of all these crosses is the same as that of the Lindisfarne cross, shown in Fig. 2.4, and the drawing sequence is the same as that illustrated in Fig. 2.5. If the bands of interlacing are treated as single cords the interlacing patterns for the three crosses are as shown in Fig. 4.46. However, the artist has used another level of interlacing that means that the design involves interlacing the fine lines at the edges of the main band. The final result (Fig. 4.47) corresponds to the cross in the centre of the top border of f. 291v.

The cross in Fig. 4.48 is on one of the most magnificent pages in the Book of Kells (f. 292r). The page has a bewildering variety of designs of all kinds and includes the opening words of the Gospel according to St John, *In principio erat Verbum* – 'in the beginning was the Word'. The design of the interlacing that ornaments the cross is closely similar to the crosses on the previous page (f. 291r) with double interlaced borders to the main band. The cross is part of a very intricate design and is surrounded by many other panels. The shape of the cross was produced using the construction lines set out in Fig. 4.50 and the interlacing is formed on a grid of two sets of equal-spaced parallel lines at 77.5° to each other (Fig. 4.51). Every part of the design

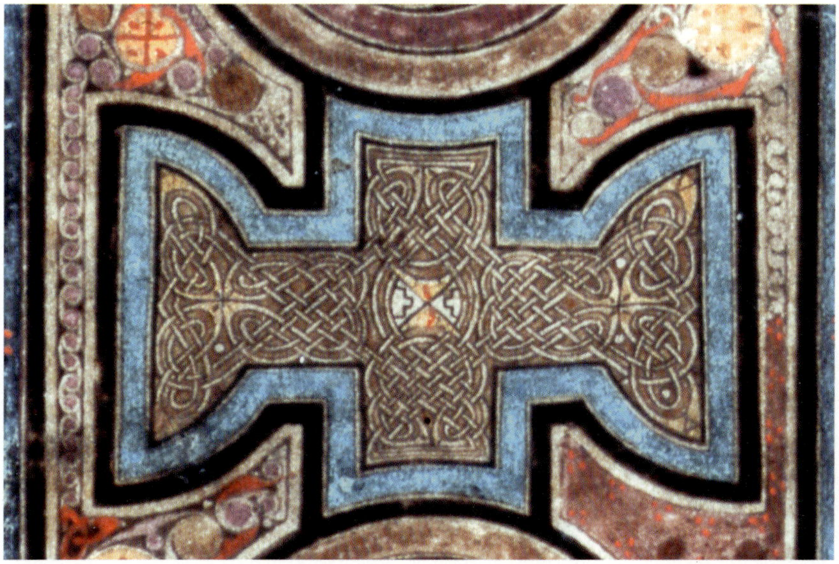

Figure 4.48
Photograph of a detail of f. 292r of Book of Kells (by permission of the Board of Trinity College Dublin). The width of the cross is 48 mm.

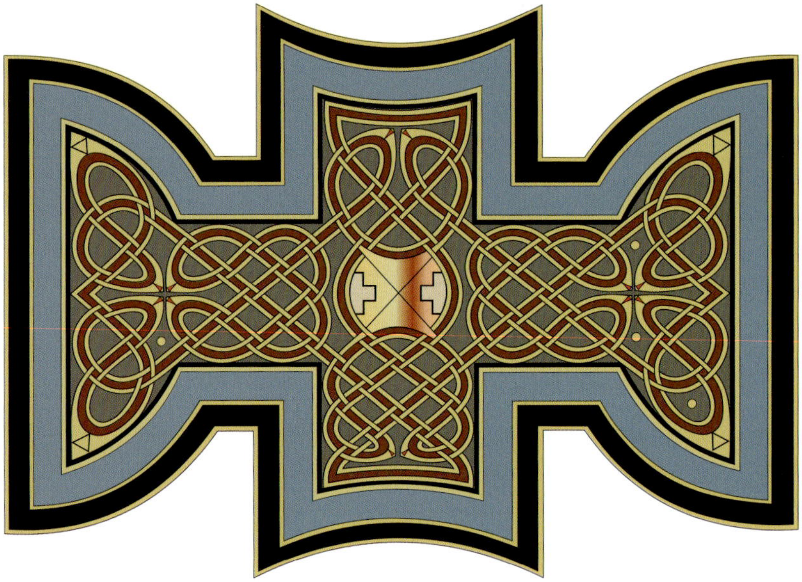

Figure 4.49
Drawing of cross shown in Fig. 4.48.

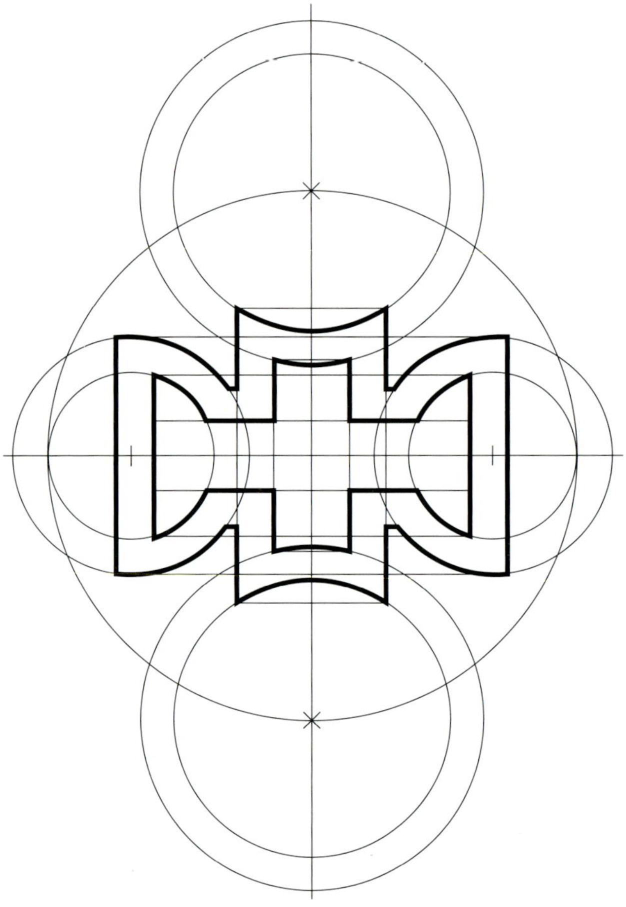

Figure 4.50
Construction lines for cross in Fig. 4.49.

Figure 4.51
Grid for interlacing pattern for cross in Fig. 4.49.

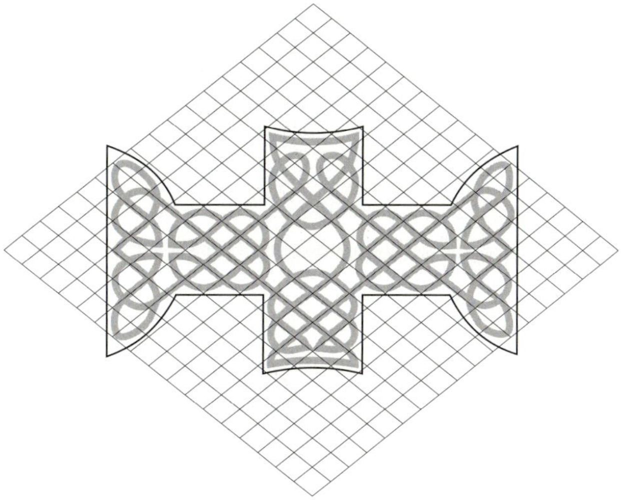

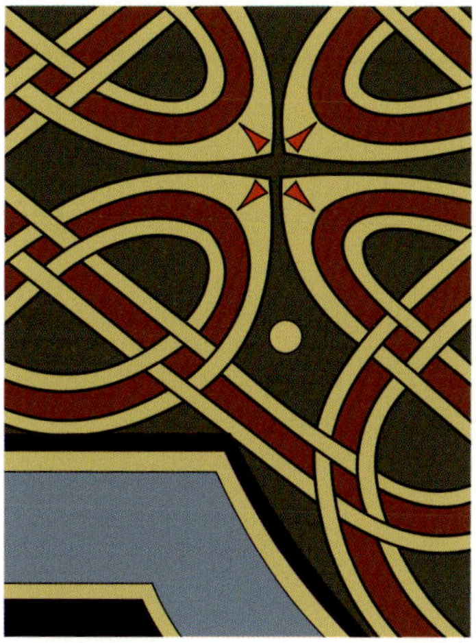

Figure 4.52
Magnified view of part of Fig. 4.49.

of this page is worthy of the highest praise, particularly when account is taken of the scale of the detail. The cross is only 48 mm (less than two inches) across, so that the artist worked at a scale that is barely resolvable by the naked eye. Some idea of the quality of the detail is evident in the magnified view (Fig. 4.52) of part of the image in Fig. 4.49. Naturally, the ninth-century artists were not able to produce lines as smooth as those in Fig. 4.52, nor presumably would they wish to, but magnified views of the actual manuscript show that the quality of the detail is exceptionally high.

ZOOMORPHIC AND FOLIACEOUS OR FOLIATE PATTERNS

Many of the topics described earlier in this chapter, such as symmetry, repetition and translation, and the under-and-over rule, apply equally to zoomorphic and foliate designs. In some respects these patterns appear to be less constrained geometrically because they reflect the shapes and forms of a wide range of animals and plants. Nevertheless, it is important to identify the underlying patterns and set these out before developing fine detail, particularly the interlacing sequences. From earlier chapters, repetition is evident in the processions of animals shown in Fig. 2.31, two- and threefold symmetry is present in the zoomorphic panels of the St Petersburg Gospel book (Fig. 3.22) and the Faversham gold pendant (Fig. 3.1) respectively, and the under-and-over rule is fully applied in the zoomorphic designs in the Lindisfarne Gospels (Fig. 3.5). As with iconic motifs, individual zoomorphic and foliate motifs are usually unconstrained geometrically but when they are grouped in a design the result may have strong geometric features.

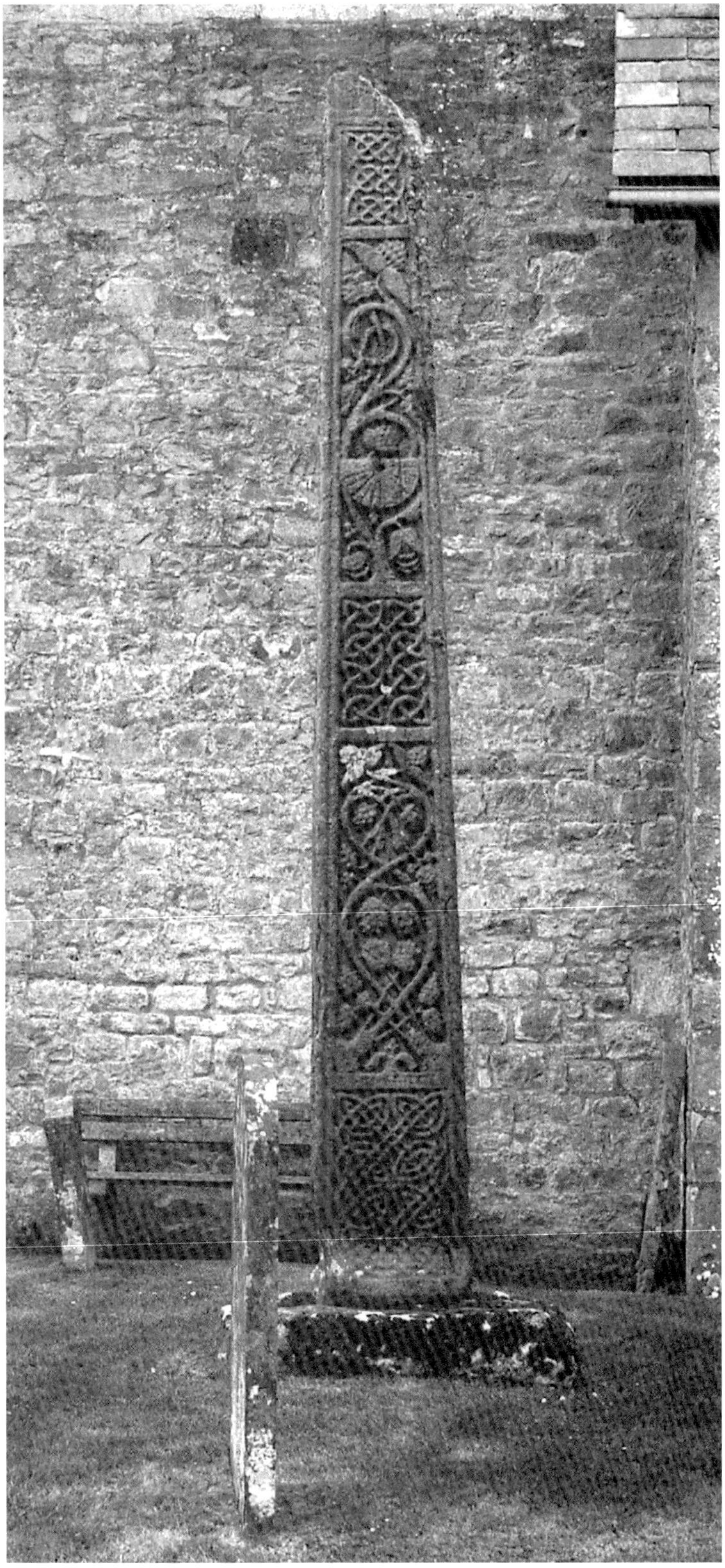

Figure 4.53
Bewcastle cross, Cumbria, England.

By far the most common foliate motif is the vine. At first sight, representation of vines has little geometric relevance, for they appear to consist of a freehand array of curving branches, with or without embedded animals. However, this is far from correct. Later in this section the design of vines on the Bewcastle cross is used to highlight some of the issues that are common to the ornamentation of a large number of stone monuments, particularly in the Anglo-Saxon regions.

The Bewcastle cross is in the graveyard of St Cuthbert's church in a remote part of Cumbria a few kilometres north of Carlisle and Hadrian's Wall. The cross-head has been lost but the remaining shaft is in remarkably good condition. There is a recess in this 3.5 m high slender tapering shaft indicating that the cross-head was carved as a separate piece that was fitted to the top. It is usually dated to the first half of the eighth century and is often compared with the equally splendid Ruthwell cross. There is a vast amount of literature on both crosses and it is clear that dating has been, and remains, the subject of intense interest and debate.

It is important to recognise that the work of the Bewcastle artist and sculptor is of a high geometric standard. All four sides of the slender tapering

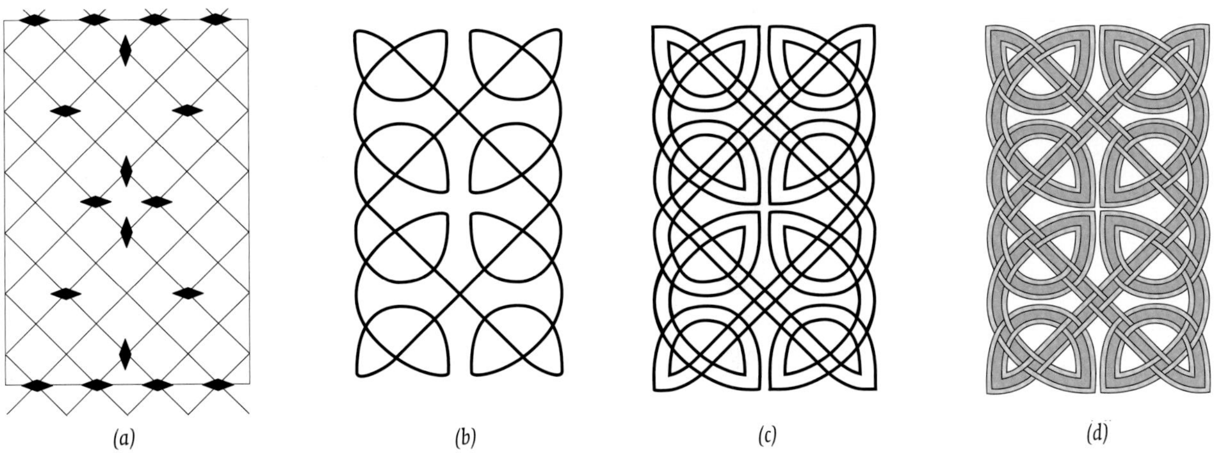

Figure 4.54
Lower, interlacing-filled panel, on south face of column of the Bewcastle cross. (a) Grid formed by eight-cord plait. (b) Formation of basic interlacing design by breaking and joining at the intersection points of the grid. (c) Form of pattern before interlacing. (d) Final design.

column (Fig. 4.53) have regular and precise panels ornamented with a range of motifs. On the south-facing side there are three panels filled with regular interlacing and two panels with vine motifs. A clear indication of the geometric standards of this work is found in the construction of the bottom interlacing-filled panel on the south side, as illustrated in Fig. 4.54. Using the descriptive approach developed in the previous section it follows that the panel is based on an eight-cord plait (Fig. 4.54a) and that the break-and-join sequence required to produce the basic configuration, shown in Fig. 4.54b, is [nnnn/opo/oooo/non/oooo/opo/onno/opo/oooo/non/oooo/opo/nnnn].

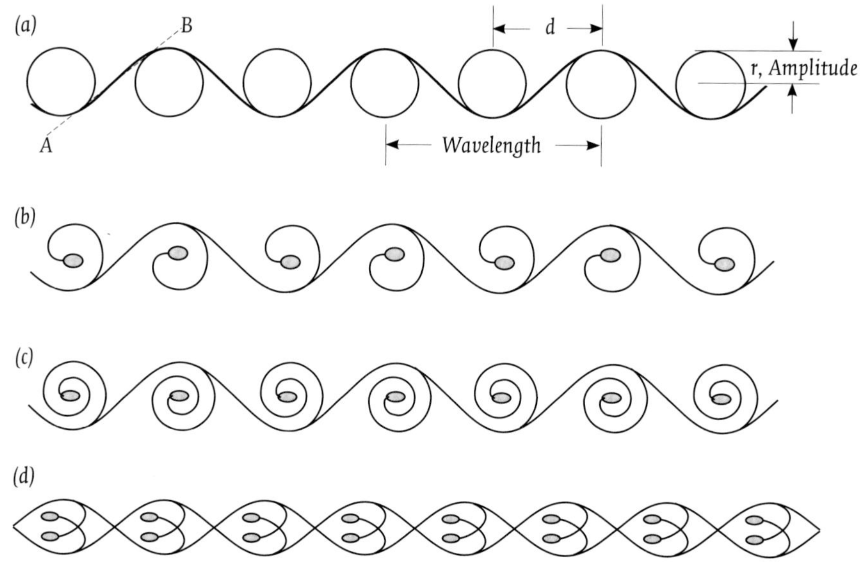

Figure 4.55
Curves used to create vine patterns. (a) Formation of a regular wavy curve. (b) Single curve with regular curved branches with single pendants, typically bunches of grapes. (c) Single curve with regular spiral branches. (d) Double curves each with single curved branches.

In the final design (Fig. 4.54d) the sides of the cords have been highlighted and then interlaced. Because the shaft of the Bewcastle cross tapers, the panels are not rectangular and further refinement is required to fit the interlacing to the panel. This is achieved by changing the shape of the initial grid (Fig. 4.54a) as described previously.

Before considering the rather sophisticated example of the geometry of the vine on the Bewcastle cross, which is framed by a non-rectangular panel, a simple form of the design must be introduced. Vines in rectangular panels can be drawn using the simple construction shown in Fig. 4.55a. This consists of a series of equal-sized, equal-spaced circles with diagonal lines, such as AB, tangential to the circles. Joining the tangent lines and the segments of the circumference of the circles forms a continuous wavy line. For spacing of circles comparable to those in Fig. 4.55a this construction produces a wavy line that approximates closely to a sine wave. This is described mathematically as $y = \sin x$, where y is the perpendicular distance from a line through the centre of the circles and x is the distance along this line. The two main characteristics of such regular waves are called amplitude and wavelength. The amplitude is equal to the radius of the circles (r) and the wavelength is twice the distance between the centres of the circles (d). The ratio d/r is a property of the wave. It can be varied by the artist according to the effects required. In the representation of vines the curve forms the main stem of the vine, which is then decorated with fruit, leaves and animals. Three simple constructions are shown in Fig. 4.55b-d.

The fine detail of the decoration of vines provides an important method in archaeological studies for analysing the origin and provenance of Anglo-

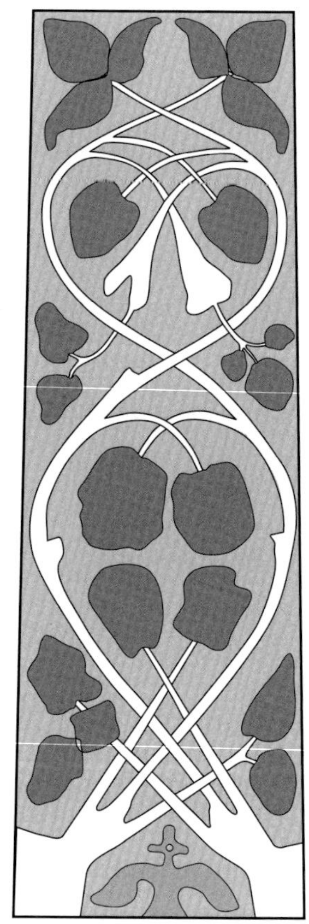

Figure 4.56
Double vine ornamentation on Bewcastle cross shaft.

Saxon stone monuments. Thus, for example, Cramp (1984, 1991) offers a detailed classification of the representation of plant structures, including 58 shapes in which leaves and leaf compositions have been carved. This type of classification has little direct relevance to geometric issues.

For the curves in Fig. 4.55a-c, $d/r = 3.2$ and for the curves in Fig. 4.55d, $d/r = 3.7$. On stone monuments with regular vine designs the value of d/r varies between about 2.1 and 3.5. Typical values from stone shafts in the north of England with well-formed patterns are Irton 2.5, Ruthwell 3.0, Ilkley 2.1, Otley 3.2 and 3.4 for two different panels, Durham Cathedral 2.3, and Acca 2.1 and 2.5 for two different panels. The appearance of these stones is illustrated and described in detail by Collingwood (1927).

There are examples on the Bewcastle cross of panels decorated with single (Fig. 4.55b) and double (Fig. 4.55d) vines. A simple example of a double vine (Fig. 4.56) is in the panel immediately above the interlacing panel (Fig. 4.54). The carving shows detail of the fruit and leaves on the vine that has been omitted from Fig. 4.56. The main interest in this illustration is the display of a mirror line in the arrangement of the vines and branches and the application of over-and-under interlacing of the stems. The interlacing does not fully conform to the rules because some of the stems terminate inside closed loops (see Fig. 4.40).

The taper in the panel, evident in Figs. 4.56 and 4.57, is an important element in the geometric design of the single vine example. The east side of the shaft has a single panel decorated with a vine inhabited by birds and animals. Construction of this design is sophisticated because in constructing the wavy line that forms the main vine, using the approach described above (Fig. 4.55), each circle has a different diameter, decreasing towards the top of the shaft, with a corresponding decrease in the spacing of the circles. In other words the wavelength and the amplitude change progressively. How can this be achieved using only a straight-edge and compasses? There are three variables – the taper of the panel, the diameter of the circles and the spacing of the circles. To achieve a uniform taper (Fig. 4.57a) the ratio of the diameters of successive circles (for example $2r_2/2r_1$) and the ratio of the spacing of successive circles (d_2/d_1) must be constant and equal to each other for all the circles in the shaft. Once the value of $r_2/r_1 = d_2/d_1$ (or more generally in mathematical terms $r_{i+1}/r_i = d_{i+1}/d_i$, where i refers to the ith circle and spacing in the column) is fixed, the taper of the panel is also fixed. The Bewcastle artist used $d/r = 3.0$ with $r_{i+1}/r_i = 0.95$ so that the size and spacing of the circles decreased by 5% or 1/20th successively.

A simple geometric construction can be used to determine the diameters and spacing of all the circles on the shaft (Fig. 4.58). Take any straight line OA and step along its length, with compasses or dividers, twenty equal spaces.

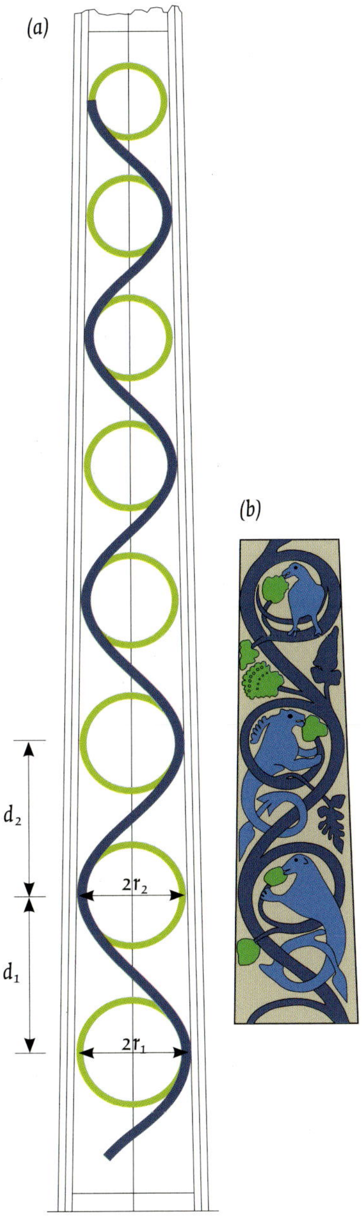

Figure 4.57
Single vine ornamentation on Bewcastle cross shaft. (a) Construction of wavy curve using a column of progressively decreasing circles. (b) Inhabited vine design.

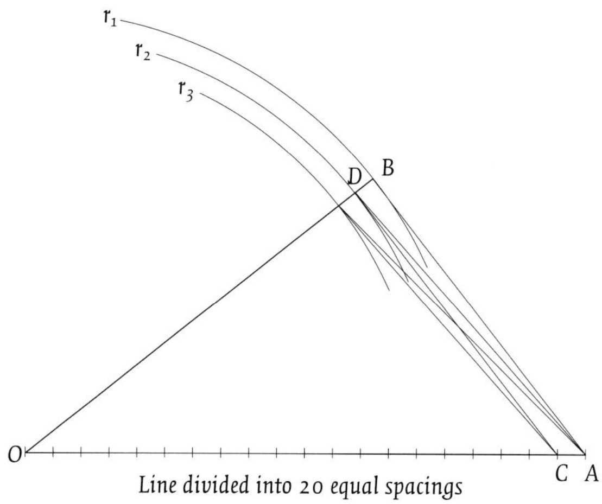

Figure 4.58
Method of reducing length of a line to 95% of the original length.

Draw any other straight line OB and mark off on this line the radius (r_1) of the bottom circle in the column. Join AB and then draw line CD parallel to AB. It follows that OD is the radius (r_2) of the second circle in the column such that $r_1/r_2 = 0.95$. This procedure is then repeated successively. The same approach can be used for the spacing of the circles. A series of circles produced in this way results in a taper of $\pm 1.03°$, which is close to the actual taper of the stone shaft. Some idea of the distribution of birds and animals that inhabit the vine is given in Fig. 4.57b. These are interlaced with the vine. Foliate ornamentation was also used in manuscripts and there is a review of the use of vine-scroll ornament in the Book of Kells in a paper by Mac Lean (1999).

CONCLUDING OBSERVATIONS

In this chapter it has been established that the use of motifs – key, spiral, interlacing, zoomorphic and foliate – in Insular art involves the application of the principles of symmetry and repetition. An understanding of these principles makes it possible to discover the methods used to create fascinating and complex designs. As alluded to earlier, the elements of symmetry – translation, rotation, and reflection – are not always easily grasped and it is often difficult to recognise these elements in more complex designs. This theme is developed further in the next chapter. As demonstrated in the simple cross design on the Ulbster stone, it is important to identify the level of detail that is being considered when describing the symmetry properties.

Different aspects of simple and, occasionally, not so simple geometric principles are involved in forming the motifs. Key patterns are constructed, primarily, from straight lines mapped out on grids. Here it is necessary to understand ideas about angles and the creation of regular arrays of equal-spaced straight lines. A high level of precision is required to create regular patterns that fill panels with pre-determined shapes. Spirals are quite complex shapes although they are observed widely in naturally occurring phenomena. It is difficult to draw regular equal-spacing spirals. Some elements of the methods described earlier were probably used in Insular art. The practical approach of drawing the path of a tightly coiled string or rope provides an important freehand method of drawing spirals.

The accuracy of Insular artists in following the under-and-over rule in designs using interlacing is remarkable. Simple geometrical constructions are required to create the basic paths of the cords of the interlacing. The early artists must have based some of their ideas on braiding patterns created in woven materials. It is more difficult to envisage the creation of complex knot designs without some understanding of the break-and-join ideas. This rather formal approach is a valuable tool for understanding the important features of these designs and for creating new designs that follow the same principles. Geometric concepts are equally important in the layout and construction of zoomorphic and foliaceous patterns. Obviously there is a greater emphasis on freehand work in these designs but regular arrays of plant and animal motifs require the creation of well-defined grids. Drawing vine scrolls in tapering panels requires some precise geometric constructions.

It is not necessary to understand the underlying geometric principles to appreciate the beauty of Insular art or to admire the superb craftsmanship involved. However, the ability to describe these works is enhanced once the geometric concepts have been recognised. The use of the language of geometry allows more precise descriptions of the layout of panels and the motif patterns and is an invaluable aid in reconstructing patterns in damaged works of art.

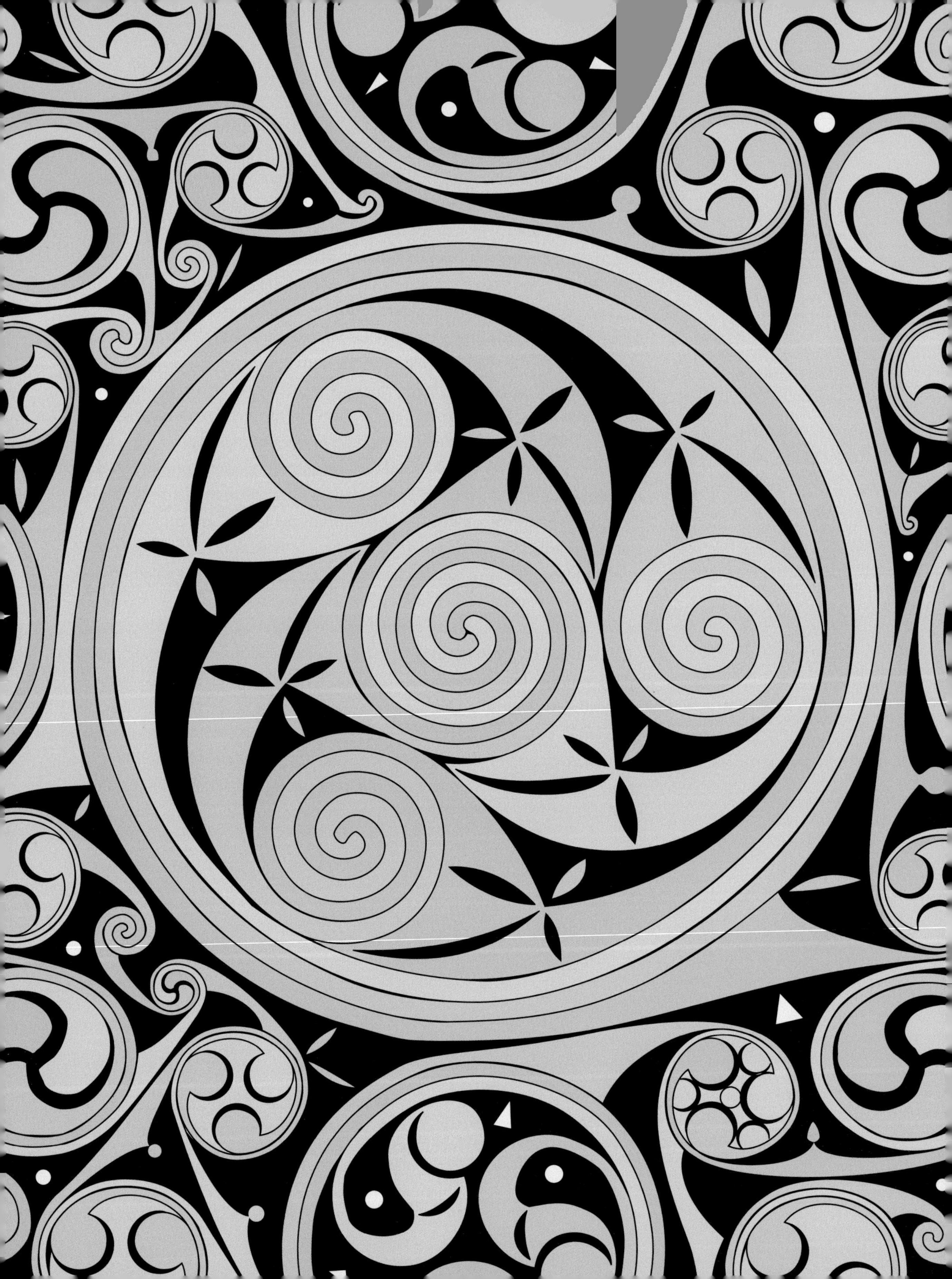

5
Transparent complexity

RULES AND COMPLEXITY

In previous chapters it has been shown that in geometric art, well-defined motifs, arranged to produce patterns obeying a variety of rules, are bounded by regular and irregular borders to form panels. This rather pedestrian description neglects many facets of Insular art, which cannot be captured in a book of this kind, that make it both original and magnificent. Nevertheless, there are aspects of this art, relating to geometric topics, which can be appreciated by a detailed exploration of illuminated manuscripts and sculptured stones. In the next two chapters ideas developed in previous chapters are used to understand and interpret some more complicated designs.

Complexity comes in many forms. In this chapter complexity that is transparent, in the sense that the details of the designs used by the artist are unambiguous and clear-cut, is considered. In Chapter 6 the emphasis is on interpreting the geometric details of manuscripts and stone monuments where, because of factors such as damage and deterioration, it is impossible to be entirely confident of the intentions of the artists. Both chapters are restricted to art that is consistent with the rules developed in Chapter 4. It is the application of these rules that makes it possible to interpret the details in very complex patterns and in work that is incomplete through damage, loss or decay.

Complexity is divided into three parts to give emphasis to different, though overlapping, issues: first, the progressive breakdown of symmetry as the scale of observation increases, so that designs that appear symmetrical and well ordered at low magnification are often full of ingenious and intriguing variations when viewed in detail at high magnification; second, the formation of patterns that are so full of detail that reproduction and unravelling is a challenging task even when it is clear that simple rules are being followed; third, the special case of crosses that are embedded in other patterns intentionally or otherwise.

CHANGES WITH SCALE

Some simple examples of changes with scale have been described in previous chapters. Figure 3.12 shows that the central panel of the Rosemarkie stone contains an equal-armed cross with a fourfold rotation point. However, the detail of the interlacing pattern is not the same in the small panels around the cross and the level of symmetry is lower. Similarly, the four crosses in the border of the St John portrait page of the Book of Kells (Fig. 4.45) have exactly the same shape, and are arranged symmetrically in the border, but there are three different interlacing patterns based on the same fine-scale grid. This approach is common to much of this art. Although the primary pattern of, for example, a cross-carpet page is based on a well-defined grid, with the finer scale design of individual panels following finer grids, the details of the patterns in the finer grids may display a range of variations. This undoubtedly helps to make the overall work intriguing, to the point of being mystical, and elevates it above the ordered and routine conformity of conventional patterns. In this section there are two examples from the Lindisfarne Gospels and the Book of Kells respectively: first, the cross-carpet page f. 210v of the Lindisfarne Gospel, described in Chapter 2, which provides an outstanding example of different levels of complexity at different scales; second, the eight-circle cross of the Book of Kells f. 33r. The details in this pattern are less accessible at a fine scale and only part of the overall design is considered.

Lindisfarne Gospels, f. 210v

It has been shown that by choosing different sequences of square-sided spirals and conventional spirals it is possible to produce subtle differences in the design of panels, as in rectangular panels (Fig. 3.2) and L-shaped panels (Fig. 3.4). Even more intriguing are the variations in the arrangement and ornamentation of the birds in the border panels that form a background to the cross and the other panels.

In her book on the Lindisfarne Gospels, Backhouse (1981) refers to a 'seething maelstrom of multicoloured birds'. If maelstrom means turbulent confusion one has to disagree, although at first sight the artist has succeeded in giving this impression. The distribution of birds is more accurately described as ordered chaos: ordered because the pattern is not random, and chaos because at no place in the pattern is it possible to predict unambiguously the orientation or decoration of the birds. As mentioned in the discussion of Fig. 3.5, there are two kinds of birds: one set has multicoloured plumage and the other has two-colour plumage. The distribution and orientation of the two sets of birds within the square grid of

Figure 5.1
Outline grid of cross-carpet page f. 210v of Lindisfarne Gospels, reproduced from Fig. 2.3, showing the orientation and distribution of two sets of birds.

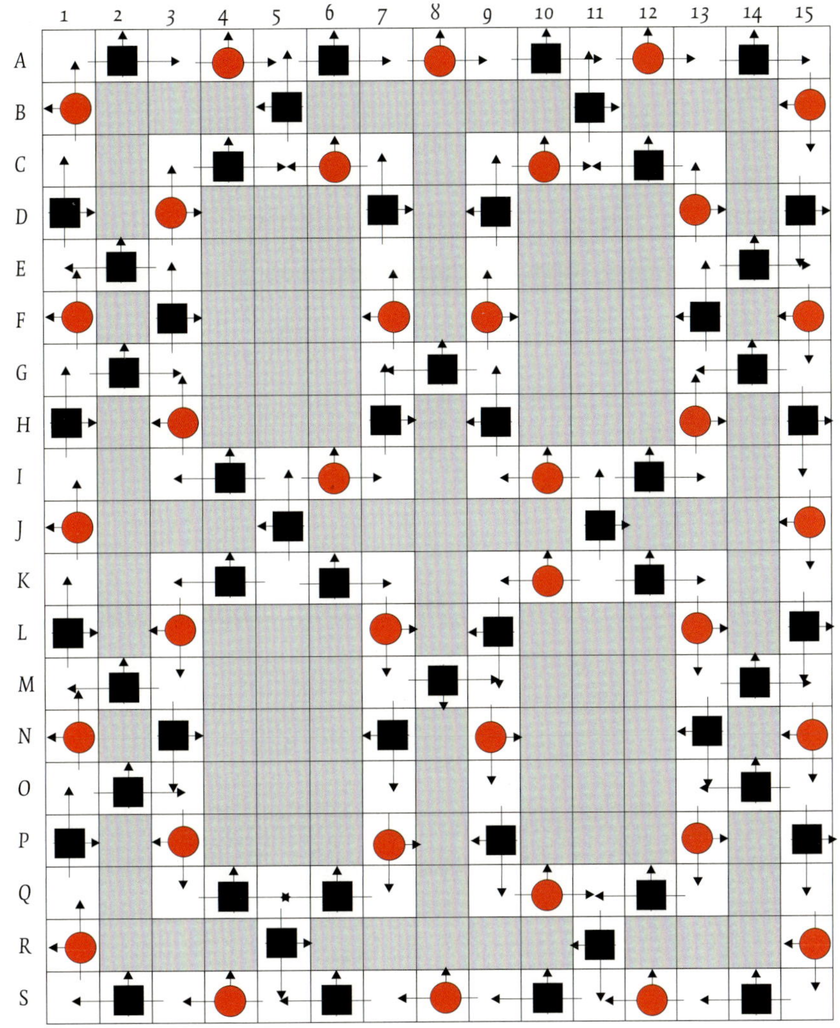

the carpet page is shown in schematic form in Fig. 5.1. An explanation of the symbols is included in Fig. 5.2; black squares represent the multicoloured birds and red circles represent the two-coloured birds. The long arrow indicates the direction that the bird is facing and the short arrow the position of the top of the bird.

Each bird takes up a row or column of three squares of the grid (Fig. 5.2a) with the body occupying the centre square. The neck and head occupy one square, as do the tail and legs. Four examples of birds showing a variety of features are shown in Fig. 5.2b. The birds are separated and are not interlaced with each other. In the actual design of the carpet page, the two outer squares overlap each other and the head and tail features of the birds interlace, as illustrated previously in Fig. 3.5. The drawing in Fig. 3.5 corresponds to squares E(1,2,3), F(1,2,3) and G(1,2,3) in Fig. 5.1.

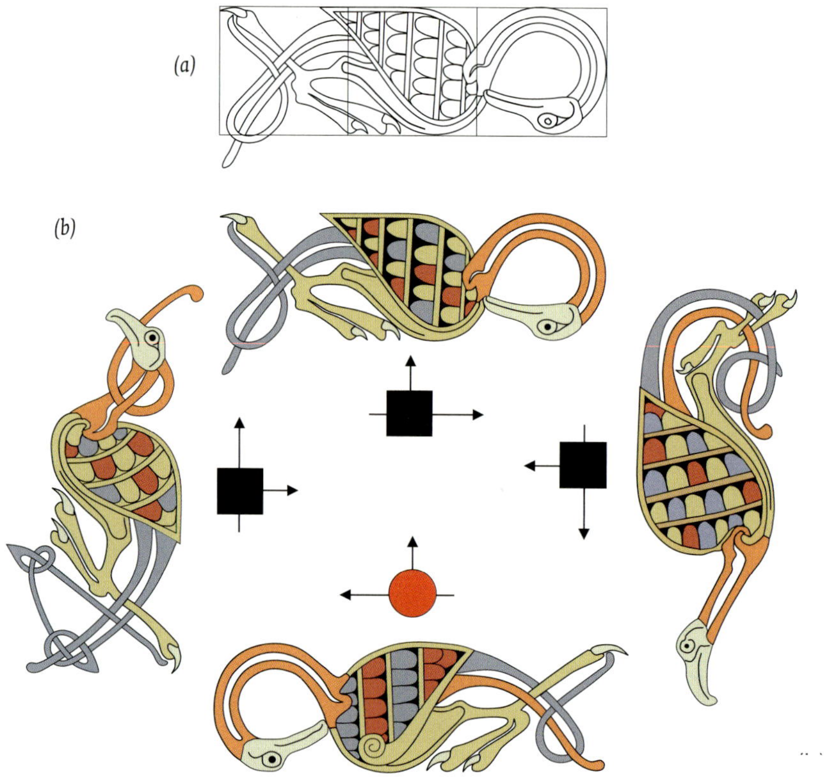

Figure 5.2
Birds of Lindisfarne f. 210v. (a) Three squares of the primary grid showing position of a bird. (b) Four birds displaying a variety of orientations and decorations. The symbols used to illustrate the orientations and decorations of the birds in Fig. 5.1 are shown alongside the birds.

In the outer squares of the main grid the two species of birds alternate perfectly around the whole of the grid and all the birds face in the same clockwise direction. Thus, for example, along the top row, squares A2, A6, A10 are filled with the bodies and wings of multicoloured birds and squares A4, A8, A12 are filled with the bodies and wings of two-coloured birds. In the top row all the birds have their backs facing to the outside whereas in the side rows the backs face inwards and outwards alternately. In the bottom row the backs of all the birds face upwards. The birds also alternate in the squares around the panels, with the exception of the bottom left-hand rectangle. Here there are two places where birds of the same set are placed side by side. The orientation of the birds around the rectangles is more complicated, but the distribution shows some symmetrical features. All the birds in the connecting squares between the outer border and the borders around the rectangular panels, such as E2, G2, G8, E14 and G14, are multicoloured with their backs facing the top, with the exception of the bird at M8, which faces downwards, and those at B5, B11, J5, J11, R5 and R11, which face to the sides.

So, although the shape and distribution of panels and finials of f. 210v have a high degree of order and symmetry, the order is not maintained to the same extent in the distribution and orientation of the birds. A further reduction in order is found when the ornamentation and shape of the birds is considered. The artist has used many different features to make each bird unique. Some of these features are illustrated in Fig. 5.2b. Most of the birds have red necks and blue tails but some have mixed red and blue necks and tails and D1 has a blue neck and B1 has a red tail. The birds at F7 and F9 have mixed green and red necks and the birds at D7 and D9 have mixed red and green tails. Some of the birds have only one tail feature and the number of toes varies between one and three. A few of the birds have a top-knot (crest or plumes). By choosing different numbers of toes, top-knots and tails, and by varying the length and amount of interlacing of these features, the artist has achieved an elegant balance of space-filling so that no part of the design looks overcrowded or empty. The choice of colours is less easy to explain. In noting that the wings of the bird at F7 have red and blue stripes without the stripes being ornamented with coloured scales or feathers, Backhouse observes that 'it seems feasible to suppose that Eadfrith [the artist] was practising the humility of avoiding absolute perfection in the mammoth task which he had undertaken'. However, there are so many variations of detail, at all levels, that this explanation seems somewhat inadequate. Equally, the quality and perfection of the draughtsmanship and skill in the painting as a whole suggests strongly that these differences in detail cannot be attributed to artistic carelessness. They add much fascination to the work and as one explores this detail one engages with the artist of the scriptorium – so much so that one often asks, why did he do this?

Book of Kells f. 33r, the eight-circle cross

The eight-circle cross is the central feature of the ornamented page (Fig. 5.3) next to the monogram page f. 34r at the beginning of the Gospel according to St Matthew. It is the only carpet page in the Book of Kells. The monogram page is widely regarded as one of the most complicated and beautiful pages of decoration ever produced. The ornamentation is so complex that it has defied reproduction by the most dedicated and skilful draughtsmen. In his book *The Book of Kells* (1920), Sullivan includes a commentary by Johan Adolf Bruun who observes, of the monogram page, that 'It is a page to discourage even the most accomplished and most enthusiastic of modern draughtsmen. In nine out of ten cases he will break down before his work is half finished...' In my view the eight-circle cross-carpet page is no less complicated in relation to the detail of the ornamentation of the cross. The complexity makes a complete representation almost impossible. Nevertheless, it can be used to illustrate how complexity increases as the scale of observation increases. To quote Henry (1967), discussing the monogram page,

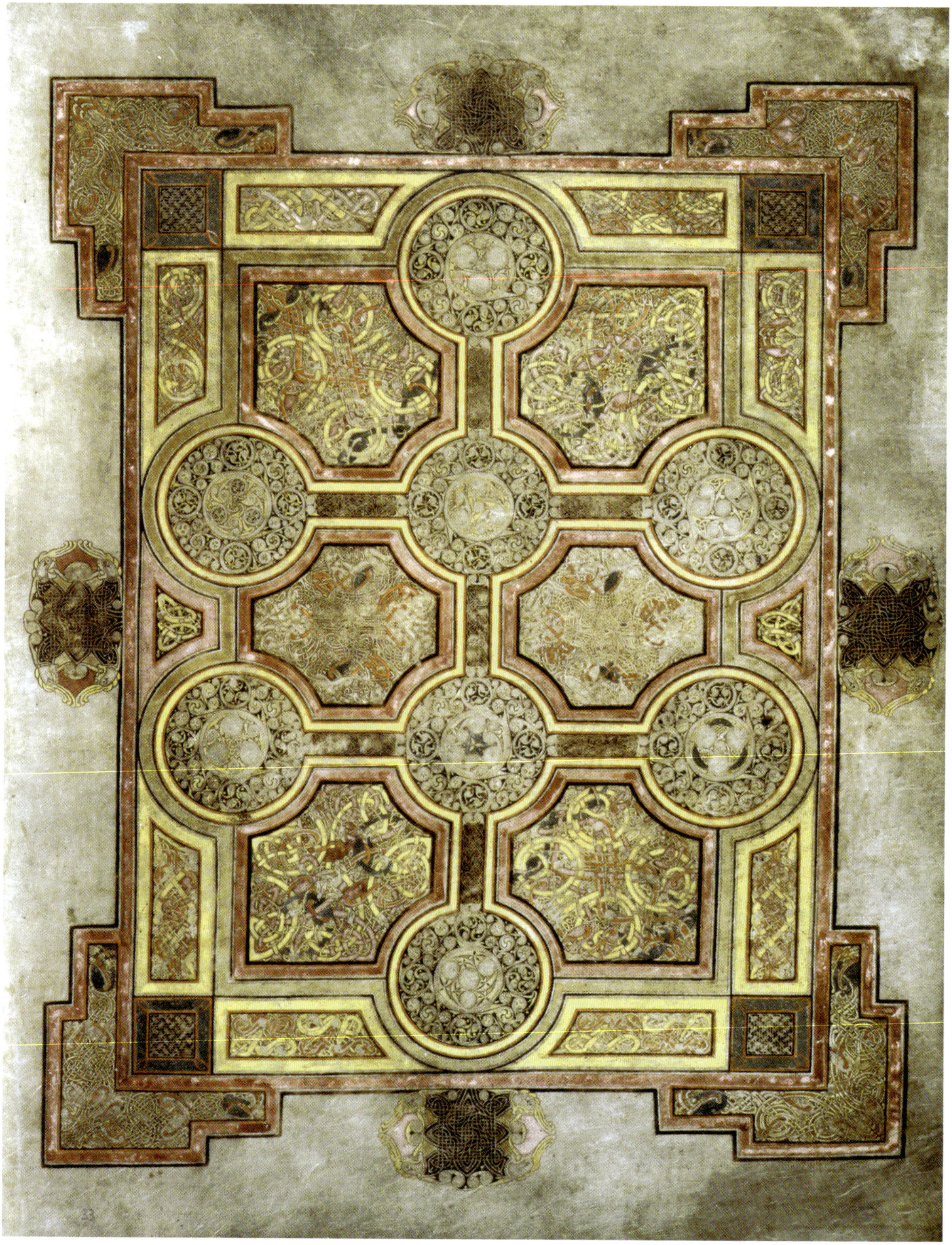

Figure 5.3
Photograph of f. 33r of Book of Kells (by permission of the Board of Trinity College Dublin).

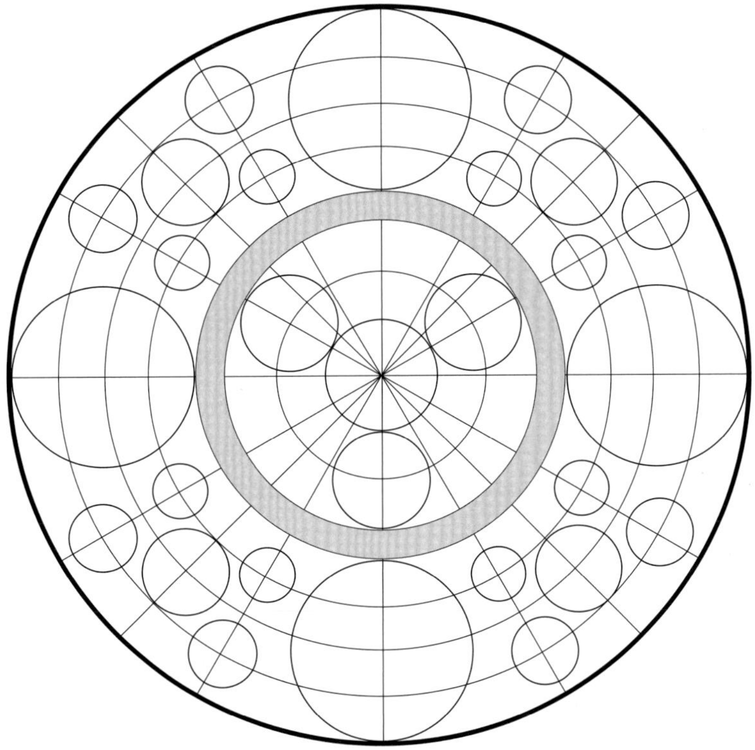

Figure 5.6
Distribution of spirals in each of the eight circles of the cross in Book of Kells, f. 33r.

Each of the large circles is filled with a swirling array of interconnected spirals. The artist has used a straightforward space-filling approach with progressively smaller spirals filling the spaces between larger spirals. Beyond the stage represented in Fig. 5.6 there are even smaller spirals arranged in a more random manner.

The details of the ornamentation are significantly different in the large circles beyond the primary configuration. Figure 5.7 shows the spiral design in the bottom circle of the cross. This illustration has some elements of interpretation and is shown without the connecting arm containing the interlacing pattern. It was developed from first principles using the rules set out in Chapter 4. The overall design conforms to the Kells original and the details of the spiral connections are fully consistent with the geometric requirements. However, the work in Kells is on such a fine scale, as can be seen from the dimensions shown in the caption to Fig. 5.7, that it was not possible to resolve and reproduce accurately some of the detail, such as the number of coils in many of the spirals and the patterns in the centre of the spirals.

Each of the three spirals around the central spiral is connected to the central spiral by S-shaped connections and to spirals in the outer border by C-shaped connections, which spiral round the central group. The threefold symmetry of the central region is retained even when the detail of the design is included. However, this threefold arrangement is not compatible with the

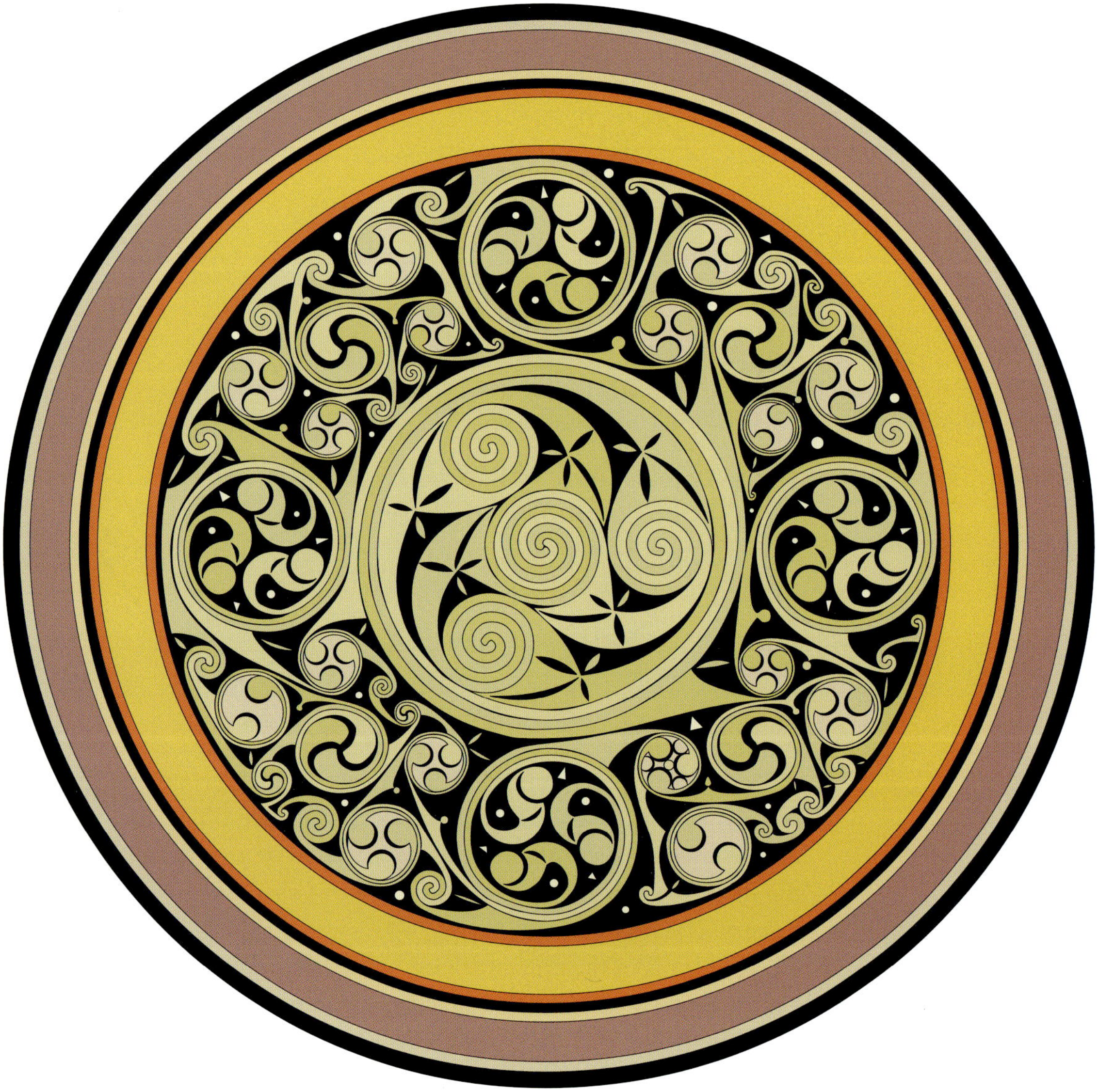

Figure 5.7
Complete design of bottom circle of eight-circle cross in Book of Kells, f. 33r. The arm, ornamented with interlacing, joining this circle to the next has been omitted. Diameter of outer circle is 50mm.

fourfold order of the border, so it is inevitable that the details of the patterns in the four quadrants of the border are different, albeit with some intriguing repetitions and symmetry as well as unexpected irregularities. Although the eight circles have the same overall arrangement of spirals there are numerous distinctive features that make each of the designs unique. The artist has used a whole range of small changes in drawing the patterns at the fine scale, which gives the work, as a whole, an intriguing impression of complexity and abstraction. It is as though the detail can, at one and the same time, be grasped and yet be beyond grasping.

TRANSPARENT COMPLEXITY

Four examples are considered in this section to illustrate different aspects of complexity achieved by Insular artists. In reproducing the work of these early artists one can never be fully confident that the intentions of the artists have been understood, but in the following examples there is little ambiguity and the details are consistent with the rules outlined in Chapter 4. Some of the most sophisticated interlacing designs are to be found on the Pictish sculptured stones of Class II (Chapter 3). According to Allen and Anderson (1903) the three circular designs on the lower part of the Aberlemno No. 2 cross (Chapter 4) are 'the most elaborate interlacing patterns in sculptured stone work'. The cross also has other panels ornamented with less complicated interlacing patterns and two panels with a key pattern that has an element of complexity not considered so far in this book. Accordingly, the first example is a fairly detailed account of Aberlemno No. 2 including an extension of the application of the breaking and rejoining approach to the design of panels filled with interlacing. The second example is the six-square cross (f. 2v) in the Lindisfarne Gospels that illustrates the use of a key pattern on a fine scale. The distribution of colours in the key pattern strongly influences the appearance of the cross. The configuration of the elementary motifs has produced an interesting example relating to ideas of continuity, which may or may not have been in the mind of the artist. The final two examples are also from the Insular manuscripts (Lichfield Gospels and Lindisfarne Gospels) and are used to illustrate the complexity achieved using designs based on zoomorphic interlacing.

Aberlemno No. 2 cross-slab

The sculptured stone cross-slab, referred to by Allen and Anderson as Aberlemno No. 2 (Fig. 5.8), is in a churchyard in Aberlemno in the east of Scotland. Even though it is exposed to the weather it is well preserved and most of the detail of the design is evident. Nowadays it is covered in the winter for protection. The cross on the front face has been carved so that it stands out in relief from the main part of the sandstone slab. The remainder of the face is decorated with some simple, yet elegant, zoomorphic interlacing. On the back face there is a battle-scene with figures on foot and on horseback. At first sight the cross appears to have a simple shape but this is misleading. In particular, there are two features of the shape, illustrated in Fig. 5.9, which must have influenced the development of the ornamentation of the panels. First, the side arms are not perfectly rectangular or aligned to the main axis of the cross, so that the simple key pattern had to be modified to fit the space in the panel. Second, although the top panel is rectangular,

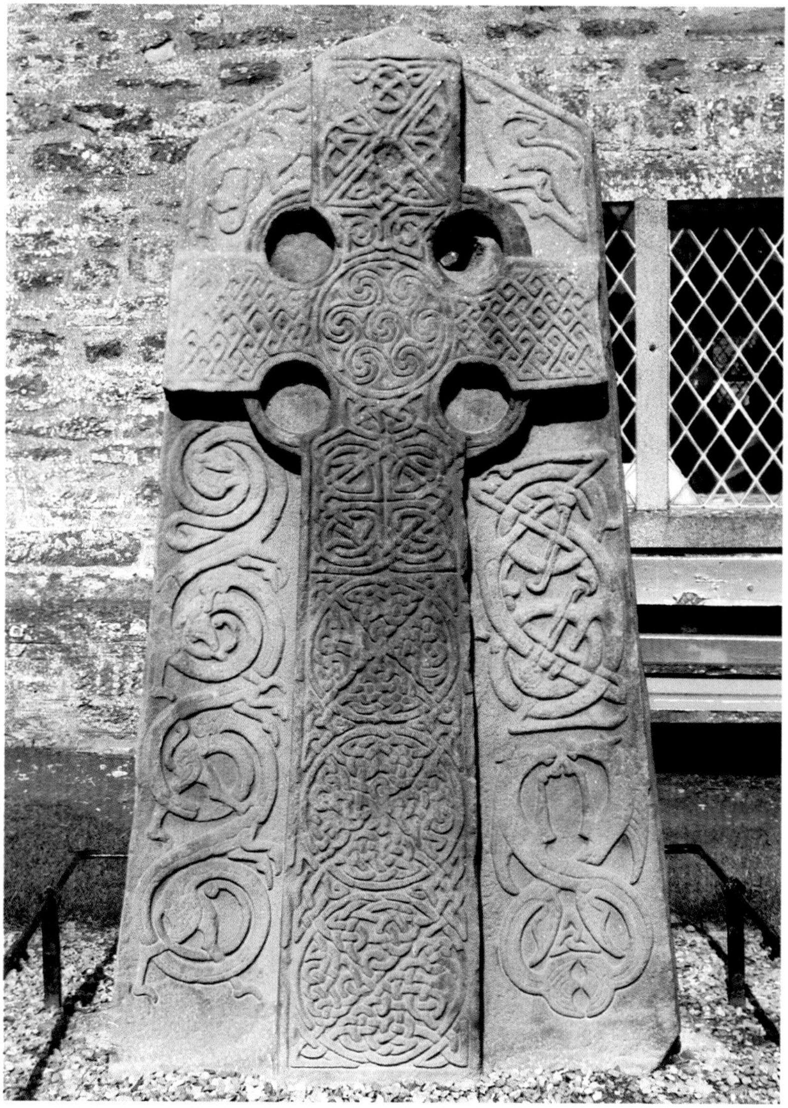

Figure 5.8
Front face of sculptured cross-slab in churchyard at Aberlemno (Aberlemno No. 2).

the main shaft of the cross, below the central spiral, tapers ±2° so that the size of the three circular panels (F, G and H) increases progressively towards the base. The details of the spiral design (marked C in Fig. 5.9) in the central panel have been described in Chapter 4. In this section emphasis is given to the development of interlacing designs, particularly in the panels marked A, F, G and H, and the key pattern in the panel marked D.

The principles used in the ornamentation of panels with interlacing designs are the same as those used for borders. The starting point is a grid with setting-out lines. In more complicated interlacing designs, the grid may include both curves (usually segments of circles) as well as straight lines. The approach is illustrated in the relatively simple design in Fig. 5.10. The basic

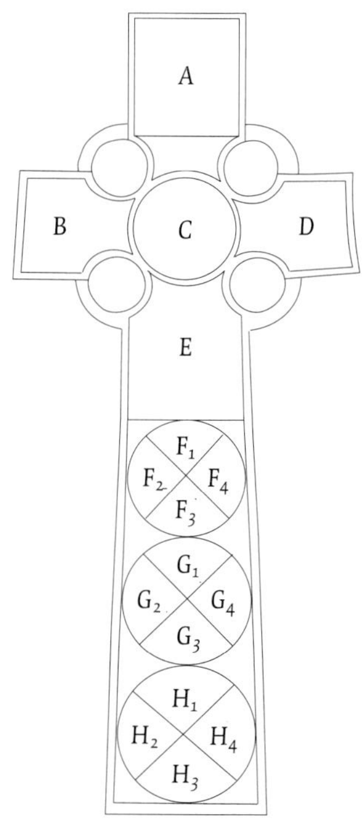

Figure 5.9
Outline of Aberlemno No. 2 showing shape of cross and distribution of main panels.

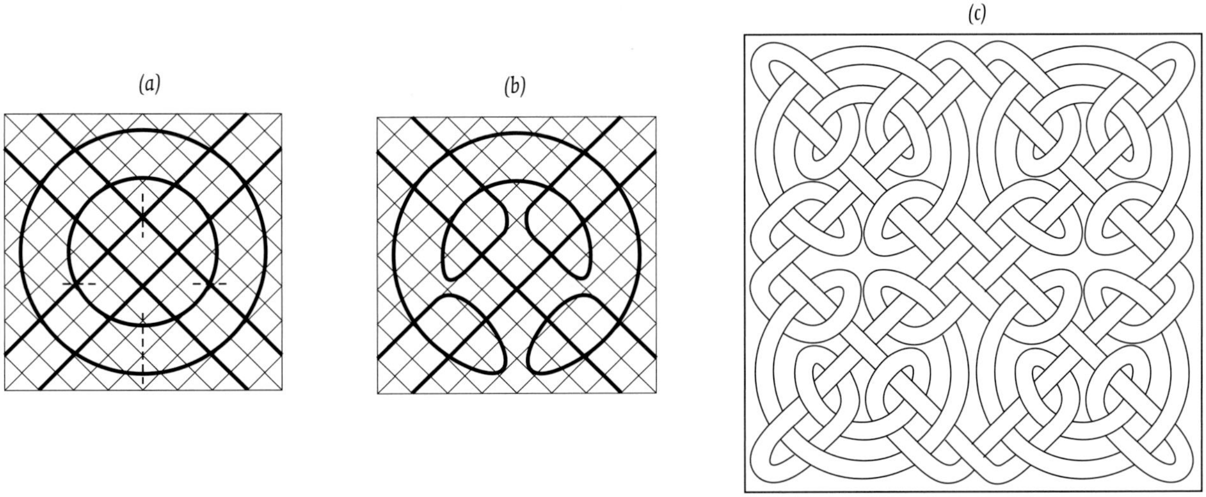

Figure 5.10
Development of a panel ornamented with an interlacing design. (a) Grid and setting-out lines. (b) Example of a pattern formed by breaking and joining. (c) Final design for a panel using the unit pattern in (b).

unit of the pattern in Fig. 5.10c is shown in Fig. 5.10a on a diagonal square grid. The pattern is developed from two sets of diagonal straight lines and two concentric circles. Breaking and rejoining the lines at the positions marked by the dashed lines and smoothing the curves produces the pattern in Fig. 5.10b. The final design is achieved by combining four of these basic units. Numerous different patterns can be drawn from the same set of lines by selecting different breaking and rejoining positions and combining the basic units in different ways.

Identifying the grids used for the more complicated interlacing designs used in Aberlemno No. 2 is more difficult and it may be that much of the work was done freehand. Panel A at the top of the cross is rectangular. The pattern (Fig. 5.11a) can be divided into four triangular segments with matching top and bottom segments and matching left and right side

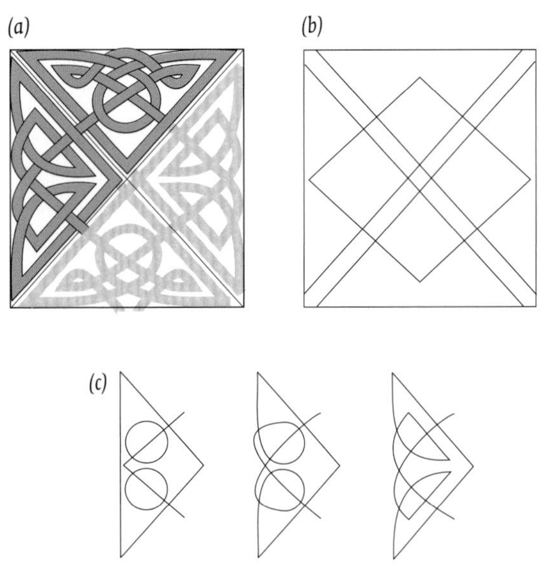

Figure 5.11
An approach to construction of design of top panel (A) of Aberlemno No. 2. (see Fig. 5.9). (a) Panel divided into four segments showing two designs with and without interlacing. (b) Setting-out lines. (c) A breaking and joining sequence to produce the design used in the left- and right-hand segments.

segments. The overall pattern is based on the outline in Fig. 5.11b but this is not sufficient to form the interlacing pattern. One possible approach to producing the pattern in the side segments is shown in Fig. 5.11c. It involves breaking and rejoining followed by reshaping to produce an aesthetically pleasing arrangement.

The interlacing design in panels F, G and H is even more complicated. Each of the circles can be divided into four segments or quadrants as shown in Fig. 5.9. The following description, based on that given by Allen and Anderson, reflects the skill and precision of Allen's work in unravelling the detail of these patterns. The pattern consists of three circular triangular knots repeated in a vertical column, the spandrels being filled with a separate knot design. The pieces of interlaced work (Fig. 5.11), which fill the upper and lower quadrants of all three circles, (F_1, F_3, G_1, G_3, H_1, H_3), are the same. In the case of the upper quadrant of the middle circle, two of the cords cross over into the adjoining quadrant on the left; and in the case of the lower quadrant of the bottom circle two of the cords cross over into the adjoining quadrant on the right. The interlaced work in the left-hand and right-hand quadrants of the upper circle (F_2, F_4) differs, one to the other, but corresponds with the circle next below it (G_2 and G_4 respectively). The interlaced work in the right- and left-hand quadrants of the bottom circle (H_2, H_4) differ from each other and from all the rest. Thus five distinct designs of interlaced work are used for filling twelve quadrants, one design being repeated six times, two others twice, and the remaining two used only once. It is clear therefore that, notwithstanding the apparent complication of the arrangement of cords, the design was not arrived at by any haphazard method, but was carefully thought out beforehand. The slight variations prevent absolute uniformity, and yet at the same time do not detract from the beautiful effects derived from apparent symmetry and rhythmic repetition.

The overall design of the cross with panels filled with interlacing, spirals and key patterns is shown in Fig. 5.13. The interlacing pattern in the upper and lower quadrants of all the circles can be constructed from a set of smaller circles (Fig. 5.12a). Inserts in the corners between the circles (spandrels) complete the pattern. Figure 5.12b-c shows that the pattern of the lower quadrant is the same as that of the upper quadrant and is related to it by a 180° rotation. Incidentally, the interlacing shown in the right-hand quadrant of the lower circle (H_4), and the associated spandrel, is not the same as that illustrated in Allen and Anderson. In this part of the stone the detail is not so clear because of damage but there can be little doubt that the drawing shown in Fig. 5.13 is closer to the original than the interpretation used by Allen and Anderson.

The design of the key pattern in the arms of the cross raises more fundamental matters of interpretation and can be used to illustrate the

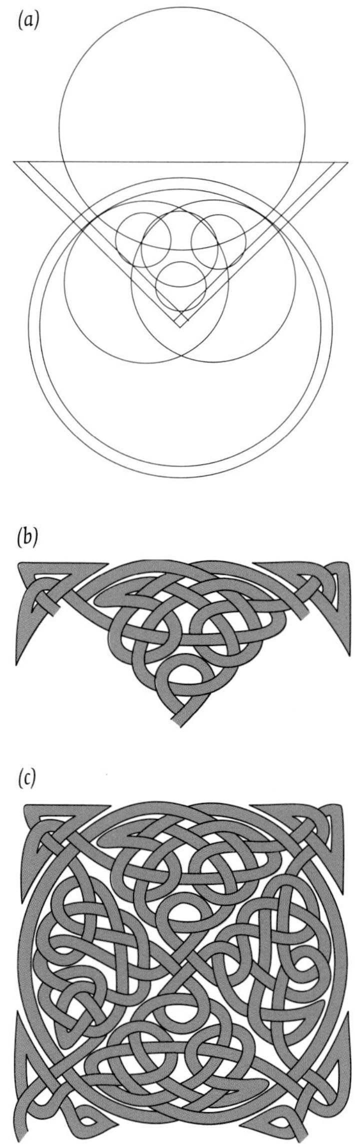

Figure 5.12
Interlacing design of panel F (see Fig. 5.9) of Aberlemno No. 2. (a) Set of circles used in construction of interlacing. (b) Interlacing pattern in quadrants F_1 and F_3. (c) Full interlacing pattern.

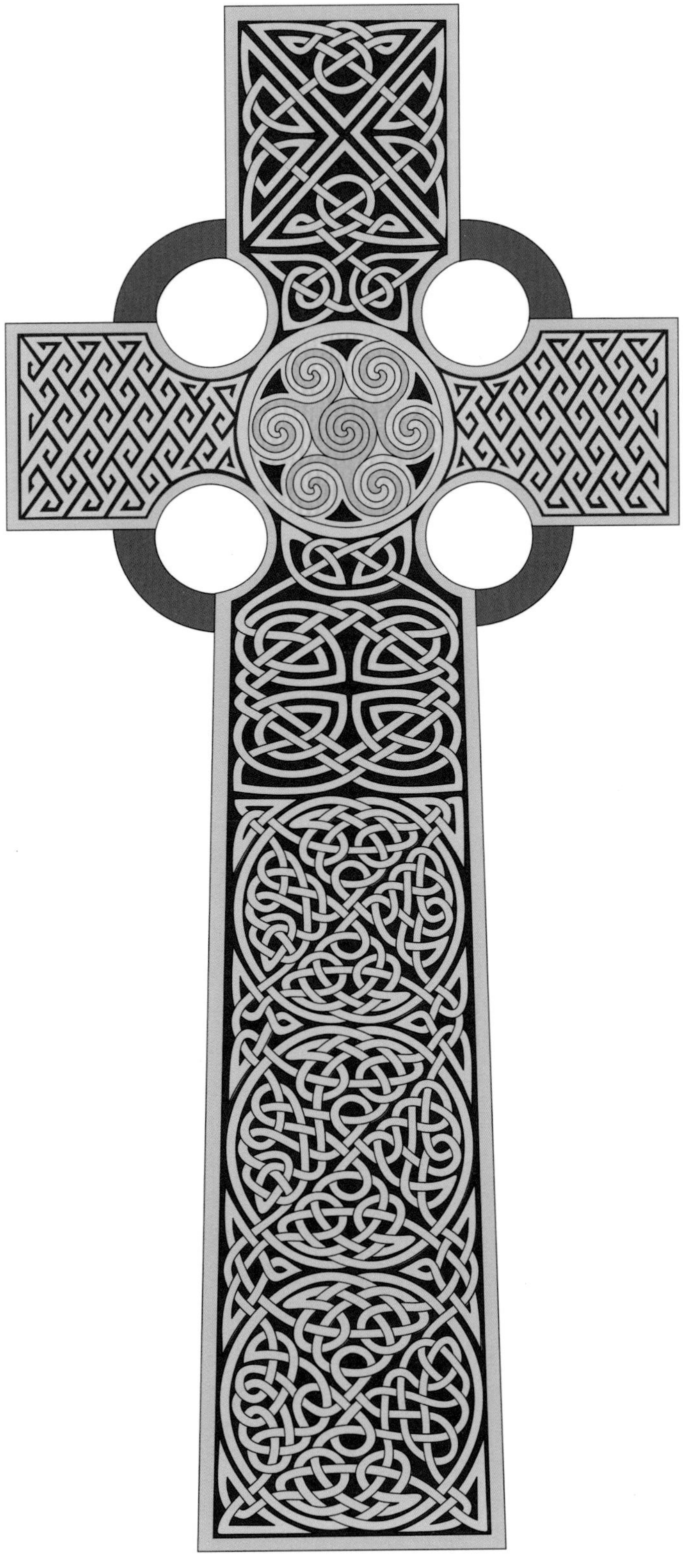

Figure 5.13
An impression of the complete design of the front face of Aberlemno No. 2. Note that the arms are shown as symmetrical and rectangular whereas in the actual cross they are not so.

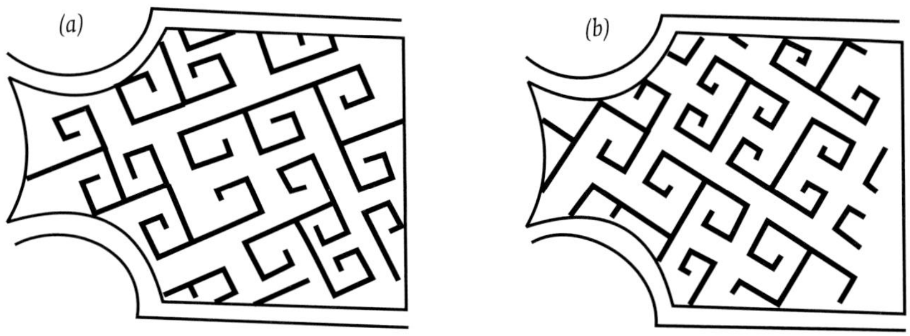

Figure 5.14
Examples used by George Bain (1951) to illustrate what he refers to as 'travesties of Pictish art', from (a) Sculptured Stones of Scotland Vol. 1, *Stuart (1858), and (b)* Stone Monuments of Angusshire, *Chalmers in Jones (1856).*

difficulties of reproducing these designs for those who do not have some understanding of the principles involved. As noted earlier, in describing the spiral pattern at the centre of the Aberlemno cross (Chapter 4), George Bain was highly critical of early attempts to illustrate the patterns on sculptured stones. He was particularly critical of the two attempts shown in Fig. 5.14 to illustrate the key patterns in the right-hand arm of the Aberlemno cross. They are, indeed, very crude and were not drawn with any real insights into the way that these patterns are developed. A cursory examination of the photograph in Fig. 5.8 suggests that the right-hand arm of the cross has a regular, geometrically satisfying key pattern constructed in an organised way from a simple unit motif. That it is not quite so straightforward is evidenced by the problems of earlier illustrators; even Bain's interpretation is not entirely satisfactory.

The pattern shown in Fig. 5.13 was produced using methods of construction similar to those used to ornament the rectangular panel in the Lindisfarne Gospels, f. 210v (Fig. 3.2) and the crescent-shaped panel on Rosemarkie No. 1 cross-slab (Fig. 3.17), with some important differences. The initial unit is formed from two straight-sided spirals on a square grid with a 1:2:3:4:5 sequence (Fig. 5.15a). The shape in Fig. 5.15b was produced either by repeating the sequences on a diagonal grid, with two sets of equal-spaced parallel lines at 74°, or by transforming the original shape (Fig. 5.15a) by rotating 45° and then scaling such that vertical dimensions increased by the ratio 4/3 compared with the horizontal dimensions. This transformation produces an angle θ of 74°. The final pattern (Fig. 5.15c) is produced from an array of units and is in two parts. The upper group (coloured blue) has the same arrangement as the lower group (coloured red). The two groups are related to each other by a rotation of 180°.

This pattern was fitted to the shape of the panel shown in outline in Fig. 5.15c. To match the actual design and the shape of the arm the angle θ has to be 74°. Any other angle requires a different shape of panel. This is clearly demonstrated in Bain's interpretation of this design. For his illustration he used a value of θ of about 80° and the resulting panel has a different shape

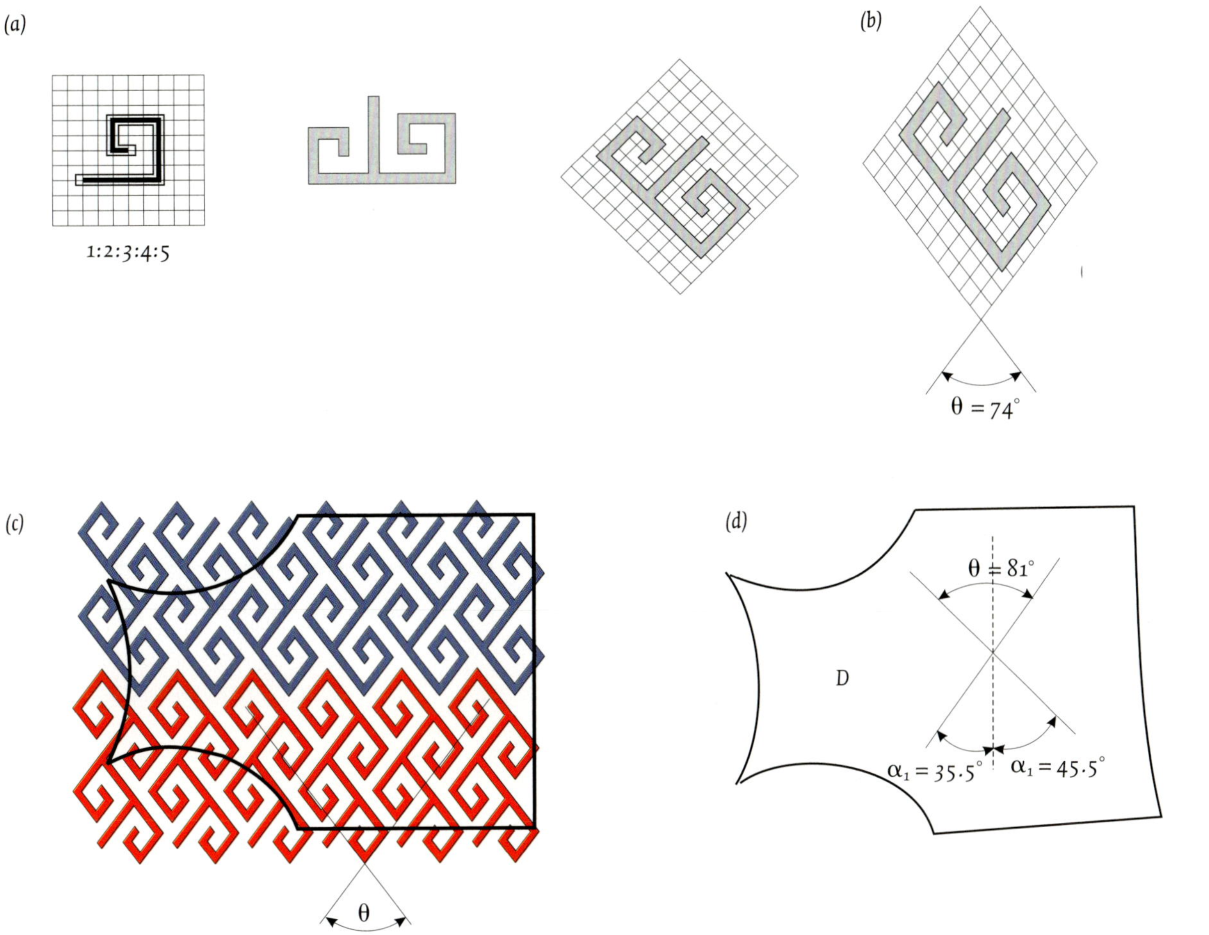

Figure 5.15
Development of key pattern for right-hand side of cross on Aberlemno No. 2. (a) Unit motif based on two 1:2:3:4:5 square spirals. (b) Change of shape of unit motif to match pattern on stone cross. (c) Array of unit motifs set in the shape of the panel. (d) Corresponding shape and angles taken from actual sculpture.

from that of the right-hand arm of the cross and so, in this respect, is not correct.

In reality the design on the cross is even more complicated because, as mentioned earlier, the arms of the actual cross are not truly rectangular (Fig. 5.15d) and the key pattern is not symmetrical in relation to the shape of the panel or the axes of the cross. The angle θ is about 81° but α_1 is not equal to α_2 ($\alpha_1 = 35.5°$, $\alpha_2 = 45.5°$). All these considerations mean that the basic pattern is distorted within the panel and that precise reproduction of the pattern can be achieved only by conventional tracing of a photograph or from a rubbing rather than geometric construction. One can only wonder at the intentions of the artist.

In the interpretation in Fig. 5.13, a regular pattern has been used and fitted to a rectangular panel with proportions and dimensions as close as possible to the original. The pattern on the left-hand arm of the stone is difficult to resolve because the cross-slab has been damaged and so no attempt was made to determine the fine detail of the pattern. It is closely

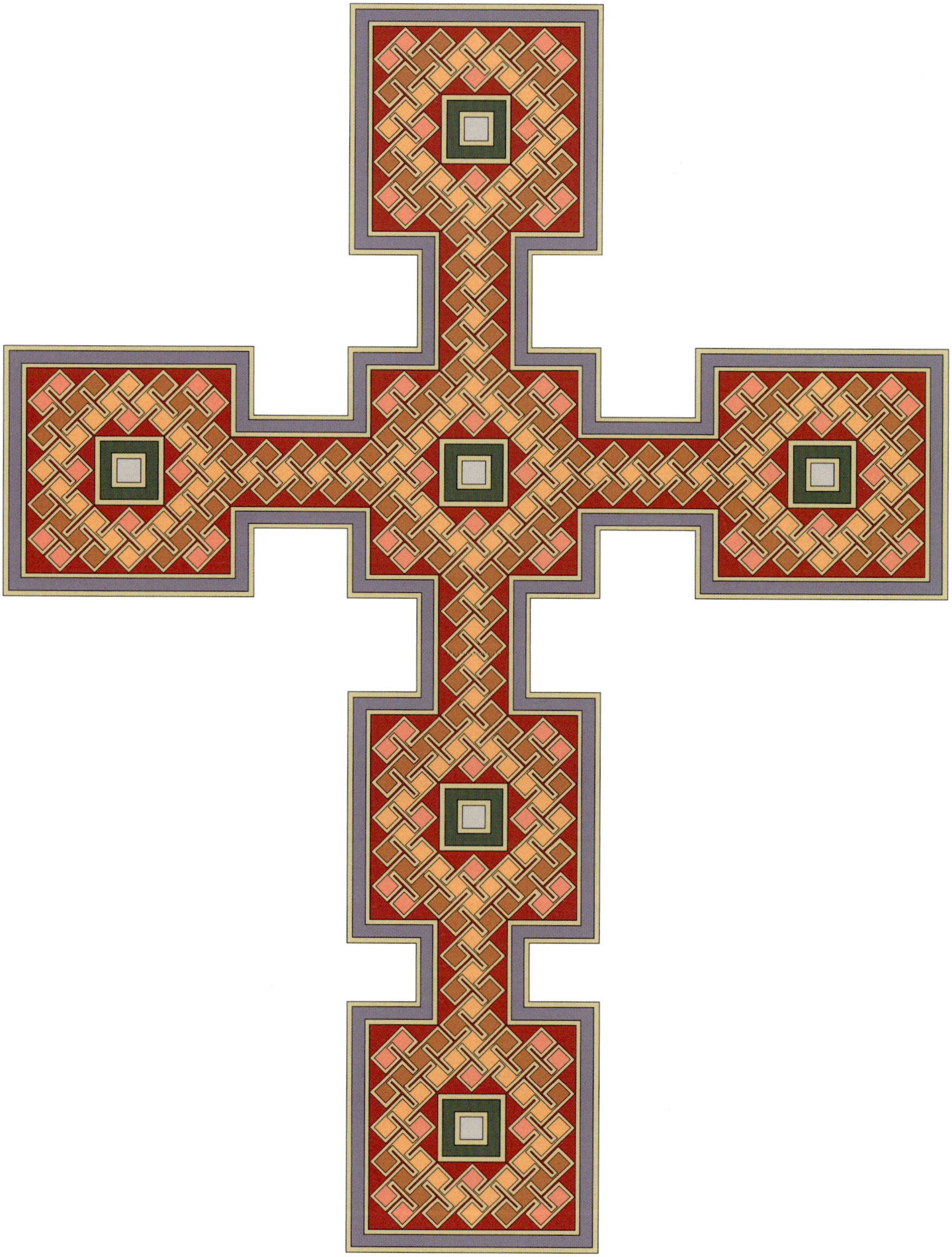

Figure 5.16
Six-square cross on cross-carpet page f. 2v of Lindisfarne Gospels.

similar to the right-hand arm and, for Fig. 5.13, it was produced by 180° rotation of the pattern in the right-hand arm.

Lindisfarne f. 2v six-square cross

The complexity of this beautiful cross, which is the central feature of the cross-carpet page introducing St Jerome's letter to Pope Damasus at the beginning of the Lindisfarne Gospels, is fully transparent although the detail of the pattern is on a very fine scale. The overall layout of the cross-carpet page is described in Chapter 2. The key pattern within the cross, shown in Fig. 5.16, can be built up using a number of different approaches. The method used in the present work is illustrated in Fig. 5.17. Each square of the cross is divided into a diagonal square grid and the key pattern forms a maze around the smaller squares (coloured red) in the grid (Fig. 5.17a). The basic unit consists of three squares that are placed diagonally and developed as in Fig. 5.17b. These units are then arranged in sequences of translations (Fig. 5.17c) and mirror reflections (Fig. 5.17d) to form the complete pattern. It is essential that the bands (coloured grey) form a continuous path, or paths, so that every

Figure 5.17
First stages in construction of key pattern for page f. 2v of Lindisfarne Gospels.

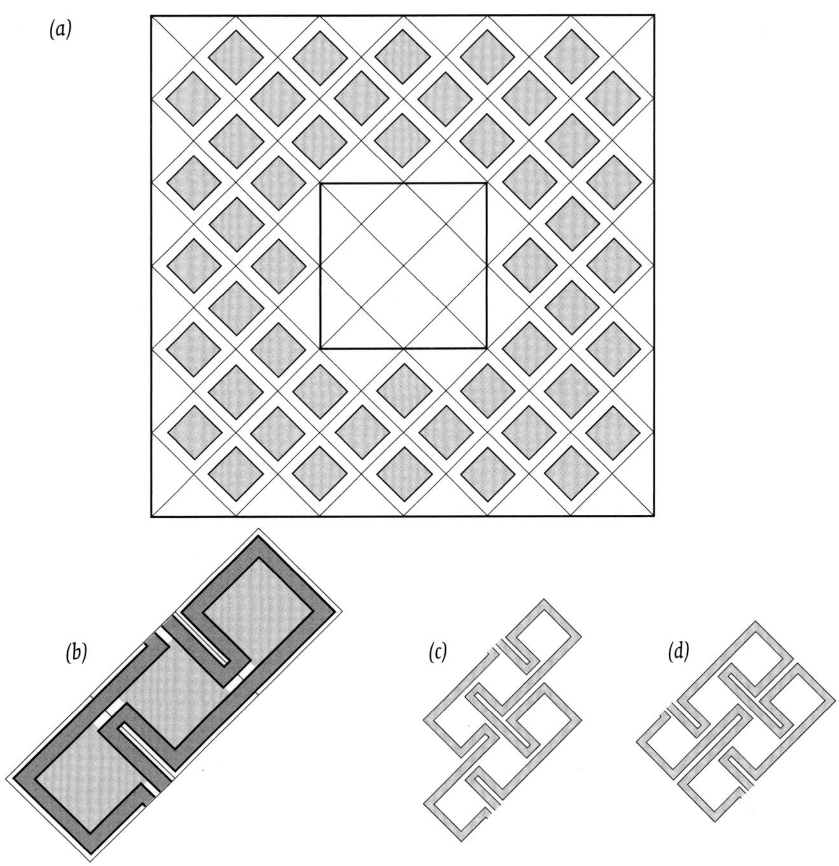

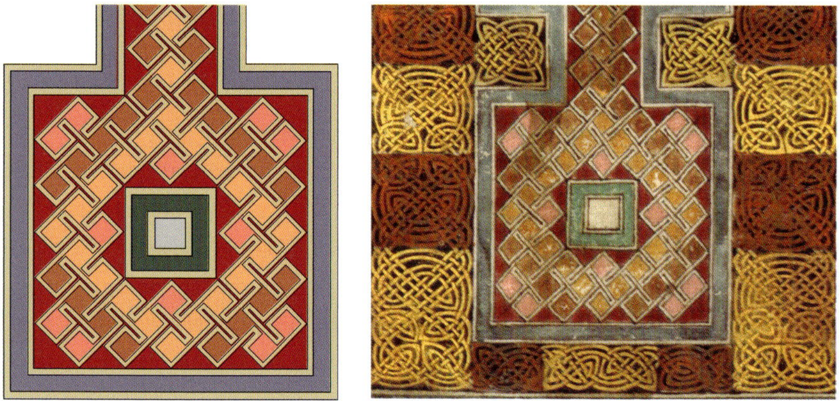

(a) (b)

Figure 5.18
Detail of key pattern in bottom square of six-square cross, f. 2v of Lindisfarne Gospels. (a) Drawing. (b) Photograph (by permission of British Library).

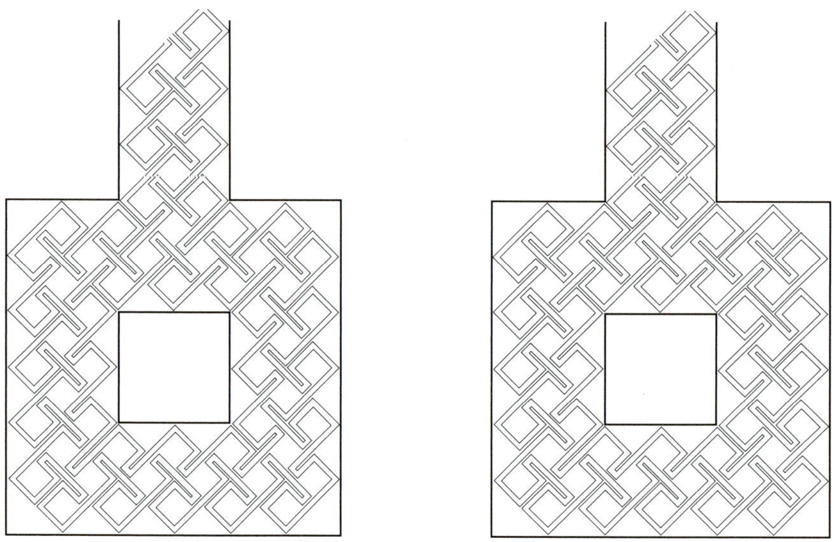

(a) (b)

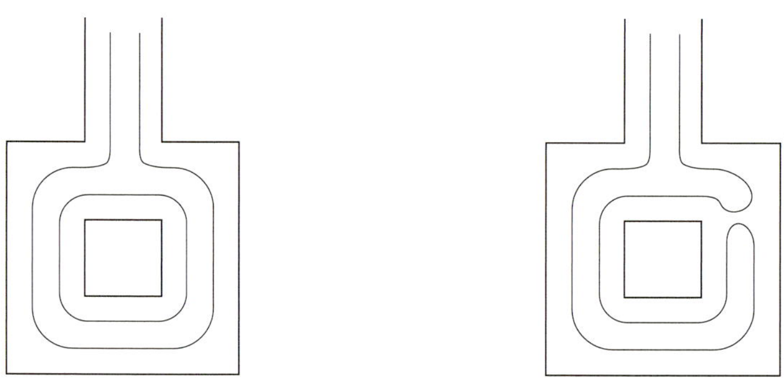

Figure 5.19
Illustration of change of paths in a maze achieved by one small change in key pattern.

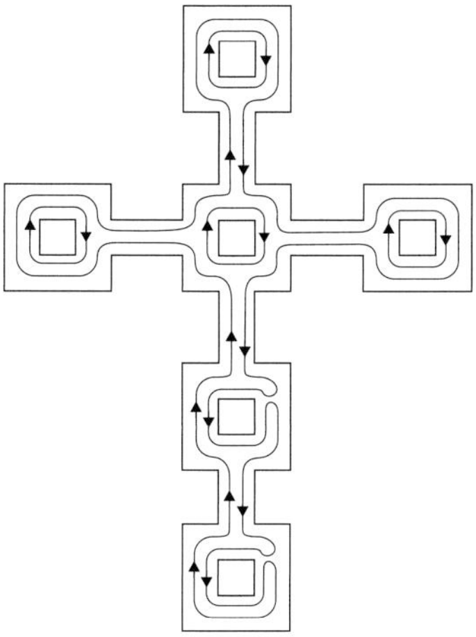

Figure 5.20
Independent paths in key patterns of the cross, f. 2v of Lindisfarne Gospels.

open end of the basic units is joined to an open end of another unit. The arrangement of the units in one of the squares of the cross is shown in Fig. 5.18a and this may be compared with the original in Fig. 5.18b. It is similar in each of the squares of the cross but there are intriguing differences.

The formation of the continuous paths of the 'maze' depends on the arrangement of the basic units and the way that they are joined together. Small changes lead to different paths in the maze. This is illustrated in Fig. 5.19 for the key pattern in the bottom square of the cross. In Fig. 5.19a there are two paths in the maze whereas in Fig. 5.19b there is only one path. This change is achieved by one small change in the joining of units in the top right-hand corner of the square. Applied to the whole of the cross this approach shows that there are five closed paths, as illustrated in Fig. 5.20. Again one can only wonder about the intentions of the artist. It seems likely, because of the simplicity and order of the paths in Fig. 5.20, that the choice of paths was deliberate.

Lichfield Gospels cross-carpet page: six-square cross

The Lichfield Gospels, dated to the middle of the eighth century, are held in Lichfield Cathedral and displayed in the Chapter House. They were probably produced at Lindisfarne but there is no real consensus among experts about this. There is only one cross-carpet page remaining. The shape of the cross is almost identical to the six-square cross of the Lindisfarne Gospels (Fig. 5.21). When the shapes of the two crosses are compared two small differences are apparent. First, in the Lichfield cross, arms of the same length separate the squares whereas the arm separating the two bottom squares of the Lindisfarne cross is 25 per cent shorter than the other arms. This difference is related to the way that the rest of the carpet-page has been designed. Second, the left-hand 'square' panel of the Lichfield cross is not square. The artist seems to have made a simple error in the setting-out stage so that the panel is longer than the other panels by an amount equal to the thickness of the border around the cross. The thickness of the border is one third of the dimensions of the squares of the primary grid. A mistake of this kind could not have occurred in the Lindisfarne cross because the detail of the key pattern defines the shape of the panels and the arms of the cross. The zoomorphic ornamentation in the Lichfield cross is quite flexible and places no such restriction on the shape of the cross.

Apart from the finials, the whole of the cross-carpet page in the Lichfield Gospel is ornamented with well-ordered zoomorphic designs of great complexity. Various kinds of birds, intricately interlaced, fill the panels and arms of the cross and interlaced birds and animals decorate the background panels around the cross. Although the interlacing is on a fine scale it is

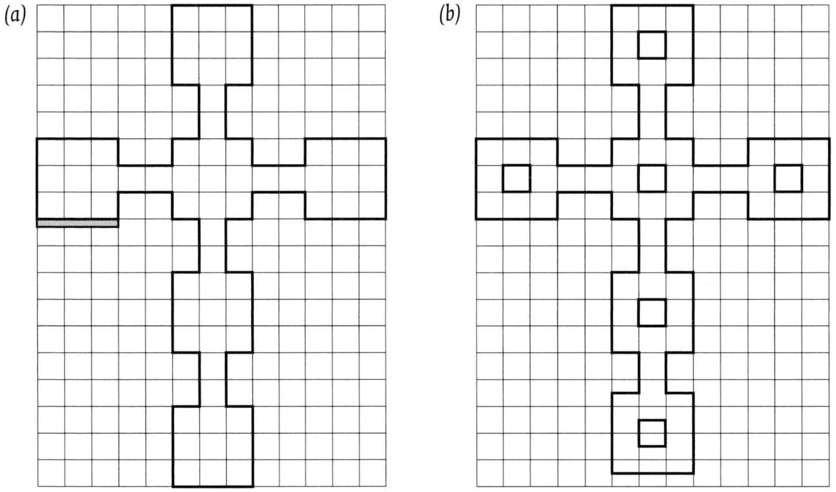

Figure 5.21
Comparison of shapes of six-square crosses. (a) Lichfield Gospels. (b) Lindisfarne Gospels f. 2v.

possible to follow the detail with considerable accuracy. There are elements of repetition and symmetry but in the fine detail the artist has used local variations in a way similar to that described in Chapter 2 for the birds of Lindisfarne f. 210v cross-carpet page. Thus, for example, the distribution and arrangement of the four interlaced birds that fill the six squares of the cross is the same for each square but there are many variations in the plumage of the birds and the patterns of interlacing surrounding them.

As an example of some of the geometric aspects of the zoomorphic interlacing consider the arrangement of the birds in the six squares. For simplicity the interlacing between the birds in the arms separating the squares with those in the squares is ignored so that each square can be treated as a separate panel. As mentioned before each square contains four birds. The birds have extended top-knots and very long necks. These form the basis for the interlacing pattern that extends throughout the panel. The most remarkable feature is that the birds are almost identical. A simple

Figure 5.22
Development of zoomorphic interlacing in panels of the six-square cross of Lichfield Gospels. (a) Layout lines. (b) Shape of a single bird. (c) Pattern formed by combining four birds in mirror orientations.

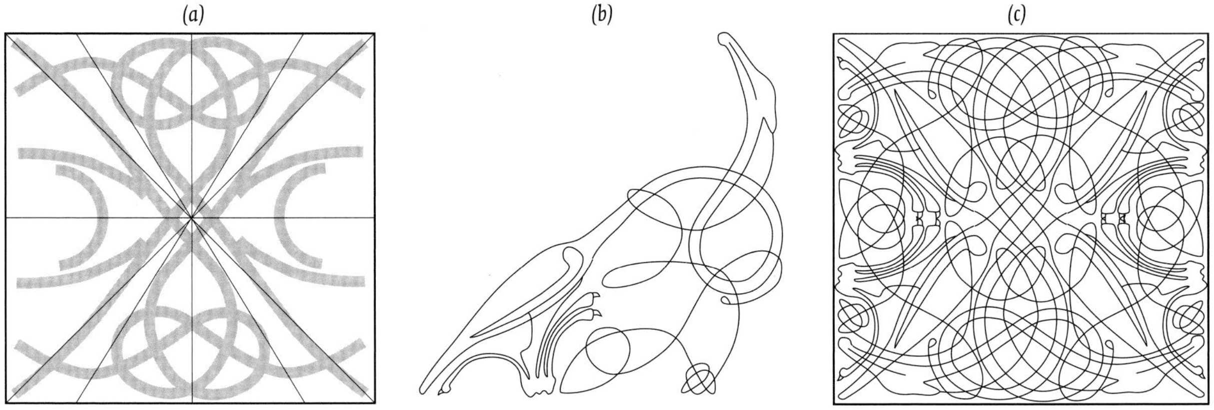

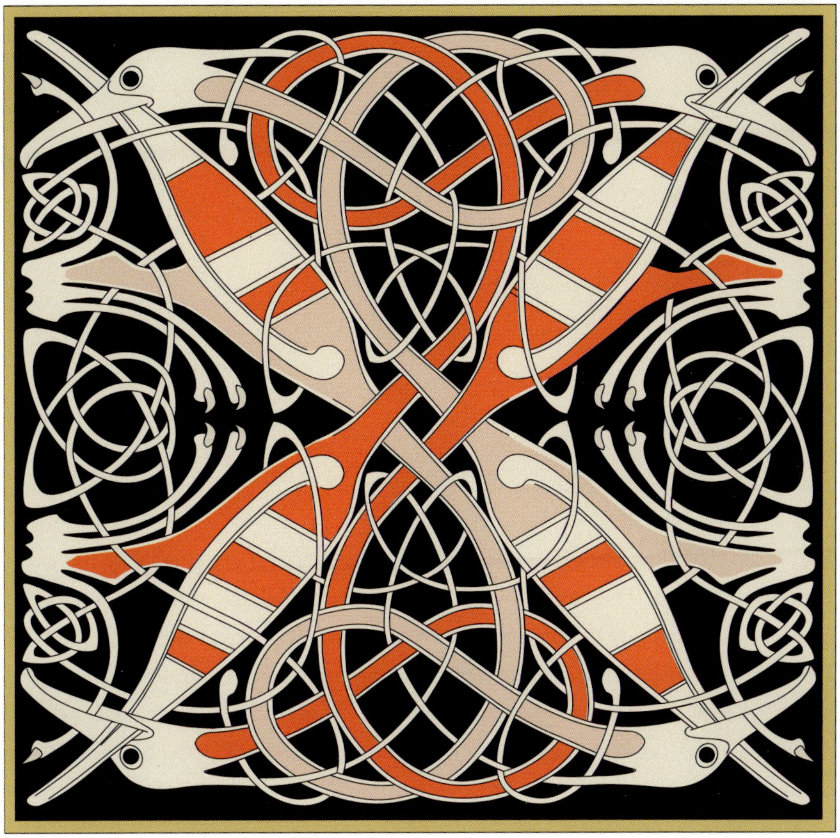

Figure 5.23
Impression of zoomorphic interlacing designs in the square panels of Lichfield Gospels. Note that interlacing with other birds in the arms between the squares of the cross has been omitted.

arrangement of setting-out lines, which can be used to construct the design, is shown in Fig. 5.22a. An outline of one of the four birds is shown in Fig. 5.22b. When this is reproduced in mirror orientation and the two birds then reproduced in another mirror orientation the pattern becomes that shown in Fig. 5.22c. In the final design all the features in Fig. 5.22c have to be interlaced, as illustrated in Fig. 5.23.

Lindisfarne Gospels, f. 26v medallion cross

Like the six-square cross in the Lichfield Gospels, the medallion cross on f. 26v of the Lindisfarne Gospels introducing the Gospel of St Matthew is ornamented entirely with zoomorphic interlacing. The surrounding panels are similarly ornamented and the finials on the border have conventional interlacing.

The cross is formed from six linked panels all based on circles (Fig. 5.24). The setting-out lines, used to locate the centre of the circles, are shown in Fig. 5.24a. Unlike the other crosses in the Lindisfarne Gospels illustrated elsewhere (f. 2v, f. 138v, f. 210v), it is not possible to identify a simple square or rectangular grid on which the pattern is based. The setting-out lines in

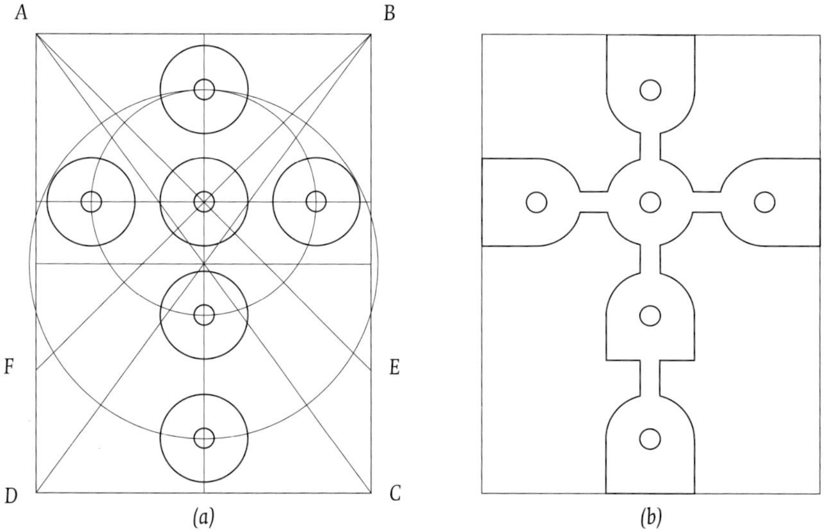

Figure 5.24
Cross-carpet page of Lindisfarne Gospels f. 26v. (a) Setting-out lines. (b) Outline of cross.

Fig. 5.24 provide a simple construction sequence and are probably the ones used by the artist. The centre of the internal frame ABCD, which excludes the border and finials, is determined from the intersections of the diagonals AC and BD. The centre of the symmetrical arrangement of five circles at the top of the cross is at the intersection of AE and BF, which lie at 45° to the sides of the rectangular frame. A circle centred on intersection AE/BF is used to locate the centres of the four circles around the central circle and another circle centred on the intersection AC/BD then locates the centre of the bottom circle. The diameter of the six circles that form the basis of the cross must have been chosen to give an aesthetically pleasing shape. This construction ensures that the distance from the centre of the four outer circles to the sides of the frame is the same so that the proportions of the related dome-shaped medallions are all the same. The connecting arms between the five top circles are all the same length. They are shorter than the arm between the bottom two circles.

The construction shown in Fig. 5.24a is not the same as that proposed by Stevick (1994). He gives a long account of a less obvious sequence of setting-out procedures and compares his proposals with those of Bruce-Mitford (see Kendrick, 1956–60), arguing that they are more convincing. However, Bruce-Mitford's work is concerned primarily with the evidence of prick-marks and other markings in relation to the methods used by the artist for the detailed zoomorphic ornamentation of the cross and the surrounding panels.

The zoomorphic patterns of the cross consist of interlaced animals resembling dogs, possibly some kind of hound. It would seem that, as with most zoomorphic ornamentation, the artist has made little effort to make the animals appear realistic. The interlaced dogs span regions within the panels and the connecting arms between the panels. The illustration in Fig. 5.25b is an example of one of the dogs, which has been 'extracted' from the cross at

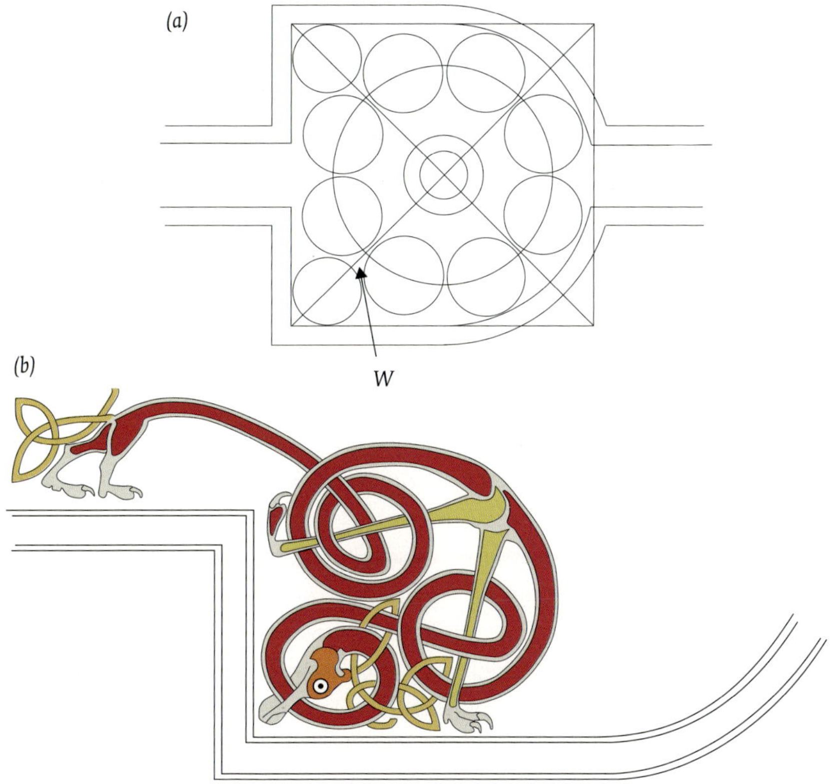

Figure 5.25
Cross-carpet page of Lindisfarne Gospels f. 26v. (a) Setting-out lines for detail in one of the medallions. (b) Four-legged animal forming part of the zoomorphic interlacing at position W in (a).

the position W in Fig. 5.25a. The laying-out lines in this diagram are the same as those shown in Bruce-Mitford's work although they were determined independently. The interlacing relates to the single animal and does not represent the interlacing in the actual artwork involving other animals.

EMBEDDED CROSSES

At the end of a substantial essay, which was the basis of his 1981 Oliver Davies Lecture, Stevenson (1981–82) makes the following observations concerning the subject of embedded crosses and related topics:

> *I should prefer to think of it as a profounder rationality, which acknowledges and demonstrates the mystery behind appearances, but by insisting on the accurate over-and-under of the strands symbolizes an underlying regularity such as the providential ordering of things; and by repeated Crosses, hidden and half-hidden as well as clear, insists on the all-pervasive presence of the victorious life-giving Redeemer.*

Stevenson considers the way that cross-shaped motifs are included in artwork of the first millennium and supposes that this is deliberate rather than the consequence of other aspects of the design. However, the extent of the deliberate use of inset and negative crosses must be a matter of conjecture. Like many other commentators on Insular art, Stevenson uses much imaginative argument. In this particular essay the emphasis is on identifying examples of embedded crosses from a wide range of sources. A few examples are described in this section where a cross can be identified with relative ease though the intention of the artist can only be presumed.

Cross-shaped features can be found in almost all designs that include elements with fourfold symmetry. By far the most common are so-called 'negative' crosses in interlacing designs. The term 'negative' is used because reversing or changing the emphasis in the patterns, using different colours, reveals the cross form. Allen and Anderson, in their description of interlacing constructions, referred to interlacing patterns derived from plaits with 'cruciform breaks' at regular intervals. There is a simple illustration in Fig. 4.41f and there are many other examples in earlier chapters. There are nine identical negative crosses in the arms of the cross at the centre of the cross-carpet page f. 210v of the Lindisfarne Gospels (Fig. 2.4). Part of one arm of this cross is reproduced in Fig. 5.26a with two negative crosses highlighted. Similarly, there are four negative crosses in one of the four crosses that form part of the border of the St John's portrait page of the Book of Kells (Figs. 4.44 to 4.47). It is possible to identify negative crosses in all the crosses in this border but the most obvious are those reproduced in the

(a)

(b)

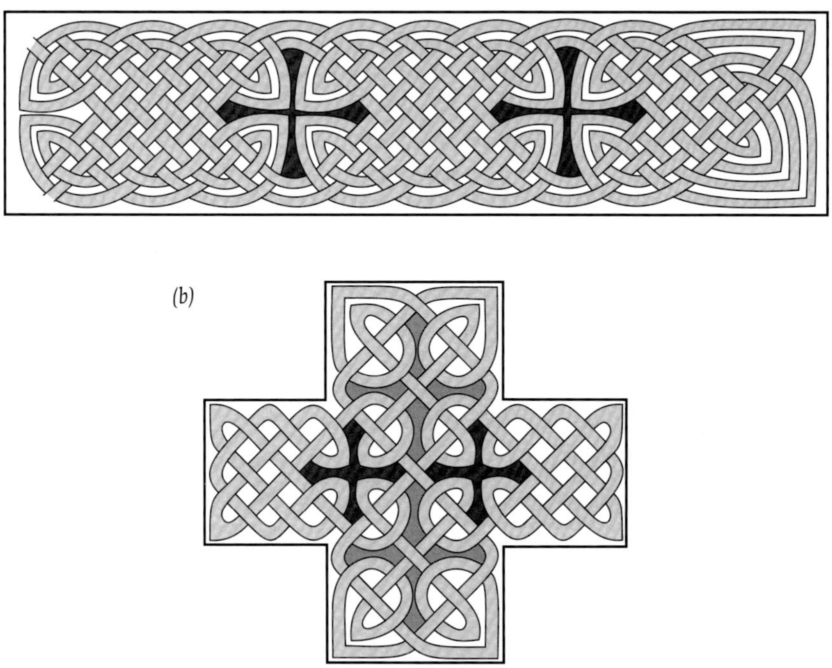

Figure 5.26
Negative crosses formed by 'cruciform breaks' in regular interlacing patterns.
(a) Lindisfarne Gospels f. 210v.
(b) Book of Kells f. 291v.

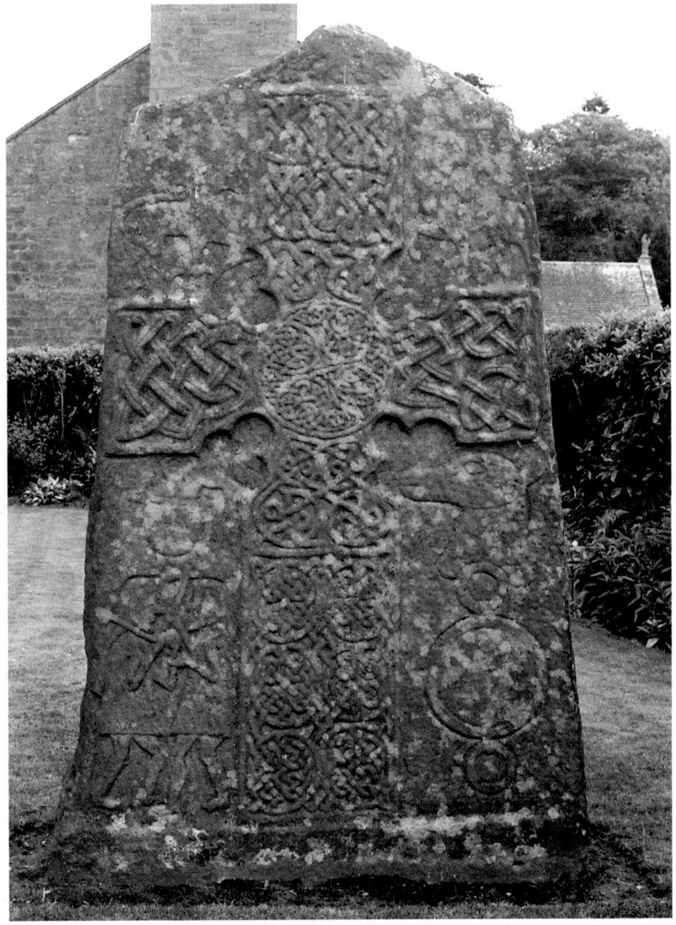

Figure 5.27
Glamis No. 2 cross-slab near Glamis Castle, Scotland.

cross in Fig. 5.26b where two different cross patterns have been highlighted.

There are also many examples of simple negative crosses in interlacing designs on sculptured stones, as for example in the panel below the central medallion of Aberlemno No. 2 shown in Fig. 5.13. A rather more complicated example is the medallion in the centre of the cross on Glamis No. 2, a red sandstone cross-slab which now stands in the garden of the old vicarage in the village of Glamis near Glamis Castle in Forfarshire, Scotland (Fig. 5.27). The cross is surrounded by carvings of animals and symbols. The panels of the cross (Fig. 5.28) are filled with a variety of interlacing patterns, some of which show negative crosses. As with Aberlemno No. 2 the arms of the cross are not exactly at right angles and the panels in the side arms are not truly rectangular. Of greater interest is the apparent lack of symmetry in the orientation of the design of the interlacing in the central medallion. The design is shown in outline in Fig. 5.28 and in more detail in Fig. 5.29. It is constructed by breaking and joining a series of circles. With and without the under-and-over interlacing the pattern has a fourfold rotation point. A negative cross has been highlighted

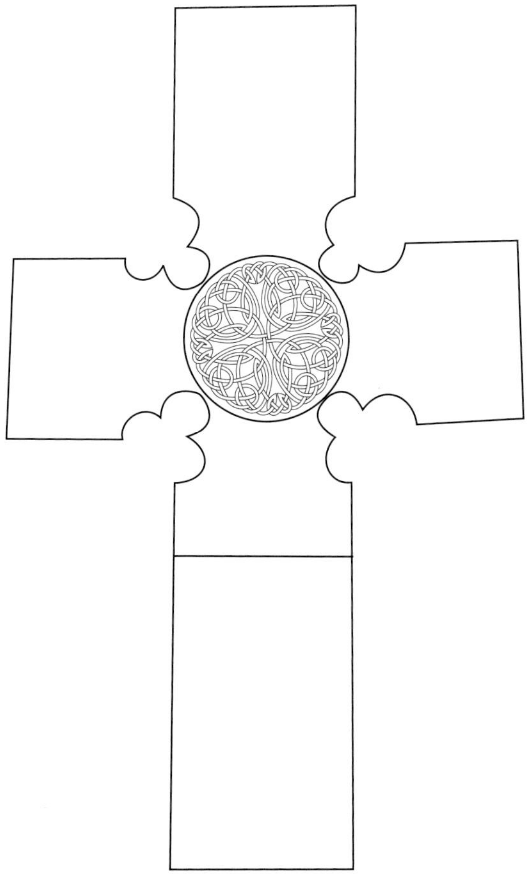

Figure 5.28
Outline of cross on Glamis No. 2 cross-slab showing shape of the non-symmetrical arms and the orientation and position of interlacing design with a negative cross.

in Fig. 5.29. The anomaly of the design is that the axes of this cross are not parallel to the axes of the main cross. The angle between the two sets of axes is about 12°. As always, one can only wonder why the sculptor produced this excellent cross-slab with such an obvious anomaly.

In the next example of embedded crosses there is little ambiguity about the intention of the artist. Figure 5.30 shows the bottom of one of the columns of the canon table (f. 12) of the St Petersburg Gospel book (Fig. 3.21). The crosses are 'embedded' in a fairly random interlacing pattern. The interlacing is of poor quality in that there is little evidence of symmetry and it is made up of many independent cords, showing many changes of colour in individual cords.

The interpretation of the example illustrated in Figs. 5.31 to 5.34 is less clear. The shapes of the crosses are similar to those in the St Petersburg Gospel but the intention of the artist is obscure. The design is from the carpet page f. 248r of the Book of Durrow. In the magnificent facsimile edition (Luce, 1960), the leather covering of volume 1 has been embossed with this design. The pattern is based on a primary grid, five squares wide by eight squares long, and consists of a trellis of rectangular interlacing (Fig. 5.32). The trellis is based on a secondary grid of diagonal squares (Fig. 5.33)

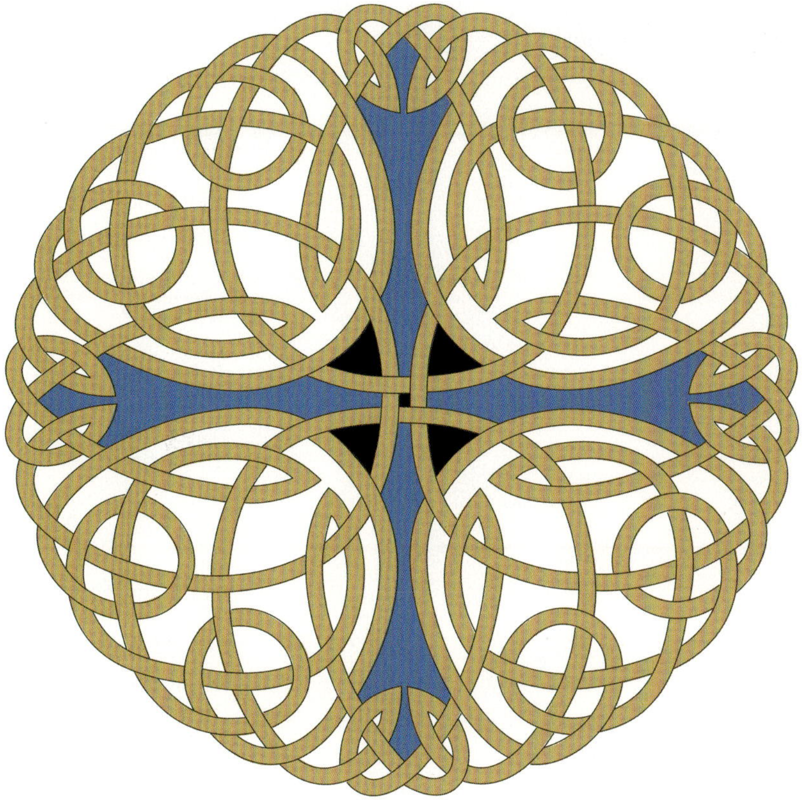

Figure 5.29
Negative cross in interlacing design in the central medallion of Glamis No. 2 cross-slab. The pattern is shown on the cross-slab.

producing seven rows of diagonal crosses with four crosses in each row. As noted by Meyer (see Luce, 1960) in his description of this carpet page, 'the stocky shape of the crosses almost degrades the symbolism; it might be intentional, but it might be nothing more than the space left between the band-ornament'. As a piece of ornamentation this carpet page does not

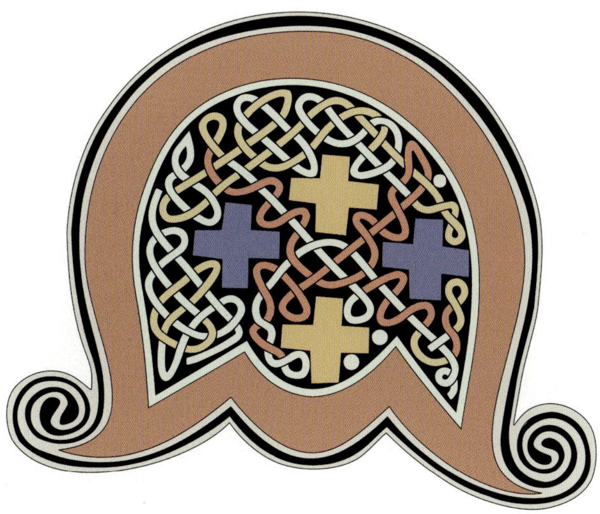

Figure 5.30
Conventional equal-armed crosses embedded in random interlacing in one of the panels at the foot of the column in the canon table of St Petersburg Gospel book, f. 12, (see Fig. 3.21).

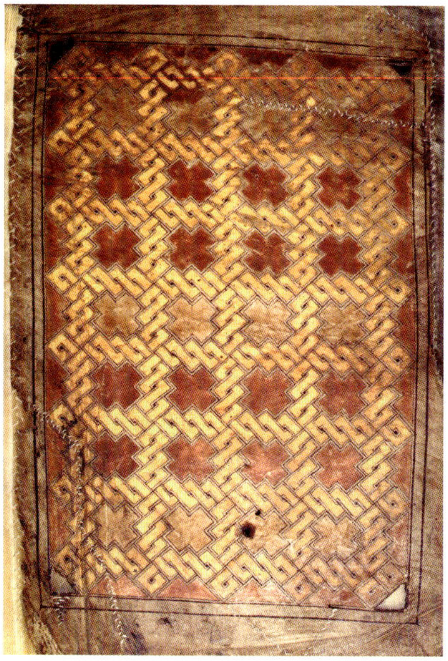

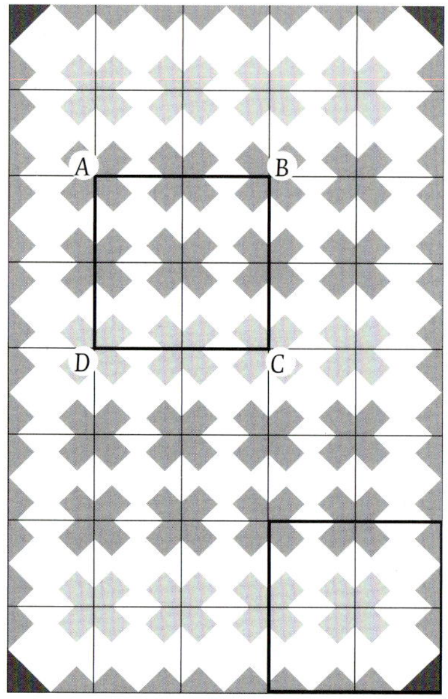

Figure 5.31
Photograph of carpet page f. 248r of Book of Durrow (by permission of the Board of Trinity College Dublin). The page measures 245 mm by 145 mm.

Figure 5.32
Layout of embedded crosses in carpet page f. 248r of Book of Durrow based on a square net. Square marked ABCD corresponds to square in Fig. 2.17.

appear to be highly regarded by the experts. Bruce-Mitford (see Kendrick, 1956–60) describes it as 'a relatively dull design in only two colours'.

The detail in Fig. 5.34 shows a small section of the carpet page corresponding to the bottom right-hand corner and also illustrates the three colours used to decorate the crosses and borders. The top, middle and bottom rows of crosses are olive green. The corners are emerald green and the other crosses and borders are brick red. There is a closed path of rectangular interlacing around each diagonal cross and a continuous strand of interlacing makes a closed path around the perimeter of all 28 crosses.

There is an interesting additional detail relating to this carpet page already referred to in Chapter 2. The page appears to be severely distorted, so that the individual crosses and the trellis of interlacing also appear distorted. In fact, many of the pages of the Book of Durrow show evidence of distortion, water

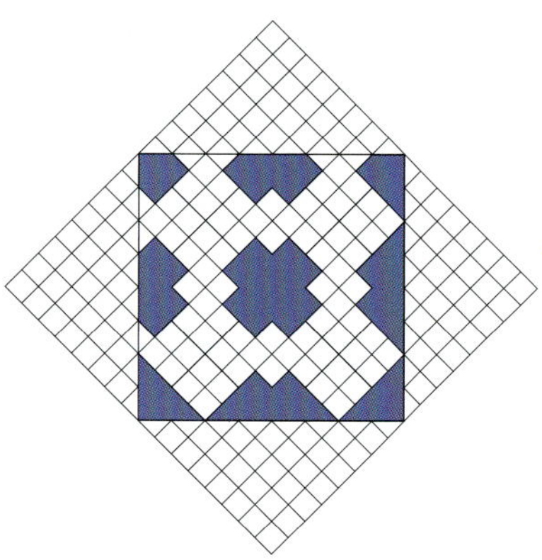

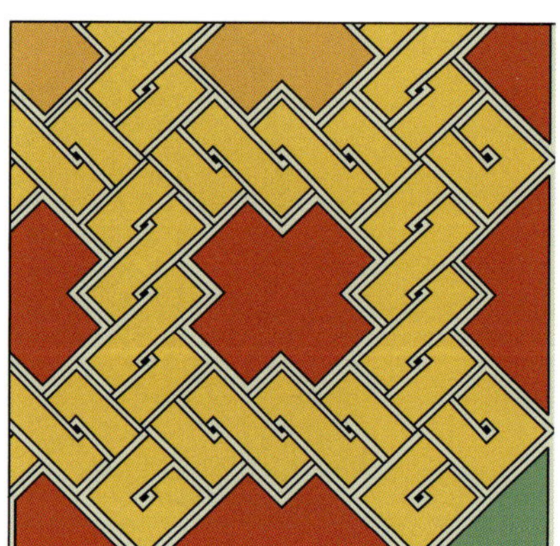

Figure 5.33
Secondary grid of diagonal squares used to construct the trellis in Fig. 5.31.

Figure 5.34
Detail from bottom right-hand corner, outlined in Fig. 5.32, showing diagonal embedded cross and part of the trellis of regular interlacing.

damage and mechanical damage by wear and tear. The design outline in Fig. 5.32 represents the shape of the page without distortion. The square marked ABCD corresponds to the square in Fig. 2.17 that was used to illustrate the way that the amount of distortion can be determined.

The final example is from portrait page f. 32v of the Book of Kells. Two small circular panels with cross-shaped designs (Fig. 5.35) form part of a secondary frame around the portrait. The pattern is a modified circular key or Greek fret. The construction is similar to that illustrated in Fig. 4.14d with reference to the carving on a stone in Cloon Lough (see Fig. 4.15). Unlike the Cloon Lough design, which has a threefold rotation point, the circular key pattern in Fig. 5.35 is divided into quadrants by a cross. Diagonally opposite quadrants have the same pattern. As with so much of the artwork in the Book of Kells the detail is on a very fine scale. The interlacing has been drawn as a single cord.

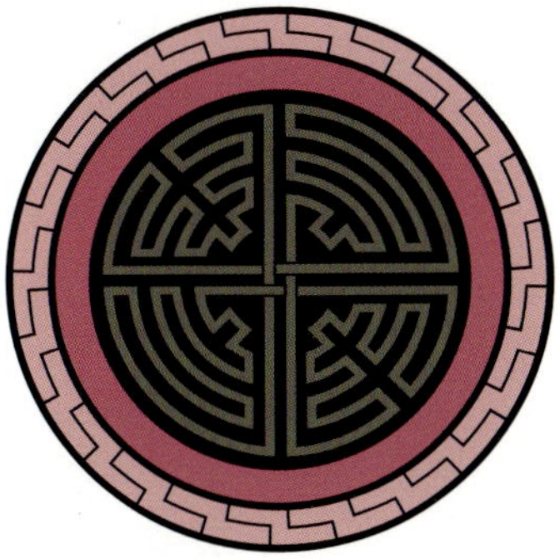

Figure 5.35
Cross formed in a circular key pattern, Book of Kells, f. 32v.

The level of geometric complexity in the examples used in this section on embedded crosses is small compared with the examples in previous sections. Nevertheless, the geometric constructions involved are far from trivial and an appreciation of the underlying geometry provides a framework for describing the designs. The more complex aspects of the examples in the earlier sections testify to the incredible sophistication of Insular artists. Because the complexity is 'transparent' it is possible to unravel these 'fantastically confused patterns', to explore the detailed geometric methods that must have been used, to gain insights into the creative instincts of the artists, and to wonder, yet again, at the level of skill, dedication and commitment that was involved in creating early medieval art.

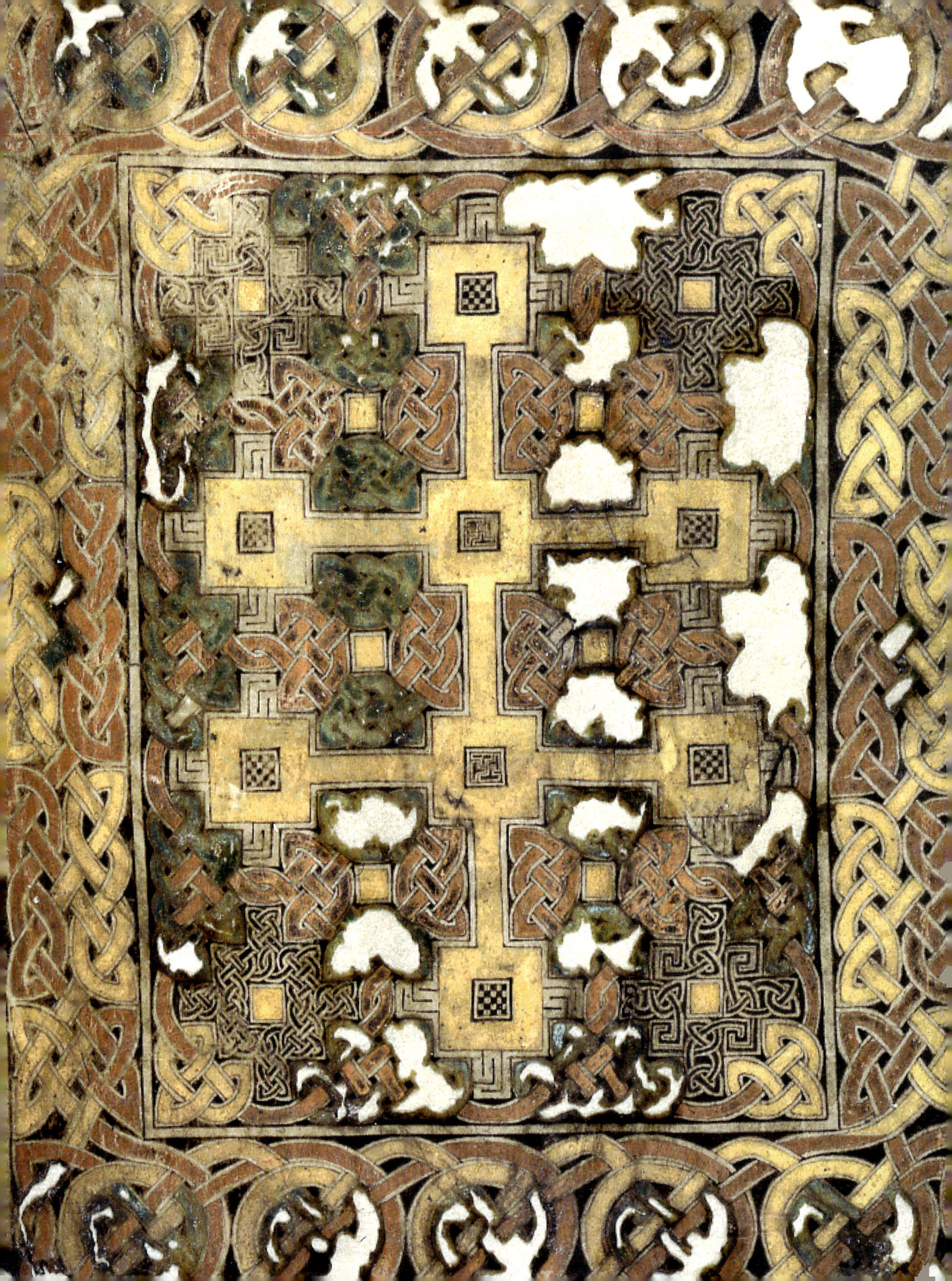

6

Interpretation and reconstruction

DAMAGE AND DETERIORATION

Many stone crosses and cross-slabs have been so badly affected by the ravages of weather, and by inadvertent and wanton mechanical damage, that one cannot, with confidence, describe the designs or patterns created by the early stonemasons. However, it is often possible, using the geometric rules described in earlier chapters, to make an informed attempt to recreate these patterns. Damage has two main forms: first, progressive weathering in which erosion and frost result in the removal of surface layers of the stone and elimination of the fine detail of the carving; and second, fracture and loss of parts of the stone so that neither the original form of the monument nor the details of the pattern is available for examination. A considerable amount of deterioration has occurred in the past two centuries since the stones were first studied and drawn by the early enthusiasts. In this respect the older representations may be more accurate, but there is little evidence that nineteenth-century artists, who had to rely on drawing to record the details, had sufficient insight into the geometric aspects of the patterns to produce acceptable interpretations. This is amply illustrated by the drawings in Fig. 5.14.

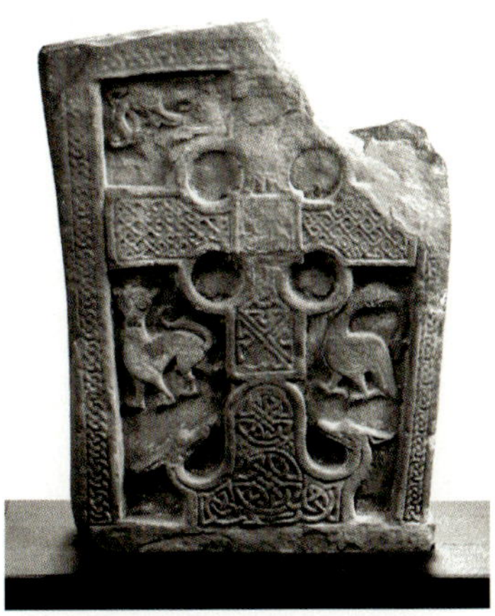

Figure 6.1
Meigle No. 5 cross-slab in Meigle Museum, Scotland.

Six examples from stone monuments are used in this chapter to illustrate aspects of interpretation and reconstruction. The most straightforward is the cross-slab at Meigle in Scotland referred to as Meigle No. 5 (Fig. 6.1). The top corner of the cross-slab has been broken off and lost so that details of parts of the cross are no longer available. The carving on the rest of the stone is worn and damaged but the detail is sufficiently clear to make a reconstruction of the pattern on the whole of the cross providing certain assumptions are made. Two examples from Wales, the Hywel ap Rhys cross at Llantwit Major and the Abraham stone in St David's Cathedral, are treated in a similar way. A more complicated example of the same sort of problem is the shaft of the Leeds Museum cross. Only a few relatively small fragments of the shaft remain. A reconstruction proposed by Collingwood (1927) is used to illustrate a possible pattern for the whole of the shaft. Even more complicated is the Kilnave cross on Islay, an island in the Inner Hebrides, which has been damaged extensively by the effects of weather and man. Here it is impossible to achieve a complete reconstruction so the final result is incomplete and some of the panels remain blank. Finally, the magnificent stone cross-slab at Nigg in Scotland is used for an interpretation of the zoomorphic design on one of the side arms of the cross. Parts of this cross-slab have been broken and lost but much of the carving on the remaining pieces is well preserved. However, the arms of the cross show the effects of severe weathering and a complete interpretation will always remain problematic. The account offered in this chapter is but one possibility.

Deterioration is also a problem in manuscripts owing to the effects of dampness and mistreatment. Reference has been made already to changes in the shape of vellum that occur during ageing, particularly in humid environments. This has only a secondary effect on the interpretation of the patterns although it has some relevance to the study of the geometric methods used to produce the patterns. In the context of the present chapter the most significant kind of damage relates to the use of aggressive pigments for painting manuscripts. This is well illustrated by the formation of large holes caused by corrosion associated with the use of green pigments in cross-carpet page f. 1v of the Book of Durrow. The damage is equivalent to the loss of fragments from stone monuments described above. It is possible to reconstruct the pattern by comparison with parts that remain.

Corrosion, erosion and mechanical damage are also serious sources of deterioration in metallic artefacts. Corrosion, by rusting, is a particularly serious problem for iron-based work. Some aspects of the design of the bronze Donore disc described in Chapter 2, in relation to geometric methods, were based on interpretations because parts of the disc, particularly around the outside, have corroded away. Much of the jewellery from Anglo-Saxon sources is damaged; decorative inlays and precious stones have been lost.

The approach to reconstruction used in this chapter is not without its dangers. Although geometric aspects may be the dominant factor in determining the pattern, the application of the rules does not necessarily result in an unambiguous design. This is amply demonstrated by the observations on the three circular knot patterns at the bottom of the shaft of the cross on Aberlemno No. 2 described in Chapter 5. Thus, there are five distinct designs in the 12 quadrants and there is no obvious reason for the way that these are distributed. And yet, in this case, the cross is sufficiently well preserved that there can be little doubt about the accuracy of the representation of the interlacing in the overall design and of the intentions of the artist and sculptor. However, because of the variety of possibilities implicit in the artist's approach to design, it follows that there would have been no way of predicting the details of the pattern if part of the stone had been damaged or lost. Nevertheless the main features of the pattern could be predicted. This consideration applies to all the reconstructions and interpretations described in this chapter. So one can say with confidence that an interpretation or reconstruction of a piece of work obeys the rules but the result is not necessarily the pattern produced by the original artist.

In addition to damage and loss of detail for various reasons, there is another aspect of interpretation that is particularly relevant to manuscripts. Some of the artwork, as for example in the Book of Kells, is on such a fine scale that even at greatly increased magnification the pattern is not entirely resolvable. Using the rules of geometric art it is possible to make an informed interpretation of the work and so determine the main intentions of the artist. However, there are some cases where this remains obscure and one is left with highly speculative constructions. An example of the former is the small cross-shaped feature in the centre of f. 27v in the Book of Kells, decorated with a key pattern, and an example of the latter is the equal-armed cross decorated with a zoomorphic design in f. 129v also in the Book of Kells.

APPLICATION OF ALLEN AND ANDERSON'S APPROACH TO CLASSIFICATION

Meigle No. 5 is an old red sandstone Class II upright cross-slab now displayed in a small museum in the old school room in the village of Meigle between Perth and Forfar in Scotland. The museum has a collection of Class II and Class III monuments most of which are only fragments of the originals. Meigle No. 5 has a central place in the museum. Part of the stone has been lost and some of the carving has been severely damaged. The carving on the front face shows an ornamented cross surrounded by four panels decorated with zoomorphic forms. To reconstruct the pattern on the cross the approach of Allen and Anderson (1903) is used. It provides a good example of the value of their work. As mentioned in an earlier chapter, they described over a thousand patterns and catalogued the early stone monuments of Scotland using their own classification.

Allen and Anderson describe the front face of Meigle No. 5 cross-slab as follows:

> *Within a border is a cross of shape No. 102A (with a base having beasts' heads projecting on each side), divided into six panels, containing (1) in the centre of the head, spiral-work No. 1082; (2) on the top arm, sculpture defaced; (3 and 4) on the left and right arms, diagonal key-pattern No. 971; (5) on the bottom arm at the top, knot No. 249, and below, triangular interlaced-work No. 727; and (6) on the base, circular interlaced work No. 711.*

Some of the patterns on the stone are still clearly visible although part of the stone is defaced and part is broken off. It follows that in producing a reconstruction one has to make some assumptions about symmetry and repetition.

The design illustrated in Fig. 6.2 is based on the above description using the patterns illustrated by Allen and Anderson (Fig. 6.3). The correlation between the patterns in Fig. 6.3 and those on the cross in Fig. 6.2 is clear but there are aspects of the design that are not fully covered by a simple

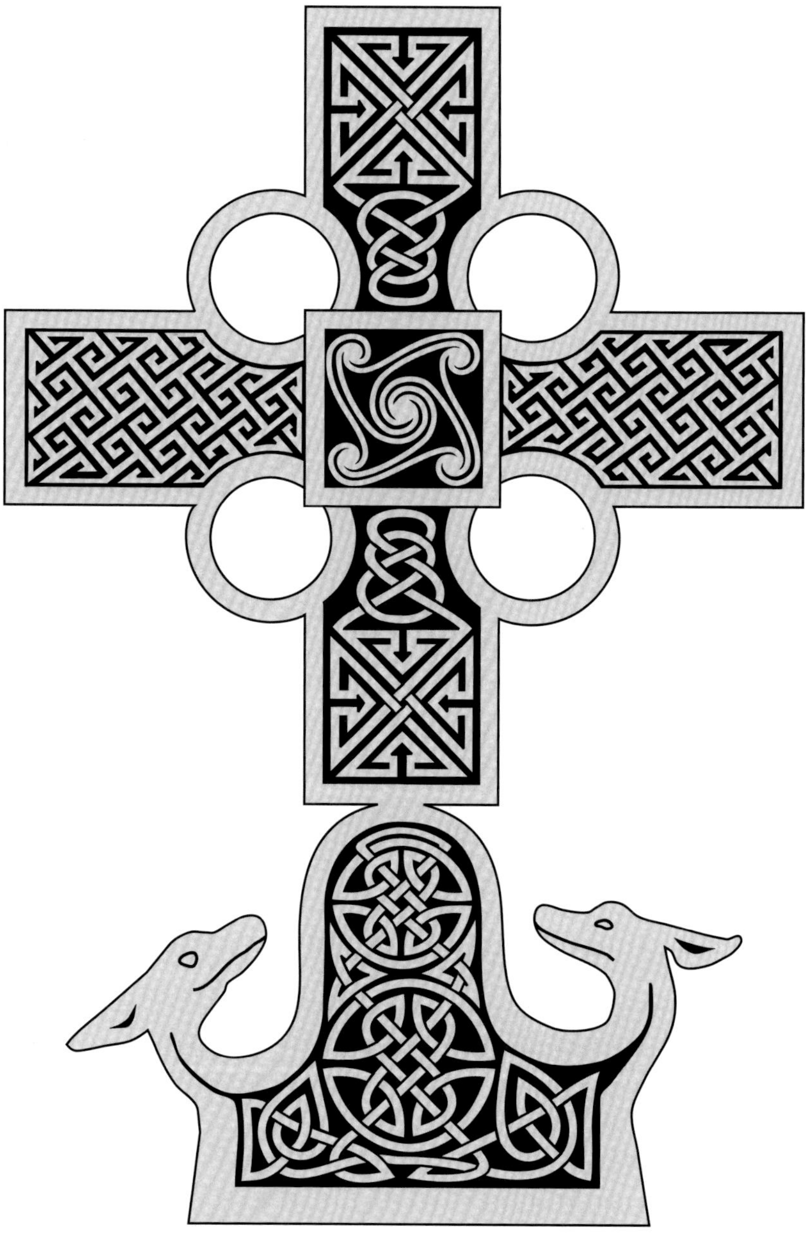

Figure 6.2
Reconstruction of Meigle No. 5 based on the description by Allen and Anderson using their classification of basic shapes (see Fig. 6.3).

(a)

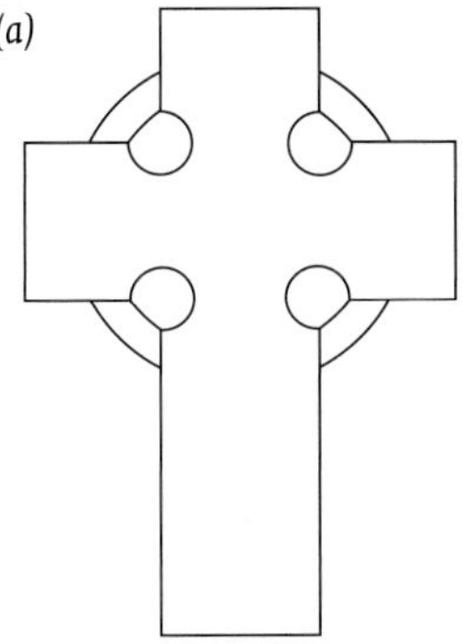

No. 102A – Cross with round hollow angles and connecting ring (with shaft).

(b)

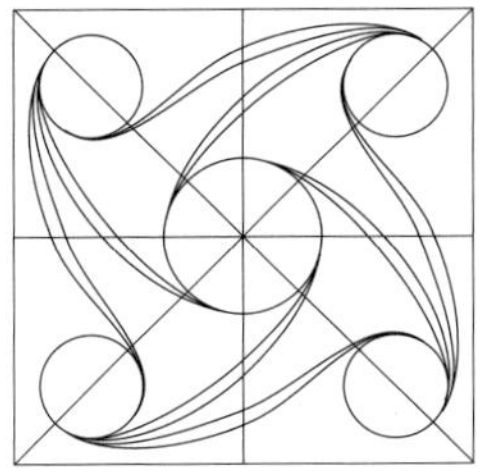

No. 1082 – A large quadruple spiral in the centre surrounded by four smaller triple spirals one in each corner of the square. The central spiral is connected with those surrounding it by C curves arranged swastika fashion, and the four outer spirals are connected with each other by S curves.

(c)

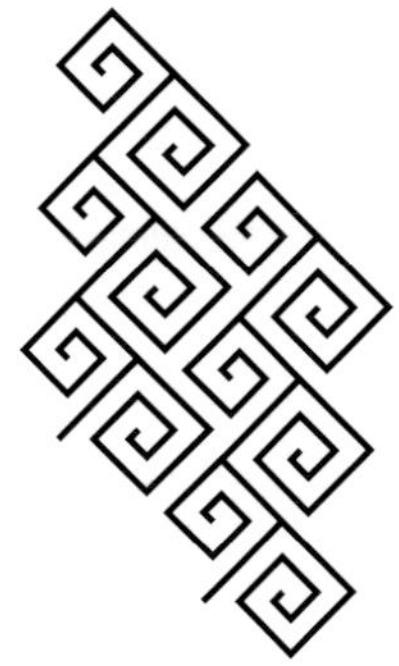

No. 971 (modified) – The actual pattern is a development of pattern No. 837A.

(d)

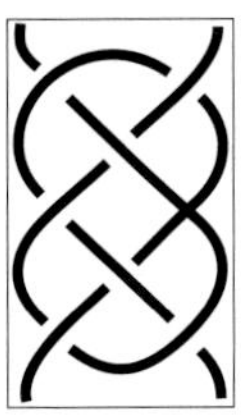

No. 249

(e)

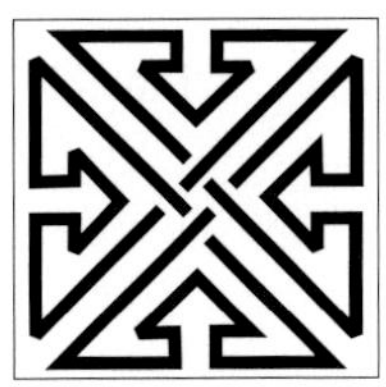

No. 727 – The same as No. 724, but with a square-headed indentation in each of the triangular loops.

(f)

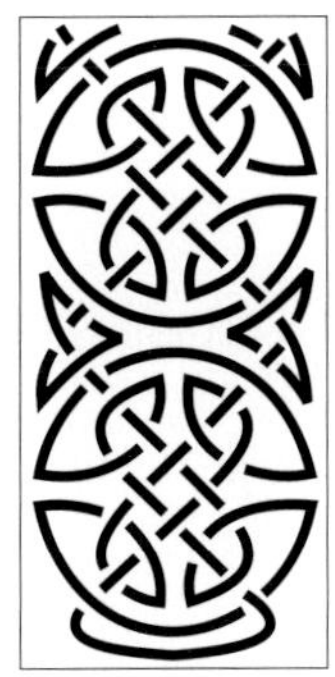

No. 711 – Pattern formed by repeating No. 430 in a single vertical row, all the circular knots being placed facing the same way.

Figure 6.3
Basic patterns used to construct the ornamentation on Meigle No. 5. The captions to each pattern are those used by Allen and Anderson (1903) with the exception of No. 971.

transfer of the patterns to the panels of the cross. Three features are worthy of mention. First, the heads of the two beasts at the foot of the cross and the interlacing pattern in the bottom panel are not fully symmetrical. The lower of the two circular knots in the panel is larger than the upper knot and the two knots are not aligned on the axis of the cross. Second, the arms of the cross are of different lengths and shapes; this has not been included in the reconstruction. Third, and most important in relation to producing an accurate reconstruction, the Greek fret pattern in the arms of the cross does not conform to a simple arrangement. Some of the difficulties of reproducing these patterns were described in relation to Aberlemno No. 2 (see Fig. 5.15). The key pattern shown in Fig. 6.3c is a modified version of that illustrated by Allen and Anderson because their diagrams of these patterns are not sufficiently precise or accurate to use for reconstruction. Even so it has not been possible to reproduce fully the actual key pattern on Meigle No. 5. The basic grid is not orthogonal and is rotated about 6° relative to the axes of the cross. In addition, the sequence of square spirals is irregular and is different in each arm. The construction in Fig. 6.2 includes some of these features but it cannot be claimed to be an accurate reproduction. The pattern in the left-hand arm has been drawn the same as in the right-hand arm with 180° rotation.

This approach to reconstruction may offer insights into the design methods of the early sculptors and artists. It may be that a collection of patterns was available to these artists, rather like the catalogue produced by Allen and Anderson. Such a collection could have provided a basis for developing new designs. However, it seems clear that the artists were not constrained by the strict geometric requirements of repetition and symmetry. In later works of art the artists deviated strongly from the 'rules' of the early days and introduced many other features.

RECONSTRUCTING PATTERNS ON BROKEN STONES

The four examples in this section are from widely spaced locations and reflect many historical events. There is evidence on some of the stones for a Viking influence, indicating that they were carved after the start of the Viking invasions and migrations. Some of the developments in geometric art under the influence of the Vikings are discussed in the next chapter. Here the emphasis is on examples where the geometric rules can be applied with confidence. There are hundreds of broken and damaged stones all over the islands. The examples described here were chosen because they illustrate the complexity of reconstruction and also demonstrate geometric features not presented in earlier chapters.

Leeds Museum cross

This example is taken from Collingwood (1927). The Leeds Museum cross is in a chapter on 'Anglo-Norse' stone carvings. It may be inferred that the carving was influenced by the work of masons centred on great monastic sites such as Lindisfarne, Jarrow and Whitby, and by sculptors of the Scandinavian tradition. By 'Norse' Collingwood means the Viking-descended peoples of Ireland, the Isle of Man, the Hebrides and west coast of Scotland who settled in the western parts of northern England during the tenth century. According to Collingwood, in AD 940–50 Leeds was a border town between the Danish (Viking) peoples and the Norse (Viking) migrants.

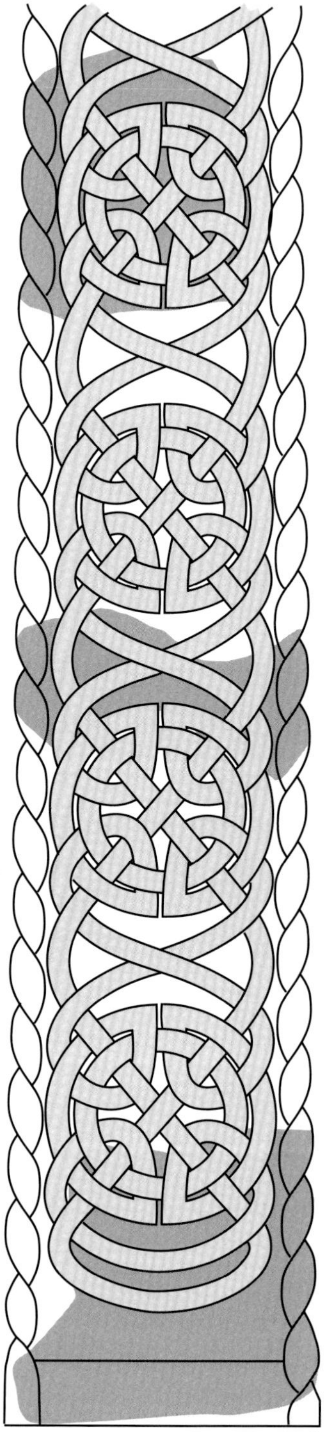

Figure 6.4
Reconstruction of Leeds Museum cross by Collingwood (1927) based on the design on three remaining fragments.

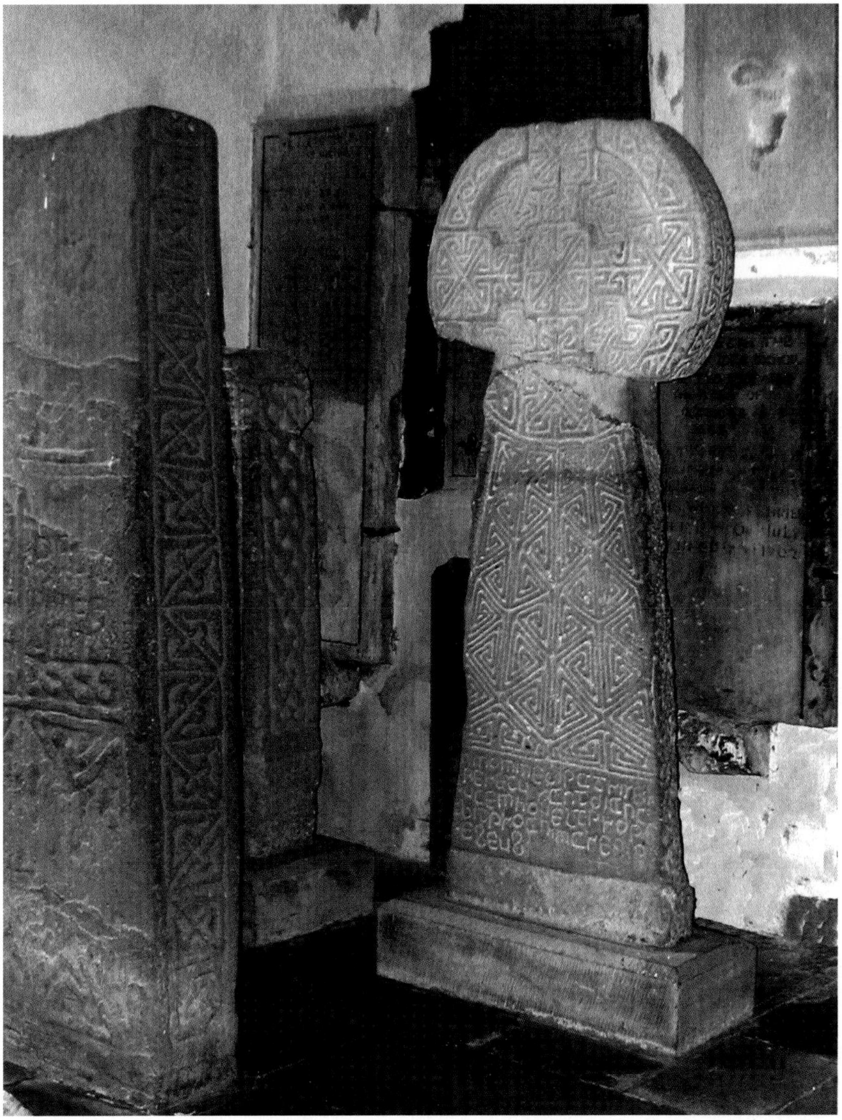

Figure 6.5
Hywel ap Rhys cross surrounded by other crosses, including Samson cross (Fig. 4.42c) on extreme left, in St Illtud's church, Llantwit Major, Wales.

Collingwood was a master of reconstruction and his skills are admirably demonstrated in the Leeds Museum cross. Only three small fragments of the shaft of the cross remain. The shaft has the form of a slender column that tapers slightly towards the top. It was almost certainly topped with a cross set in a ring. The drawing in Fig. 6.4 is based on Collingwood's reconstruction. Shading indicates the position of the remaining fragments. The unit or basic pattern is evident in the upper fragment. This pattern is repeated four times, with a progressive increase in size, to fill the slight taper of the panel. The resultant design is consistent with the patterns on the other fragments. Incidentally, the knot that forms the basic pattern is No. 410 in Allen and Anderson's catalogue, referred to in the previous section. Allen and Anderson do not cite any examples of the use of this pattern. The most interesting feature of the design is the use of a closed loop in the centre of each knot. Closed loops are a common feature of Viking Age designs. In other respects the knot is similar to many examples in manuscripts and on stones from earlier works, and its construction can be followed from a grid similar to Fig. 5.10a using an appropriate break-and-join sequence or alternatively from an eight-cord strand (Fig. 4.54).

Hywel ap Rhys (Houelt) cross

This is the cross of Hywel ap Rhys, ruler of Glywysing, who was present at the court of Alfred of Wessex in AD 884. According to the inscription on the bottom of the stone Hywel prepared this cross for the soul of Rhys his father. The cross, made of local grit stone, is in St Illtud's parish church in Llantwit Major in South Wales (Fig. 6.5). The monument is in the form of a disc-headed cross-slab. Many years ago the disc-head was broken from the shaft and part of the stone is now missing. It has been reassembled by inserting a wedge of reconstituted stone between the two pieces. A cast of the stone is in the National Museum of Wales in Cardiff. It is said to be one of the finest and earliest of the Welsh Group III monuments. A corpus of early Welsh monuments was produced by Nash-Williams (1950), and a new, three-volume corpus is currently in preparation under the auspices of the University of Wales Board of Celtic Studies and National Museum and Galleries of Wales. Redknap (1991) has published an excellent summary of Welsh monuments.

Nash-Williams was an admirer of Allen and Anderson's work and used their classification to describe the front of the stone as follows:

> *The cross-head comprises five squares of swastika key-pattern (No. 995), linked by opposed T's (No. 908), with four-lobed plain twists (No. 501) filling the arc of the wheel and large double-beaded triquetra-knots (No. 798) in the interspaces. The shaft below is filled with a double vertical band of well-executed triangular fretwork (No. 979) widening towards the bottom so as to fit the splayed face.*

A complete reconstruction of the design on one face of the stone is shown in Fig. 6.6.

The design of the triangular pattern on the shaft is of particular interest. Nash-Williams described this pattern as fretwork and Allen and Anderson call it a key pattern. The pattern is unique to this stone although the approach to the design is essentially the same as that used for patterns based on the Greek fret. It is made up of clockwise and anti-clockwise triangular spirals. The detail is far from trivial. To understand the method of construction consider a

Figure 6.6
Final reconstruction of the pattern on Hywel ap Rhys cross.

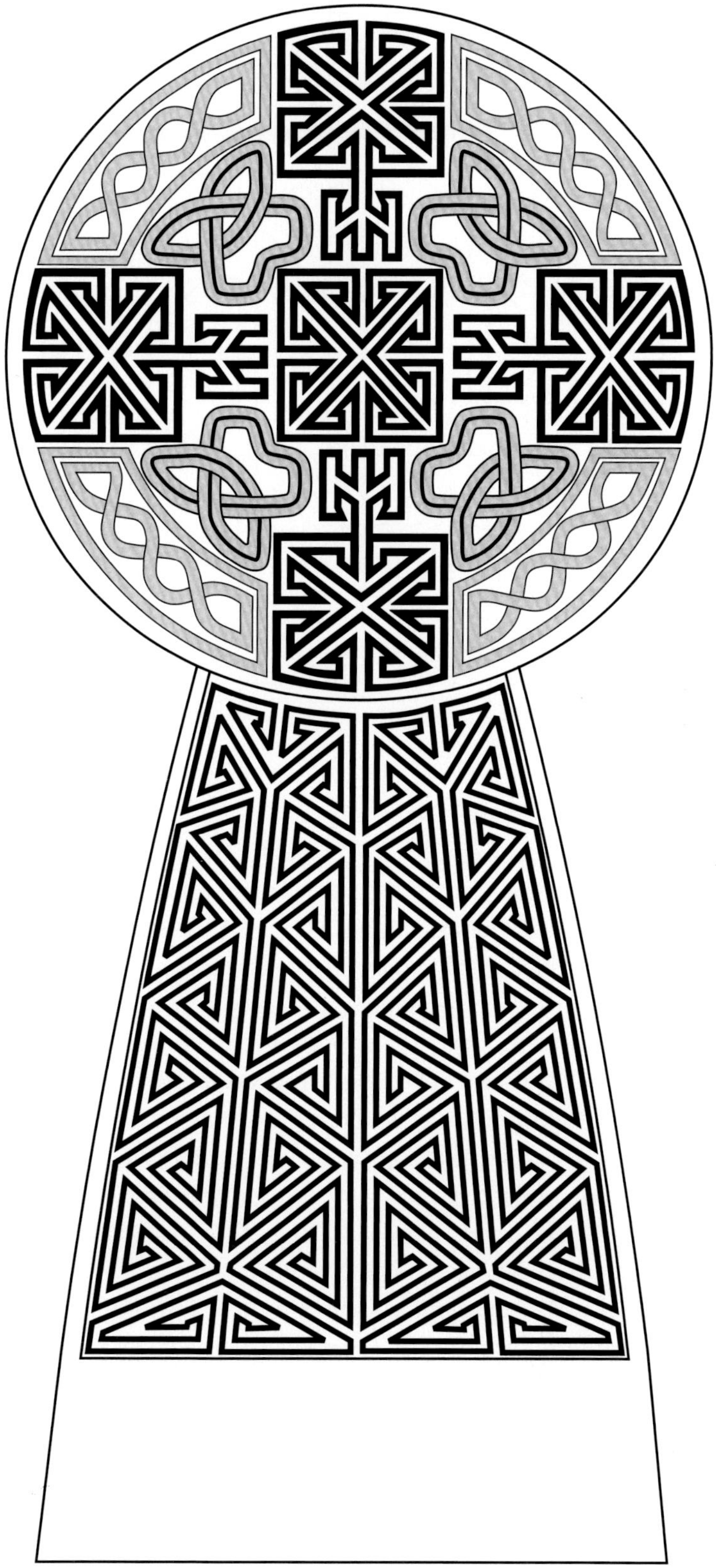

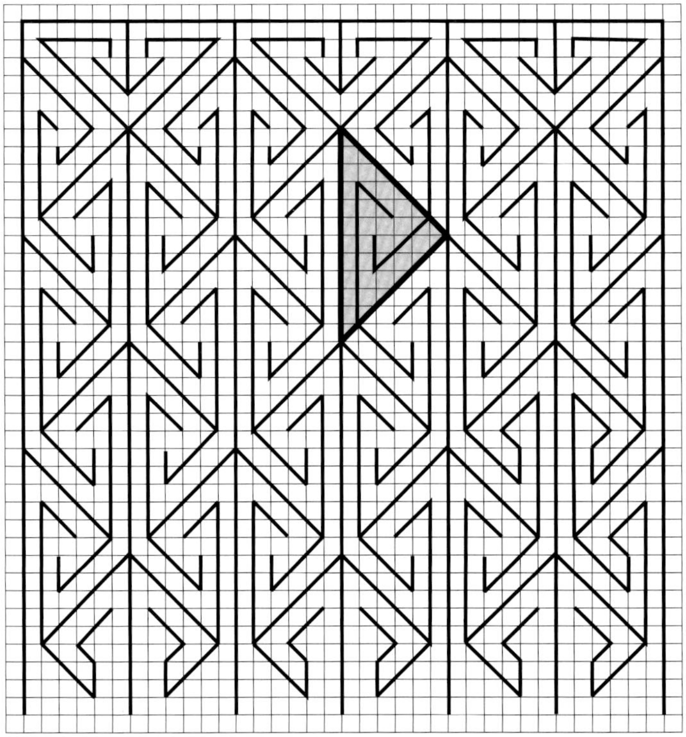

Figure 6.7
Pattern No. 979 from Allen and Anderson (1903).

basic pattern formed on a square grid with a set of vertical lines and two sets of lines at ±45° to the vertical lines (Fig. 6.7). Because of the way that the straight-sided spirals are formed in this construction adjacent vertical lines of the triangular spirals are separated by a distance (a) equal to the length of the sides of the squares of the primary grid (Fig. 6.8a). The lines at ±45° are separated by a distance equal to the length of the diagonals of the squares ($a\sqrt{2}$) of the primary grid. However, the spacings of the spirals on the Hywel ap Rhys cross are independent of their position and orientation. This means that the elementary approach of Fig. 6.7 is inadequate.

The solution to this difficulty is to recognise that the key pattern in Fig. 6.7 can be treated as a set of triangles, one of which is highlighted. These triangles completely fill the space except at the upper boundary. Each triangle is filled with a double straight-sided spiral (Fig. 6.8a and b). To form spirals, with lines spaced equally, each triangle is filled with a grid as illustrated in Fig. 6.8c. Three sets of equal-spaced lines are aligned parallel to the sides of the triangle and form the grid. The approach can be applied to all shapes of triangle (Fig. 6.8d).

With this method of construction it is possible to consider the approach required to produce the pattern on the shaft of the Hywel ap Rhys cross. The following features are noted: (1) the pattern is made up of four columns of triangular spirals, (2) the shaft tapers towards the top and the triangles

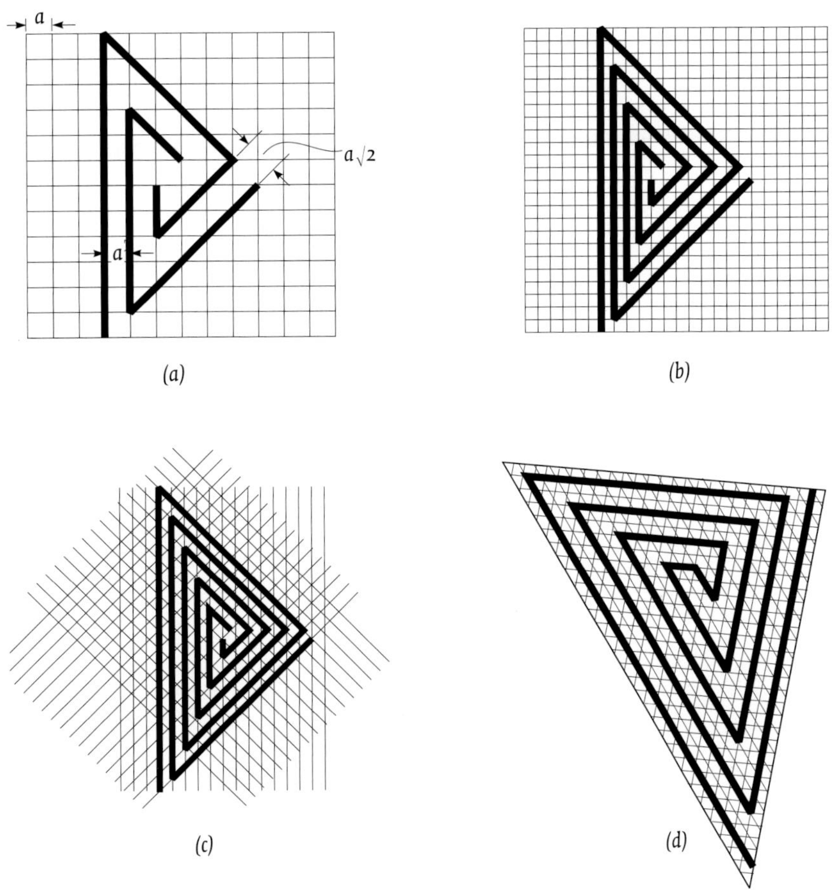

Figure 6.8
Grids used to produce straight-sided triangular spirals. (a) Straight-sided triangle double spiral, as shown in Fig. 6.5, produced using a square grid. Spacing of vertical lines is a, spacing of ±45° lines is a√2. (b) Straight-sided triangle double spiral as in (a) drawn on a finer grid. (c) Similar straight-sided spiral constructed on a grid of three sets of equal-spaced lines parallel to the sides of the triangle. The spacing of the vertical and ±45° lines is the same. (d) Spiral formed in a triangle with three non-equal sides. Note that the width or thickness of the bands in both the primary and complementary (or reciprocal) spirals is a matter of choice.

decrease in size, (3) at the top of the shaft the shape of the triangles follows the shape of the circular cross-head, and (4) the overall design is influenced by the arrangement of the individual triangles. It follows that each triangle has a different size, shape and orientation. The first step in drawing this design from first principles is to form a grid to represent the arrangement of the triangles on the stone (Fig. 6.9a). The network is somewhat arbitrary and was produced directly from the pattern on the stone but modified slightly so that the pattern is symmetrical about the centre line. It deviates from a network such as that in Fig. 6.9b, which is based on progressive scaling. Double spirals are then formed in each triangle separately by forming a grid of three sets of equal-spaced lines parallel to the sides of the triangle. The spacing between the lines is the same for all the triangles. The choice of spacing influences the number of lines within the triangle (*cf.* Fig. 6.8a and b) and was determined by reference to the number of lines found on the stone. For the purposes of calibration one of the two central triangles on the stone was used to determine the spacing and this was applied throughout the construction. The resulting design is shown in Fig. 6.10. The detail is in good

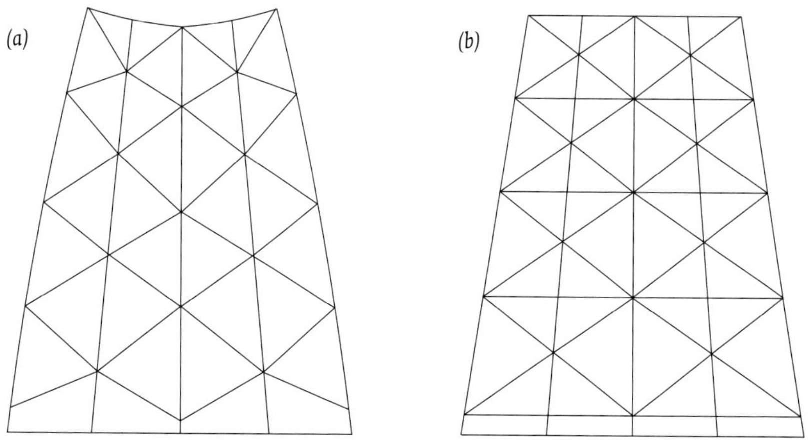

Figure 6.9
Grids of triangles that form the basis of the design on the shaft of Hywel ap Rhys cross: (a) actual shaft, (b) ordered grid produced using a scaling rule.

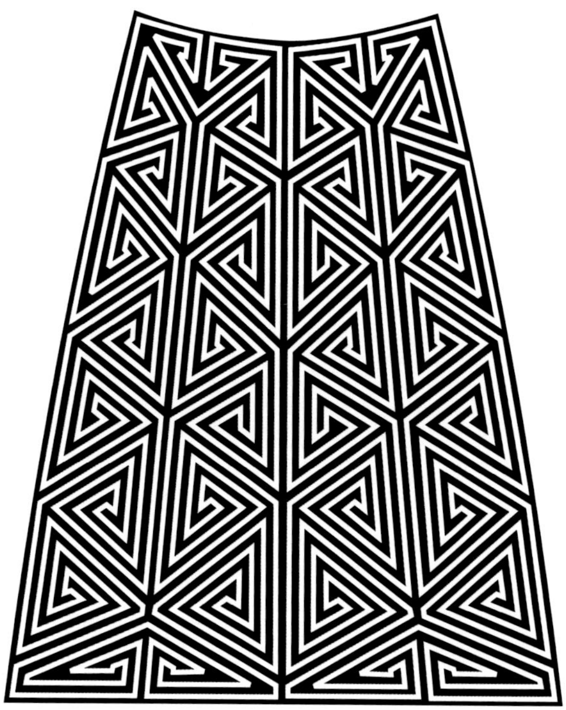

Figure 6.10
Reconstruction of key pattern on shaft of Hywel ap Rhys cross.

agreement with the pattern on the stone and provides strong evidence that the original artist adopted a similar method of construction.

As described by Nash-Williams, the design on the disc head is based on a cross of five squares filled with a key pattern with arms featuring another key pattern. This is surrounded by panels filled with a simple twisted cord and four triquetra knots. Although part of the stone is missing, reconstruction of the whole of the pattern is relatively simple apart from the key patterns. These can be constructed using a similar approach to that described above for

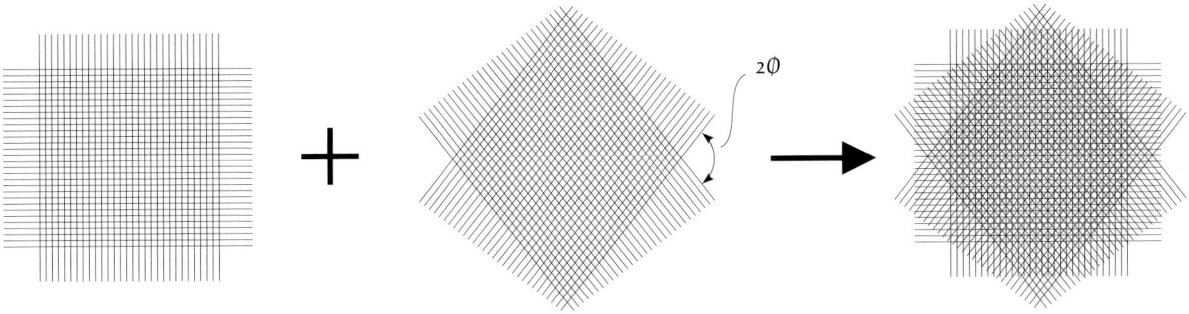

Figure 6.11
Formation of key pattern in the arms of Hywel ap Rhys cross.

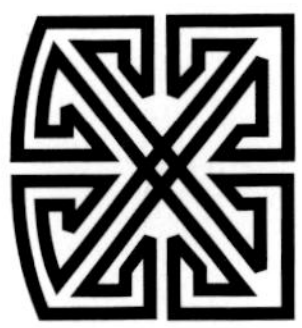

straight-sided spirals. The critical step is the construction of a grid. The panels are distorted rectangles that vary in size and orientation. The two panels in the horizontal arms are the same size and the designs are mirror images of each other. The outer parts of the 'rectangles' follow the circular shape of the cross-head. The upper and lower 'rectangles' are slightly smaller and larger, respectively, than the rectangles on the side arms and the patterns are mirror related also. The central 'square' is rectangular and the pattern has the same form as those of the outer panels. The approach to the construction of the key pattern is illustrated in Fig. 6.11. The grid is formed by sets of equal-spaced lines parallel to four directions in the key pattern; two sets are orthogonal and two sets lie at 2ϕ to each other. In the outer panels $2\phi = 104^\circ$ and in the central panel $2\phi = 95^\circ$. The final design is combined with the key pattern on the shaft to give the complete reconstruction (Fig. 6.6).

Abraham stone

For many years this stone was embedded in the wall of the south transept of St David's Cathedral in Pembrokeshire, Wales. It was moved in the year 2000 to form a central feature of a small museum in the thirteenth-century bell tower attached to the fourteenth-century gateway of the cathedral grounds. The design of the cross is now used widely as a symbol of the town of St Davids, being carved in Welsh slate by a local sculptor and engraver, John Williams.

The stone is the gravestone of Hedd and Isaac, sons of Bishop Abraham who was killed by the Vikings in 1080. About 25 per cent of the stone, which was carved in low relief, is missing. A reconstruction is shown in Fig. 6.12a. Nash-Williams described the design as a wheel cross in a debased Anglo-

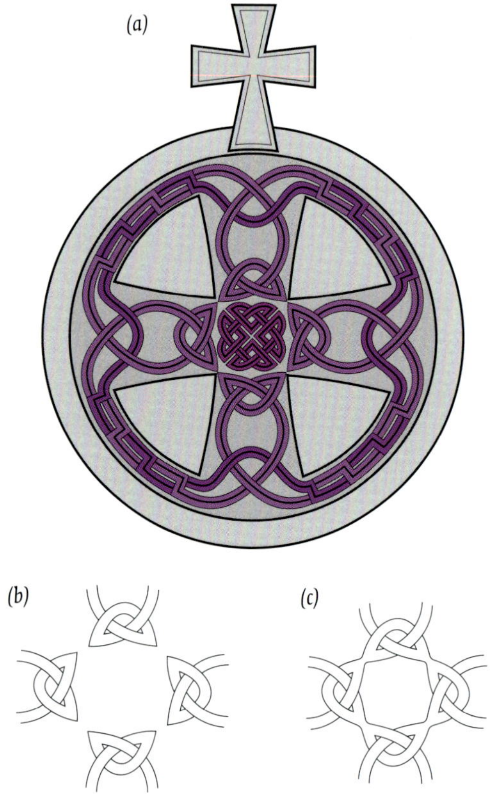

Figure 6.12
Abraham stone, St David's Cathedral. (a) Complete pattern. (b) Interlacing design with four Stafford knots. (c) Interlacing design with bifurcations.

Norse form. The central knot is typical of designs from the seventh to ninth centuries but the interlacing of the cross, with slightly splayed arms, and the surrounding ring suggest a Viking influence.

A feature of particular interest is the evidence for bifurcations in the double beaded cords of the interlacing. As sketched in Fig. 6.12b, there are four loops of interlacing, forming Stafford knots around the central motif. Alternatively, the design can be drawn as in Fig. 6.12c with bifurcations in the cords instead of independent Stafford knots. Even by close examination of the stone it is not possible to establish unambiguously which of the two representations the artist intended. Nash-Williams opts for the design with bifurcations.

Kilnave cross

This cross stands outside a ruined chapel set in a walled burial ground in the fields that slope down to the beautiful Loch Gruinart estuary in the west of Islay in the Inner Hebrides (Fig. 6.13). There are a number of important sculptured stones on Islay and they were recorded in the late nineteenth century by an enthusiastic antiquarian (Graham, 1895). Even at that time Graham was complaining about the state of the carvings which were 'trodden upon and scratched by boot-nails, and they suffer from the umbrella points and pocket-knives of over-zealous tourists, anxious to make clear the earth-filled or lichen-covered scroll'. The location and design of the Kilnave cross evoke many thoughts of times past and of the beauty of times present. In a recent account Lamont (1972) reviewed the evidence for the chronology and provenance of the stones and, in particular, dates the Kilnave cross to the second half of the eighth century. The design of the carving has many of the characteristics of manuscript art of this period, notably the Lindisfarne Gospels and the Books of Durrow and Kells.

The most recent and complete record of the Kilnave cross is in RCAHMS (1984). The cross is carved from a thin slab of Torridian flagstone, which is local to the present site. It is supported by a base of stones and is severely damaged. Weathering has resulted in flaking-off of the surface of the stone, removing much of the detail of the carving. Parts have also been lost by mechanical damage. And yet the broken and damaged cross remains a supreme monument to the spirit of the Christians who worshipped and witnessed on Islay over twelve hundred years ago.

Only the east-facing side of the stone appears to have been carved. The design is divided into eight panels ornamented mainly with spiral and key patterns. Any reconstruction is inevitably suspect but the design in Fig. 6.14 is consistent with the residual marking on the stone and also with the interpretations illustrated in RCAHMS (1984).

The panel in the upper arm of the cross is almost complete. The design consists of an array of spirals joined by C-curves (peltae). A similar panel of spirals has been carved in the centre of the shaft. The detail is not so evident, particularly in the centres of the four spirals in the corners of the rectangular panel. There are three roundels, with spiral designs, in the arms and centre of the cross. The central roundel is quite well defined and has threefold rotational symmetry. The detail in the smaller roundels is less clear, with the north arm completely destroyed by flaking. They have been drawn with threefold symmetry. These roundels are surrounded by an indeterminate pattern. It may be a fine-scale key pattern similar to that in the panels above and below the central roundel or, possibly, an interlacing pattern as in the background to the cross in the central panel of the Rosemarkie stone. Parts of the pattern that are beyond reconstruction are shown by cross-hatching.

Only small regions of the key pattern in the panels above and below the central roundel have survived. Sufficient detail remains to show that the pattern is set at ±45° and is based on a 1:1:2:2:3:3 square spiral. This has been fitted into symmetrical hourglass-shaped panels. Accurate reproduction is impossible. The key pattern in the lower panel is formed by 180° rotation of the pattern in the upper panel.

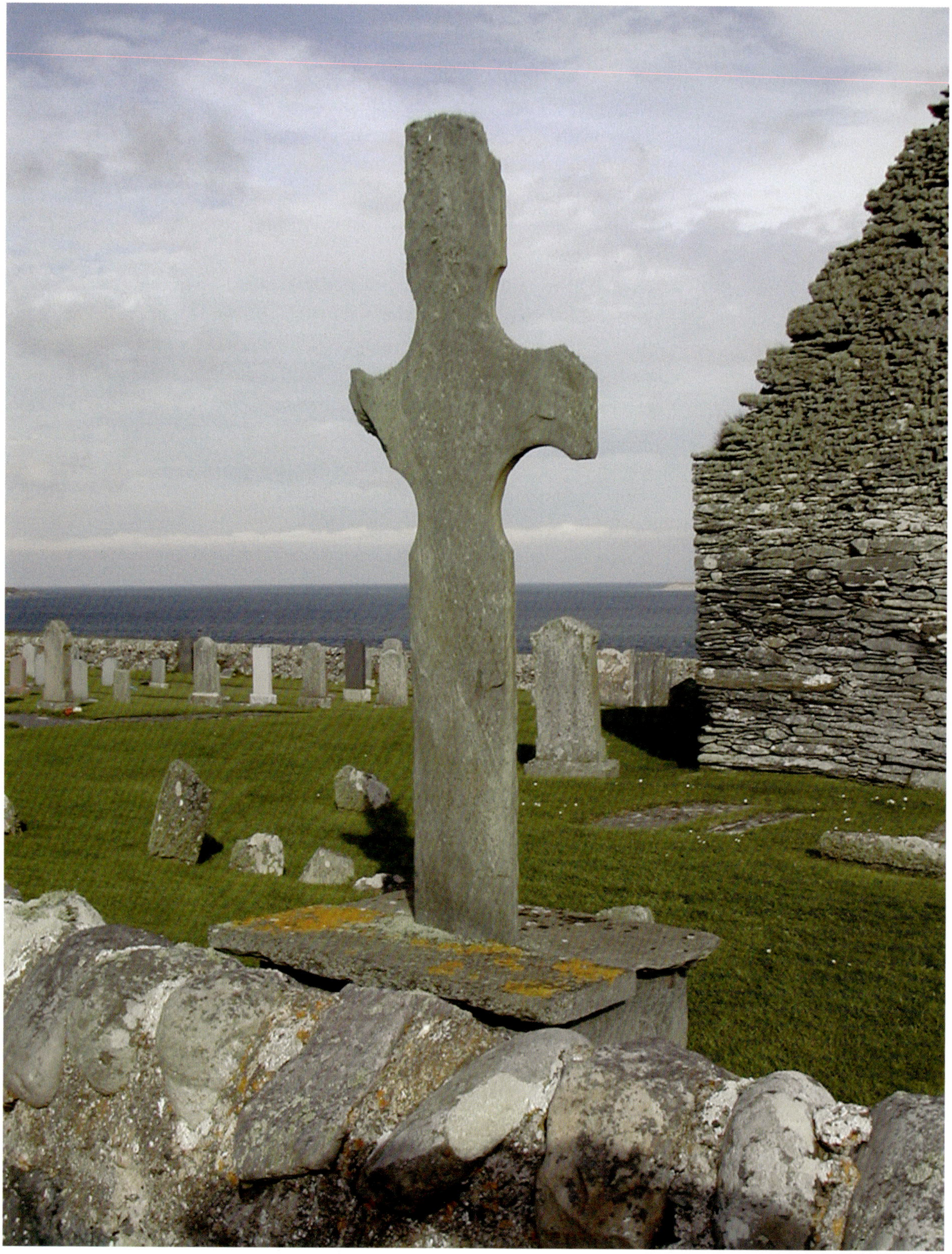

(a)

(b)

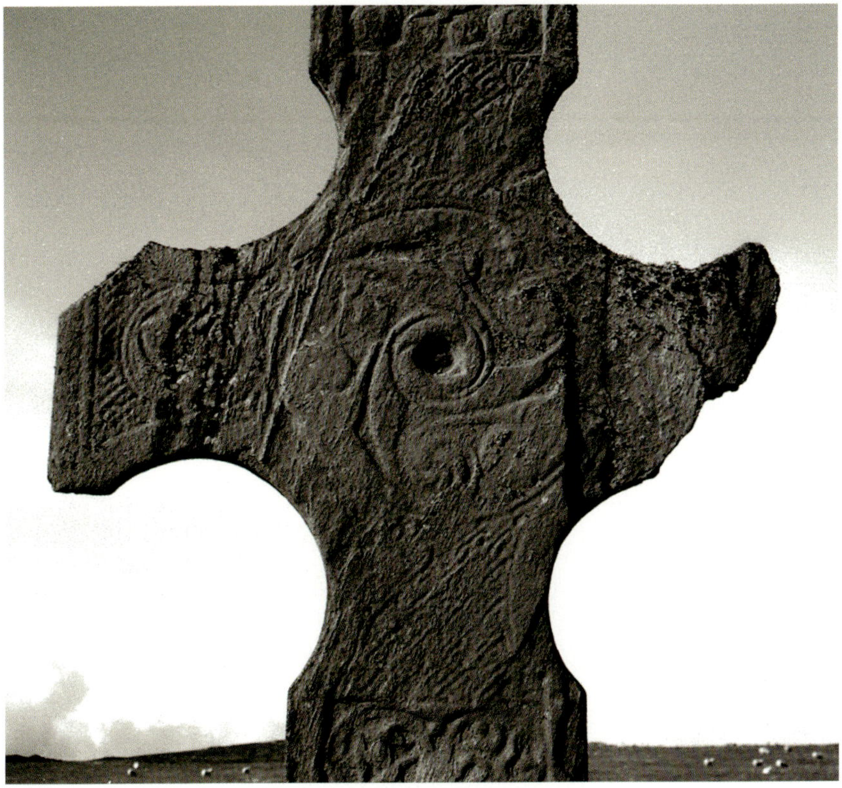

Figure 6.13
Kilnave cross on Islay. (a) A view looking east to Loch Gruinart. (b) Part of the cross showing residual markings on the east face, photographed in oblique sunlight to reveal as much shadow detail as possible. (c) Edge view of stone showing the pronounced lamination of the Torridian flagstone used for this cross.

(c)

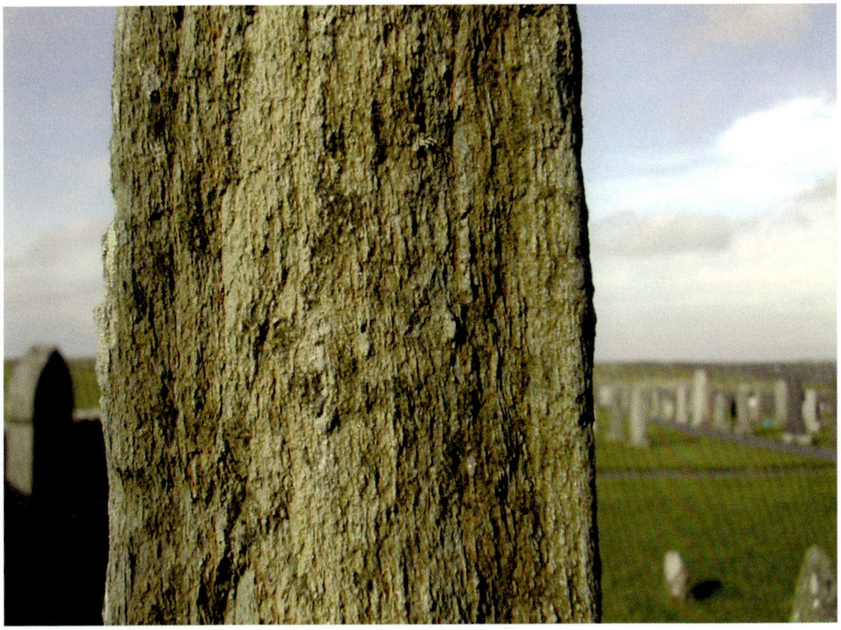

Figure 6.14
Proposed reconstruction of the design on east face of Kilnave cross.

ZOOMORPHIC INTERPRETATION AND RECONSTRUCTION: NIGG CROSS-SLAB

There are many aspects of the cross-slab at Nigg (see Fig. 2.28) that invite attempts at reconstruction and challenge one to discover the geometric methods used by the artist. Many antiquarians have produced drawings of the stone and some have made casts of it that have been included in museum collections. Stuart (1858) recalls that the stone was 'thrown down by a hurricane in 1727'. There is an engraving in Cordiner, *Remarkable Ruins and Romantic Prospects of North Britain* (1795), suggesting that at this time the stone was unbroken. At some stage it was placed against the east gable of the church in Nigg. It was later broken when it was being moved and a substantial piece was lost. Part of the lost piece was recovered as late as 1998.

As with the Aberlemno No. 2 cross-slab, the early drawings of the Nigg cross-slab are, understandably, far from accurate with regard to the detail of the designs. However, some of the evidence in the drawings and descriptions of the stones in the early accounts provide the only record of detail now lost forever. This is demonstrated admirably by the contribution of Petley (1857). His paper was presented to the Society of Antiquaries of Scotland in 1831, a year after his death, and there is a letter at the end of the published account that makes it clear that the original drawings were made by Petley around 1811–12. Reference is made later to some of the detail of Petley's drawings with regard to the reconstruction of the design on the right-hand arm of the cross. Figure 6.15a records the outline of the stone as drawn by Petley in 1811–12. The stone was in two pieces and a small piece was missing. In Stuart (1858) the stone is shown as in Fig. 6.15b, indicating that further damage and loss had occurred. By the time Allen and Anderson produced *Early Christian Monuments of Scotland*, at the beginning of the twentieth century, the stone had been reassembled and cemented together without a gap for the missing pieces. In the most recent drawing of the stone by I. G. Scott in RCAHMS (1999) the small fragment, recovered in 1998, is included and the remaining pieces shown in their proper positions as in Fig. 6.15c.

The layout and quality of the ornamentation of the cross-slab closely resembles the art of the early manuscripts, most notably the cross-carpet pages of the Lindisfarne Gospels. In his book *Remarkable Ruins*, mentioned above, Cordiner observes, 'The monuments around this obelisk had been wrought with great mathematical accuracy; and raised with such labour as to indicate no small proficiency in the art of sculpture'. An added level of geometric complexity, compared with manuscripts, was involved in carving ornamentation on curved surfaces, as in the numerous raised bosses that adorn the panels that surround the central cross. The ornamentation of the

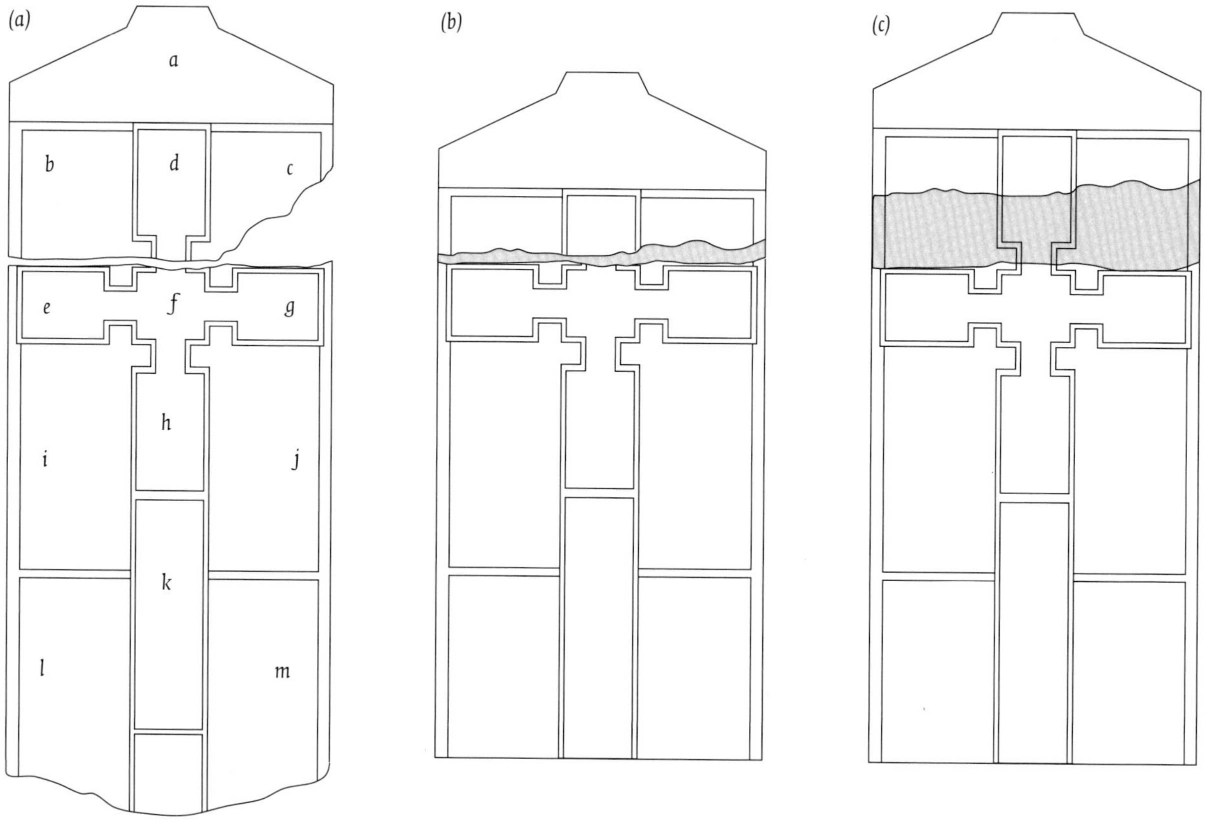

Figure 6.15
Outline drawings of Nigg cross-slab. (a) Arrangement based on Petley's drawings of 1811–12. (b) Arrangement according to photographs taken about 1902. (c) Arrangement shown in a recent drawing by Scott (1999) with the two remaining pieces separated so that the panels are in their correct positions as recorded by Petley (a). The stone in the church at Nigg is now displayed (Fig. 2.28) with a spacer to show the original positions of the two large pieces.

panels can be summarised as follows, by reference to the labelling used in Fig. 6.15: (a) two symmetrically placed, bearded human figures bowing; (b) four bosses with spirals around a diamond-shaped region with a key pattern of square spirals; (c) similar to (b) but the bosses are ornamented with key patterns, interlacing and spirals; (d), (e), (g) and (h) interlaced beasts; (f) three-by-three square array of circular knots; (i) four circular bosses around a lozenge-shaped boss, embedded in numerous smaller spiral bosses, the whole ornamented with tightly interlaced snakes or serpents; (j) eight circular bosses with snakes; (k) a key pattern based on straight-sided spirals set at $\pm 51°$; (l) and (m) arrays of bosses with spirals.

The confusion evident in previous attempts to unravel the details of the zoomorphic ornamentation can be illustrated by reference to one of the panels in the arms of the cross. Figure 6.16a is a photograph of the right-hand arm, panel (g), taken with oblique illumination. The first recorded drawing of the same panel by Petley in 1811–12 is shown in Fig. 6.16b. This drawing suggests that Petley had difficulty 'interpreting' the pattern on the stone so that the result is incomplete and unsatisfactory. Gibb's drawing, dated 1853, in Stuart's *Sculptured Stones of Scotland* (1858), is shown in Fig.

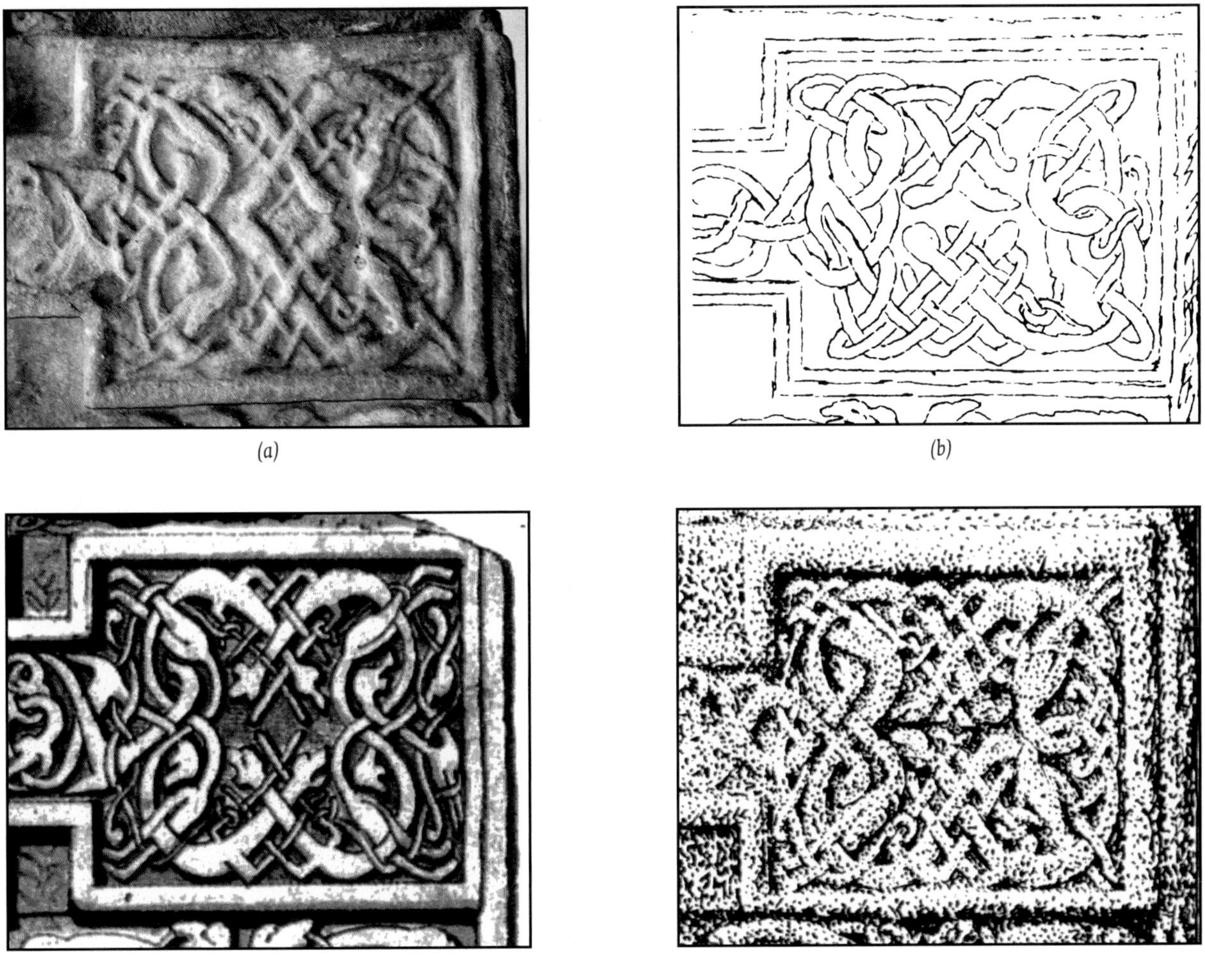

(a) (b)

(c) (d)

Figure 6.16
Impressions of zoomorphic pattern on right-hand arm of Nigg cross-slab. (a) Photograph 1999. (b) Petley's drawing 1811–12 (courtesy RCAHMS). (c) Gibb's drawing 1853 (courtesy RCAHMS). (d) Scott's drawing 1999 (Crown Copyright). (e) Interpretation 2002.

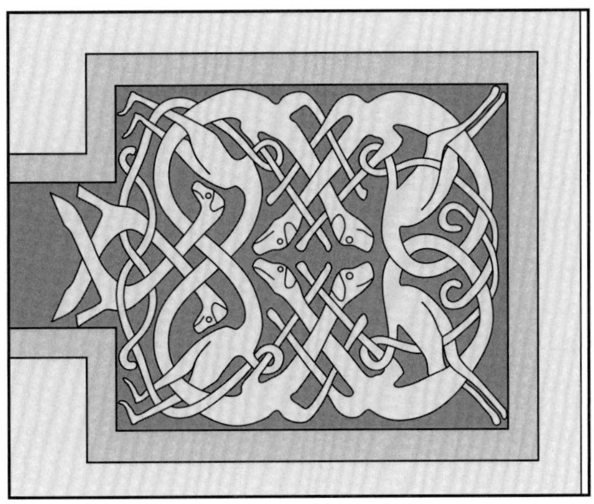

(e)

6.16c and is more convincing, and in many respects quite admirable, but it is far from satisfactory. Allen (1903) describes the design on this panel as 'four pairs of beasts interlaced'; he may have been relying on Gibb's drawing. In fact there are only three pairs of beasts. The recent interpretation (Fig. 6.16d) by Scott (see RCAHMS, 1999) was produced using the techniques of present-day archaeological illustration described by Scott (1997).

The evidence of past attempts to illustrate this panel indicates that one cannot assume that a casual study of the stones will reveal the patterns created by the original stonemasons. The process of discovery, even for skilled illustrators of the calibre of Ian Scott, requires an insight into the way that these patterns were created, the rules that were followed and the potential sources of inspiration. A starting point in interpreting the pattern on the actual stone (Fig. 6.16a) is to suppose that it consists of interlaced beasts and that the beasts are 'dog-like'. If it is further supposed that the style of illustration resembles that used by the Lindisfarne artist in, for example, the medallions of the cross on cross-carpet page f. 26v (see Figs. 5.24 and 5.25), then one can 'expect' to see beasts with four legs, extended necks and bodies, and a tail, all interlaced with similar beasts and arranged in geometric order.

With these insights it can be seen that the design is symmetrical about a horizontal axis through the middle of the panel and that there are three beasts in each half. The shape of one such beast, taken from the bottom right-hand corner of the panel, is illustrated in Fig. 6.17. A mirror reflection of this beast reproduces the beast in the top right-hand corner. Following these procedures and then interlacing using a rigorous under-and-over discipline produces the simple line drawing in Fig. 6.16e that defines the basic features of the design but gives no indication of the cross-sectional shape of the carving on the stone.

A second important zoomorphic form on the Nigg stone is the snake or serpent. Dome-shaped bosses on the stone are ornamented with interlaced snakes that spread out from the bosses and form a background design by interlacing with snakes from other bosses. There are many examples of this form of ornamentation from Iona, Ireland, Islay and north-east Scotland, most notably the St Andrew's sarcophagus, the St John's cross on Iona, the Kildalton cross on Islay and crosses at Clonmacnois, Ireland. In a paper entitled 'Snake-Bosses and Redemption at Iona and Pictland', Mac Lean (1993) reviews the arguments and counter-arguments for the chronology and provenance of this form of sculpture, along with a consideration of iconographical issues, which is the stuff of art-historical and archaeological study. It is not so relevant to an awareness of the geometric implications.

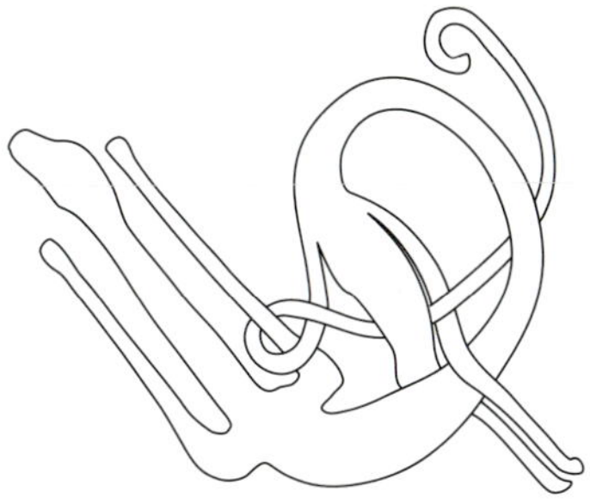

Figure 6.17
Zoomorphic form, resembling a 'Lindisfarne' dog, extracted from lower right-hand corner of panel shown in Fig. 6.15.

It seems likely that the stonemasons started with thick slabs of stone and dressed them down to produce a surface with dome-shaped features arranged in well-defined arrays. The patterns would then have been mapped on this surface in preparation for the intricate task of carving the fine detail. A simple illustration of a snake pattern is shown in Fig. 6.18a. The shaded boss is surrounded by a flat surface. The heads and tails of three snakes emerge from the interlacing on the boss. The geometric arrangement is closely analogous to simple interlacing patterns on flat surfaces. A variety of patterns can be generated using different break-and-join sequences. Clearly the interlacing pattern must satisfy a continuity rule such that all the strands of the pattern are included in the bodies of the snakes. This is readily established by following the path of each snake as demonstrated in Fig. 6.18b.

To create these patterns on a curved surface it is necessary to form a grid of equal-spaced lines on the actual surface of the stone. This is straightforward on cylindrical surfaces but is more complicated on surfaces, such as a hemisphere, with double curvature. Sets of equal-spaced lines are required so that the width and spacing of the bands (the bodies of the snakes) is the same over the whole surface. Illustration of the patterns on bosses is difficult and the interpretation of the patterns is even more difficult, particularly on weather-beaten stones created over a thousand years ago. No completely satisfactory interpretations of snake bosses are available. The difficulties of illustration are the same as those experienced by the cartographer who has to map, on a flat surface, the shape of features on the earth. This is almost impossible without the use of specialised methods of projection. The problem can be understood by reference to Fig. 6.19, which represents a section through a hemisphere. Points A, B, C etc are spaced equally on the curved surface and correspond to a set of equal-spaced lines on the spherical surface AB = BC = CD etc. In plan view the corresponding spacing of these lines is

Figure 6.18
Illustration of a snake boss. (a) Three snakes, interlaced on a boss, with heads and tails spreading out from the boss. (b) Paths of interlacing on the boss demonstrating that all of the cords belong to the three snakes.

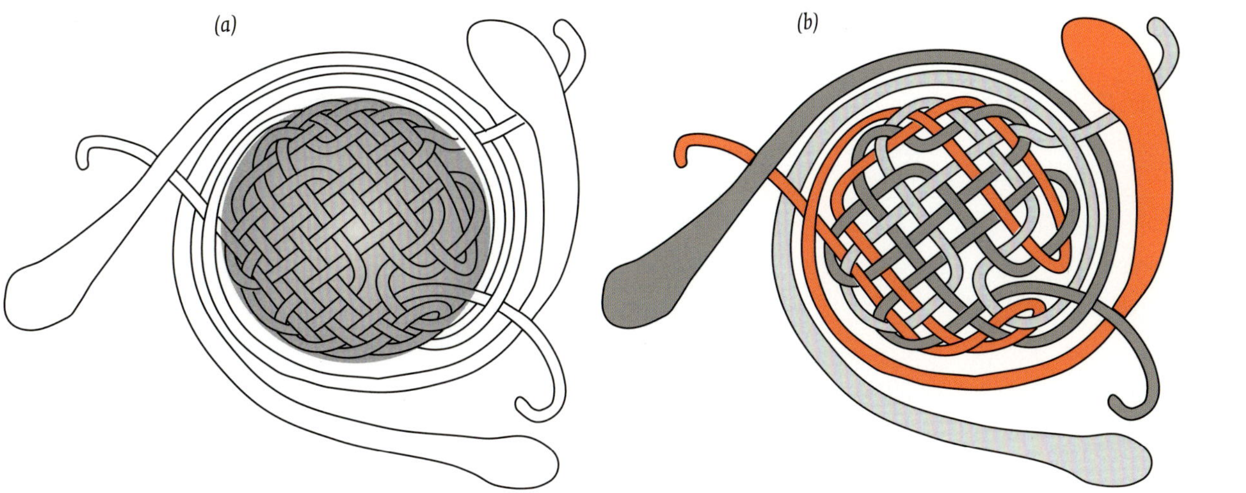

A′B′, B′C′, C′D′ etc. Clearly in plan view the lines are not equal-spaced and when the lines are treated as cords of finite width they will merge together towards the outside of the dome. For a dome with the shape of only a small part of a sphere, as in Fig. 6.19b, the effect is not so marked.

Few observations have been made of the cross-sectional shapes of the domes on carved stones. Petley observed that on the Nigg stone 'the circles and lozenges in the compartments on each side of the cross [are] an inch and a half above the level of the base'. This indicates that the shape of the bosses was similar to the shape illustrated in Fig. 6.19b. Such other evidence that exists suggests that the shapes of the bosses range from shallow domes to protruding domes, as on the Kildalton cross (Fig. 6.20).

The Nigg stone also displays domes ornamented with other motifs such as spirals and key patterns. The geometric constructions for these patterns are similar to those described in earlier chapters for flat surfaces. As always, the essential first step is the creation of a grid. The problem of illustrating these patterns remains.

CORRODED MANUSCRIPTS: BOOK OF DURROW

The cross-carpet page that now opens the Book of Durrow (Fig. 6.21) has been severely damaged by the corrosive effects of the copper salts in the emerald green pigments used in colouring. Parts of the vellum have been completely eaten away, leaving large holes roughly the shape of the pattern. In addition, as with other pages of the manuscript (see Fig. 2.17 relating to f. 2.48r) the page has been distorted by the combined effects of ageing and moisture. Nevertheless, reconstruction of the page is relatively straightforward once the main features of the design have been identified. The procedures, described in more detail elsewhere in this book, have been followed to

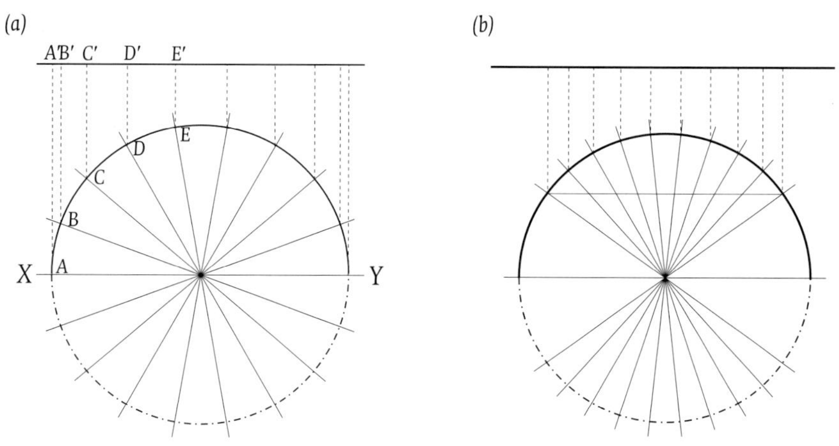

Figure 6.19
Projection of part of a sphere onto a planar surface.

produce a reconstruction of the central panel of the page containing an eight-square cross resembling a Patriarchal cross.

Westwood (1868) included f. 1v of the Book of Durrow in his reproductions of illuminated pages of early medieval manuscripts. It is not a true facsimile because, in reproducing f. 1v, Westwood reconstructed those

(a)

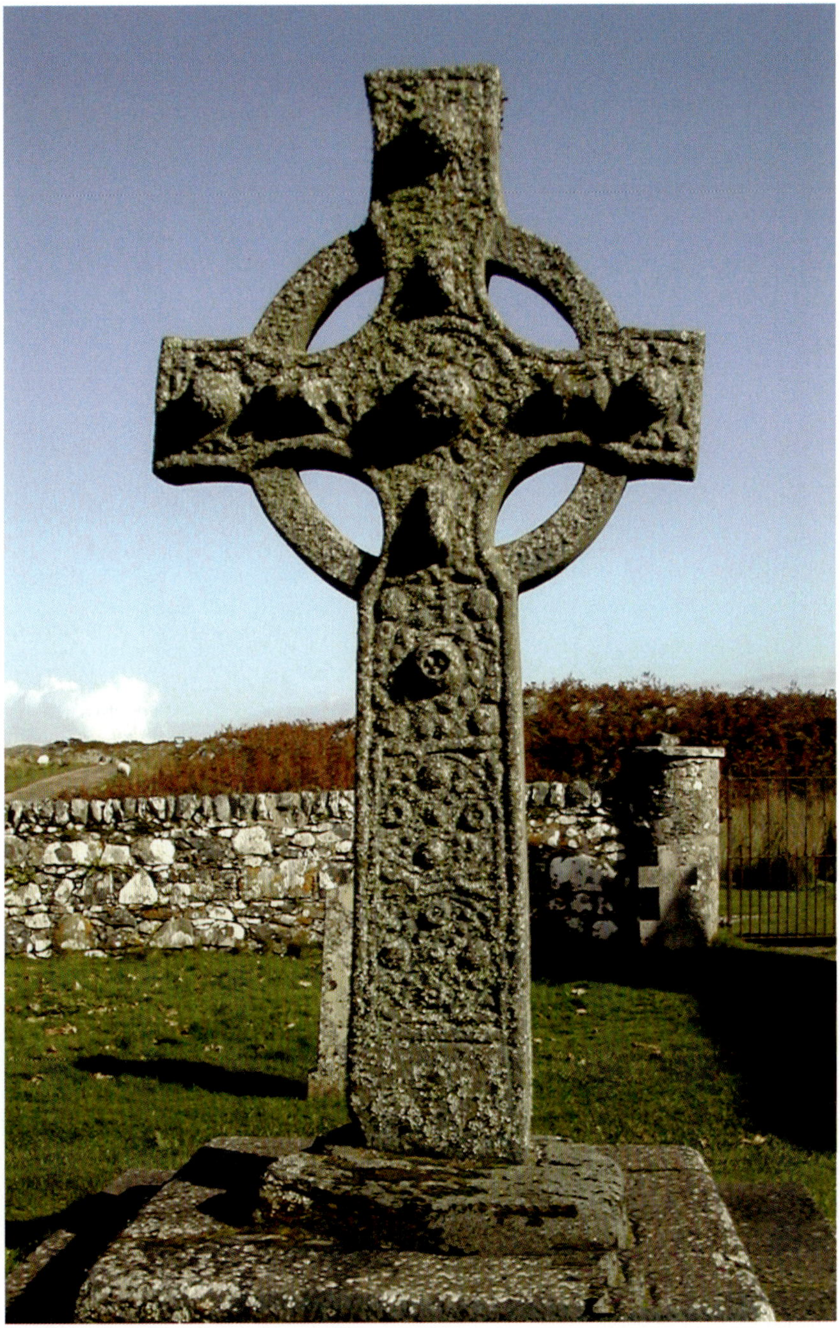

(b)

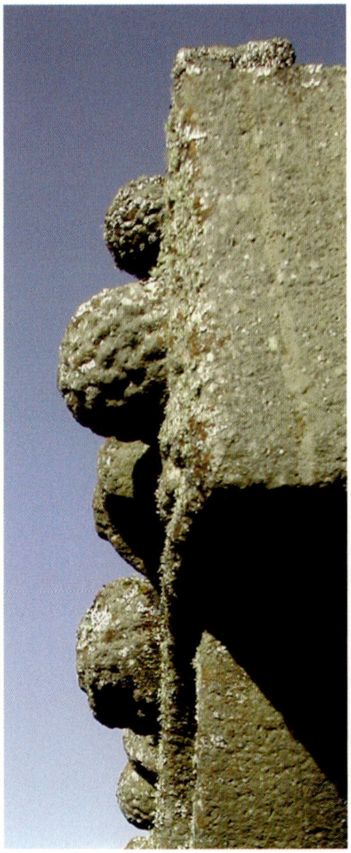

Figure 6.20
Kildalton cross on Islay, Scotland. (a) General view. (b) Side view of a boss.

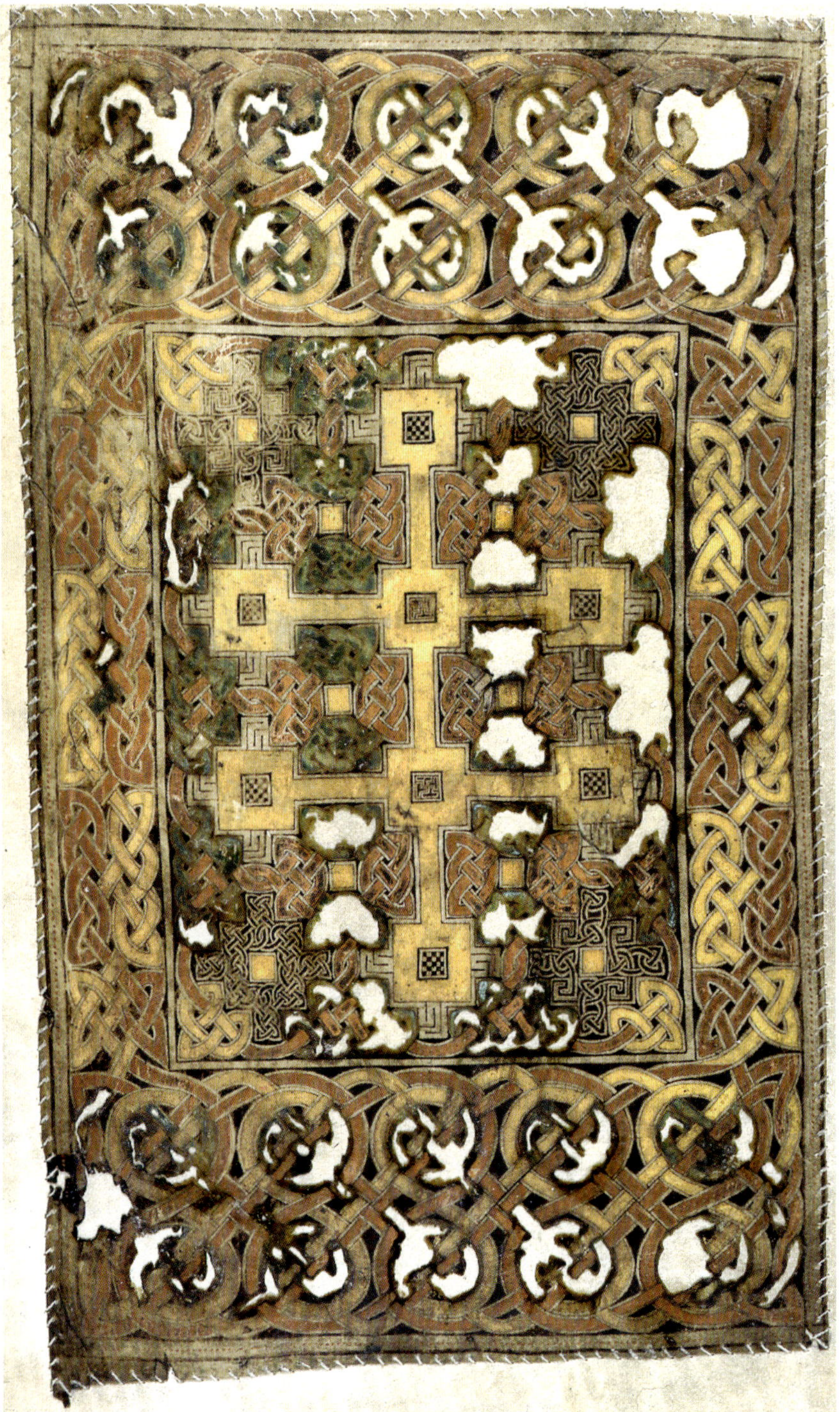

Figure 6.21
Photograph of cross-carpet page, f. 1v, of Book of Durrow (by permission of the Board of Trinity College Dublin).

parts destroyed by corrosion. He also corrected some of the features of the pattern affected by shrinkage and distortion. In the reconstruction described here a photographic image of the original manuscript and the various commentaries on the manuscript in Luce (1960) were used. It is to be noted that, in producing the photographic record, each leaf of the book was flattened and repaired, resulting in a further change of shape.

The whole of the carpet page is filled with simple motifs. The central panel is based on a 19-by-26 square grid and the eight-square cross conforms precisely to the grid (Fig. 6.22) in the same way as the cross in the *Persian Diatessaron* (Fig. 2.2). The main outline of the cross and surrounding panels have two mirror lines, through the centre of the rectangular panel, parallel to the sides of the rectangle. This mirror-image symmetry does not apply when fine details of the pattern, such as the interlacing sequences and the ornamentation of the small equal-armed stepped crosses in the corners of the rectangle, are taken into account. Two different interlacing patterns are used in these corners and they are arranged such that diagonally opposite crosses have the same design. The small squares in the centres of the large squares of the cross are filled with either chequer-work millefiori or swastika-like fret patterns. These, and the empty squares elsewhere, correspond in size and position to the individual squares of the primary grid. The chequer-work and swastika patterns are based, respectively, on five-by-five and eight-by-eight square grids (Fig. 6.23).

Remarkably, the pattern as a whole, even when scrutiny is extended to the fine detail in the individual motifs, has a twofold rotation point. Similarly, the interlacing patterns around the cross, ignoring the detail associated with linking with adjacent interlacing motifs, show fourfold rotation symmetry so that, starting with a simple unit, the pattern is developed by rotating, successively, by 90° (Fig. 6.24). It follows, with this level of symmetry and repetition throughout the design, that reconstruction (Fig. 6.25) can be achieved, with a high level of confidence, even though large parts of the page have been badly damaged.

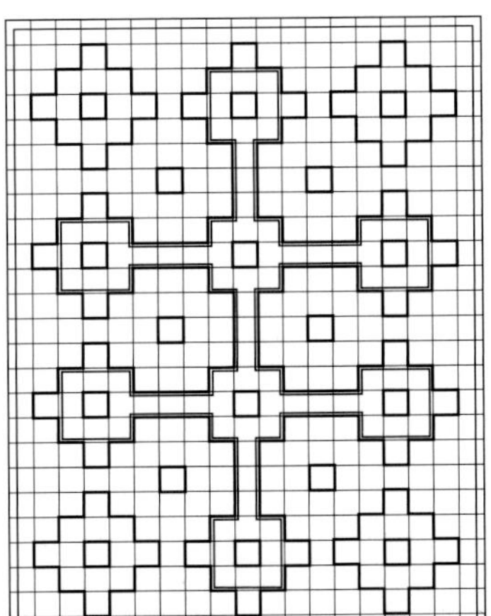

Figure 6.22
Outline grid of central panel of cross-carpet page f. 1v of Book of Durrow showing the position of the eight-square cross and other smaller panels.

There can be little argument about the geometric construction of this central rectangle although reference should be made to the layout constructions proposed by Stevick (1994). Basically, Stevick proposed that the shape of the central rectangle is based on the ratio $\sqrt{2} = 1.414...$ (an irrational number) as a result of a construction with compasses and a straight-edge. Measurements made on the facsimile edition show that the rectangle is distorted and that the ratio is close to 1.40. A grid of 26 squares by 19 squares gives a ratio of 1.368... Because of the distortion any one of these ratios could apply, but the evidence is strongly in favour of the interpretation, used here, based on a regular square grid.

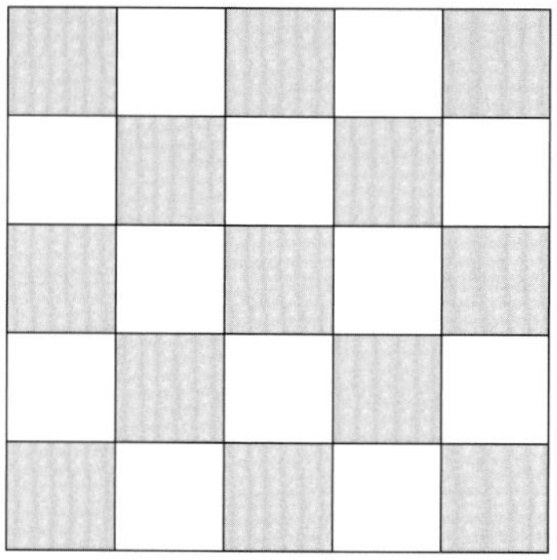

(a)

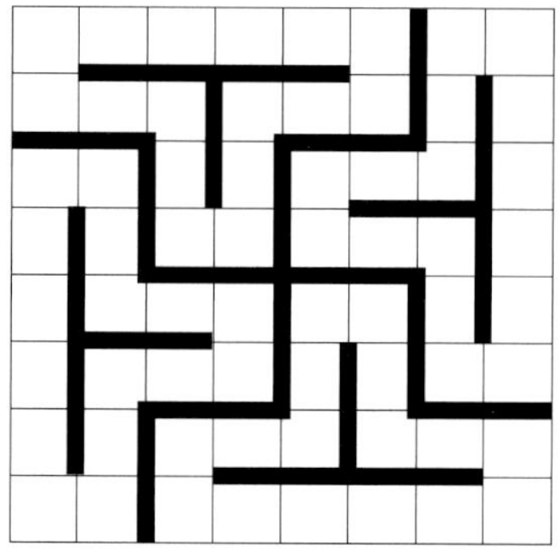

(b)

Figure 6.23
Illustration of grids used for (a) chequer-work, and (b) swastika-like patterns on f. 1v of Book of Durrow.

The pattern has many symmetrical features including the distribution of colours. It is to be noted that the broad bands of interlacing distributed around the cross consist of 25 separate cords. The artist has avoided emphasising continuity of the interlacing by changing the colours along single cords.

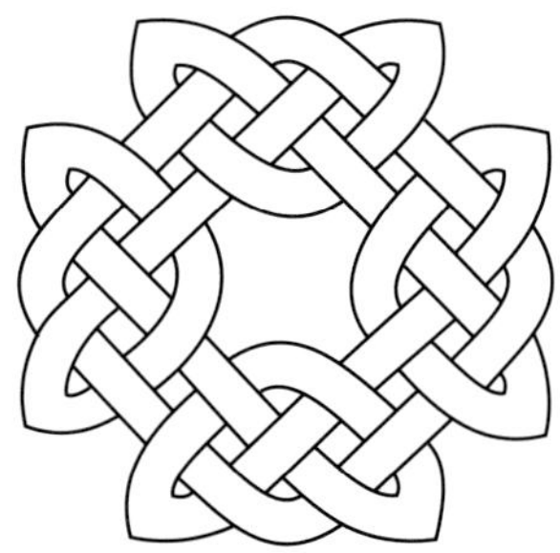

Figure 6.24
Formation of one of the simple interlacing patterns on f. 1v of Book of Durrow by rotation and repetition of a basic motif.

FINE-SCALE REPRODUCTION IN MANUSCRIPTS: BOOK OF KELLS

Reference was made in Chapter 5 to the incredible complexity of so much of the illumination of the Book of Kells. The work is less transparent than the equally magnificent and elegant Lindisfarne Gospels but it is on such a fine scale that the detail is barely resolvable even with a magnifying lens. There is also evidence of deterioration, with age and use, resulting in loss of detail and distortion, although the manuscript has survived far better than the Book of Durrow.

In this section an attempt is made to interpret the details in a small cross-shaped feature in f. 27v (Fig. 6.26). This page is dominated by symbols of the four Evangelists – man, calf, lion and eagle representing Matthew, Mark, Luke and John. The cross is ornamented with a conventional key pattern but the fineness of the detail and deterioration mean that interpretation is not straightforward. It seems that the artist has used some ingenuity to fit the zigzag key pattern to the stepped shape of the panel.

The layout of f. 27v is based on a square grid (Fig. 6.27). Symbols of the Evangelists occupy the four main panels. The borders are divided into panels ornamented with motifs – key, spiral, interlacing and zoomorphic – drawn to a very fine scale with a high level of geometric order and symmetry. The shape of the stepped central panel results from the layout of the main panels and the borders. It is no surprise that Sir Edward Sullivan (1920) observed:

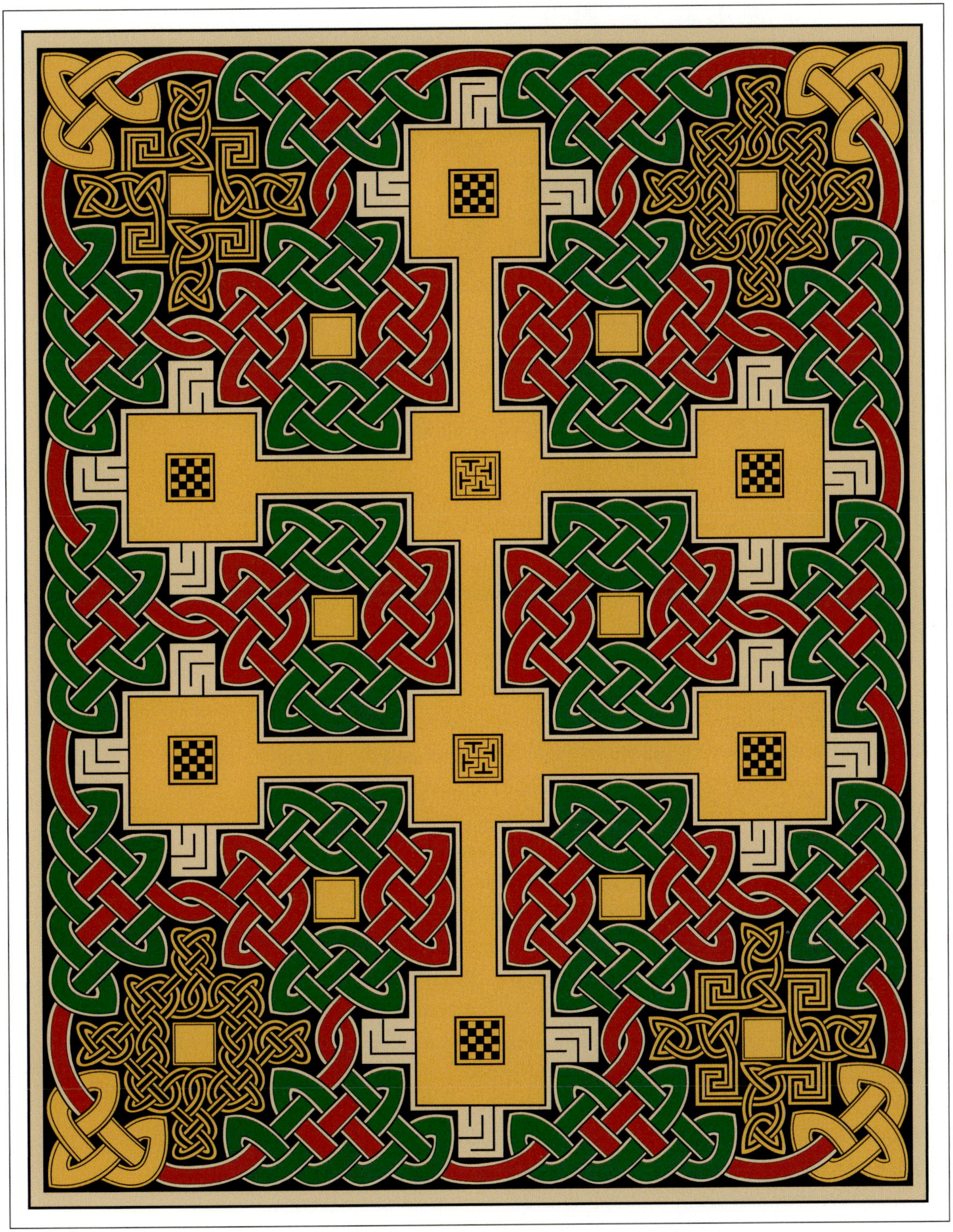

Figure 6.25
Reconstruction of f. 1v of Book of Durrow.

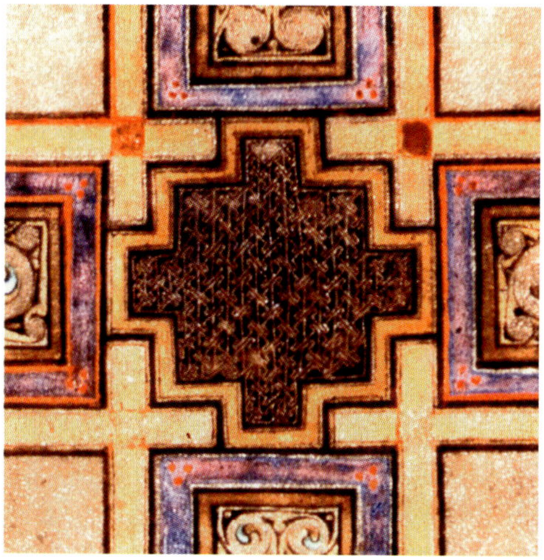

Figure 6.26
Photograph of small cross-shaped panel at centre of f. 27v in Book of Kells (by permission of the Board of Trinity College Dublin). The panel is 30 mm across.

'The central and some of the other panels in the borders of this page contain miniature work of an outstanding perfection'.

It is just possible in the facsimile edition of the Book of Kells (Henry, 1974) to recognise a zigzag key pattern in the stepped cross of the central panel. The basic unit of this pattern (Fig. 3.8b) is a familiar feature in Insular art and is transformed into a continuous design by simple repetition and translation (Figs. 3.7, 3.20, 4.8 and 4.10).

A natural approach to fitting this pattern to the step-shaped central panel of f. 27v is to identify a square grid with the unit dimensions of the square in Fig. 3.8b. Such a grid is shown in Fig. 6.28a. The result is close to the pattern evident in the manuscript but it is not entirely satisfactory because the mitres are wrong. In his reproduction of the same panel Bain (1951) assumed that the cross fitted a grid as shown in Fig. 6.28b and so achieved correct mitring. This approach is not satisfactory either because the resulting shape of the cross does not correspond to the shape in the manuscript. The problem is resolved by choosing a grid with both square and rectangular elements as in Fig. 6.28c. The central square of the cross has a 12-by-12 square grid (length of sides a) and the side arms have a four-by-four rectangular grid (length of sides a and $3a/4$). In this way the overall shape of the cross is achieved with an even number of grid elements and the corner designs satisfy mitring and aesthetic requirements. This construction (Fig. 6.25d) is in good agreement with the cross in f. 27v but the fine detail of the zigzag pattern does not match perfectly. Many of the small differences can be attributed to lack of precision by the artist who was working at such a fine scale. The most obvious anomaly is in the lower left-hand corner of the central square. The artist has introduced some extra lines so that the pattern has broken down in this region. Many of the other small differences can be attributed to the difficulties the artist must have faced in fitting the pattern to a non-regular grid.

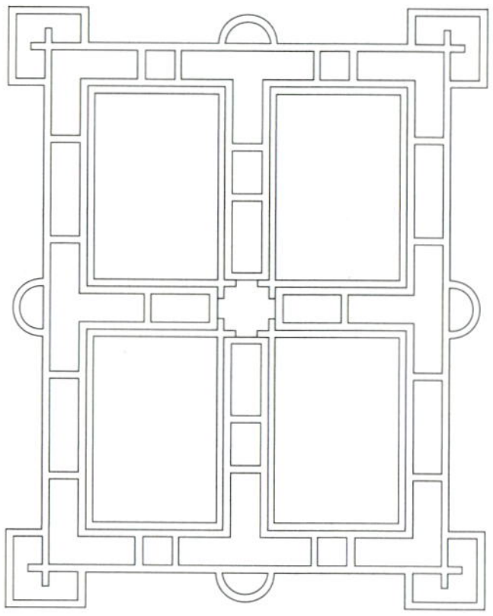

Figure 6.27
Layout of f. 27v of Book of Kells.

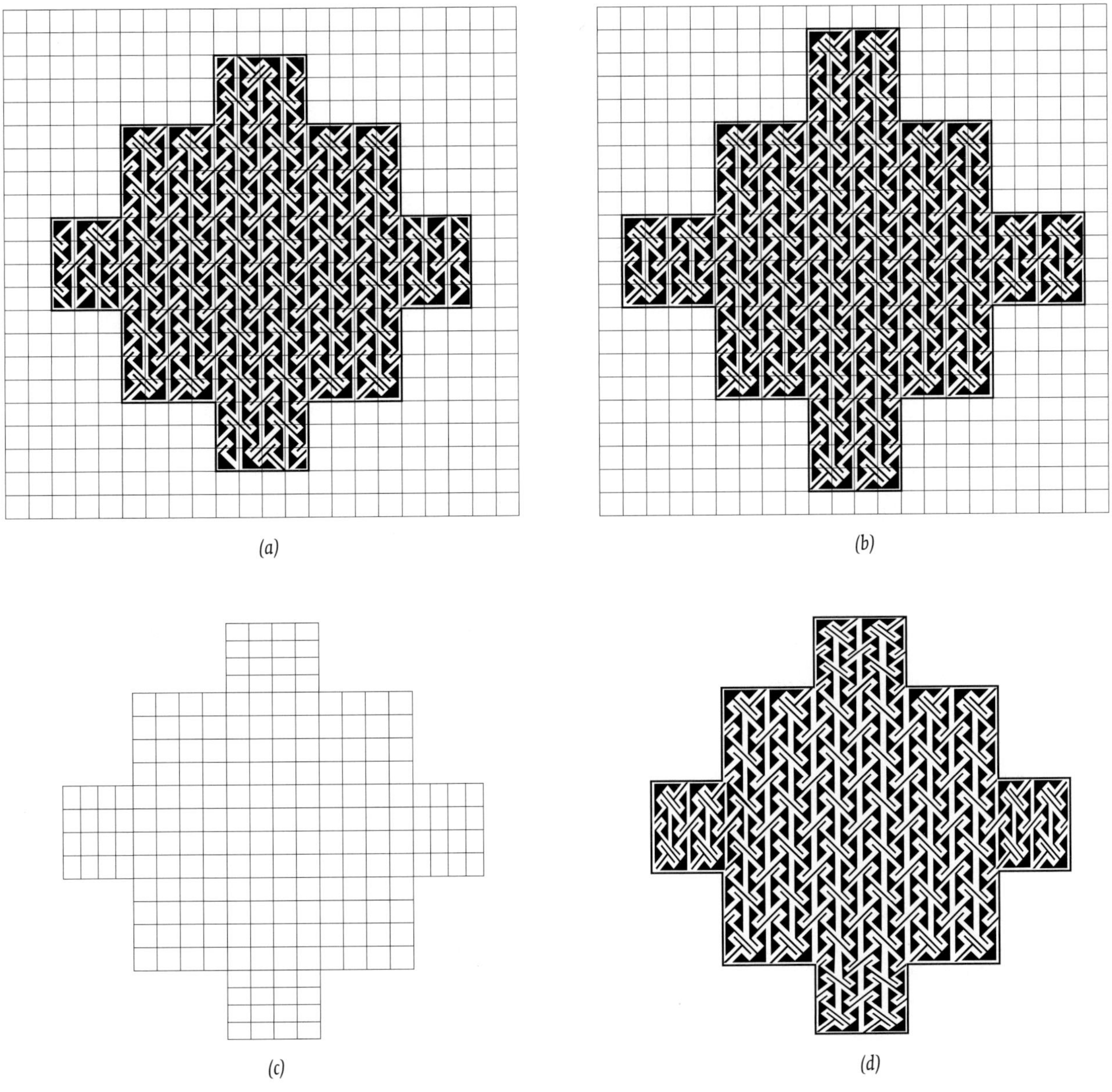

Figure 6.28
Illustration of aspects of construction of zigzag key patterns in cross-shaped panel of f. 27v of Book of Kells (see text for details).

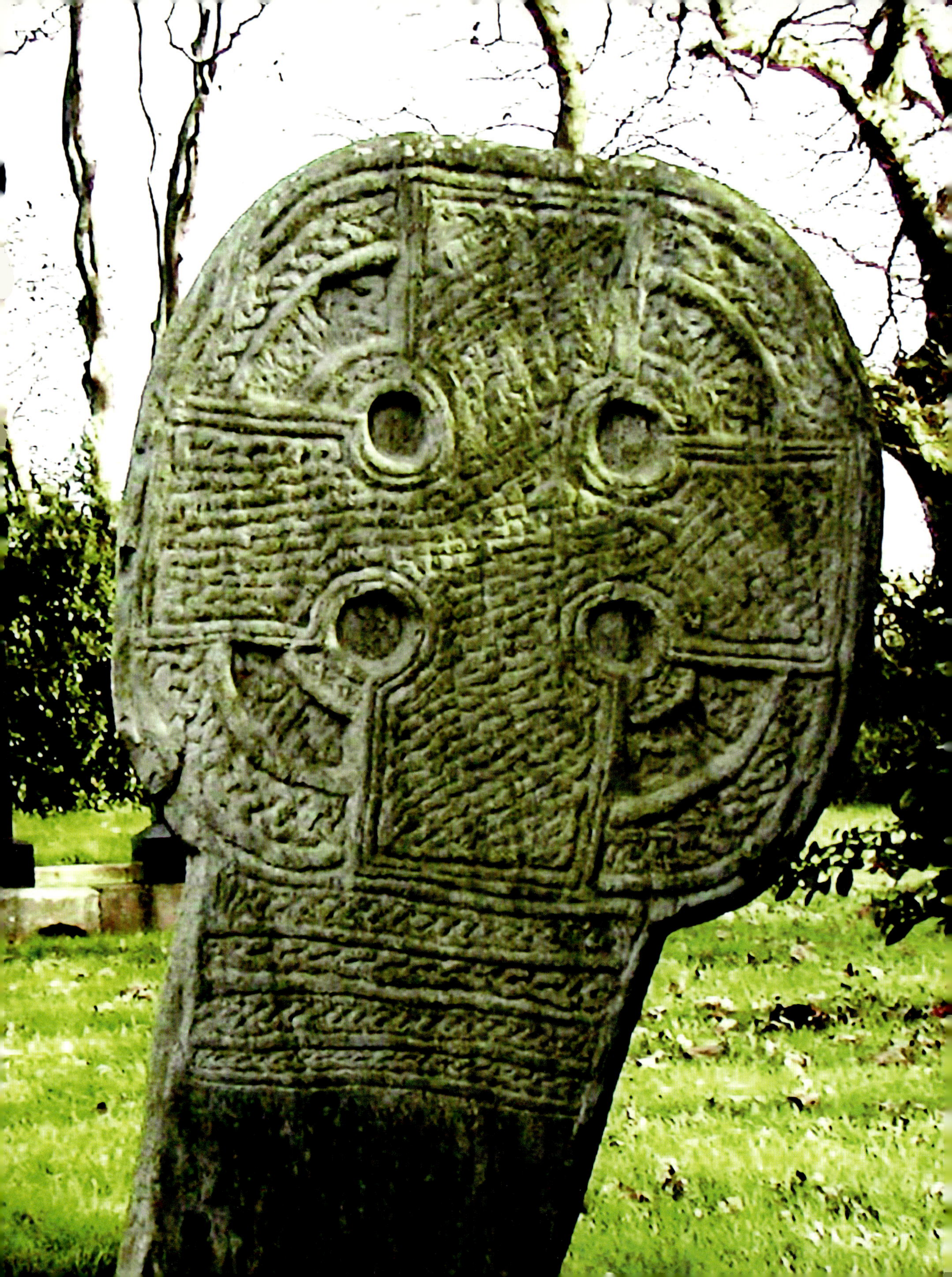

7

Distortions with time and breaking the rules

INTRODUCTION

The application of geometry and rules suggests some degree of order and organisation. But, as seen throughout the preceding chapters, even with a high level of conformity the sterile formation of regimented patterns does not follow and the artistic dullness of perfect patterns can be avoided and transcended. Geometry and rules then become the servants of art and not its masters (Read, 1931). They provide an underlying framework for artists and craftspeople working in a wide variety of media. Small changes in detail transform highly ordered patterns into intriguing new creations. In a sense one might argue that the evidence for the use of geometry and rules in early medieval times is, at best, circumstantial, but this evidence is nevertheless profound. There can be little doubt that straight-edge and compasses were fundamental tools used for laying out designs and creating the fine grids used in masterpieces as varied as the manuscripts of Durrow, Lindisfarne and Kells, the stone cross-slabs of Rosemarkie and Nigg, and the metalwork of the Hunterston and Kingston brooches and the Donore disc.

There are few examples in manuscripts, stone and metalwork that reach the high levels of perfection and aesthetic quality evident in the examples mentioned above. Equally, the quality of the application of rules and geometry almost invariably falls short of the standards set by these works. In this chapter some aspects of deviations are described. These are sometimes referred to as degradation and degeneration, or even debasement, particularly in the context of the way the art form has developed from one generation to another. There are many aspects of deviations that are more properly related to changes in style, differences in approach to design, and the influence of other schools of design, most evident in the changes that occurred following the Viking invasions and migrations. Even here geometry and rules continued to provide a framework for the art and can still be used as a basis for considering deviations in style, quality of craftwork and technique, and evolutionary changes.

Consider first features that might be classified as either intentional or genuine mistakes, best described as 'breaking the rules', where it is obvious from the rest of the work that the artist is fully conversant with the principles of geometry and the rules. Thus, for example, many apparent mistakes may have resulted from inadvertent errors that could not be removed because of the difficulties of making corrections once the work had been executed. This must be the explanation of the extraordinary error in the layout of the cross on the cross-carpet page of the Lichfield Gospel (Fig. 5.21). Once the ornamentation of the page had started the artist had little alternative, apart from abandoning the work, but to continue. There are many strange 'errors' in the art of Pictish cross-slabs that are more difficult to categorise, such as, for example, the non-symmetrical arrangements of the interlaced knot on Glamis No. 2 (Fig. 5.28) and the key patterns in the arms of the cross on Aberlemno No. 2 (Fig. 5.15). The overall quality of the carving on both these cross-slabs is of the highest order so it seems unlikely that the apparent errors are the result of carelessness. One possible explanation is that the sculptor was working from patterns or templates created by another artist and did not recognise the symmetry in the patterns or the requirement for symmetry overall.

There is also the possibility that these 'errors' were deliberate and used to achieve a particular aesthetic effect or to avoid 'perfection'. This is the argument cited in Chapter 5, and used by Backhouse (1981) to explain apparent anomalies in cross-carpet page f. 210v of the Lindisfarne Gospels. It is suggested that the artist was practising the humility of avoiding absolute perfection. In some cases it is hard to avoid the conclusion that the artist was being thoroughly mischievous.

Whatever the explanation it is important to distinguish mistakes of this kind from those associated with carelessness, poor workmanship and a lack of appreciation of the art forms the craftsmen were attempting to emulate. Gombrich (1960) has emphasised the confusion that arises in repeated copying by those who have not been trained in classifying the objects they were observing. In other words, without an understanding of the underlying principles, distortion and confusion set in and the final results bear little relation to the original. To quote Bruce-Mitford (see Kendrick, 1956–60), 'styles become sterile, flabby and degenerate once discipline and concentration falter and apathy and laziness take over'. In a similar and more extreme vein Nash-Williams (1950), writing about the changes in key patterns on stone monuments, observes that 'all forms become debased as time goes by, and finally degenerate into mere rusticated patterns'.

Clearly, thoughts of this kind were in the minds of Kermode (1907) and Nash-Williams (1950), when they studied, copied and reproduced the stone monuments of the Isle of Man and Wales respectively. They refer constantly, in describing the stones, to degradation and degeneration. In the next two sections there is a discussion of some aspects of so-called degeneration of interlacing and key patterns using stones found in the Isle of Man and Wales as examples. The designs on these stones are also used to introduce aspects of rules, related to geometry and the grammar of ornament, not yet considered. It seems that in these examples, the distinction between degeneration, associated with incompetence, and progressive change, owing to deliberate evolution of methods and styles, is not clear.

A different aspect of the breakdown of the conventional rules and practice involves the combination of motifs within a single panel that must have been associated with the evolution of style. Evolution becomes a major feature of the stonemason's art when the influence of Viking styles is introduced. Much of this art is on the edge of our subject, both in time and in style. Examples from the Isle of Man, Cumbria and North Wales are used to introduce some of the characteristic features of Viking-influenced work to demonstrate the nature of the changes that occurred.

It is worth recording that developments in style and form also occurred as a result of interactions with other cultures and societies. Most notable was the influence of Carolingian art on indigenous Anglo-Saxon art towards the end of the first millennium. Here there was a move towards more naturalistic art characterised, for example, by the introduction of foliate ornamentation such as the acanthus. The whole process is elegantly summarised by Kendrick (1949) as follows:

> *at the time of the appearance of Viking art, Northumbrian art was moving in the direction of a Carolingian style, that is to say it was forsaking, although with appreciable hesitation, the barbaric style for the classical style. Had it not been for the Vikings in York the acanthus would have flourished in the place of the withered vine-scroll, and there would have been a Northumbrian Winchester style [a style that combines the abstract geometric patterns of Insular art and the Carolingian style of tenth- and eleventh-century France and Germany with its fluent acanthus plant decoration]. It was the Vikings who put back the clock. Themselves loving barbaric art, they welcomed an English revival of it in the provinces they occupied. The timid Carolingian experiments were forgotten, and it was with the ancient art of the Columban missionary St Aiden, not that of the Francophile Alcuin, that the Saxon sculptors met the challenge of the Northmen.*

METAMORPHOSIS: INTERLACING AND KNOTS

Under the influence of heat and pressure rocks change their internal order – a silaceous sandstone becomes a quartzite and a limestone becomes a marble. The 'heat and pressure' for metamorphosis in early medieval geometric art has many forms, from the creative instincts of artists and patrons to the introduction of new motifs and styles by migrating peoples. The nature of this metamorphosis is elusive. It is only possible to touch the surface of the subject using a few examples to illustrate the nature of the changes.

The key rule of interlacing is the successive under-and-over movement of the cords. As demonstrated in Chapter 4, the formation of interlacing patterns is best understood using a regular grid as a starting point. It is possible, using different break-and-join sequences, to transform this grid into many designs. A regular sequence produces a repeating pattern. Allen and Anderson (1903) observed that 'the worst class of [interlacing] work, from a decorative point of view, is that in which the breaks in the plait are made without any apparent method, as in many of the Welsh and Cornish stones'. However, it does not follow that regular decorative patterns are the most pleasing aesthetically.

It is sometimes argued that a Celtic knot is made of a single cord, and is referred to by some Celtic enthusiasts as 'the thread of life'. Unbroken lines are said to symbolise the process of man's spiritual growth and the repeated crossing of the physical and the spiritual are expressed in the interlacing in knots. Unbroken lines are also seen as a symbol of eternity. This theme is developed by George Bain (1951), who cites examples that suggest that the artists of Pictland deliberately altered the break-and-join sequences in the interlacing to ensure that the pattern was made up of a single cord. He calls it a sacred Celtic line. Later in this section an approach to achieving single-cord patterns is described. However, one cannot assume that single-cord designs are in any way universal; the interlacing around the eight-square cross on f. 1v of the Book of Durrow (Fig. 6.21) has 25 separate cords.

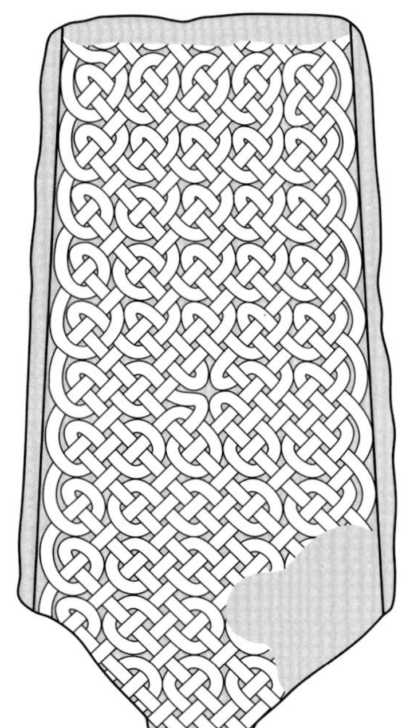

Figure 7.1
Reconstruction of the interlacing pattern on the remaining fragment of the Llangenydd stone based on a photograph of a cast of the stone in Nash-Williams (1950). The stone tapers towards the top.

Llangenydd stone, south Wales

As an introduction to a detailed discussion of the great cross at Lonan in the Isle of Man, two examples are considered that provide insights into aspects of metamorphosis. Figure 7.1 is a reconstruction of the pattern on a stone fragment found at Llangenydd in Glamorgan, Wales. The stone is recorded as No. 209 by Nash-Williams (1950). Using the approach described in Chapter 4 the pattern on the undamaged part of the stone can be described as a 22-cord plait with the following break-and-join sequence:

*[oooooooooo/ononononono/nooooooooo/popopopopop/oooooooooo/oooooooooo
o/nononononono/popopopopop/oooooooooo/ooooooooooo/nononononono/pooopopop
op/opoooooooo/ooooooooooo/nononononono/pooopopopop/opoooooooo/oooooooo
ooo/nononononono/popopopopop/oooooooooo/ooooooooooo/nonooonono/pooopo
opop/ooooonnoooo/oooonpooooo/nonooooooo/poooooooooop/ooopopopoo/ooooo
oooooo/nononononono/pooooooooop/opoooopoo/ooooooooooo].*

A more illustrative representation of the break/join sequence is shown in Fig. 7.2. Here the parallel (p) and normal (n) break/joins are marked by symbols. The final result is identical to the sequence described above. In both cases every detail of the design is given so that it can be reproduced precisely by an artist or craftsperson. The sculptor of the Llangenydd stone has

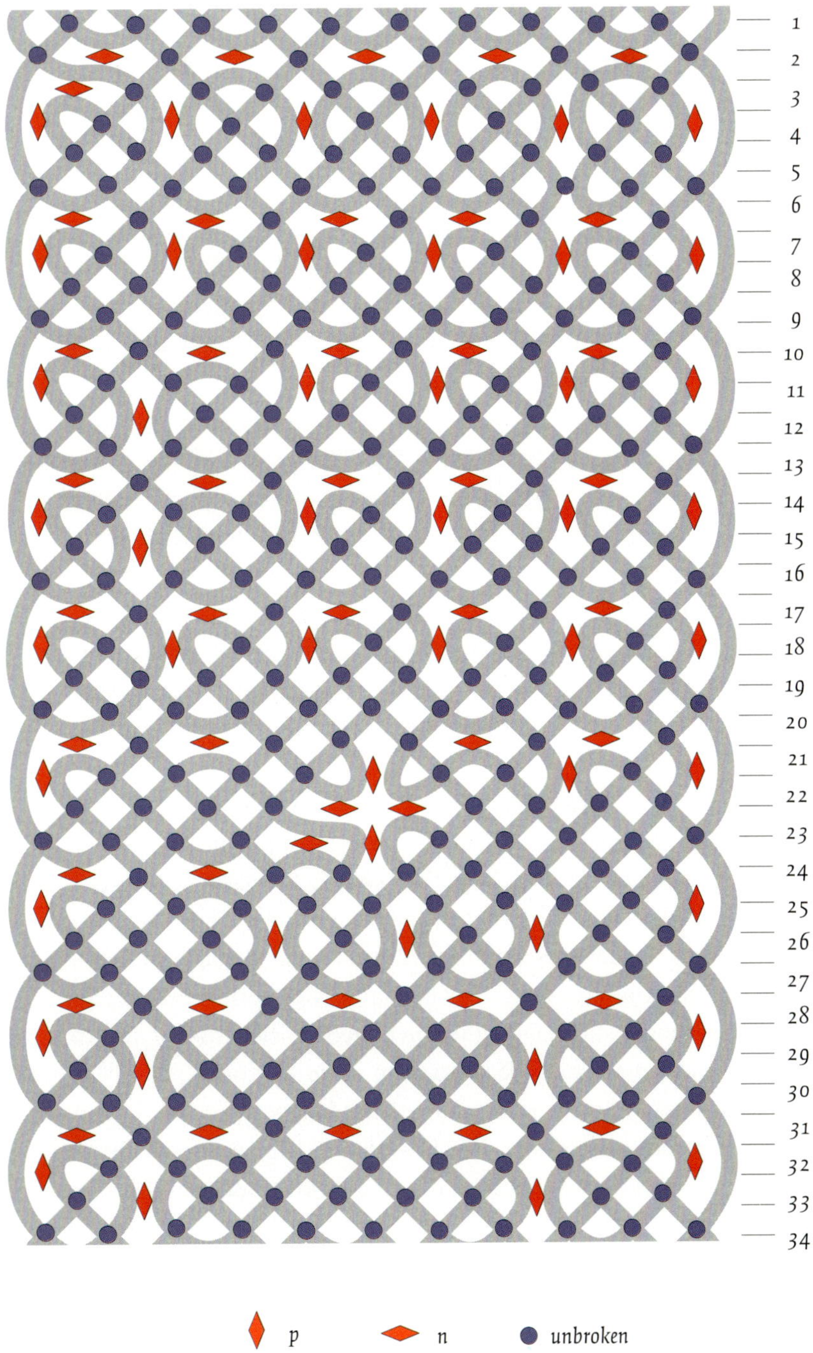

Figure 7.2
Break-and-join sequence on the undamaged part of the Llangenydd stone using a square grid and a 22-cord strand.

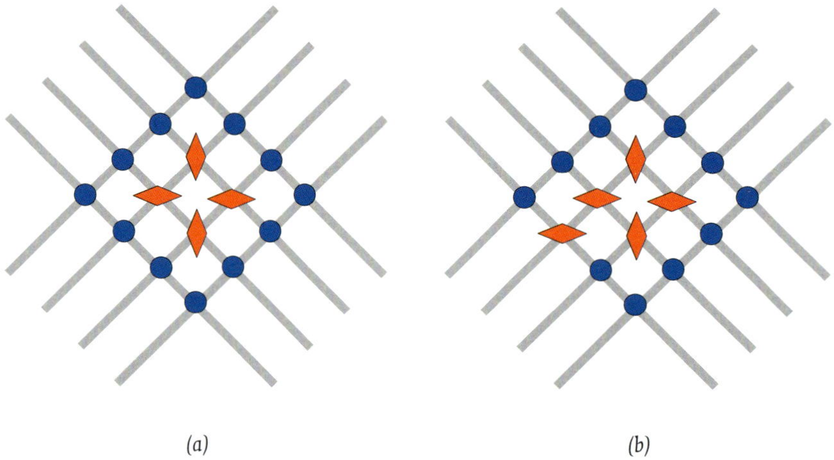

Figure 7.3
Break-and-join sequences for (a) regular and (b) distorted embedded crosses.

complied fully with the over-and-under rule of interlacing and yet the distribution of break/joins seems haphazard. The high quality of the work indicates that the position of the break/joins must have been determined before the work started and one is left wondering – one can only wonder.

There is a group of break/joins near the centre of the stone that is suggestive of a set of cruciform breaks as described in Chapter 5 for embedded crosses. Here again there is some mystery, for the choice of breaks produces a distorted cross, as illustrated in Fig. 7.3b. Thus, in the upper left-hand corner of the 'embedded' cross, there is an isolated closed loop of cord. Incidentally, the design on the stone is somewhat more sophisticated than the pattern in Fig. 7.2 because the stone tapers. This means that to accommodate the pattern the artist must have used a non-square grid.

Margam (Conbelin) cross, south Wales

The five-square cross set in a ring of interlacing (Fig. 7.4) was probably carved at the end of the ninth century or early in the tenth century at Margam Abbey in south Wales. It is No. 234 in Nash-Williams' corpus. The original monument is in the Margam Stone Museum and a cast is in the National Museum and Gallery, Cardiff. The name Conbelin recalls part of an inscription on the stone. Only the wheel-head of the cross is shown in Fig. 7.4b. On the actual stone the interlacing in the bottom square of the cross continues into a narrow panel on the shaft below the cross. In the central square of the cross there is a raised boss that is displaced from the main axes of the cross. This must surely have been a deliberate feature of the design.

The panels of interlacing in the squares of the cross, the arms joining the squares, and the arcs of the outer ring provide interesting insights into metamorphosis of interlacing patterns. Although each panel is different the over-and-under rule has been strictly obeyed. The four approximately square panels at the ends of the arms of the cross are used to illustrate the nature of metamorphosis. A similar analysis applies to all the other panels.

For convenience the notation adopted to describe borders of interlacing in Chapter 4 is used and each of the interlacing patterns in the squares is treated as a development of a border from a multi-cord strand. Consider then the changes in design and style of interlacing evident in the sequence of patterns displayed in squares marked (i) to (iv) in Fig. 7.5. In panel (i) the interlacing is formed from a 10-cord strand. The cords are arranged in a

(a)

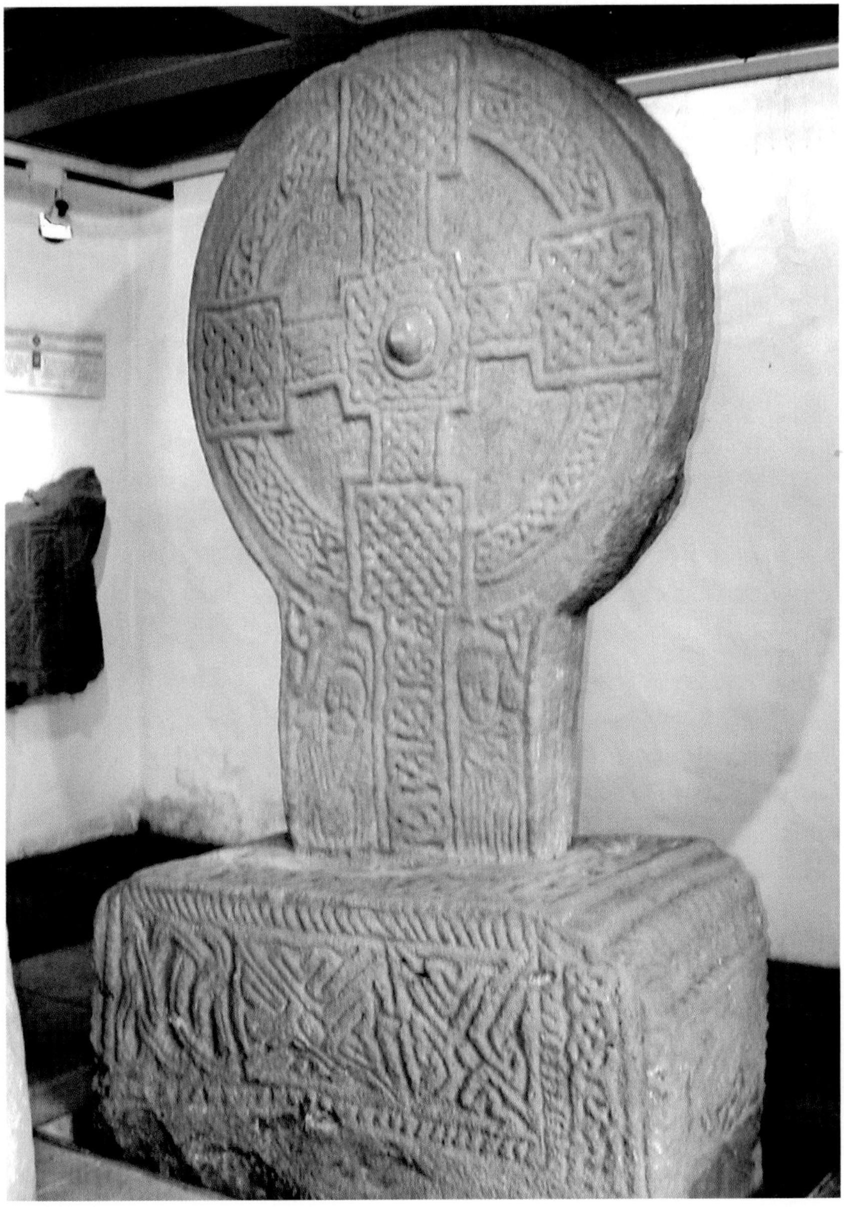

(b)

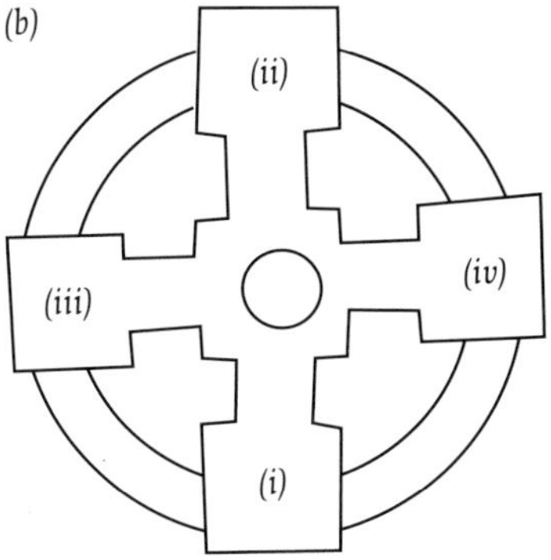

Figure 7.4
Photograph (a) and outline (b) of the Margam (Conbelin) cross showing the distribution of panels filled with interlacing.

regular and symmetrical way following a square grid without any breaks-and-joins. This is the simplest form of interlacing and, because the strand is not continuous, the loops at each end mean that the resulting interlacing within the panel consists of five separate loops.

The interlacing in panel (ii) is formed from a 12-cord strand using a square grid similar to that in (i). It is distinguished from (i) because there is a vertical break/join in the centre of the panel. Without the break/join the design is formed from a continuous loop. The break/join transforms this to two closed loops. In panel (iii), formed from a 10-cord strand on a diamond-shaped grid, there are five break/joins. These transform four separate loops of interlacing into three loops. One of the loops forms a closed circle. In this panel the shape of the loops and the decorative effects have been changed further by the use of a strong and deeply incised line down the centre of the

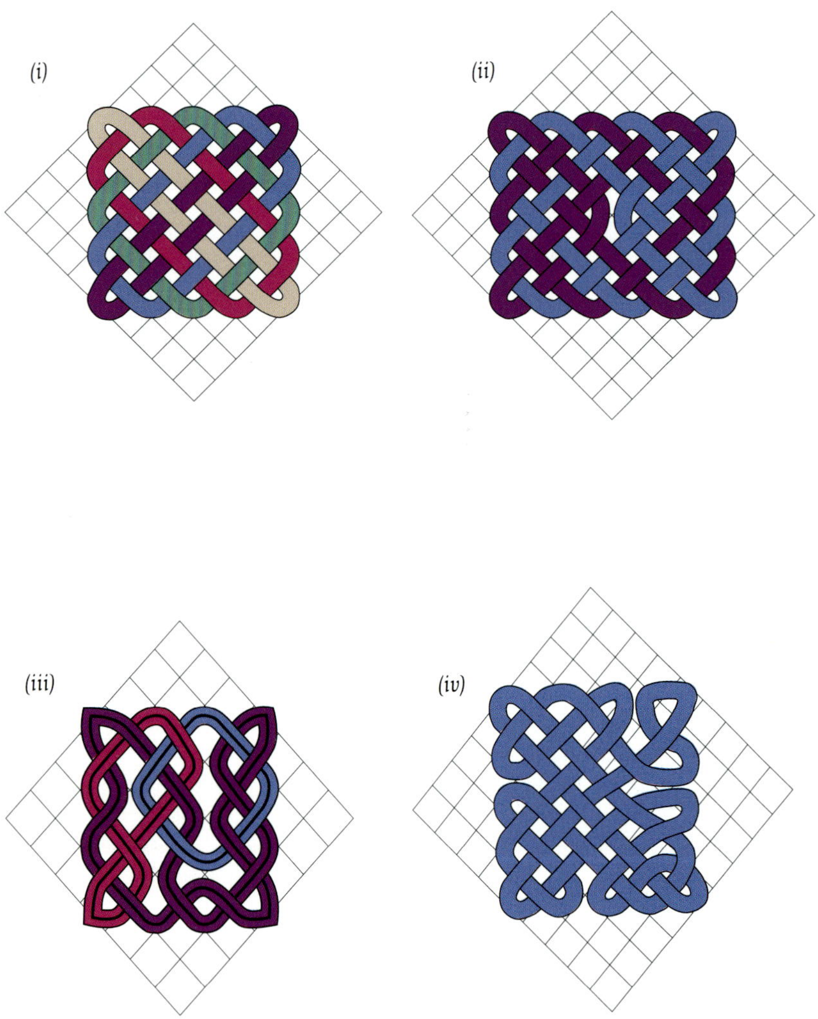

Figure 7.5
Details of the interlacing in the four 'square' panels of the Conbelin cross showing the progressive change of geometric detail and artistic style within a single piece of work.

cords and the arrangement of the cords is less ordered than in (i) and (ii). Finally, in panel (iv) a 10-cord strand, based on a slightly distorted diamond-shaped grid, has been transformed so that the left-hand side is regular and ordered with only two break/joins and the top right-hand corner is formed from a twisted loop with little regard for the conventional patterns of interlacing. The whole consists of a single loop.

The closed circular loop of panel (iii) and the irregular interlacing in (iv) have similarities with ornament on sculpture that is known to have been influenced by the art of the Vikings. There is a sense that, in presenting the work in this way, the artist is reflecting the passage of time and the inevitability of change. Whatever the intentions of the artist the impression is left that the changes have real significance and are not the idle results of poor workmanship, poor reproduction of standard patterns, or a deliberate disregard for the conventions of the past.

Lonan Old Church Cross, Isle of Man

This cross stands in the grounds of St Adamnan's church close to the coastal path in the Isle of Man. The church is said to be dedicated to St Lonan, or Adamnan, an Irish saint who was Abbot of Iona at the latter end of the seventh century, and the cross is dated some time between the seventh and ninth centuries. The photograph in Fig. 7.6 shows a very rugged cross set in a crude circle with a short stem. It appears to be tilting but no amount of realignment would makes it appear genuinely upright. In other words, that is the way it was made. The cross is designated No. 57 by Kermode (1907), who carried out a vast amount of research, involving meticulous copying, of all the stones on the island. A new numbering system was introduced by the Manx Museum and the cross is now designated No. 73.

Kermode's description of this cross is very informative and justifies an extensive quotation:

> *the stone, with pure plait-work decoration is remarkable for the badness of its workmanship... a large wheel-cross, ninety-nine inches in total height; the head is thirty-eight inches across, the fust twenty-four inches, and the stone is four inches thick... This is by far the most difficult piece of plait-work I have had to trace, and it has taken me many weary months to do so. At one time I was inclined to think that it was merely a pseudo-plait, in reality a hopeless tangle of discontinuous bands. Upon finally completing my full-sized drawing with the aid of the cast and many tracings, I was however, able to account for each particular portion of every band, and found the plait to be composed of no fewer than nineteen separate straps or strands, most of which form 'dead-ends' against other straps... there were many instances of irregular lapping over, or under, two or even three times in succession, while some straps are very short. The best part*

of the work is the head, which is quite regular. Evidently this is where the carver began his work, but before long he lost himself entirely. It looks as though the design had been correctly drawn, but the lines had got erased, the workman perhaps being ignorant or careless. This also will account for the more simple portions in the smaller spaces between the limbs being correctly carved. Two of the strands are continuous through the lower limb which is also fairly good, the left arm being the most confused.

The interpretation of the ornamentation on the cross in Fig. 7.7 is based on the drawing by Kermode following his painstaking work using rubbings and direct observations. It was copied by tracing Kermode's drawing rather than drawing from first principles. The design lacks geometric rigour and the under-and-over rule has not been obeyed fully. Kermode's drawing is not entirely clear

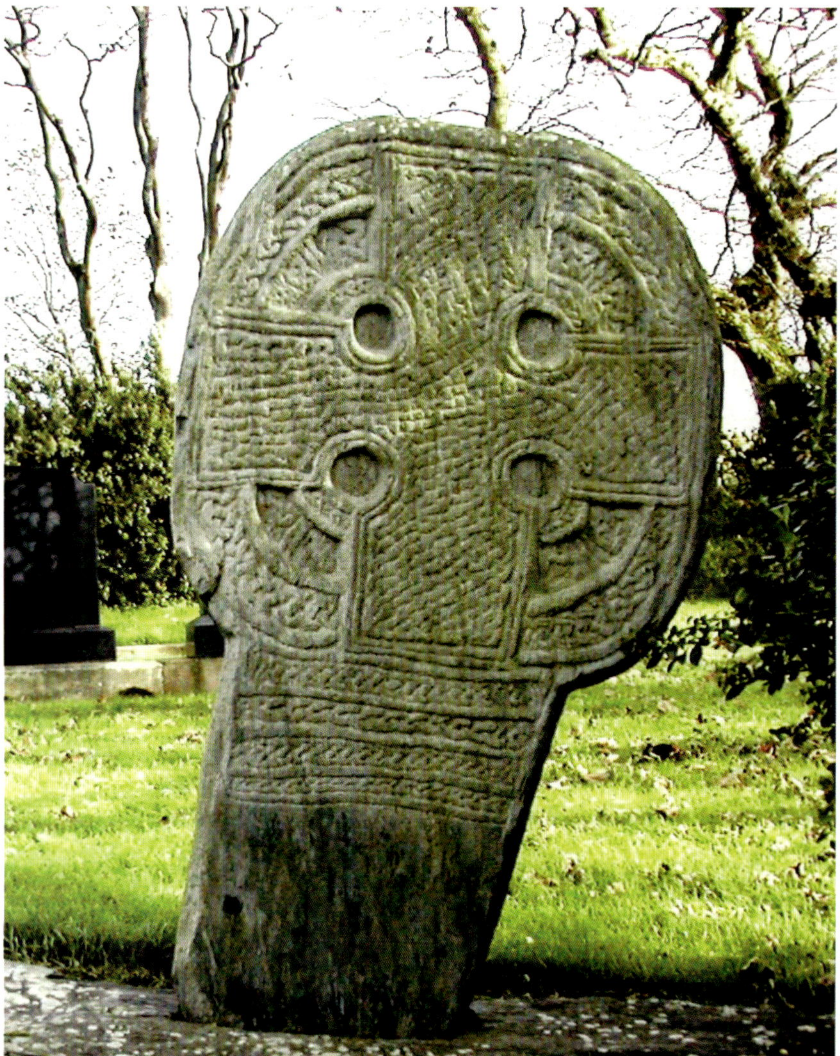

Figure 7.6
A rugged cross in the churchyard of Lonan Old Church in the Isle of Man. Dappled winter sunshine has revealed details of the design on part of the stone.

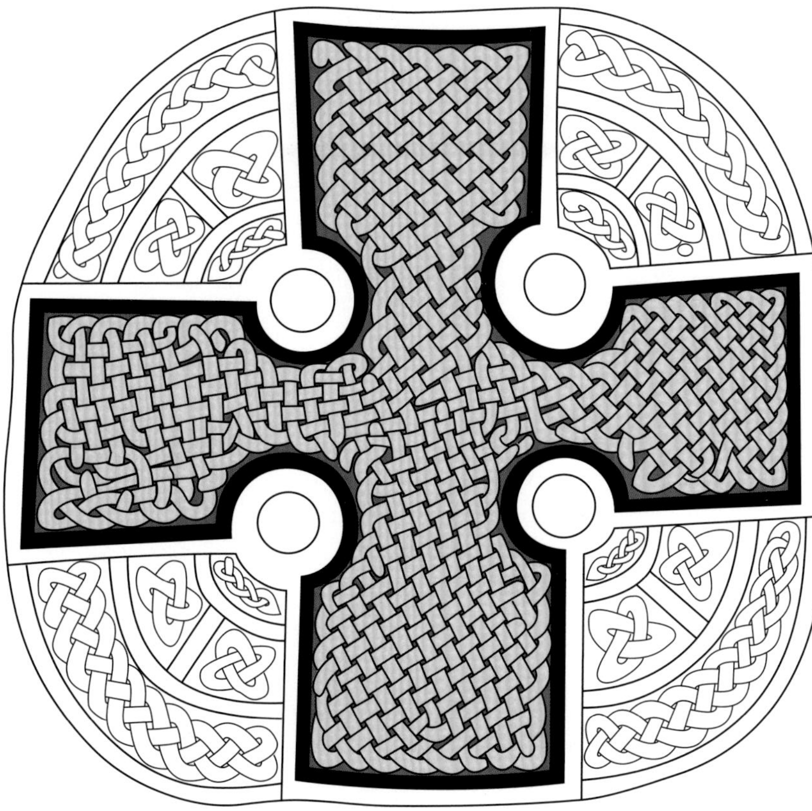

Figure 7.7
Tracing of the interlacing on the Lonan Old Church cross based on the work of Kermode (1907).

and it seems likely that he has relied to some extent on interpretation. In drawing Fig. 7.7, the individual cords of the interlacing have been made slightly narrower than on the stone to make the detail less confusing.

Kermode attributes the lack of perfection in the design to poor workmanship. However, it may be, as suggested for the Conbelin cross, that the progressive change in the quality of the interlacing is deliberate. One has an image of an imperfect cross, a broken cross for a suffering world, a weary man struggling with the change and decay that is the fate of all mankind – a metaphor in stone for the human condition.

Continuous paths

A surprising feature of the Lonan cross, particularly in view of the traditional Celtic views about continuity referred to earlier, is the total breakdown of any sense of continuity of the interlacing. This is most evident in the lower parts of the design as the interlacing becomes progressively more contorted and irregular. It is, of course, relatively easy to produce a design that fills a panel, in the shape of a cross, with a continuous band of interlacing. Indeed, Bain (1951) produced an elegant design with continuous interlacing, based on the

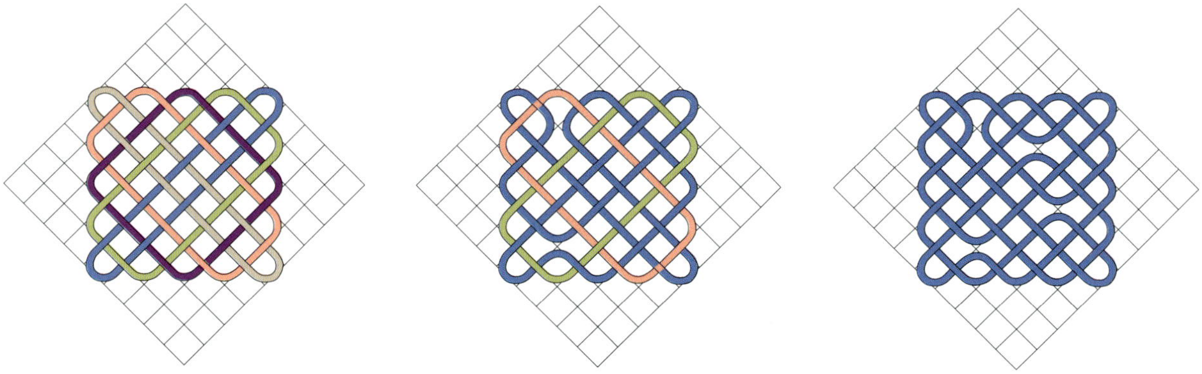

Lonan cross, which he used for a greetings card. It is formed from a single cord and has a high level of order and symmetry.

A design with multiple cords can be transformed to one with a continuous loop, as illustrated in Fig. 4.37 for the formation of a triquetra knot from three interlocking loops. This transformation involves two break-and-joins. The general rule, referred to in Chapter 4, for transforming a set of loops into a single loop can be applied to the interlacing in the square panels of the arms of the Conbelin stone. Thus the interlacing in panel (i) of Fig. 7.5 consists of five separate paths (n = 5). To transform it into a single loop requires (5 – 1 = 4) break-and-joins. An example is illustrated in Fig. 7.8.

Figure 7.8
Transforming an interlacing pattern made up of five separate cords into a pattern with the same basic geometry but with only one cord. (a) Five cords. (b) Two break-and-joins transform the five cords in (a) to a design with three cords. (c) Four break-and-joins in (a) produce a design with a single cord.

METAMORPHOSIS: SQUARE KEY PATTERNS

In the context of this discussion a square key motif is simply a square motif ornamented with a key pattern. A selection of such motifs, found on carved stones in Wales, is illustrated in Fig. 7.9. They have been constructed from square grids and display different levels of symmetry. Thus, for example, the pattern in Fig. 7.9a has a twofold rotation point and two mirror lines and the pattern in Fig. 7.9b has a fourfold rotation point and four mirror lines. The 'swastika-type' step pattern in Fig. 7.9c has only a fourfold rotation point and can been drawn in a clockwise or anti-clockwise sense.

In stonework and manuscripts these motifs have been used separately and in combination as rows, columns and two-dimensional arrays. An example of an array of motifs in the form of a cross is illustrated in Fig. 4.12 from the Macdurnan Gospel book. Two-dimensional arrays of motifs are used in the central panels of two crosses in Wales, at Nevern and Carew. They are of particular interest, for here a progressive development of the design that creates additional complexity can be discerned. Some may call this work degenerate but in a very real sense it is both fascinating and original.

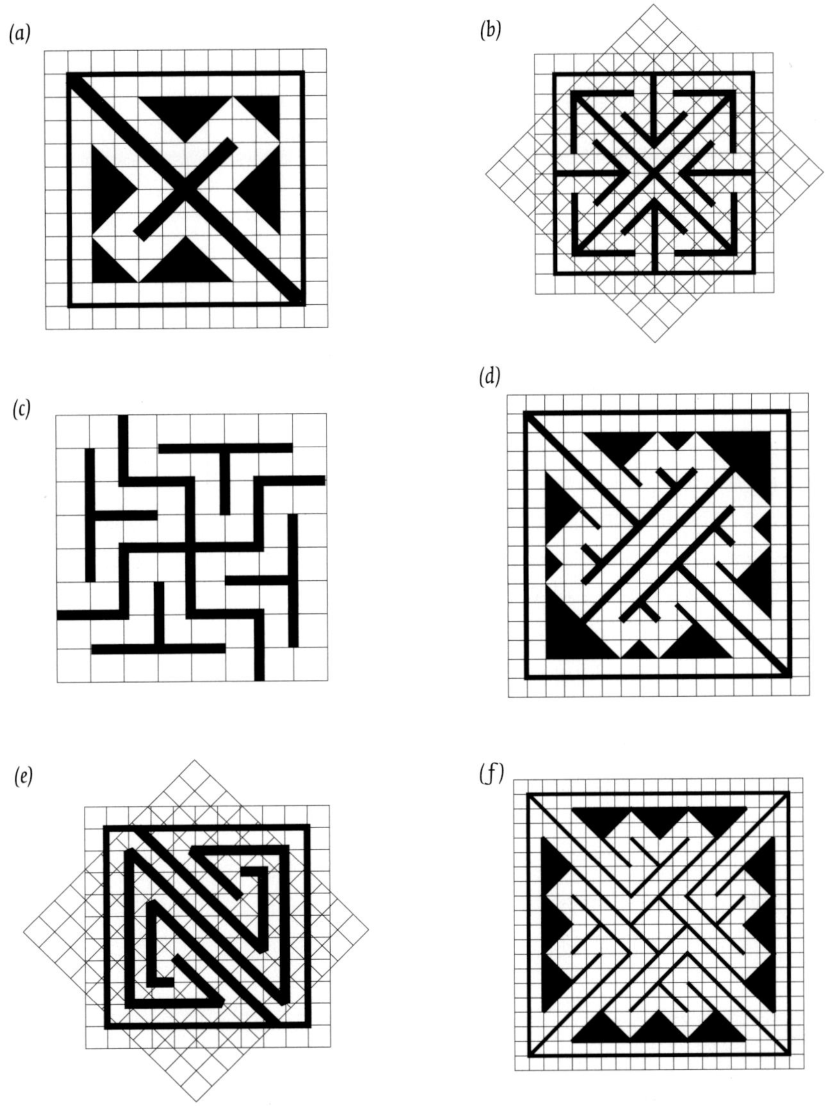

Figure 7.9
Selection of square key patterns from stone monuments in Wales.

It seems likely that the Nevern cross, outside St Brynach's church in the little village of Nevern between Cardigan and Fishguard, and the Carew cross, which stands in a small walled enclosure at the edge of a field close to Carew Castle near Pembroke, were made at the same monastery workshop. They have been dated to the second half of the tenth and early eleventh centuries (Nancy Edwards, private communication; Redknap, 1991). The shafts of these crosses have rectangular cross-sections and all four faces are ornamented with interlacing and key patterns in a range of styles. Some of the interlacing designs are precise and well ordered, some have irregular breaks and some have inscribed lines in the middle of the bands. The range of styles is similar to those described in the previous section for the Conbelin cross. The cross-head of the Nevern cross, ornamented with triquetra knots, was used in Chapter 4 (Fig. 4.39) to describe the formation of designs with continuous loops.

The layout of the panels on the front face of both stones is illustrated in Fig. 7.10. Westwood (1876–79) was the first to produce detailed drawings of these stones. Allen (1899) described the patterns on the stones using the same approach that he used in his later work with Anderson. Line drawings of the patterns on the Nevern and Carew crosses, by Worthington G. Smith (WGS), the draughtsman of the Cambrian Archaeological Association, are included in Allen's article and are reproduced in Nash-Williams (1950). The outline drawings in Fig. 7.10 are based on Smith's work.

The most prominent panels on both stones, shaded in Fig. 7.10, are filled with a zigzag key pattern as shown in the photographs in Fig. 7.11. The structure of these patterns is not immediately obvious. The pattern on the Nevern cross is more ordered than that on the Carew cross, suggesting that Nevern was produced before Carew. In simple terms the panel on Nevern is made up of six squares of key patterns in a two-by-three array (Fig. 7.12a) and the Carew pattern is made up of a three-by-three array (Fig. 7.12b). In both, the squares and the resulting panels are distorted. Outlines of the actual patterns are shown in Figs. 7.12c and d. The starting point for interpreting these patterns is an understanding of the construction of the square key patterns. An important requirement is that at the corners of the squares the diagonal lines combine to form a swastika-like arrangement, as at X in Fig. 7.12c.

The basic unit of the design is created from a square grid (Fig. 7.13a) and has a fourfold rotation point. It can be represented in an anti-clockwise sense (as in Fig. 7.13c) or a clockwise sense. The diagonal lines intersect the

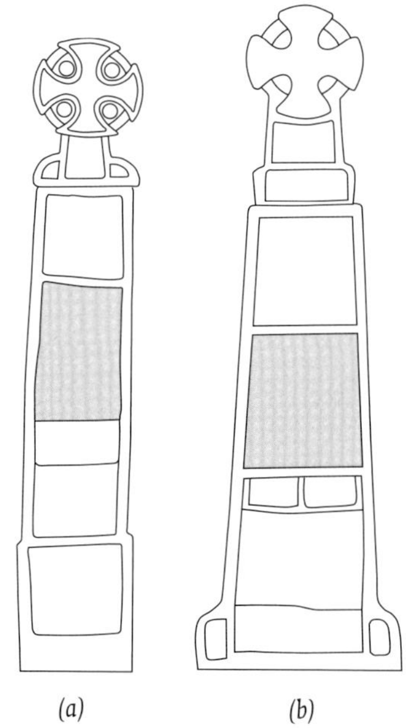

Figure 7.10
Layout of panels on front faces of (a) Nevern cross and (b) Carew cross.

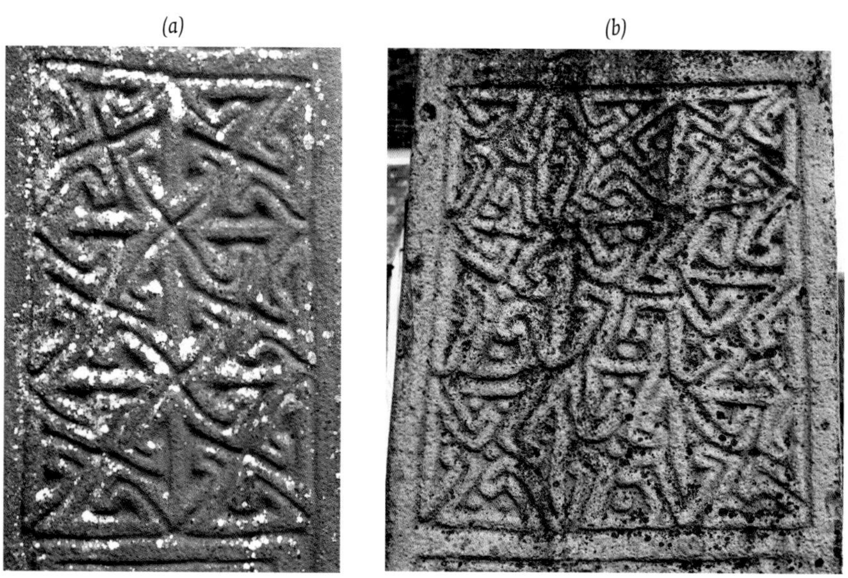

Figure 7.11
Photographs of irregular zigzag key patterns on front faces of (a) Nevern cross and (b) Carew cross.

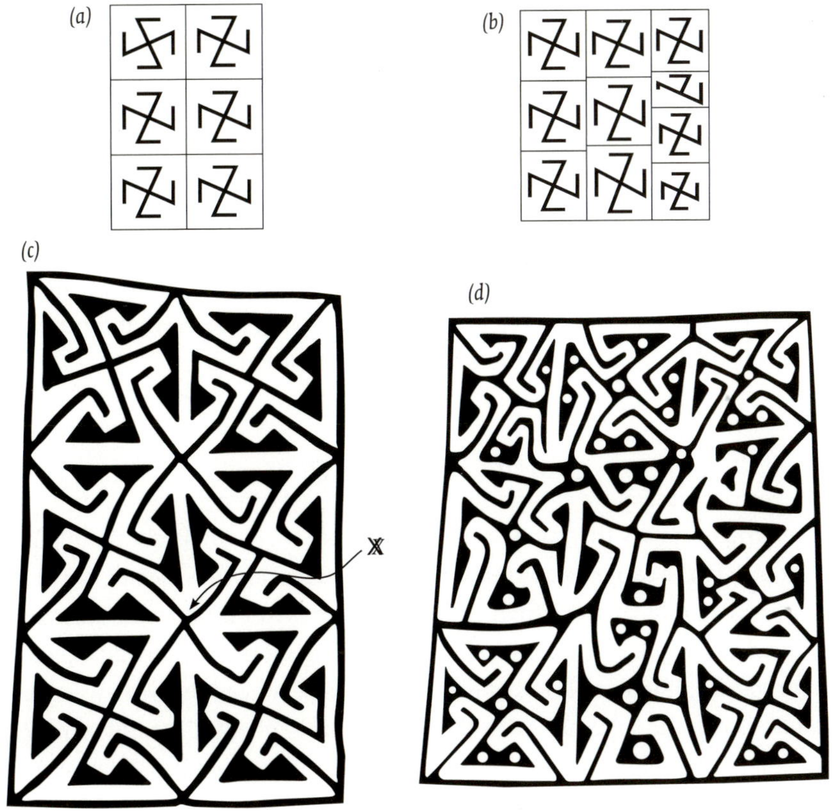

Figure 7.12
Arrangement of zigzag patterns on (a and c) Nevern cross and (b and d) Carew cross.

corners of the outer square and a small square, oriented diagonally, is formed in the centre. This square is not present in the designs on the Nevern stone. The key pattern has been modified, as in Fig. 7.13b and c, with curving lines. The size of the diagonally oriented square can be changed by modifying the curvature. A range of designs, based on the same unit square grid, are evident on the Carew panel.

The artist developed the designs further by varying the way that the squares were combined to form the panel, as illustrated schematically in Fig. 7.12a and b. In the Nevern panel the zigzags in the squares are arranged in an

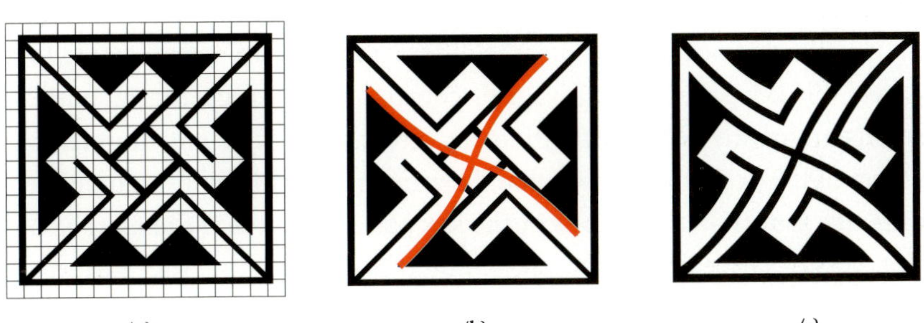

Figure 7.13
Development of zigzag squares for designs on Nevern and Carew crosses.

anti-clockwise sense except in the top left-hand corner which is in a clockwise sense. The zigzags in this square are in a mirror orientation to the zigzags in the other squares. In this way the artist has created asymmetry and a sense of mystery. In the Carew panel all the zigzags are arranged in the same sense but the squares are distorted and part of a square has been inserted in the column of squares on the right-hand side. The square in the lower left-hand corner is the most geometrically precise. Insertion of the extra half square has created distortion and confusion so that the design cannot be understood so easily. Small pellets, arranged somewhat randomly, have been included between the zigzags of the Carew panel.

MIXING MOTIFS

It is a truism to say that 'one needs rules before one can distort them'. The examples in the two previous sections demonstrate this very clearly, for there can be no doubt that the final designs were based on patterns that were ordered and regular. The convention of confining motifs to individual panels was retained. It is also clear that the artists who produced the work were very familiar with the rules although they clearly broke them. Consider now the designs on two crosses, from Inchbrayock in Scotland and Penally in Wales, in which the ornamentation is mainstream in relation to the geometric art of the early medieval period and yet the artists have broken even more of the established rules and conventions.

The Inchbrayock cross is now in the museum at Montrose having been found on an island in the estuary close to Montrose in Scotland. There is also a cast of the cross in the museum, which provides facilities for making rubbings of this replica. The drawing in Fig. 7.14 is based on a rubbing and photographs. An accurate interpretation is not possible because the stone has been damaged by erosion and wear. The main features are undoubtedly correct. Allen and Anderson (1903) make a half-hearted attempt to describe the ornamentation as follows: 'a diagonal key pattern in the centre of the head developing into spiral work (too irregularly disposed to be capable of being classified) on the four arms'.

Unlike conventional designs, the different motifs are not separated into panels, the key pattern is only vaguely constrained to a regular grid, and the spirals are poorly developed with many bifurcations. The most interesting aspect of the design is the way that the artist has combined two completely different motifs so that bands of the key pattern flow into the spirals and vice versa. There is a dynamic about this design and the pattern is 'unpredictable'. It would not be possible to reconstruct any part of the design if the stone had been broken and pieces lost.

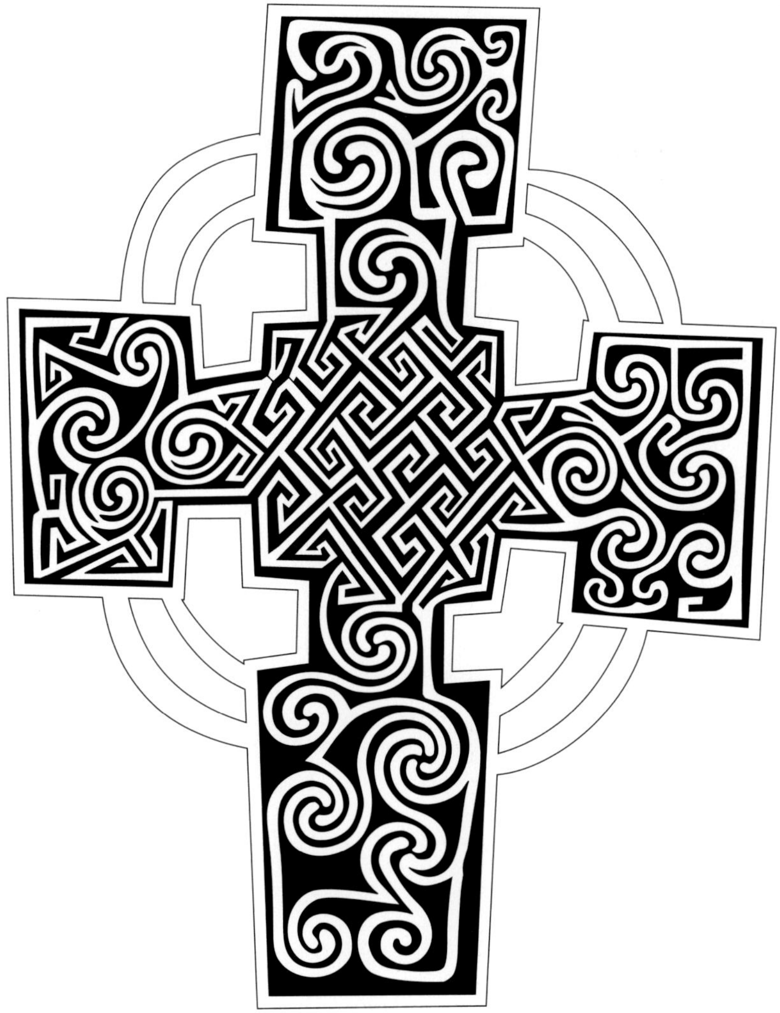

Figure 7.14
Drawing of Inchbrayock cross, Montrose Museum, Scotland.

The mixing of motifs is even more pronounced on the Penally stone fragment illustrated in Fig. 7.15. There are two important carved stones at Penally, near Tenby in South Wales, now displayed in the south transept of the beautiful old church of St Nicholas. There are cast replicas of the stones in the National Museum and Gallery, Cardiff. The stones have many unique features. One of the stones is a thin monolithic cross with a ring-head and a slightly tapering shaft that is ornamented with either interlacing or vine motifs on all four sides. The other stone is a fragment of a cross-shaft that is also ornamented on all four sides. On one of the narrow sides there is a well-ordered key pattern which establishes that the sculptor was able to produce high-quality work fully matching the geometric standards of this art. The two faces illustrated in Fig. 7.15 are of a different kind. The drawings in Fig. 7.15 are based, like those of Nevern and Carew (Fig. 7.10), on the work of Worthington Smith one hundred years ago (see Allen, 1899 and Nash-

Williams, 1950). Smith was able to produce an interpretation of the design, even though the surface of the stone was severely damaged by scaling. The drawings in Fig. 7.15 differ slightly from Smith's work but the differences have little consequence in the context of the present discussion. Because of the weathering damage not all the detail in Smith's drawings can be confirmed by observation.

Like the Inchbrayock cross, the different motifs on each face of the stone merge into each other and the whole is contained in a single panel. Some of the detail is not immediately evident even in line drawings. At the top of one face (Fig. 7.15a) there is a diagonal key pattern that merges into spirals. Below this is a pair of 'confronting' animals that are biting the tails of the other animals, possibly serpents. Westwood (1876–79) described these animals as dragons with gaping mouths vomiting smaller dragons. This is followed by some interlaced plant-scrolls. At the top of the other face (Fig. 7.15b) there is a six-cord triple-beaded plait. Below this there are spirals that

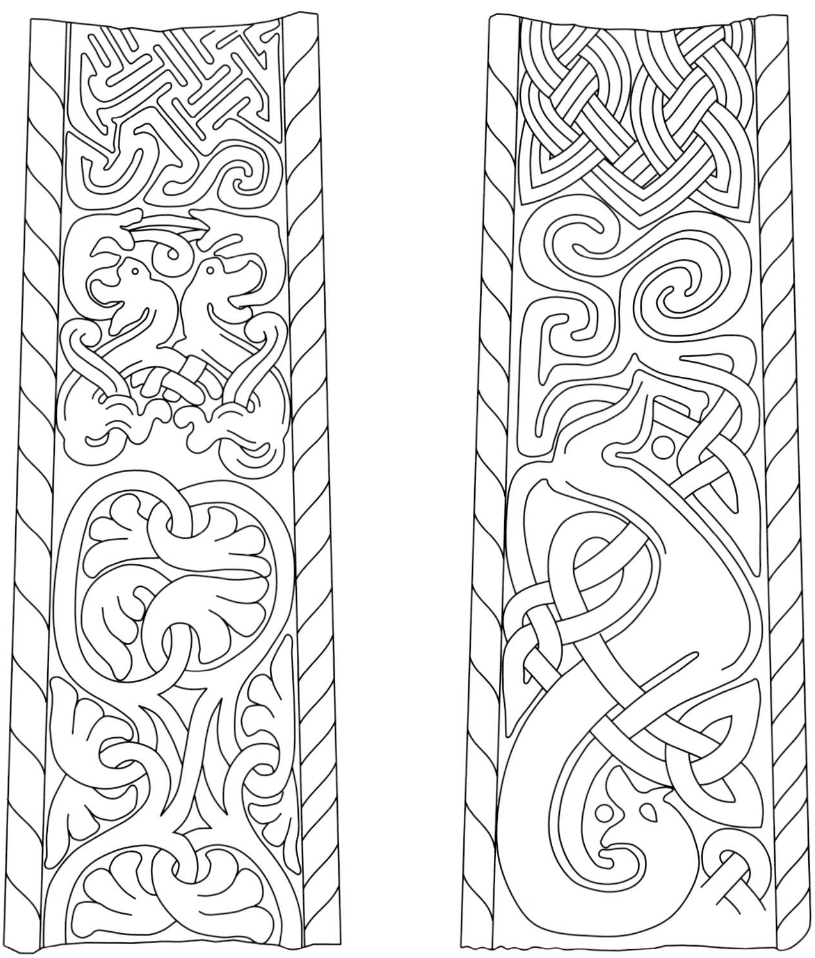
(a) (b)

Figure 7.15
Mixed motifs on two faces of a fragment of a stone shaft, Penally, Wales.

eventually bifurcate and form an elaborately interlaced tail of an animal, with front and hind legs, closely resembling the dog-like figures of many of the animals in the Lindisfarne Gospels.

In using all the conventional motifs – key, spiral, interlacing, zoomorphic (animal and reptile) and vegetal – with a range of styles, the artist has demonstrated his awareness of ornamentation from many parts of the islands and, more importantly, has touched on the contributions of many different cultures, including Anglo-Saxon. In bringing them together in a single piece of stone carving, in such an intimate way, there is a sense of unity and ecumenicity.

VIKING INNOVATIONS: ISLE OF MAN AND CUMBRIA

The rich variety of gold and silver artefacts of the early medieval period and the Viking era, displayed in the Gold Room of the Historiska Museet (Museum of National Antiquities) in Stockholm, are guarded by two superb grill-doors. One grill has a regular interlacing design and the other a ring chain design. For a visitor from the islands, these doors are reminders that interlacing is not unique to the art of the islands and that other motifs have been developed elsewhere.

It is not surprising that there is extensive overlap of Scandinavian art and the early medieval art of the islands. The early Anglo-Saxon migrations resulted in new styles and zoomorphic forms from northern Europe that are reflected in early metalwork and manuscripts. The later migrations of Vikings, starting with the raids on Lindisfarne in 793, resulted in the introduction of new motifs and styles.

The example of the design on a runestone in Fig. 7.16 represents the final development of a whole series of styles, Borre, Jellinge, Mammen, Ringerike, and Urnes, evident in Viking art stretching from the art of Scandinavia in the fifth century, through the Viking period to the eleventh and twelfth centuries. They relate primarily to zoomorphic forms, some of which resonate closely with early jewellery and manuscripts, but many of which are foreign to the art of early medieval work in the islands. The style of the runestone is attributed to the Urnes style. These stones were painted, as in Fig. 7.16, with a beast, painted red, interlaced with snakes, painted black. The runic inscription tells the purpose of the stone: 'Holmfast had the stone erected in memory of Igulger, his father, and Torbjörn'. There is ample scope for speculation on the creative influences that emerged when wood carvers and sculptors, trained in the traditional Viking styles, interacted with the artists active in the islands.

(a)

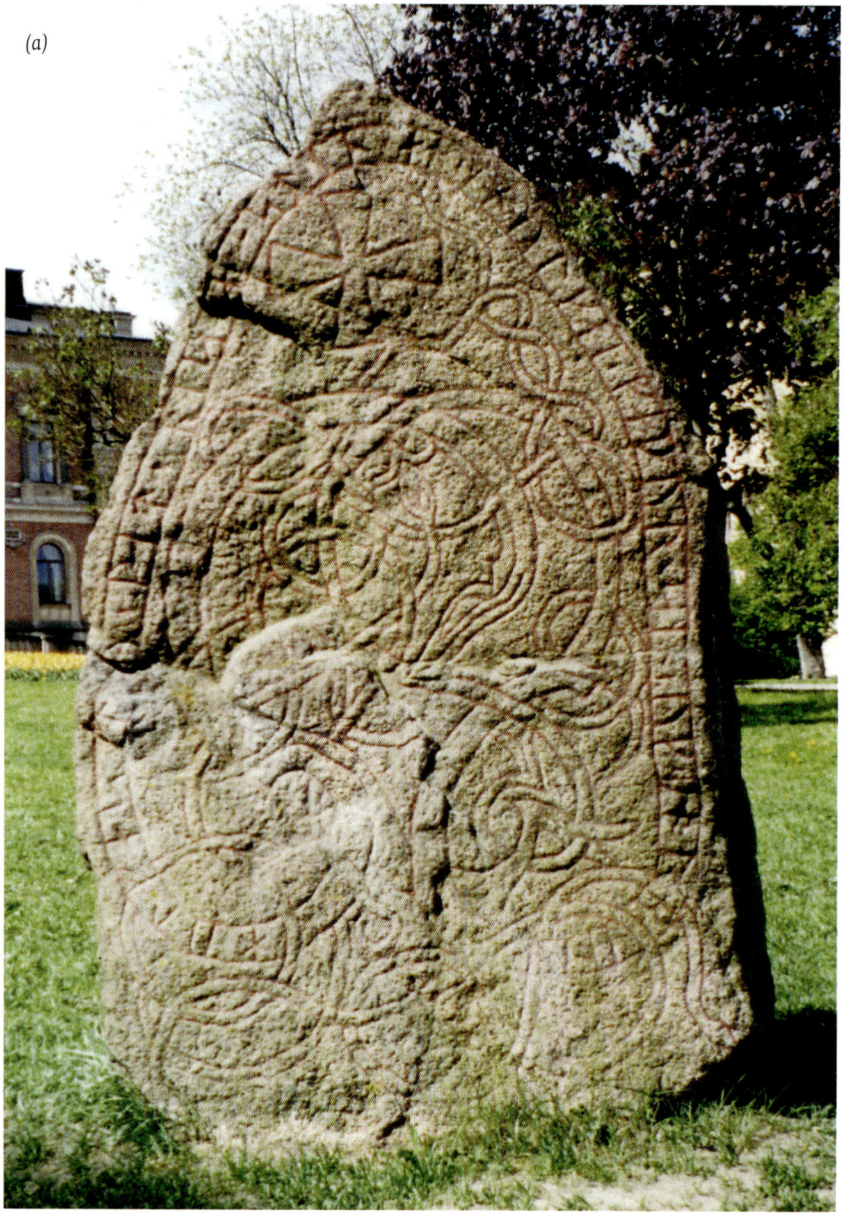

Figure 7.16
Runestone (U938) in University Park, Uppsala, Sweden. (a) Photograph. (b) Illustration of zoomorphic ornamentation showing a runic animal and snakes.

Evidence for the blending of motifs and styles from the tenth century onwards can be found in many parts of the islands. The effects are found, in particular, in the Isle of Man where extensive Viking settlements were established. Kermode (1907) divided the stone crosses on the Isle of Man into two main classes: Pre-Scandinavian and Scandinavian. Some modern scholarship (Trench-Jellico, 1985) suggests that some of the sculpture without Viking features was more or less contemporary with Viking cross-slabs. The Pre-Scandinavian work is similar to that described in the preceding chapters of this book, with extensive evidence for the creative

(b)

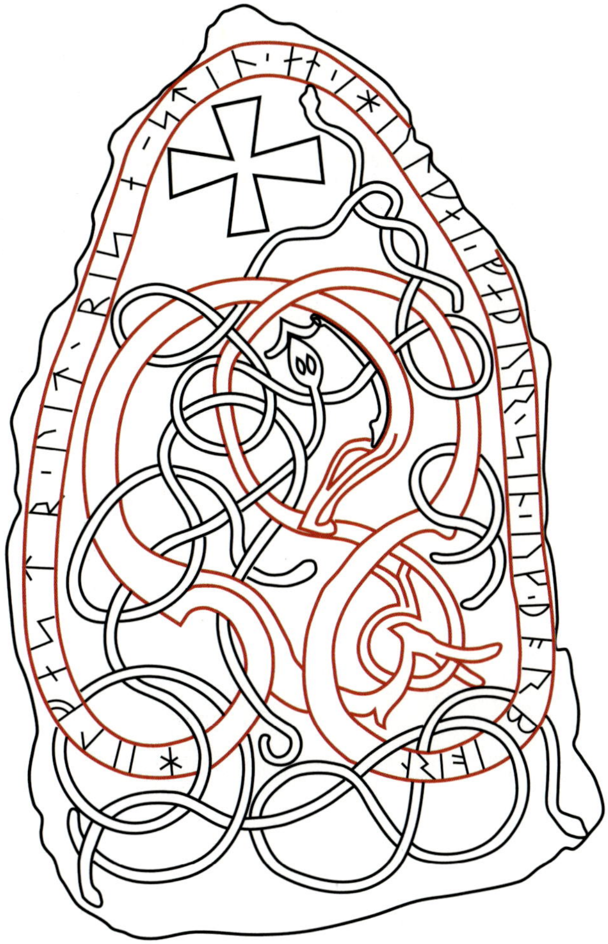

developments of style, as in the cross at Lonan Old Church (Fig. 7.7), suggesting that much of this work was produced after corresponding work elsewhere in the islands. There are new styles and motifs in the Scandinavian work and, to quote Kermode (1907), 'As regards execution and workmanship, one notices as a characteristic less regard for accuracy of detail and careful finish, less formality and stiffness, a bolder treatment, and a greater freedom than in our earlier period'.

The above comments are borne out by a slate cross-slab at Michael in the Isle of Man (Fig. 7.17) that is typical of many of the stone carvings on the island. According to the inscription, in runic script, on the edge of the stone and around the top of the cross, 'Mael Brigde, son of Athakan, the smith, erected this cross for his own soul [and that of] his brother's wife. Gaut made this stone and all in Man.' Gaut was a leading sculptor and seems to have had a major influence on the development of sculptural work in the island. The cross-slab is in the north transept of the church in Kirk Michael. There are obvious differences in style in the interlacing on the cross and on

Figure 7.17
Gaut cross-slab, Michael, Isle of Man. (a) Photograph in St Michael's church showing a cross, surrounded by Runic script, embedded in block of concrete. (b) Drawing based on detail evident in photograph.

(a)

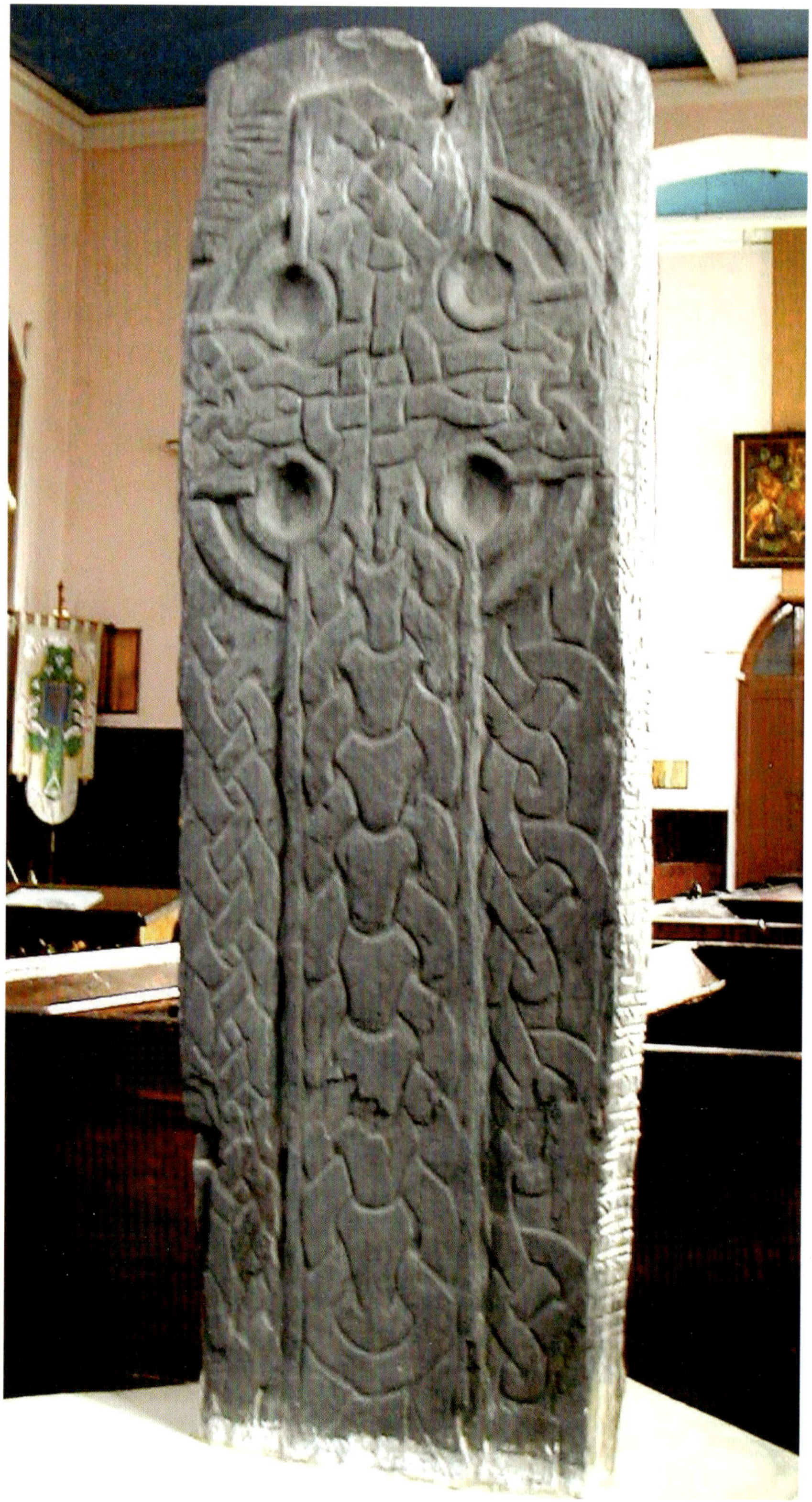

(b)

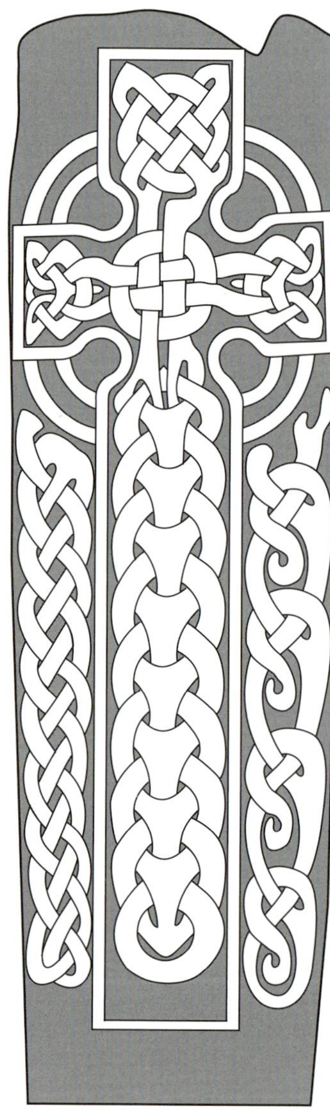

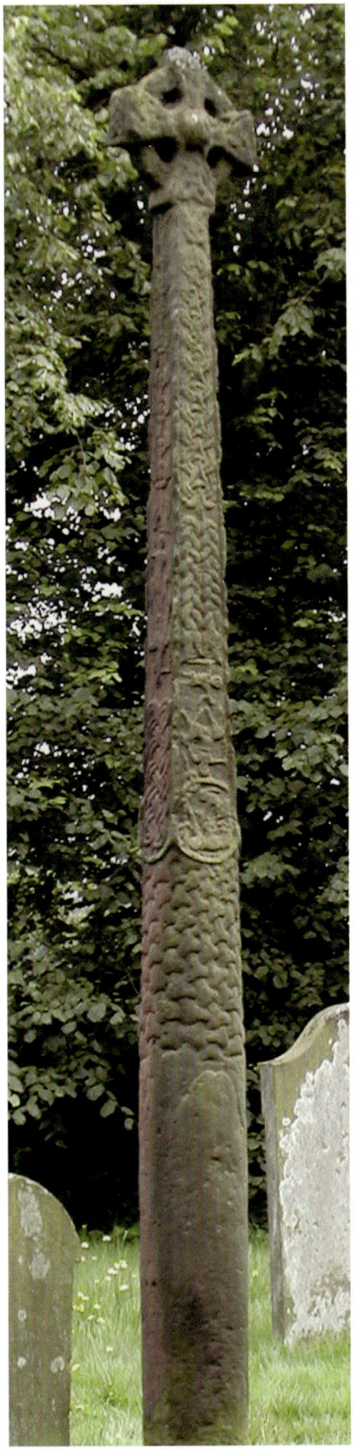

Figure 7.18
Gosforth cross outside St Mary's church, Gosforth, Cumbria, England.

the four-cord interlacing in the plait on the left-hand side of the shaft of the cross. The ring-chain pattern, on the shaft of the cross, and the strange tendril-like interlacing of bifurcating cords in the panel on the right-hand side, are new motifs. Many similar motifs are displayed on other stones in the Isle of Man. To discover the methods of constructing the ring-chain pattern, and the diversity of forms of this pattern, one must travel eastwards to Gosforth in Cumbria.

The Gosforth cross (Fig. 7.18) is in the grounds of St Mary's church in the village of Gosforth at the western end of the Lake District National Park in northern England. It is a red sandstone column, over 4.5 m high, topped with an equal-armed ring cross. The bottom of the column is smooth and almost cylindrical and this merges into a section, also with a circular cross-section, ornamented with a ring-chain design that spreads around the slightly tapering column. Above this, the cross-section of the column becomes square. The four faces of the shaft are ornamented with a whole range of motifs and scenic designs. The overall shape of the column has suggested to some that the sculptor was imitating roods carved from the trunk of a tree.

The first detailed description of the Gosforth cross is by Revd W. S. Calverley (1883), who records how he and Dr C. A. Parker, a local doctor, started their discovery of the secrets of this superb stone:

> *I have a very vivid recollection of going to Gosforth one dull wet day in the late autumn of 1881, when I thought that the continuous damp and rain of the previous weeks would have softened the lichens which had filled every sculptured hollow on the cross-head, and of standing with Dr Parker beneath the cross, whilst his coachman, up aloft, with a dash of a wet brush to the right and to the left hand scattered the softened mosses, and revealed – what none had seen clearly perhaps for centuries – the sign of the ever-living Trinity, the triquetra of the Book of Kells and other MSS. of the early Christian church.*

The illustrations in Calverley's paper which were used for the drawings in this section were based on drawings and measurements made by Dr Parker and engravings by Magnus Petersen of Copenhagen.

The Gosforth pillar is clearly of Christian origin and the cross (Fig. 7.19) was carved with a high level of geometric order and symmetry, fully meeting the rules of interlacing. There is no suggestion of the artistic developments of the kind demonstrated in the cross at Lonan Old Church. Below the cross on the east face of the column there is a well-ordered four-cord plait with interlacing far superior, in geometric terms, to that on the Michael cross-slab (Fig. 7.17). However, the interlacing is terminated with the heads of beasts and a warrior carrying a spear holds the jaws of the lower beast apart.

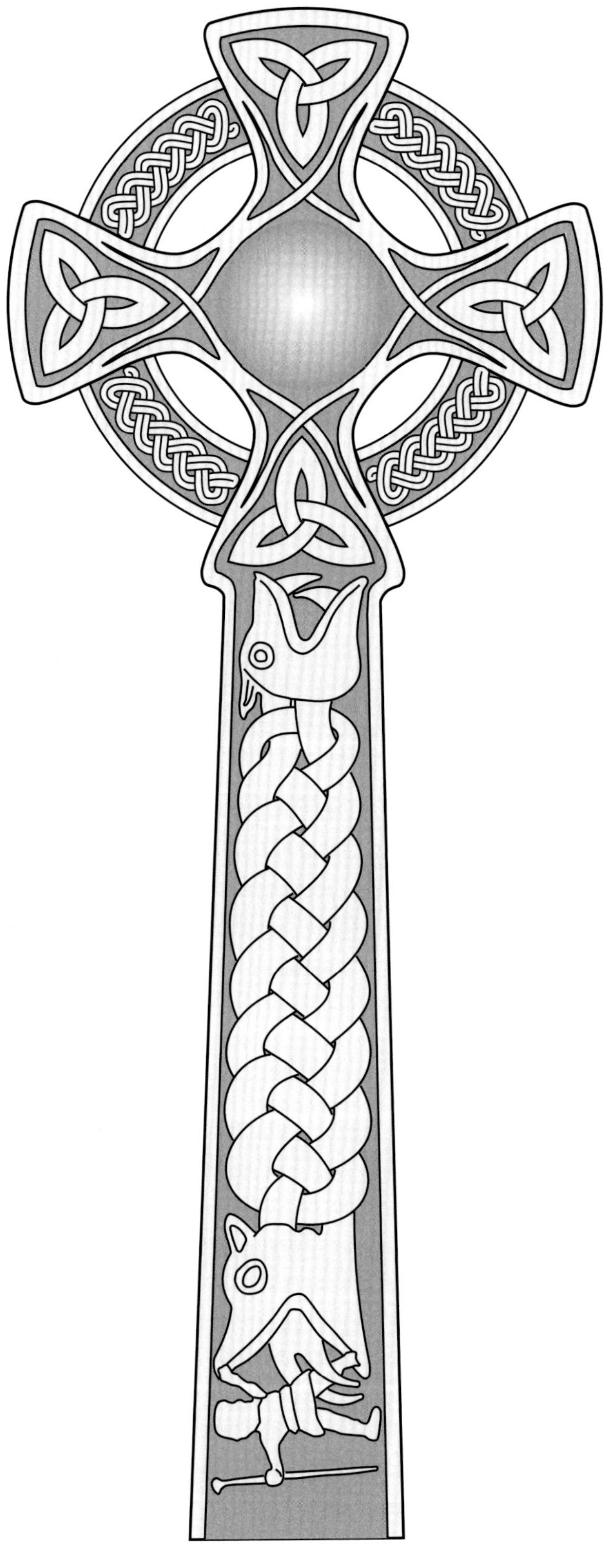

Figure 7.19
Drawing of cross and upper part of east-facing side of the shaft of Gosforth cross.

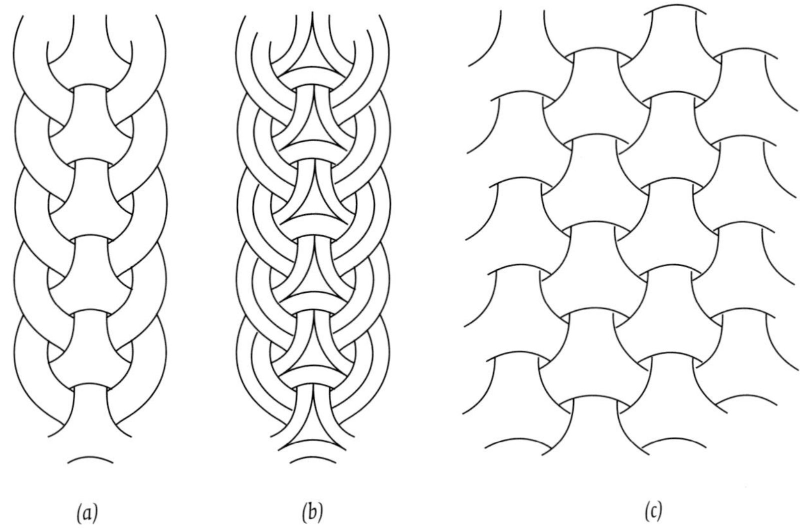

Figure 7.20
Ring-chain designs used on Gosforth cross.

There are many picture stories on all four faces of the Gosforth column. Calverley interpreted the pictures, with the help of scholars from Denmark, in terms of the myths and legends of Scandinavia. The warrior illustrated in Fig. 7.19 is Vidar, the silent god and a son of Odin, and the beast is a wolf that has swallowed Odin. But the picture stories have a double meaning, for the myths of Scandinavia resonate with the myths of Christianity and so, for example, a scene on the east side can be seen to depict both Odin hanged from a tree and the crucifixion of Christ.

The faces of the column are remarkable also for a display of various forms of ring-chain designs. Three examples are illustrated in Fig. 7.20. Most of the patterns are linear arrays of linked rings, the exception being the pattern on the lower part of the shaft, which has a 'two-dimensional array' of rings formed on a curved surface. If the shaft is treated as being cylindrical the pattern can be represented on a planar surface. The geometric construction of these patterns can be understood using the sequence shown in Fig. 7.21. For a linear array the starting point is a link formed from a set of rings (Fig. 7.21a). A series of links are joined together in an ABC sequence and interlaced to form the repeating pattern (Fig. 7.21b to d). A similar ABC sequence is used to form a planar array, as illustrated in Fig. 7.22. The appearance of ring-chain designs can be changed by altering the shape of the rings, the width of the bands and, in the linear arrays, the length of the band joining the links. A linear array with elliptical rings was used for the ring-chain on the Gaut cross-slab (Fig. 7.17). The ring-chain merges with interlacing.

Two further features of the ring-chain design are illustrated in Fig. 7.23, taken from the south face of the Gosforth cross. First, the chain is in a

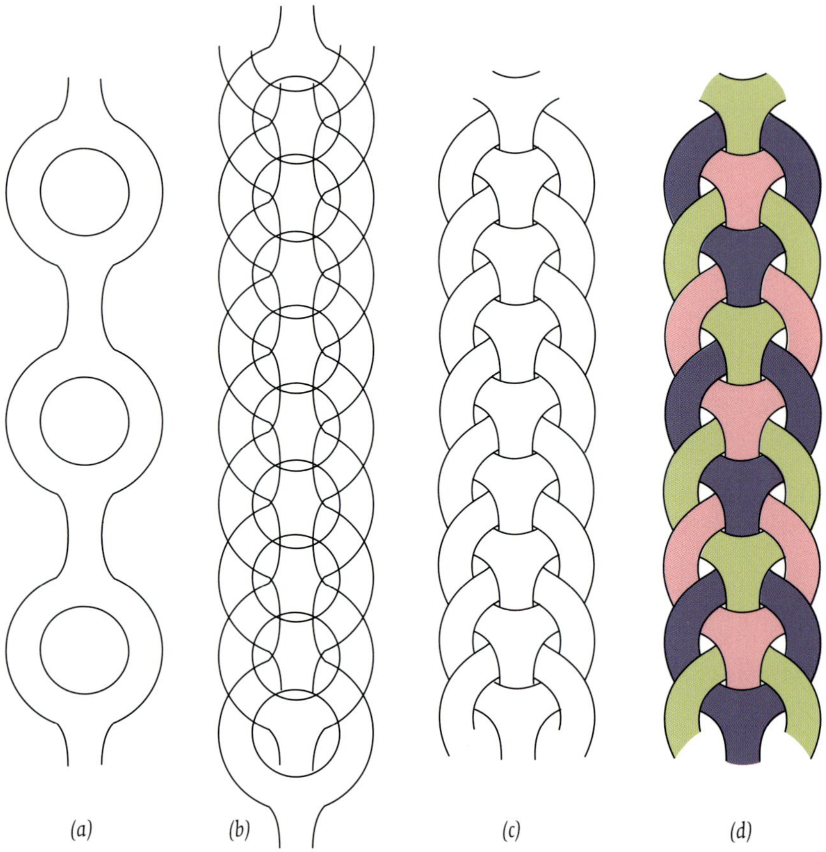

Figure 7.21
Formation of a linear ring-chain design.

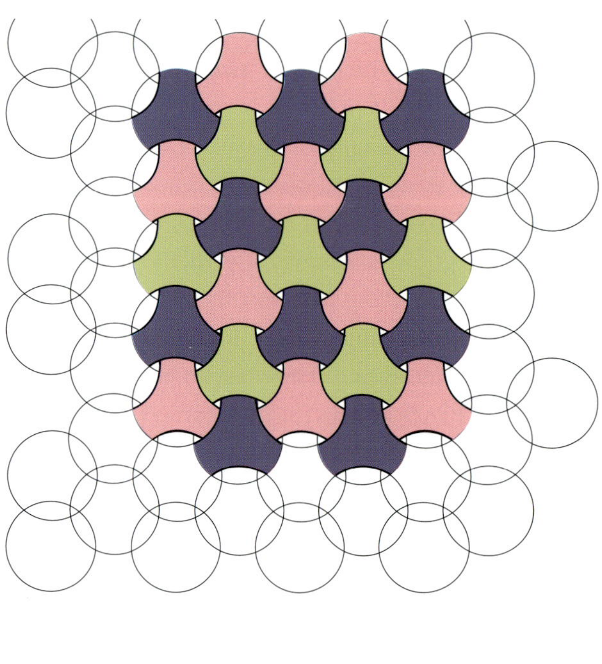

Figure 7.22
Formation of a planar ring-chain design.

slightly tapering panel so that the artist had to use rings of different size. Second, the chain terminates in a wolf's head. Calverley sees the rings of the chain as the vertebrae and ribs of the wolf and the head, gagged and not showing teeth, as another part of the mythological story. The planar ring-chain at the bottom of the Gosforth shaft is not as regular as that shown in Fig. 7.22, partly because the shaft is not perfectly cylindrical.

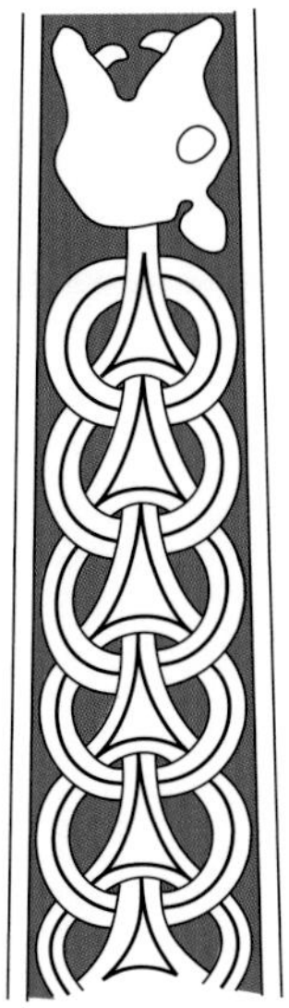

Figure 7.23
Drawing of one of ring-chain designs on Gosforth cross.

VIKING INNOVATIONS: MAEN ACHWYFAN

In the opening paragraphs of this book reference was made to the red sandstone monolith standing in the middle of a field near Whitford in North Wales, whose ornamentation reflects something of the spirit of the time when it was first erected about a thousand years ago. The earliest known drawings of the Whitford cross, also known as Maen Achwyfan or 'Stone of

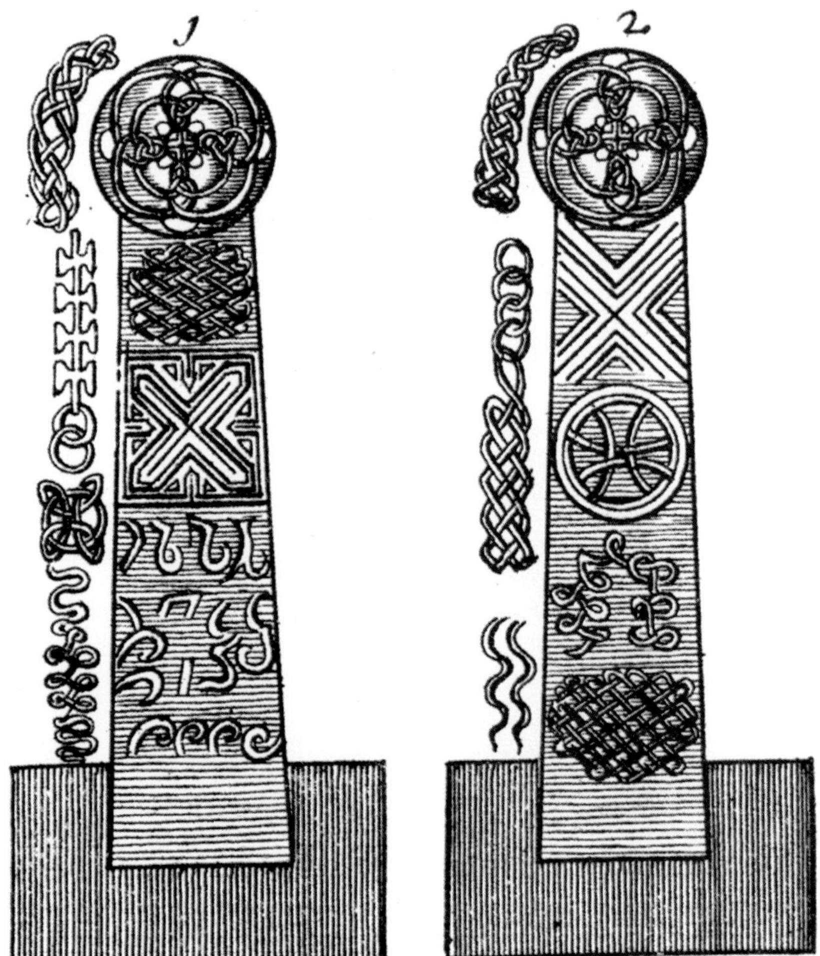

Figure 7.24
Drawings of the two main faces of the cross at Whitford, Wales as recorded in Edmund Gibson's edition of Camden's Britannia (1695).

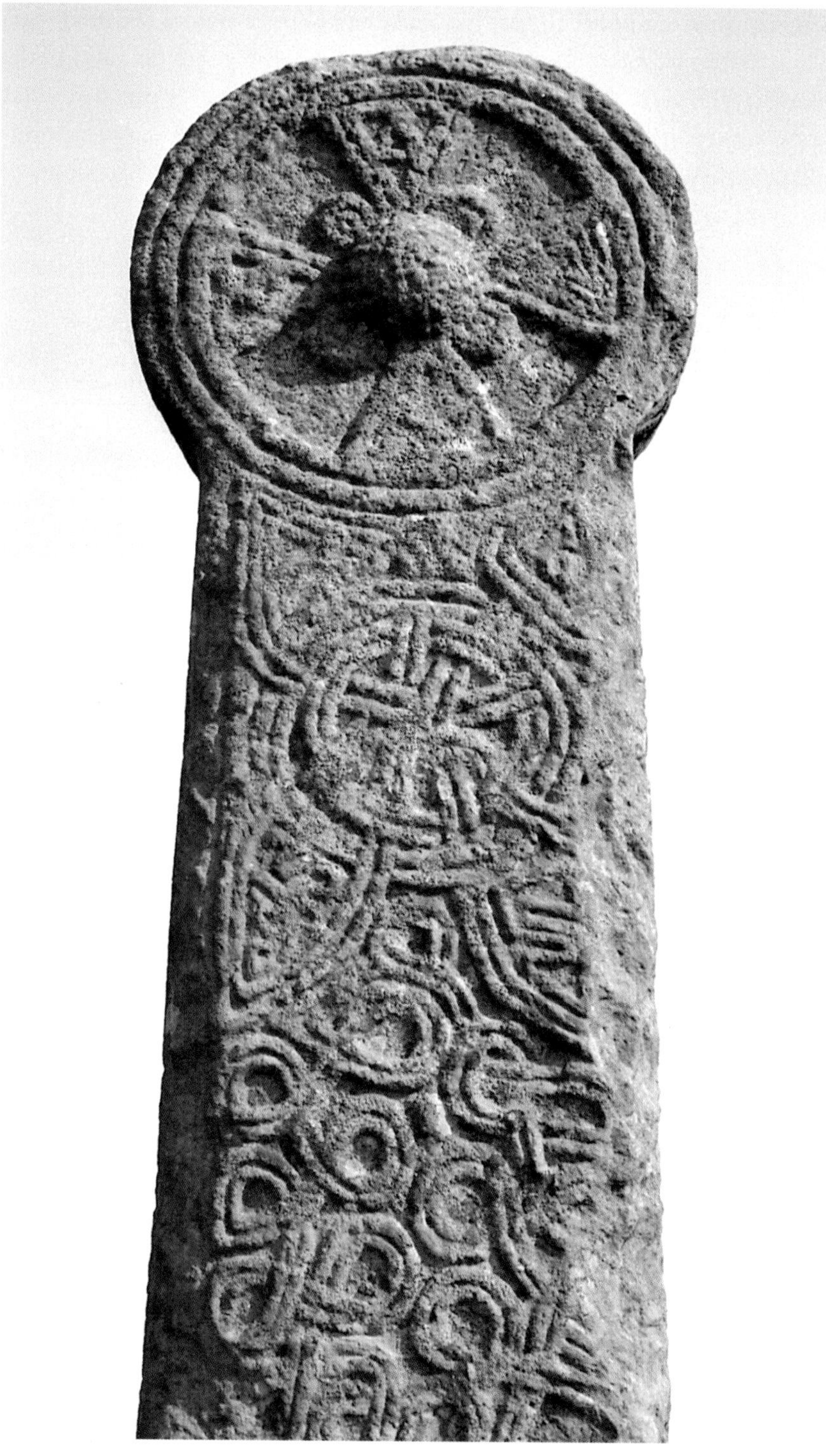

Figure 7.25
Photograph of part of the west-facing side of Whitford cross for comparison with drawing in Fig. 7.24.

Lamentations', are reproduced in Fig. 7.24 from *Camden's Britannia* (1695) which is an early antiquarian's travel guide to Britain. They are the work of a Welsh antiquarian, Edward Lhuyd (1660–1709). Nash-Williams (1950) describes the cross as a 'disc-headed pillar cross'. It is 3.3 m high and has a rectangular cross-section; all four sides are ornamented with a variety of abstract and iconic motifs. The cross is probably in its original position and the two main sides, 1 and 2 in Fig. 7.24, face east and west respectively.

Although the drawings in Fig. 7.24 are inaccurate in many respects, as can be seen by comparing them with the photograph of part of the west-facing side shown in Fig. 7.25, they give a clear indication that the ornamentation is distinctly different in style to earlier stone sculpture. The appearance of the interlacing in the top panel below the cross on the east-facing side was used in Chapter 1 to explain the breakdown of the 'rules' for interlacing. This is another aspect of the metamorphosis described earlier.

Figure 7.26
Sketch of distorted patterns on part of west-facing side of Whitford cross.

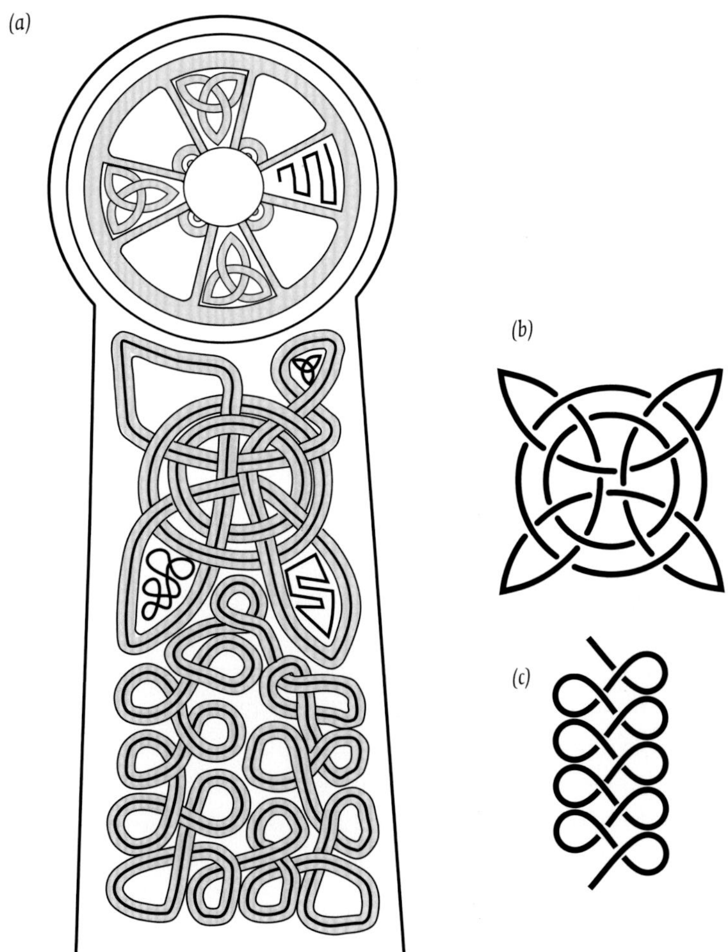

Some parts of the ornamentation obey the geometric rules quite closely. Thus, the square diaper key pattern in the panel below the interlacing is well produced and is in the same class as other diaper patterns from stones in Wales, shown in Fig. 7.9. Similarly, the ring crosses on both sides of the stone are symmetrical equal-armed crosses ornamented with well-formed symmetrical triquetra knots. The sculptor has, rather mischievously one feels, included a different form of ornamentation in one of the arms of each cross. On the east face the top arm of the cross has looped-knot work instead of the triquetra knot and on the west face the right-hand arm of the cross has a key pattern. Also, the axes of the crosses are not aligned accurately with those of the main shaft. Each of the crosses has a central boss. On the east face the boss is flattened and has two sets of straight lines, at right angles, incised across it. The boss on the west face is hemispherical and is ornamented with interlacing, as in the bosses of Nigg, and others, described earlier.

The ornamentation on the rest of the stone is less ordered and includes a number of Viking-related figural representations. Below the cross on the west face there are two patterns that are, in effect, highly distorted forms of conventional motifs. These are illustrated in Fig. 7.26. The top pattern is a distorted form of pattern No. 772 in Allen and Anderson (1903), with double-beaded cords forming two closed loops around a four-lobed knot, reminiscent of the Ringerike style (Fig. 7.26b). The lobes are further ornamented with a triquetra knot, a key pattern and irregularly looped cords. Similarly, the lower pattern is essentially a double row of closed loops, as in Allen and Anderson's pattern No. 550 (Fig. 7.26c). The cross feature shown in the 1695 diagram (Fig. 7.24) is a figment of the artist's imagination.

Thus the origins and features of the abstract motifs, icons, and styles of ornamentation on the Whitford cross, the Stone of Lamentations, bridge many cultures and ethnic groups.

CONCLUDING OBSERVATIONS

The examples used in this chapter illustrate the many ways that Insular art developed. The highly structured and disciplined approach evident in the Lindisfarne Gospels and many of the Pictish sculptured stones is not nearly so apparent in the sculptured stones of Wales and the Isle of Man. Archaeologists and art historians use this as one approach to establish a chronological framework. It cannot be overemphasised that metamorphosis, involving progressive change, is best understood by starting with well-defined and ordered patterns. It seems highly improbable that regular patterns, such as the key patterns in the bottom panel of the

Rosemarkie stone (Fig. 3.20) or the precisely defined interlacing that ornaments the small cross at the centre of cross-carpet page f. 210v of the Lindisfarne Gospels (Fig. 2.4), could ever be created by a process of metamorphosis starting from a more chaotic pattern. Thus, evidence for metamorphosis gives a strong indication for the imprint of time in dating early medieval art.

Similar reasoning applies to the development of designs, such as those on the Penally and Inchbrayock sculptured stones, that combine different motifs within a single panel. It is inconceivable that a regular zoomorphic-ornamented panel, such as the rectangular panels of the Lichfield cross (Fig. 5.23), could ever evolve from the far less rigorous zoomorphic designs on the Penally stone.

Concepts of change and the passage of time have been applied also to the apparent 'debasement' of sculptured work referred to earlier in this chapter. However, the relative skills, styles and tastes of individual artists make rigorous application of this approach to chronology somewhat limited. It does not follow, necessarily, that a poorly executed page of manuscript illumination post-dates a more refined and elegant piece of work.

These arguments apply also to establishing the chronology of work in which new motifs and styles have been introduced. Clearly, artworks with well-defined Viking motifs are unlikely to have been produced in the islands before the establishment of Viking settlements. It does not follow that art without any evidence of Viking styles pre-dates art with these styles. There are examples of sculptured work completed within the past hundred years that follow closely the styles of work completed in the seventh and eighth centuries without any trace of Viking influence.

Finally, metamorphosis has an interest of its own quite apart from chronological implications. By introducing subtle changes artists have created intriguing new designs that prompt questions about their intentions, which will always remain a mystery.

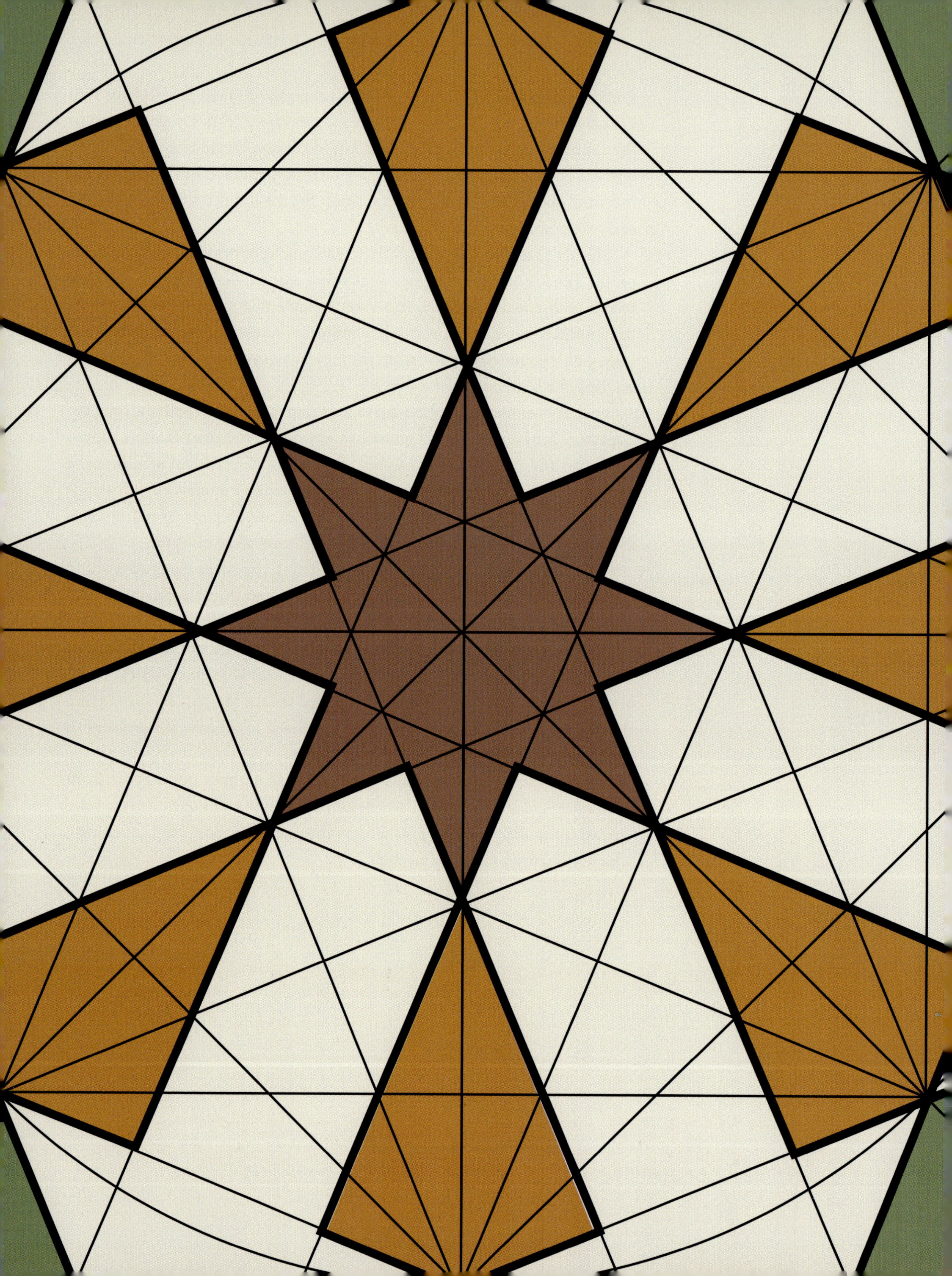

8
Epilogue

ART AND GEOMETRY

In his book *Remarkable Ruins* (1795), Cordiner describes the Nigg cross-slab (Fig. 2.28) in the following terms: 'The monuments round the margin of this obelisk had been wrought with great mathematical accuracy; and raised with such labour as indicates no small proficiency in the art of sculpture'. Mathematical accuracy derives from the informed use of geometry in constructing the layout of the cross and surrounding panels as well as in the fine detail of the ornamentation. The term 'geometric art' has been used as a convenient way to describe work in metal, stone and on vellum reflecting the creative activity, in the second half of the first millennium, of people living in the islands now called England, Ireland, Scotland and Wales. It has also been called 'barbaric art' but this term merely serves to distinguish it from classical and naturalistic art.

The level of geometry involved in early medieval art, as described in previous chapters, should not be seen as being difficult. Once it is recognised that the concepts are simple and straightforward it becomes relatively easy to follow the basic methods of construction of layout and individual motifs. The early medieval artists relied on straight-edge and compasses and restricted the use of geometry, with few exceptions, to drawing straight lines, circles, triangles, squares and rectangles. Although the constructions may at first sight appear complex it is possible, by following simple geometric rules systematically, to understand them.

As a recapitulation, consider the sequence required to produce the equilateral triangle, square and regular pentagon shown in Fig. 8.1. Incidentally, this provides an alternative method of producing a regular pentagon to that described in Chapter 2. Start by drawing a straight line AB. Draw circle C1, radius r, with the compass point on line AB and then circle C2, with the same radius r, with the compass point at the point of intersection of C1 with line AB. The line CD is at right angles to AB. Draw circle C3 (radius r) with the compass point at the intersection of C1 and C2. The construction line EF can now be drawn through the intersection of C1 and C3 and the intersection of C3 and CD, and similarly for GH. Finally, draw

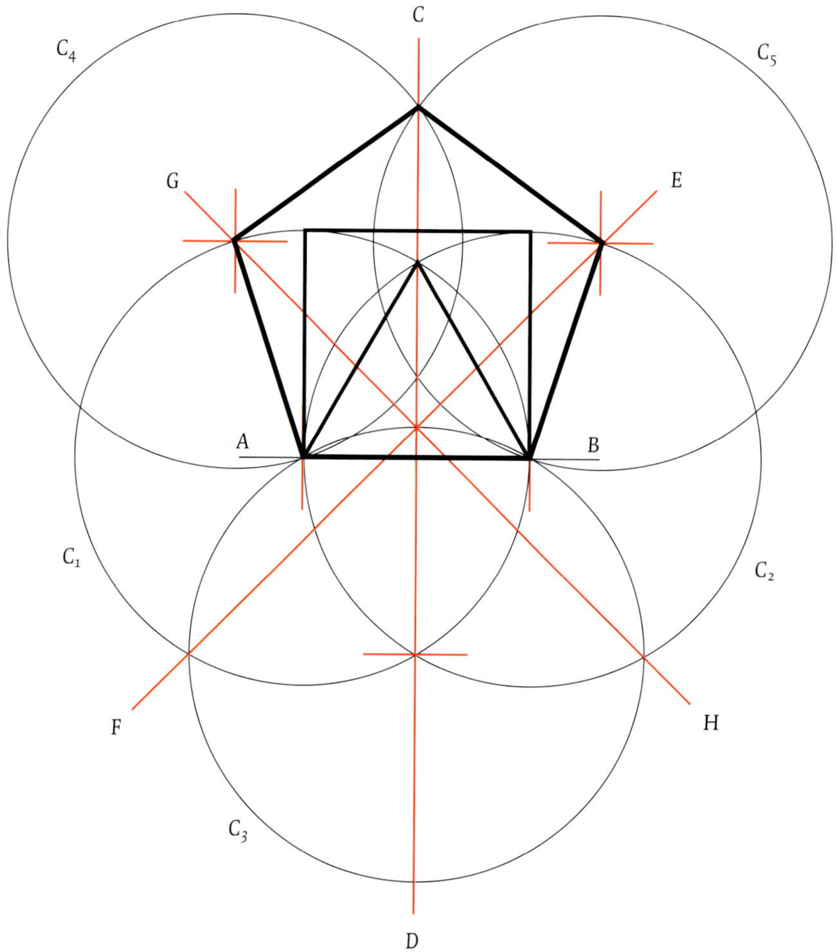

Figure 8.1
Geometric construction of equilateral triangle, square and regular pentagon using only a straight-edge and compasses.

circles C4 and C5 (radii r) centred on the intersections of C1 and GH, and C2 and EF, respectively. From this construction it follows that the sides of the triangle, square and pentagon are all the same length because they are all equal to r, the radius of the circles.

Geometric methods of this kind are simple, elegant and precise. They are based on the geometric methods of early Greek civilisations who developed their understanding from the Egyptians. The Greeks used these methods to design splendid temples and successive generations of people have used similar procedures. The proportions used in architecture often display the aesthetically pleasing golden section or golden ratio $2/(1+\sqrt{5})$, as described in Chapter 2. The construction of a golden section, using similar procedures to those illustrated in Fig. 8.1 to draw triangles, squares and pentagons, is shown in Fig. 2.11b. The pentagon construction in Fig. 2.26 required a measurement involving the golden ratio.

Because the Greeks did not have a numerical system equivalent to the decimal system they could not explain the meaning of irrational numbers such as the square root of two ($\sqrt{2}$), of three ($\sqrt{3}$), of five ($\sqrt{5}$), and so on. Pythagoras called these numbers unspeakable numbers. They can be drawn or represented by the constructions described earlier but they cannot be expressed numerically. Irrational numbers open up many fascinating fields in mathematics. For the Greek philosophers, and many others, irrational numbers and related concepts, such as the golden section or ratio and the Pythagorean golden triangle, create a sense of mystery and transcendence. They have a beauty and fascination of their own which has been called a sacred geometry (see, for example, Lawlor, 1982).

Similar construction methods to those in Fig. 8.1 have been used throughout this book in creating reproductions of the work of early medieval artists. Again, by way of recapitulation, this is demonstrated by the example in Fig. 8.2 showing a possible approach to the design of St Cuthbert's pectoral cross. This beautiful piece of jewellery is generally held to be an expression of seventh-century Anglo-Saxon Christianity (Bruce-Mitford, 1974). The cross is ornamented with cloisonné with garnet inlay and filigree borders. It was found in St Cuthbert's tomb in Durham Cathedral when it

Figure 8.2
Construction lines to draw St Cuthbert's pectoral cross.

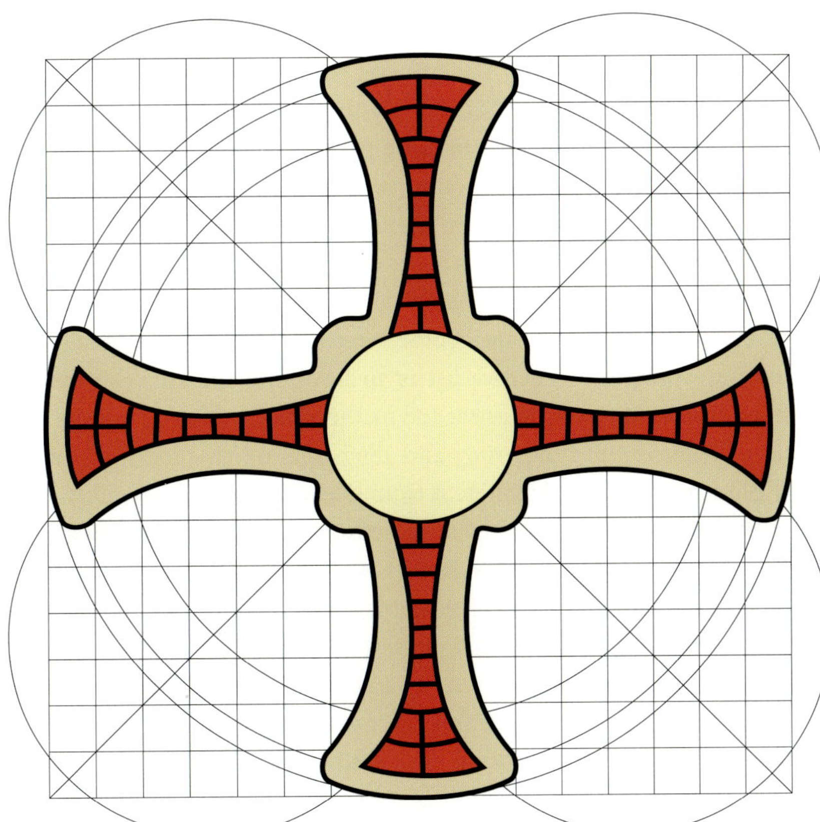

was opened in 1827. St Cuthbert was buried in 687. In the construction in Fig. 8.2 straight lines, squares and circles are combined to produce a simple and elegant cross with a high level of symmetry.

Geometric constructions are also the basis of much Islamic art, which has a beauty and richness quite distinct from the work of the Insular artists. The mysteries of geometric constructions experienced by the Greeks remain. A typical simple construction is shown in Fig. 8.3. The first steps (Fig. 8.3a) involve squares and circles. Straight lines are added, as in Fig. 8.3b and c, to create a fine network. Any number of patterns can be created in this grid. Figure 8.3d is but one example. As with St Cuthbert's cross this design has a high level of symmetry, with a fourfold rotation point and four mirror lines. The pattern in Fig. 8.3d is the basic repeat unit of the extended pattern in Fig. 8.3e. The repeat units can be added indefinitely to cover large areas such as ceilings, floors and walls and so create the beautiful art that adorns tombs, mausoleums, mosques and other buildings throughout the Muslim world.

Patterns, repeated as in Fig. 8.3e, have been the basis for the design of fabrics and wallpapers for centuries. The uniqueness of any given wallpaper design rests with the motifs or repeat units and the way these are combined. Owen Jones, in his beautiful book *The Grammar of Ornament* (1856), gives a collection of more than 2,350 classic patterns with examples from nineteen different cultures from all over the known world, including Egyptian, Persian, Greek, Roman, Byzantine, Indian, Chinese and Elizabethan. Although the styles in these patterns are distinct, and thereby characteristic of their particular cultures, it is possible to see underlying geometric constructions and the applications of symmetry in all of them.

There are numerous other areas of the visual arts that have close affinities with geometry. The whole field of perspective, developed by artists over many centuries, is based on simple geometric constructions. A particularly fascinating example of creative art is to be found in Japanese temple geometry. This is the work of artists and mathematicians during Japan's Edo period of seclusion between 1603 and 1867. In some respects, so-called *wasan* geometry is distinctly different from classical western geometry. One of the outcomes of the use of *wasan* geometry was the formulation of a wide variety of geometric problems that were inscribed on delicately coloured wooden tablets called *sangaku*. These tablets were hung under the eaves in shrines and temples and have a unique aesthetic and spiritual appeal. Other examples include the equally fascinating art created by the Dutch artist M. C. Escher, in which complex shapes are combined with extraordinary symmetry relations to produce work that is both intriguing and beautiful. Escher created this work first and foremost as art but his work has resulted in new

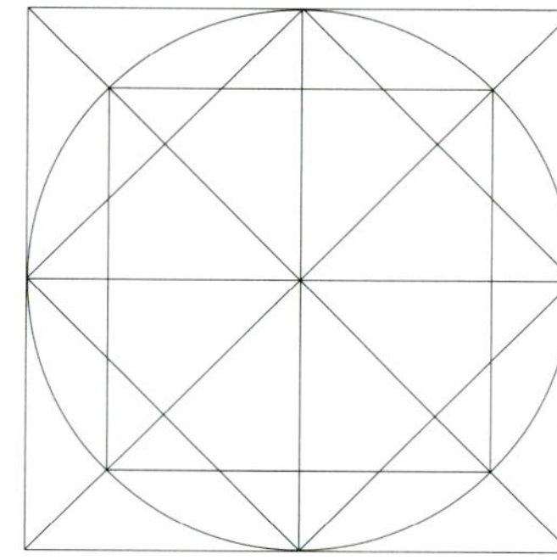

(a)

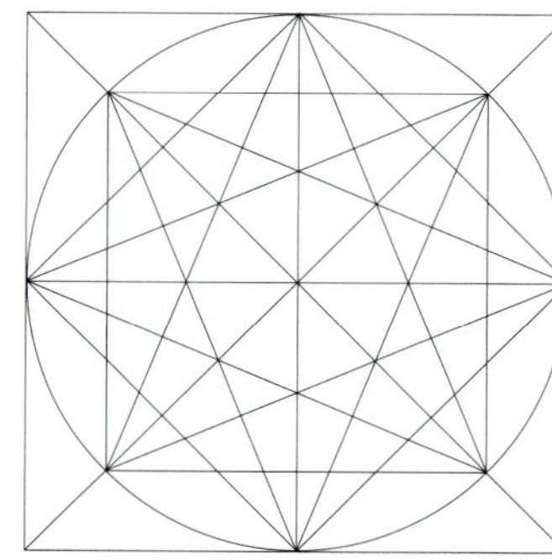

(b)

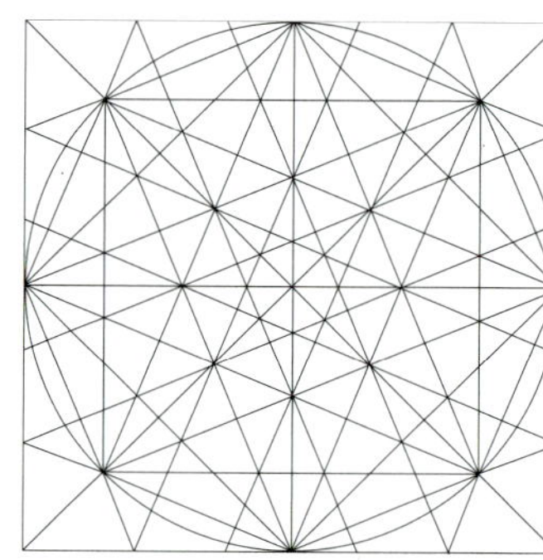

(c)

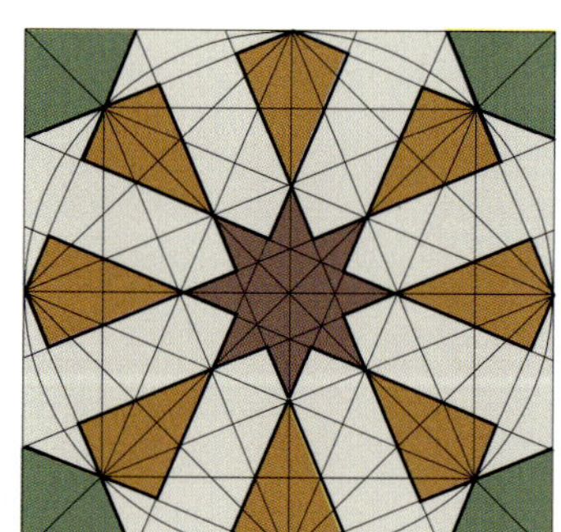

(d)

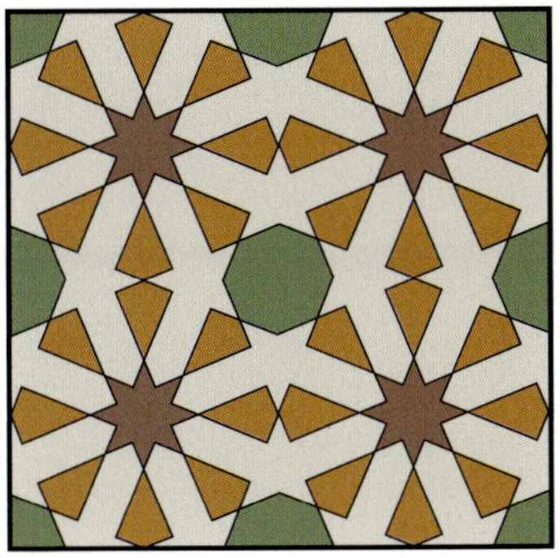

(e)

Figure 8.3
Construction lines to produce a pattern typical of Islamic art.

and important insights into the understanding of the mathematics of symmetry, notably in colour symmetry. Similarly, the fractal concepts of Mandelbrot have opened up a whole new field of images based on studies of self-similarity and scaling.

CONSTRUCTION METHODS REVISITED

At the beginning of *The Grammar of Ornament*, Jones sets out some general principles in the arrangement of form and colour in architecture and the decorative arts. Proposition 7, which relates to the decoration of surfaces, is particularly apposite to the work of Insular artists: 'The general form being first cared for, these should be subdivided and ornamented by firm lines; the interstices may then be filled in with ornament, which may again be subdivided and enriched for closer inspection'. The relevance of this proposition to Insular art is demonstrated by the examples in earlier chapters. Thus, the methods of geometric construction used in laying out carpet page f. 210v of the Lindisfarne Gospels (Fig. 2.3) with a series of well-defined panels are rigorous and formal. The panels are ornamented with motifs arranged with a similar level of precision using geometric constructions. It is the combination of the panel approach and the use of specific motifs – interlacing, spiral, key and zoomorphic – that gives the geometric aspects of Insular art its most characteristic appeal.

Many features of Insular art, and in particular the use of Christian imagery, have not been described in this book. These are, of course, of great importance in art-historical and archaeological studies but here the geometric features are less relevant. Even so there is evidence, as in the Irish high crosses of the ninth and tenth centuries (Gelly, 1995), for the use of panels and grids as a basis for arranging biblical figures.

Close inspection of the fine detail of the treatment of geometric ornamentation in Insular art gives fascinating insights into the minds of the craftspeople and artists who created them. Only a few examples, mainly from the Lindisfarne Gospels, have been included in this book, as in the treatment of the panels of f. 210v (Chapter 3), the central spiral-ornamented panel of f. 138v (Fig. 4.26) and the maze design used in the six-square cross of f. 2v (Fig. 5.16). They demonstrate that, in creating the fine detail, the artist has introduced fascinating features and puzzles that are only revealed by determined examination. Arguably, the Lindisfarne Gospels can be regarded as the outstanding example of the application of geometric methods in the whole of Insular art.

Most of Insular art can be distinguished by identification with Christianity. It flourished at a time when Christian communities were growing in the islands and much of the driving force for creating the art is readily attributed to the needs of worship and mission. The cross is the fundamental motif and biblical imagery was widely used. Most of the other motifs used in Insular art have origins in pre-Christian times. As noted in the Introduction, the central theme of the cross has allowed an extension of the consideration of the geometric aspects of Insular art beyond the period when manuscript art flourished. So it has been possible to include examples from stone monuments produced long after manuscript art declined. It is not surprising that styles changed with the passage of time as new influences and peoples changed the social, cultural and political systems in the islands.

The importance of geometric construction persisted throughout the early medieval period but the metamorphosis evident in Welsh monuments, the introduction of new Viking-influenced motifs in parts of the islands, most notably in the Isle of Man, and the breakdown of the panel conventions seen in the Penally and Inchbrayock crosses suggest that later artists were not constrained by earlier practices.

Another fascinating aspect of the art of early medieval times is the way that successive artists working in metal, stone and vellum in widely separated parts of the islands over many centuries created motifs and patterns that used closely matched geometric methods. Consider, by way of example, patterns based on the spiral motif. In their monumental work, Allen and Anderson (1903) have catalogued hundreds of spiral patterns produced in a variety of media. Pattern No. 1096 (Fig. 8.4) consists of three triple spirals and three hooks arranged around a triple spiral in the centre. This pattern, with small but significant differences, occurs on a bronze disc brooch found in Ireland (Fig. 3.1c), in the centre of the Kilnave cross on Islay (Fig. 6.13), in the centre of the circles of the eight-circle cross of f. 33r of the Book of Kells (Fig. 5.7) and in numerous other works, including the Book of Durrow f. 3v and the Tara brooch. Each artist has created a unique design based on underlying geometric principles that must have been understood in order to create a satisfying image. This suggests that the methods of geometry were taught in a disciplined way and passed from one generation to the next. Explanations based on routine copying and the use of templates are not acceptable except in some special cases. It is sometimes argued that templates were used in reproducing patterns on stone monuments; the poor application of templates may account for apparent errors in some carvings.

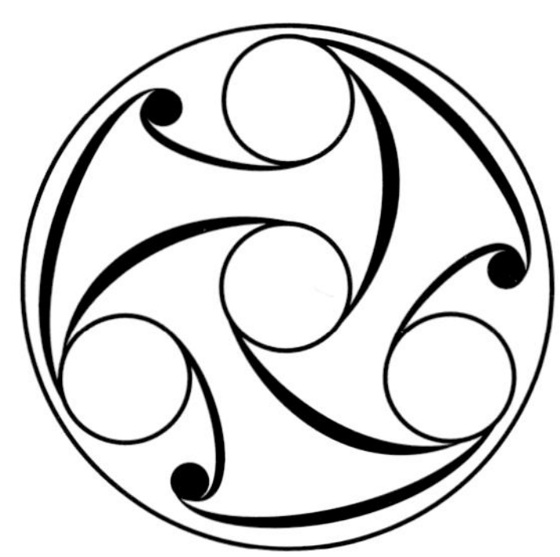

Figure 8.4
Simple spiral pattern that forms the basis for more elaborate designs.

The evidence presented in Chapters 4 and 5 for the way that motifs are drawn and combined to produce satisfying designs suggests that considerable ingenuity and skill was used. Key patterns, as illustrated in Figs. 3.8 and 4.10, are far from trivial even when they are produced in a regular grid of two sets of equal-spaced orthogonal lines. When these motifs have to be fitted to non-orthogonal panels there is added complexity. Thus, for example, the panel at the bottom of the Rosemarkie stone is not square so the artist must have used a grid with non-parallel lines. The use of polar grids to create designs in circular panels and the complex grids for ornamenting irregular panels are illustrated in Figs. 4.14 and 4.16 respectively.

Similar arguments apply to interlacing and zoomorphic designs. Some of these display exceptional complexity and it is difficult to determine the methods used to create them. The break-and-join ideas of Allen and Anderson described in Chapter 4 provide an important basis for understanding the underlying principles of interlacing. The formal treatment illustrated in Fig. 4.43 offers a powerful method for describing the break-and-join sequences in the interlacing used in borders and in square and rectangular panels that are based on multi-cord plaits. Clearly, the Insular artists had a sound understanding of the principles involved, as evidenced by their strict adherence to the over-and-under rules.

OUTSTANDING CHALLENGES

Each piece of Insular art can be the subject of Lamprecht's challenge, quoted in Chapter 1 on the subject of early medieval art: 'Fantastically confused patterns are thus evolved, whose puzzle asks to be unravelled, whose convolutions seem alternatively to seek and avoid each other, whose component parts, endowed as it were with sensibility, captivate sight and sense in passionately vital movement'. Hopefully, this book will contribute to the process of unravelling. The approach has been to select relevant examples and pursue the unravelling process using the tools of geometry and the concepts of symmetry. Innumerable examples remain, providing interesting fields for exploration.

The examples have been based, almost entirely, on work in which the geometric approach can be represented solely as a two-dimensional problem. This is perfectly adequate for manuscript art and for most work created in metal and stone, even though the creation of patterns in these media uses three-dimensional effects, as in the carving of stone and the use of cloisonné in metalwork. Some aspects of design in three dimensions have been considered (see Fig. 6.19) but this remains a significant challenge. It is particularly applicable to carvings on stone bosses as described briefly in Chapter 6. There are many bosses on stone monuments in Scotland, Iona and Ireland, but no systematic investigations have been made to measure the shape of the bosses. Casual observations suggest that most of them can be treated as parts of a sphere. Other shapes resembling parts of ellipsoids and 'torus rings' have also been used. Many of these three-dimensional surfaces are ornamented with spirals, interlacing, interlaced snakes, and key patterns. Without precise measurements of the shapes of bosses it is unlikely that the geometric detail of the designs will be unravelled.

A FINAL WORD

Remnants of the approach to art described in this book still survive today. Primary motifs, as used in early medieval art, are found in artefacts and decorations created in recent times. They include cosmetic jewellery and fabric designs, crosses in churches and in stained glass windows, carvings on gravestones and war memorials, symbols on road signs and tourist routes, table mats, prayer kneelers, menus, and even the tail planes of jet aircraft. These motifs are symbolic of a host of factors relating to perceptions of local and national identity and to many of the mysteries of life. This book is not the place in which to comment or speculate on these issues. It is sufficient to enjoy the richness and beauty of magnificent works of art and to marvel at the skill and creativity of the artists and craftspeople who created them, over a thousand years ago, using the tools of geometry to fashion the fantastic patterns that form such an important feature of their work. George Bain was a pioneer of the modern use of these motifs. Building on the work of Allen and Anderson, he provided a basis for introducing motifs into art and was dedicated to ensuring that they were applied with a full understanding of the basic rules followed by the original artists.

And so, in conclusion, we can echo the words of Sir David Wilson: 'We who study the intricacies of the art today cannot appreciate the thoughts which lay behind it, we can only marvel at the skill which fashioned it. If it is not to our taste, let us not condemn what we cannot understand.' This book provides a deeper understanding of the geometric aspects of the art – the wonder, mystery and intricacies remain.

Glossary

Carolingian	name given to the dynasty of French kings founded by Charlemagne
carpet page	decorated manuscript page reminiscent of an eastern carpet
cross-slab	stone slab ornamented with a cross and other motifs
champlevé	process of enamelling in which grooves are cut in a metal base and filled with coloured enamels
Chi-Rho	XP monogram denoting the first two characters of 'Christ' in Greek, often used as a Christian symbol
cloisonné	from *cloison* (compartment) – a design made by filling in with coloured enamel an outline of flattened wire put on edge and soldered to a metal base
colophon	an account, added to a manuscript, that identifies the date, author and place where the manuscript was written or published
damascene	ornament on metal formed by etching or by inlaying other metal, usually gold or silver
Diatessaron	a harmony of the four Gospels
escutcheon	plate or shield surrounding keyholes, handles, etc.
filigree	fine threads or beads soldered to a metal base
foliate	also 'foliaceous', representing or imitating plant forms
finial	ornament decorating the corners and sides of a geometric design
folio	sheet of vellum
grammar	fundamental principles or rules of an art or science
Hiberno-Saxon	term signifying cultural overlap between Ireland and England: Hibernia is the Roman name for Ireland
incise	produce lines and designs by cutting into a surface with a sharp tool

Insular	term signifying cultural overlaps between England, Ireland, Scotland and Wales
isotropic	the same in all directions
key pattern	motif or pattern made up of straight lines
metamorphosis	process of change – of shape, form and structure
millefiori	ornamental glass made by fusing glass rods of different sizes and colours and then drawing into thin rods that may be cut into thin slices
niello	black substance of metallic alloys with sulphur used to fill engraved or impressed designs on silver or other metal.
pelta	shape resembling the curve of a mushroom or an ancient shield
pennanular	nearly annular, of the form of almost a complete ring
reliquary	receptacle or repository for relics, especially those of saints
repoussé	raised in relief as a design in a thin piece of metal hammered and punched from the underside
sarcophagus	stone coffin
scriptorium	writing room of a monastery
spandrel	triangular shape between curved lines, as in arches, and a rectangular frame
Stafford knot	type of knot pattern
tendril	slender, thread-like leaf or stem by which a plant anchors to a support
tessellated	composed of small blocks of variously coloured material arranged in the form of a pattern.
translation	displacement (of a motif) in the plane of a drawing or illustration
triquetra knot	closed knot motif or ornament of three-lobed form
triskele	symbol consisting of three bent legs or lines radiating from a centre
trumpet	connection or scroll – pattern of curves beginning with a thin line fanning out to a shape like a trumpet
vellum	animal skin, usually calfskin, prepared to receive writing
zoomorphic	representing or imitating animal forms

References

Adcock, G. (1974), 'A Study of the Types of Interlace on Northumbrian Sculpture', MPhil thesis, University of Durham.

Alexander, J. J. G. (1978), *Insular Manuscripts: 6th to 9th Centuries*, London, Harvey Miller.

Allen, R. A. (1899), 'Early Christian Art in Wales', *Archaeologia Cambrensis*, 16 (fifth series), 1–69.

Allen, R. A. and Anderson, J. (1903), *The Early Christian Monuments of Scotland* (2 vols), The Society of Antiquaries of Scotland. Facsimile edition, Balgavies, Angus, Pinkfoot Press, 1993.

Backhouse, J. (1981), *The Lindisfarne Gospels*, London, Phaidon Press.

Bailey, R. N. (1988), *Corpus of Anglo-Saxon Stone Sculpture in England. II. Cumberland, Westmorland and Lancashire North-of-the-Sands*, Oxford, Oxford University Press.

Bain, G. (1951), *Celtic Art: The Methods of Construction*, London, Constable.

Brown, M. P. (2003a), *The Lindisfarne Gospels: Society, Spirituality and the Scribe*, London and Toronto, British Library Publishing.

Brown, M. P. (2003b), *The Painted Labyrinth: The World of the Lindisfarne Gospels*, London, British Library Publishing.

Brown, P. (1980), *The Book of Kells*, London, Thames and Hudson.

Bruce-Mitford, R. (1974), 'The Pectoral Cross of St Cuthbert', in *Aspects of Anglo-Saxon Archaeology: Sutton Hoo and Other Discoveries*, ed. R. Bruce-Mitford, London, Victor Gollancz, 281–302.

Bruce-Mitford, R. (1979), *The Sutton Hoo Ship-Burial: A Handbook by Rupert Bruce-Mitford*, London, British Museum Publications.

Bruce-Mitford, R. (1987), 'Ireland and the Hanging-Bowls – a Review', in *Ireland and Insular Art A.D. 500–1200*, ed. M. Ryan, Dublin, Royal Irish Academy, 30–39.

Bruce-Mitford, R. and others (1975–83), *The Sutton Hoo Ship-Burial* (3 vols), London, British Museum Publications.

Camden, W. (1695), *Camden's Britannia*, ed. Edmund Gibson. Facsimile edition, Newton Abbot, David and Charles, 1971.

Calverley, W. S. (1883), 'The Sculptured Cross at Gosforth West Cumberland', *Archaeological Journal*, 40, 142–58.

Coatsworth, E. (1989), 'The Pectoral Cross and Portable Altar from the Tomb of St Cuthbert', in *St Cuthbert, his Cult and his Community: To AD 1200*, ed. G. Banner, D. Rollason and C. Stancliffe, Suffolk, Boydell Press, 289–301.

Collingwood, W. G. (1927), *Northumbrian Crosses of the Pre-Norman Age*, London, Faber and Gwyer.

Cordiner, C. (1795), *Remarkable Ruins and Romantic Prospects of North Britain*, London, I. and J. Taylor.

Cromwell, P. R. (1993), 'Celtic Knotwork: Mathematical Art', *The Mathematical Intelligencer*, 15, 36–47.

Cramp, R. J. (1984), *Corpus of Anglo-Saxon Stone Sculpture in England. I. County Durham and Northumberland*, Oxford, Oxford University Press.

Cramp, R. J. (1991), *Grammar of Anglo-Saxon Ornamental: A General Introduction to the Corpus of Anglo-Saxon Stone Sculpture*, Oxford, Oxford University Press.

Douane, O. B. (1996), *Celtic Art*, Brockhampton Press.

Edwards, N. (1999), 'Viking-Influenced Sculpture in North Wales', *Church Archaeology*, 3, 5–16.

El-Said, I. and Parman, A. (1976), *Geometric Concepts in Islamic Art*, World of Islam Festival Publishing Company Ltd.

Gelly, M. A. (1995), 'The Irish High Cross: Methods and Design', in *From the Isles of the North*, ed. C. Bourke, Belfast, HMSO, 157–66.

Gombrich, E. H. (1960), *Art and Illusion: A Study in the Psychology of Pictorial Representation*, London, Phaidon Press.

Graham, R. C. (1895), *Carved Stones of Islay*, Glasgow, James Maclehose and Sons.

Guilmain, J. (1985a), 'The Composition of the First Cross Page of the Lindisfarne Gospels: "Square Schematicism" and the Hiberno-Saxon Aesthetic', *Art Bulletin*, 67, 535–47.

Guilmain, J. (1985b), 'On the Layout and Ornamentation of the Cross-Carpet Page of the Lindisfarne Gospels, folio 138v', *Gesta*, 24, 13–18.

Henderson, G. (1987), *From Durrow to Kells: The Insular Gospel-Books 650–800*, London, Thames and Hudson.

Henderson, I. (1967), *The Picts*, London, Thames and Hudson.

Henry, F. (1965), *Irish Art in the Early Christian period (to 800 AD)*, London, Methuen.

Henry, F. (1967), *Irish Art during the Viking Invasions (800–1020 AD)*, London, Methuen.

Henry, F. (1974), *The Book of Kells: Reproductions from the Manuscript at Trinity College Dublin*, London, Thames and Hudson.

Jones, O. (1856), *The Grammar of Ornament*, London, Day and Son.

Kendrick, T. D. (1949), *Late Anglo-Saxon and Viking Art*, London, Methuen.

Kendrick, T. D. (1956–60), *Evangelorium Quattuor Codex Lindisfarnensis* (2 vols), Olten, Switzerland, Urs Graf-Verlag.

Kermode, P. M. C. (1907), *Manx Crosses*, London, Bembrose and Sons.

Lamont, W. D. (1972), *Ancient and Mediaeval Sculptured Stones of Islay*, Glasgow, John Smith and Son.

Lang, J. T. (1991), *Corpus of Anglo-Saxon Stone Sculpture in England. III. York and East Yorkshire*, Oxford, Oxford University Press.

Lawlor, R. (1982), *Sacred Geometry: Philosophy and Practice*, London, Thames and Hudson.

Luce, A. A. (1960), *Evangelorium Quattuor Durmachensis (The Book of Durrow)* (2 vols), Olten, Switzerland, Urs Graf-Verlag.

Mac Lean, D. (1993), 'Snake-Bosses and Redemption at Iona and Pictland', in *The Age of Migrating Ideas*, ed. R. M. Spearman and J. Higgitt, Edinburgh, National Museums of Scotland, 245–53.

Mac Lean, D. (1999), 'Northumbrian Vine-Scroll Ornament and the Book of Kells', in *Northumbria's Golden Age*, ed. J. Hawkes and S. Mills, Stroud, Sutton Publishing, 178–90.

Meehan, B. (1994), *The Book of Kells: An Illustrated Introduction to the Manuscript in Trinity College Dublin*, London, Thames and Hudson.

Nash-Williams, V. E. (1950), *The Early Christian Monuments of Wales*, Cardiff, University of Wales Press.

Nordenfalk, C. (1968), 'An Illustrated Diatessaron', *Art Bulletin*, 50, 119–40.

Nordenfalk, C. (1977), *Celtic and Anglo-Saxon Painting: Book Illustration in the British Isles 600–800*, London, Chatto and Windus.

Nordenfalk, C. (1987), 'One Hundred and Fifty Years of Varying Views on the Early Insular Gospel Books', in *Ireland and Insular Art A.D. 500–1200*, ed. M. Ryan, Dublin, Royal Irish Academy, 1–8.

Peers, C. and Radford, C. A. R. (1943), 'The Anglo-Saxon Monastery of Whitby', *Archaeologia*, 89, 27–88.

Petley, C. C. (1857), 'Carved Stones in Ross-shire', *Transactions of the Society of Antiquaries of Scotland*, 4, 345–52.

Pinder, M. (1995), 'Anglo-Saxon Garnet Cloisonné Composite Disc Brooches: Some Aspects of their Construction', *JBAA*, CXLVII, 6–28.

RCAHMS (1984), *Argyll: An Inventory of the Monuments. V. Islay, Jura, Colonsay and Oransay*, Edinburgh, Royal Commission on the Ancient and Historical Monuments of Scotland.

RCAHMS (1999), *Pictish Symbol Stones*, Edinburgh, Royal Commission on the Ancient and Historical Monuments of Scotland.

Read, H. (1931), *The Meaning of Art*, London, Penguin Books in association with Faber & Faber.

Redknap, M. (1991), *The Christian Celts: Treasures of Late Celtic Wales*, Cardiff, National Museum of Wales.

Robinson, S. F. H. (1908), *Celtic Illuminative Art in the Gospel Books of Durrow, Lindisfarne and Kells*, Dublin, Hedges, Figgis and Co.

Ryan, M. (1995), 'The Decoration of the Donore Discs', in *From the Isles of the North*, ed. Cormac Bourke, Belfast, HMSO, 27–35.

Ryan, M. (ed.) (1987), *Ireland and Insular Art A.D. 500–1200*, Dublin, Royal Irish Academy.

Schattschneider, D. (1990), *Visions of Symmetry: Notebooks, Periodic Drawings, and Related Work of M. C. Escher*, New York, W. H. Freeman and Company.

Scott, I. G. (1997), 'Illustrating Early Medieval Carved Stones', in *The Worm, the Germ and the Thorn*, ed. David Henry, Balgavies, Angus, Pinkfoot Press, 129–32.

Seright, S. E. (1997), *George Bain – Master of Celtic Art*, Rosemarkie, Scotland, Groam House Museum Trust.

Shubnikov, A. V. and Koptsik, V. A. (1974), *Symmetry in Science and Art*, New York, Plenum Press.

Small, A., Thomas, C. and Wilson, D. M. (1973), *St Ninian's Isle and its Treasures* (2 vols), London, Oxford University Press.

Speake, G. (1980), *Anglo-Saxon Animal Art*, Oxford, Clarendon Press.

Stevens, P. S. (1981), *Handbook of Regular Patterns*, Cambridge, MA, MIT Press.

Stevenson, R. K. B. (1974), 'The Hunterston Brooch and its Significance', *Medieval Archaeology*, 18, 16–42.

Stevenson, R. K. B. (1981–82), 'Aspects of Ambiguity in Crosses and Interlacing', *Ulster Journal of Archaeology*, 44/45, 1–27.

Stevick, R. D. (1994), *The Earliest Irish and English Bookarts: Visual and Poetic Forms before AD 1000*, Philadelphia, University of Pennsylvania Press.

Stuart, J. (1858), *Sculptured Stones of Scotland*, Volume 1, The Spalding Club of Edinburgh.

Sullivan, E. (1920), *The Book of Kells*, the Studio Ltd facsimile reprint, Studio Editions Ltd, 1986

Trench-Jellico, R. M. C. (1985), 'A Redefinition and Stylistic Analysis of P.M.C. Kermode's "Pre-Scandinavian" Series of Manx Sculptures', PhD thesis, University of Lancaster.

Webster, L. and Backhouse, J. (eds.) (1991), *The Making of England: Anglo-Saxon Art and Culture AD 600–900*, London, British Museum.

Werner, M. (1990), 'The Cross-Carpet Page in the Book of Durrow: The Cult of the True Cross, Adomnan, and Iona', *Art Bulletin*, 72, 174–223.

Westwood, J. O. (1868), *Fac-Similes of the Miniatures and Ornaments of Anglo-Saxon and Irish Manuscripts by J. O. Westwood; Drawn on Stone by W. R. Tymms*, London, Quaritch.

Westwood, J. O. (1876–79), *Lapidarium Walliae: The Early Inscribed and Sculptured Stones of Wales*, Oxford, Oxford University Press for the Cambrian Archaeological Association.

Whitfield, N. (1999), 'Design and Units of Measure on the Hunterston Brooch', in *Northumbria's Golden Age*, ed. J. Hawkes and S. Mills, Stroud, Sutton Publishing, 296–314.

Wilson, D. M. (1973), 'A Stylistic Consideration of Miscellaneous Objects', in *St Ninian's Isle and its Treasures*, ed. A. Small, Aberdeen, Aberdeen University, 125–43

Wilson, D. M. (1984), *Anglo-Saxon Art: From the Seventh Century to the Norman Conquest*, London, Thames and Hudson.

Youngs, S. (ed.) (1989), *'The Work of Angels': Masterpieces of Celtic Metalwork 6th to 9th Centuries AD*, London, British Museum.

Index

Page numbers in bold indicate photographs